D1465624

Techniques of
LANDSCAPE
ARCHITECTURE

Techniques of
LANDSCAPE
ARCHITECTURE

Edited for the
Institute of Landscape Architects
by
A. E. WEDDLE

HEINEMANN : LONDON

Frontispiece   Beech trees in Savernake Forest

William Heinemann Ltd
15 Queen St, Mayfair, London W1X 8BE
LONDON MELBOURNE TORONTO
JOHANNESBURG AUCKLAND

First published 1967
Reprinted 1968, 1969, 1970, 1975
© Institute of Landscape Architects, 1967

434 92231 5

Printed in Great Britain by
Butler & Tanner Ltd, Frome and London

Foreword

LORD HOLFORD

This is a technical handbook, written, edited and illustrated by people who know that the purpose of techniques is to inform, moderate and help to carry out designs. They also know that if designs are to be comprehensive and authoritative, the technical details that make them so must be accurate and sound. So the book deals with practical matters, rather than with pure theory and criticism; but, as its subject is landscape, the practical matters include good appearance in large things as well as small.

In a foreword it is permissible to express views or make suggestions for which neither authors nor editor are responsible; and also to commend the work to architects and engineers and town planners and many others who will find it useful in the creation and maintenance of our environment. So I take this opportunity to do both these things.

First I want to suggest that some understanding on everyone's part of what it is possible to create at all scales of landscape from a small town park to a whole valley region, would be the best assurance we could have in these beautiful but congested islands, that our surroundings will not decline from good to bad and from bad to worse. Landscape can no longer be regarded as an absence of building. It represents a positive attitude toward the land, that identifies the facts of both natural and human ecology, and is aware of the responsibilities of development as well as of conservation.

Next I would like to commend to the attention of members of the land professions the advance which this book records in those aspects of the subject which the Americans call 'landscape engineering'. When combined with the traditional English skill in landscape architecture and planting, it provides a range of techniques suited to our urgent needs in the second half of the twentieth century – a century that has introduced the motorway and the high-voltage overhead transmission of electricity, and will now construct an ever-increasing volume of industrialised building.

HOLFORD

University College, London

v

Introduction

This book was commissioned by the Institute of Landscape Architects in an attempt to provide a general textbook dealing with technical aspects of landscape architecture. There are already attractive publications dealing with visual aspects of landscape design, and some specialised publications dealing with gardens, reclamation, playing fields and other subjects. This book sets out to cover the range of techniques which can be drawn upon in tackling most kinds of landscape problem. At the outset, it must be made clear that for our purpose, landscape has been very widely defined as the whole of the outdoor environment in both town and countryside. Thus, at the small scale we include pavings, fencing, the detailing and planting of open spaces in towns and around buildings, very conscious of the fact that these are seldom gardens in any normal sense, certainly not enclosed and private, but constitute the elements of townscape which can achieve both grace and durability if well designed for functional and aesthetic satisfaction. At the other extreme are the problems of conservation and management of coast and countryside, and in between comes the full range of design and layout tasks for recreation, industry, town development and the like.

At different scales these tasks are the special concern of architects, engineers, town planners, surveyors, ecologists, foresters and in fact the whole range of land-using and land-managing professions. Their skills are normally focused on solving problems within closely defined technical limits and within narrowly drawn territorial boundaries. The total result of their work is however likely to have profound influence beyond the confines of a single site or function, and it is here that the landscape architect attempts to act as a co-ordinator, foreseeing problems and conflicts and suggesting design solutions which enfold changing activities and new construction within what is already a complex and crowded landscape.

The all-encompassing nature of the landscape architect's work today inevitably means that he must draw on the skills of others and act as a collaborator. And he is limited to a large extent by specialised training and experience. In compiling this book therefore, it has been necessary both to have a range of specialists and a selection of landscape architects, with collectively a spread of skills which could not be found in a single author. Editorial guidance has attempted to coordinate these special contributions and impart a sense of continuity of subject matter and treatment.

There are twelve chapters, and it will be helpful to explain their sequence and grouping. The first three may be taken as introductory and general to the approach of the landscape architect to problems and their solution. Chapter 1, SITE PLANNING, deals with fundamental principles of technical design in the organisation of uses and spaces. Chapter 2, PRACTICE, deals with the organisation of consultations and contracts to tackle landscape problems.

Chapter 3, SURVEY, describes the special techniques of landscape survey employed as aids to appraisal and design.

'Hard landscape' or at least landscape not primarily concerned with plants, comes next, in a sequence comprising EARTHWORKS, HARD SURFACES, ENCLOSURE, OUTDOOR FURNITURE and WATER.

The group of chapters which follow is concerned with plants and planting, including separate chapters on GRASS and TREES. The final chapter outlines the processes of ADMINISTRATION AND MAINTENANCE by which landscape is managed and cared for.

Illustrations have been used to amplify the text. They comprise a selection of photographs, and specially prepared line drawings. The latter are nearly all based on actual examples, but in selection and redrawing the emphasis has been placed on illustration of technical principles involved where these are more important than the site or design illustrated.

Space available for this ambitious project has severely restricted both general treatment and individual authors, and being fully aware of our selective brevity and occasional omissions, it has been necessary to give a guide to further reading and to reference material, at the end of chapters and in a separate appendix.

Formal acknowledgments have been given wherever possible, but the Editorial Committee is further indebted to those who in many ways have contributed material and given encouragement. Special thanks are also due to John Higgins (Appendix), John Brookes (photographic illustrations) and to Geoffrey Bass who as Art Editor dealt with all line drawings.

Contents

Chapter Authors

MISS SYLVIA CROWE, C.B.E., P.P.I.L.A., Landscape Consultant to the Forestry Commission, C.E.G.B., Harlow and Washington New Towns, etc. Author of *Tomorrow's Landscape, Landscape of Power, Landscape of Roads* and *Garden Design*.

GEOFFREY A. COLLENS, M.L.A.(Pennsylvania), A.R.I.B.A., A.I.L.A., Architect and Landscape Architect. Associate, Derek Lovejoy and Associates.

NORMAN H. J. CLARKE, F.I.L.A., Landscape Architect, Hertfordshire County Council.

BRIAN HACKETT, M.A., F.I.L.A., A.R.I.B.A., A.M.T.P.I., Professor of Landscape Architecture, University of Newcastle-upon-Tyne. Visiting Professor of Landscape Architecture, University of Illinois, U.S.A. 1960–62.

TIMOTHY COCHRANE, M.L.A.(Pennsylvania) Dip. L.D.(Dunelm) A.R.I.B.A., A.I.L.A. Architect and Landscape Architect in private practice.

FREDERICK GIBBERD, K.B., C.B.E., A.R.A., F.R.I.B.A., M.T.P.I., F.I.L.A. Architect, planner and landscape consultant. Author of *Town Design, Architecture of England, Modern Flats* (with F. R. S. Yorke), *Design in Town and Village* (with Sharp and Holford).

IAN PURDY, A.R.I.B.A., Dip.T.P.(Lond.) A.M.T.P.I. City Architect and Planning Officer, Cambridge.

G. A. JELLICOE, C.B.E., P.P.I.L.A., F.R.I.B.A. (dist. T.P.), M.T.P.I. Architect, Landscape Architect and Town Planner. Author of *Italian Gardens of the Renaissance* (jointly with J. C. Shepherd); *Baroque Gardens of Austria, Studies in Landscape Design*, vols. I and II.

MRS PATRICIA BOOTH, B.Sc.(Hort), F.I.L.A. Landscape Architect in private practice.

IAN GREENFIELD, B.Sc.(Agric), M.I.Biol. Agricultural consultant, director of the Cayford Technical Service on turf. Talks and broadcasts. Author of *Turf Culture*.

MISS BRENDA COLVIN, P.P.I.L.A., Landscape Consultant to Ministry of Public Building and Works, Central Electricity Generating Board, etc. Author of *Land and Landscape*, Murray, and *Trees for Town and Country*.

J. T. CONNELL, F.Inst.P.A.(Dip.), A.M.I.B.C.A., Superintendent of Parks, Borough of Eccles.

OTHER CONTRIBUTORS:

D. J. GREIG, B.Sc.(Agric), M.Sc.(Agric. Eng.), A.M.I.Agr.E., Lecturer in Farm Mechanisation, The University of Newcastle-upon-Tyne.

G. V. DARRAH, B.A.(Nat.Sc.), B.A.(For.), South-Western Woodlands Association Ltd.

E. BRENT JONES, Civic Trust.

J. A. C. HIGGINS, A.R.I.B.A., A.A.Dip., A.M.T.P.I., Dip.T.P.(Lond.), A.I.L.A., Senior Landscape Architect, Ministry of Public Buildings and Works. Chairman of the I.L.A. Research Committee responsible for the collection of information for the Appendix of the book.

G. A. BASS, Dip.Arch.(Leicester), A.R.I.B.A., A.I.L.A. Partner, G. Alan Burnett & Partners, Chartered Architects, Structural Engineers, Landscape Architects.

Plates

Acknowledgments

Contributors

Many landscape architects and members of allied professions have been consulted and have given advice or commented on the preparation of parts of this book. Their help is gratefully acknowledged, in particular those mentioned below.

John Anthony, Brian Blaney and Brian Cato for sections of Chapter 2. D. J. Greig for the section on drainage in Chapter 4. Miss Elisabeth Beazley for help and suggestions in the preparation of Chapter 5, as well as for the inspiration afforded by her book *Design and Detail of the Space between Buildings* (Architectural Press). W. S. Brett for material in the section on planting in Chapter 5. Atlas Lighting Limited, British Lighting Council, Civic Trust, Council of Industrial Design, Mrs. Dalrimple, General Secretary—Keep Britain Tidy Group, Electrical Development Association, Federation of Quarry Owners of Great Britain, Furniture Development Council (Research and Information), H. N. Mason, B.Arch., Dip.C.D., A.R.I.B.A., A.M.T.P.I., Master Sign Makers Association, Gordon Patterson, A.I.L.A., Rowlands Electrical Association Limited, Stevenage Development Corporation, D. Thomas, B.A.(Arch.) A.R.I.B.A., Ward and Company (Letters) Limited, Peter Whitworth Esq., and G. P. Youngman, M.A., P.P.I.L.A. for data and illustrations in Chapter 7. Mr F. Tuson for assistance with the preparation of written and illustrative material in Chapter 8. Frances Perry for parts of the section on water freshness in Chapter 8. E. Brent Jones for the section on transplanting large trees in Chapter 11. G. V. Darrah for advice and help on general forestry practice. Raymond S. Balls for parts of Chapter 12 dealing with maintenance associated with new development, planning authorities and conservation.

Photographs

J. Allan Cash, *frontispiece*; Lawrence Halprin, Plate 1.1; H. S. Howgrave-Graham, 1.2; Harlow Development Corporation, 1.5, 1.6; *Country Life*, 1.8; Caterpillar Tractor Co., 4.1, 4.2, 4.3, 4.4, 4.5; N. C. K. Rapier Ltd., 4.7, 4.8, 4.9, 4.10, 4.11, 4.12, 4.13, 4.14, Architectural Press, 5.1, 5.4, 8.4; C.R.V. Tandy, 5.2, 5.3, 5.5, 9.5, 9.7, 9.8, 9.9, 12.1; Michael Brown, 5.6; Basildon Development Corporation, 5.8; Greater London Council, 5.9; Coventry Corporation, 5.10; G. S. Thomas, 6.5; Building Design Partnership, 7.1, 7.5; Frederick Gibberd, 7.2; Richard Sheppard, Robson & Partners, 7.3; Southern Stone and Concrete Ltd., 7.4; Stevenage Development Corporation, 7.6, 7.10, 10.8, 12.10, 12.11, 12.12; Monocrete Co. Ltd., 7.7; Atlas Lighting Ltd., 7.8, 7.9; Elton Civic Supplies Ltd., 7.11, 7.14; Colin Forbes, 7.15, 7.16, 7.17; H. N. Mason, 7.18; Harvey Fabrication Ltd., 7.12; Burnham & Co. Ltd., 7.13; Jellicoe & Colleridge, 8.1, 8.2, 8.5, 8.6, 8.7, 8.10; Brenda Colvin, 8.3, 11.1, 11.8; Jellicoe, Ballantyne &

Coleridge, 8.4; Gordon Patterson, 8.11; John Brookes, 9.2, 9.3, 9.4, 9.6; W. Hargreaves & Co. Ltd., 10.1, 10.2, 10.3, 10.5; Hydraumatic Seeding Ltd., 10.4; Richmond Gibson Ltd., 10.6; Wates Ltd., 10.7, 12.8, 12.9; Forestry Commission, 11.2, 11.3, 11.6; Shell, 11.4; *Scotlands S. M. T. Magazine*, 11.5; Civic Trust, 11.7; *Scotsman*, 11.9; J. T. Connell, 12 2, 12.3, 12.7; Raymond S. Balls, 12.4, 12.5; Wates, 12.6.

Site Planning

SYLVIA CROWE

1.1 Introduction

The service which a landscape architect can render his client rests on his ability to apply the principles of sound design to the use of open spaces. This entails, in addition to basic design ability, a knowledge of the materials of landscape, that is land, water and organic life. He must also understand the interaction between these materials, the climate in which they function and the human use to which they are being adapted. These factors together make up the ecology of a landscape and it is the landscape architect's function to arrange, develop and adapt them to serve the particular use for which the land space is designed. The extent of this field of work ranges from the smallest open space within urban development to national parks and the countryside as a whole.

The means by which a landscape architect will carry out his work are:

An assessment of the site and its surroundings.
A compilation and understanding of the required land use and functions of the proposed development.
The preparation of plans by which his ideas may first be conveyed to his client and then be translated to the ground.
Such supervision of the implementation of the plans as may be necessary to ensure their functioning.

1.1.1 Types of landscape site plans
The function of all site plans is to state how a given project is to be translated into good landscape. That is, a landscape which will fulfil its functions with efficiency, can be maintained in a viable condition and contributes to the welfare and good appearance of the environment. The scope and degree of detail of the plans will in each case depend on the nature of the project and the stage of development for which the landscape plan is prepared.

Master plans. These lay down the essential principles to be followed in the development and the broad lines of the design. They are not detailed. They are flexible within the limits of the basic principles and broad conception and will be subject to revision by the landscape architect as the detailing of the project proceeds.

The landscape master plan may form one element within a town planning, engineering or architectural project. In this case it may either take the form of a report and of principles diagrammatically expressed which will be incorporated into a comprehensive master plan prepared by the planning team, or it may be produced as a separate plan in consultation with the team. Alternatively, the project may be a predominantly landscape problem, entirely within the province of the landscape architect, or (more often) carried out in consultation with other professions involved, but remaining solely a landscape plan. From the master plan will evolve definitive plans for different sections of the project as they develop.

On long-term projects the plan may not be developed beyond the master plan stage, while on projects for more immediate realisation, the master plan stage will be developed, after agreement and adjustment, into working plans.

Site plans for existing projects. Ideally any landscape plan will follow early consultations with those responsible for other elements in the project. But in practice it will often be required for projects in which other elements are already completed, or planned beyond the possibilities of major adjustment. A site plan for a completed or completely planned project will usually be more rigid and detailed than those referred to in section 1.1.1, and will often be developed, with only minor revisions, directly into working plans. All site plans and master plans should be accompanied by reports. In section 1.1.1 these can be of greater importance than the plans. The material required at master plan stage may include:

Plans: Site analysis, use analysis. Small-scale location plan showing the influence of the environment on the new project, and the project's influence on the environment. Contoured site plan showing design solution.

Illustrations, sections, model: (For details of the various types of plan and presentation see Chapter 2.)

Report: The report will state the problem, the reasons for the solution, the phasing, the costs and the means of maintenance.

1

1.2 The basis of the site plan

The landscape plan evolves from two sets of factors:

(*a*) The site.
(*b*) The function.

1.2.1 The site factors (see also Chapter 3—Site Survey and Appreciation). These apply not only to the site but also to its surroundings. The relevant minimum extent of these is the visual limit into and out from the site and the character of adjacent though unseen landscape. This will influence:

Kinetic experience (e.g. passing from one urban square to another).
Use requirements (e.g. proximity of city, coast).
Ecological and climatic factors (e.g. the presence of some distant windbreak).

1.2.2 Use factors
These comprise the following:

The primary function of the site.

Subsidiary functions or multiple use.

Density of use.

Access and traffic requirements.

The appearance and well-being of the landscape both within the site and beyond it.

Capital and maintenance cost (see also Chapter 12—Administration and Maintenance).

Planning and legal requirements (see also Chapter 2—Practice of Landscape Architecture).

1.3 Information needed for preparation of site plan

1.3.1 Contoured surveys (of site and surroundings to the scope and scale appropriate to the project).
Complete details of existing and proposed buildings, with differentiation, in the case of buildings planned and not yet built, between essential features and variable ones. There may for instance be latitude in the siting or in the arrangement of some structures, while others are inexorably fixed by necessity of their particular functions. This should be ascertained from the architects or engineers.

1.3.2 Site appreciation
Climatic, soil and ecological reports are needed and the visual character and potential of the site must be assessed (see also Chapter 3).

1.3.3 Planning implications
These include the influence of the project on its environment; its relationship to other proposed developments; legal and planning restrictions; its possible influence on traffic problems. Consultations will usually be required on these points with the relevant bodies, e.g. the local planning authority, the Nature Conservancy, etc. (see also Chapter 2). The client should be informed of the proposed consultations.

1.3.4 Client requirements
To discover the client's true requirements is a matter of first asking the right questions, and then of separating the essential from the inessential and establishing the priorities. Where the client is an individual it is comparatively easy to ascertain the requirements, but in the case of a multiple body it may be more difficult and most

difficult of all is the case of unknown, future users, such as the inhabitants of a new town. Full use of research and the application of common sense must be made in these cases.

Existing examples of similar or relevant projects should be studied and their failures and successes noted. Judgment must then be used to decide how far the lessons of other projects are applicable. Allowance must be made for different soil and climatic factors and for social conditions. This is particularly important when studying examples from other countries. In all cases where uncertainty exists, the plan should allow for maximum flexibility. For instance, in planning for recreation changing habits must be taken into account, but it should also be realised that further and unexpected trends may develop, and wherever possible, plans should be sufficiently flexible to allow for future adjustment. Specialist bodies should be consulted on all subjects in which the landscape architect is not himself an expert.

For sources of information see Appendix.

Function. Where the primary function of the site lies outside the technical knowledge of the landscape architect he must acquaint himself with the factors of those functions which might influence his design of the landscape. For instance if he is dealing with a reservoir he must find out the requirements to avoid pollution, or in the case of a mineral working he must discover the working process and programme. No landscape architect can be expert in all the matters he must deal with but he can acquire the skills to extract the data essential for his purpose.

Density of use. This includes traffic density, static and in passage, residential density and visitor density.

1.3.5 Timing
The designer will be concerned with two time scales, first the period of development, which may be in phases, and second the life or expected duration of the completed project.

1.3.6 Costs
These are in two simple categories; capital costs and maintenance costs.

1.3.7 Means of maintenance
These are dealt with in detail in Chapter 12. They are fundamental and must be considered in parallel with design for function.

1.4 Site factors

1.4.1 Climate
The creation of a favourable micro-climate is one of the basic reasons for site manipulation and in attaining this the placing of shelter belts is often the first step in preparing the plan. Since a certain minimum width is required according to site conditions (see also Chapter 11—Tree Planting) they may influence all other elements of the plan including the siting of buildings. The basic pattern of the plan will also be influenced by the need for maximum sun in cool climates and shade in hot ones.

1.4.2 Site contours
The contours of a site will provide the first line of thought on how a site should be developed. They will suggest the best positions for buildings, for views, for shelter. The best use must be made of level areas of the site for large level elements such as playing fields.

The siting of roads will depend on their gradient in relation to the site gradients. If traffic separation is to be achieved by over- and under-passes the site contours will suggest the most economic siting for these. A road sited side-long to the contours will give an opportunity to run the road and footpath at different levels. If the required maximum road gradient is less than the site gradient between the road's point of entry and destination, the road will have to take a suitably extended course.

Elements such as car parks, which it is desired to conceal should be sited on the lower contours. Normally tree-screens will be sited on the higher contours. From the first tentative sketch onwards all design should be carried out on a contoured plan.

1.4.3 Existing vegetation
Where any part of the site can remain undisturbed the existing ground cover should be examined to see if it is suitable for retention. If so it must be both protected and maintained for the duration of site works. Hedges and bushes may sometimes be used in the new development and particularly on exposed sites their value as shelter for new planting may be considerable. Healthy trees should always be preserved where possible. Their position, spread and the ground level at their base must be shown on the surveys, as the need to retain approximately the same level over their root area may determine the shaping and levelling of the site. Any existing features which are to be kept must be protected by fencing before the first construction machinery reaches the site.

1.4.4 Water (see also Chapter 8—Water)
Early site investigation should ascertain whether water is available from natural sources. If it is it may form an important element in the site plan. Before including existing water, either in the form of a pond or a stream, in the new development, its seasonal variations and purity must be discovered, also whether its volume is likely to be decreased as a result of the site development. This often occurs when surface water is drained off in urban development.

1.4.5 Soil conditions
In some cases these may be a determining factor. Overall lack of soil may dictate the same type of pattern which would result from extreme aridity, that is, a pattern of localised areas where growing conditions are artificially induced, on a background of inert material or of poverty plants.

Modern techniques of soil improvement have made it possible to obtain growth on areas which would at one time have been considered infertile. The possibilities and cost of this should be ascertained in difficult cases, before the plan is evolved. But in normal cases the soil conditions should be reflected in the plan and marked differentiation of soil quality within the site will influence the siting of different elements.

The nature of the subsoil will also influence the site plan from the first. In projects where there is any question of undergrounding structures or putting roads in cutting the nature of the subsoil may be decisive. The practicability and cost of contouring and levelling will equally be affected. In considering both these operations the level of the water-table must also be ascertained.

1.4.6 Site surroundings
These will influence the visual pattern of the development which must relate the site to the surroundings; the position of screen planting, this may be needed as a visual barrier or to reduce noise or pollution (see also Chapter 11); the access or prevention of access—for instance adjacent areas

of public resort, such as commons, should influence the pedestrian way system in urban development, and equally fast traffic roads should be insulated from uncontrolled pedestrian access.

Views seen from the site will influence the siting of buildings, and the arrangement of plantings. Views into the site may have to be considered from view points some distance from the site. The importance of these will depend on distance, which will determine not only whether an object is seen at all, but also whether it is identifiable, or blurred by atmospheric perspective, on contours, or on intervening objects such as trees. The effect of new structures on distant views should be ascertained by taking out sections along a number of sight lines.

Montage on photographs, or a scale study model may also be used. In using the latter, the view point, even if some miles away can be scaled out and fixed at the correct level. The visibility of proposed structures on the model can then be ascertained. Contoured ordnance maps to a scale of $2\frac{1}{2}$ in to 1 mile will be found useful in assessing the interplay between a site and its surroundings. From these, probable view points can be picked out and then checked on site.

1.5 Use factors

These must be ascertained from the client and from those concerned with the particular use to which the site is to be put.

1.5.1 Traffic
Access for traffic and parking is now often a major site use. Requirements must be ascertained for:

Access to public road with requisite sight lines.
Access points for each type of traffic within the site. This will cover loading bays for lorries, workers' cars, residents' cars, visitors' cars.
Turning spaces appropriate to each type of vehicle.
Parking requirements.

Peripheral screening and/or trees within the car parks is desirable, as cars are a restless element in any landscape. It can be achieved with little or no loss of parking space. Screening is especially necessary for projects in the countryside (Fig. 1.1). Car parks for occasional or seasonal use need not always be hard surfaced. The site plan should differentiate between hard surfaced and green car parks. Approach roads should normally take the shortest route compatible with contours and a pleasant line. But easy deviations may be justified to avoid severing land, since land cut off by a traffic route is largely wasted.

Whether or not cycle traffic should be segregated from motor traffic and/or pedestrians depends on the amount of cycle traffic expected. Leading to some industrial sites it may be heavy and will justify separate cycle tracks. Cycle parking should be provided even for small numbers, otherwise cycles will be leant against windows and plants.

Pleasant conditions should be assured for any public footpaths through or adjacent to the site. Segregation of pedestrians and vehicles is desirable for all areas of fast or heavy traffic, and where children are concerned, even in the case of light traffic. Where possible, traffic and pedestrians should take different routes. The pedestrian routes should be more direct, but can have steeper gradients. Approaches to either under-passes or foot-bridges should be made to appear the natural and easiest route for the pedestrian by making them pleasant and gradual, with a maximum gradient of 1:10 which is

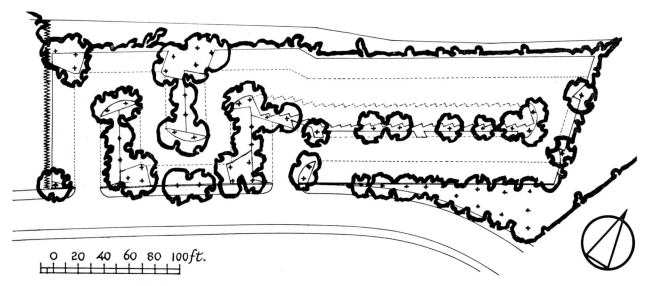

0 20 40 60 80 100 ft.

Fig. 1.1. Tree screened car park, Aldershot. Landscape Architect: Brenda Colvin.

4

Fig. 1.2. A residential area, where high density dwellings opening on to paved ways contrast with wedges of unbroken grass. Harlow. Architect: Michael Neylan, A.R.I.B.A. Landscape Architect: Sylvia Crowe.

5

Plate 1.1 A pattern where the background is hard wearing surface with plant groups superimposed. House in California. Landscape Architect: Lawrence Halprin.

Plate 1.2. Protection of growing material in a high-density area by the use of cobbles and changed level. Gossops Green. Crawley New Town.

negotiable by perambulators. In all cases there should be protection from noise and fumes between cars and pedestrians. Where they run roughly parallel, grade seperation is helpful in giving protection with economy of land use.

1.5.2 Density

Density is a factor in all planning from the simple case of the size of a family in a dwelling to the number of visitors to a National Park. There is an appropriate ecology for every density, which the site plan must evolve. In high density housing small public open spaces must be conceived as hard wearing surfaces. In a heavily used town centre for instance the whole surface is an open air floor, furnished, if at all, with well-protected trees or plants. The more difficult problems arise in housing areas with nett residential densities of 30 to 60 persons per acre where some grass surface is desired, but will only survive if sited off the main lines of access, or if protected.

The minimum viable size of grass areas is influenced by climatic and soil conditions as well as by density and siting. This factor of wear and density should influence the whole development, from the master plan onwards, since it requires a differentiation of open space into large areas not cut up with access roads and paths, where green landscape can flourish, and into small, densely used areas of hard-wearing surface (Fig. 1.2).

There is a basic division in design between a density which requires a background of wearing surface, on which living material is imposed (Plate 1.1), and a density which allows a background of living material on which a pattern of wearing surface is imposed (Plate 1.5).

Detail design can reduce the wear/density ratio by such devices as change of level or use of deterrents such as cobbles and hazards (Plates 1.2, 1.3, 1.4).

Plate 1.3. Protection of growing material by change of level at Crawley.

But the greatest prevention of wear results from providing adequate paths in the direction in which they are needed. The most direct desire routes may sometimes have to be modified but they must always form the basis of the design. Plans for rural projects, e.g. camp sites, must take account of the probable increase in density not only of the site itself but of its surroundings, and devise any necessary protection or modification of the ecology to deal with this. Methods of doing this are:

Protective planting of thickets to prevent access to certain areas.
Provision of paths.
Use of change of level, or ditches, to discourage straying.
Change or modification of vegetation.
Reduction of density by difficulty of access, e.g. allowing only rough tracks past certain points.

In the vicinity of a camp or a car park, a buffer zone must be planned for, to allow people to fan out from the access point for picnics and short walks. Particular care must be taken on geological formations liable to erosion, e.g. sand dunes.

1.5.3 Safety factors
Safety precautions will often influence and may sometimes inhibit the design. Serious physical hazards should be foreseen by the landscape architect and guarded against in the site plan. Subsequent emergency measures can ruin the design. Examples of genuine hazards are:

Access to fast traffic roads by pedestrians and especially children.
High unprotected retaining walls.
Deep water accessible to children.

Other hazards, not serious in themselves may involve legal liability. These may sometimes be dealt with by insurance.

1.5.4 Special functions
Residential. The functions of residential open space are (a) to give access and (b) to provide for outdoor living.

In (a) the needs of vehicle/pedestrian segregation must be combined with providing both forms of access to the dwellings. In (b) an important factor is whether the use of the open space is to be for privacy or sociability. Complete privacy is usually required in at least one section of private gardens. The provision of this is more important than size. Some degree of privacy is also desirable in the gardens of flats and in communal gardens, which should be designed to provide secluded sitting places.

Sociability is required in the public open space which will comprise residential courts, playgrounds and town squares, each designed for its appropriate density of use. Pedestrian ways should link the public open spaces into a connected system, to which private houses will have easy access and which will lead to the schools, the shopping centres and the recreation areas. All paths in the pedestrian system must be wide enough for two perambu-

Plate 1.4. Use of cobbles and change of level. Crawley.

lators abreast (minimum 4 ft 6 in) and the main paths will be wider.

One of the basic patterns for pedestrian/vehicle separation is the Radburn system. Many variations on this have recently been evolved.

Plate 1.5. A space large enough to use grass as a background, with hardwearing surface superimposed. Mark Hall, Harlow.

It must be ascertained in consultation with the architects, whether the architectural elements of the plan will themselves provide an interesting setting for the pedestrian way or whether space must be provided to establish planting beside the paths. Normally both methods will be employed to give variations between one section and another. In this case the width left between buildings for the path must vary. Where planting is required, ample space for whatever type is intended must be provided, both above and below ground.

Paths must be direct in their general line. In their minor deviations, devices such as changes of level and hazards must make them appear as the natural course and discourage short-cutting, which is a sign that the static and passage elements of the system have been confused (see p. 21). Steps, unless very shallow, should have a ramped alternative for perambulators.

Childrens' playgrounds of all types should be located at an early stage of the plan and linked into the pedestrian system. Similarly resting places with provision for sitting in both sun and shade should be related to shopping centres, old peoples' dwellings and to any features likely to attract onlookers.

Private gardens. The basic function of a private garden is the provision of open-air living for the inhabitants. To this may be added the client's special requirements, such as space for growing trees, fruit, flowers or vegetables, the provision of a swimming pool, tennis courts or other special features. The open-air room will require privacy, a view either looking out from the site or created within the site and direct access from the appropriate part of the house. Some form of terrace is usually required. If the terrace looks on to rising ground, sufficient space must be levelled to avoid an appearance of oppression, and drainage must be arranged to prevent water flooding into the house. There must be co-ordination between the levels of the damp-proof course (d.p.c.) and facing bricks, and of manhole covers with the finished ground level.

In all but the smallest gardens provision must be made for tool and potting sheds, compost heaps and their access paths. The need for stand-pipes must also be considered. In country house gardens and estates the client will often require only a small area needing garden maintenance, but will wish to develop additional land as amenity woodland, or grazed park. Success here will require a solution

8

to the problems of maintenance by farm and forest methods. (See also Chapter 12—Maintenance.)

Hospitals. The use of hospital grounds will be for access and car parks, patients, visitors, staff.

Patients. These need a pleasant outlook from windows, and easy attractive walks to take them out-of-doors in convalescence. Special requirements for geriatric and long-term patients include sunny terraces on which to sit. Wind shelter is essential. For mental patients small plots for gardening may be needed and safe boundaries which do not appear restrictive must be provided.

Visitors. Seating in pleasant surroundings should be provided where visitors and patients can sit together.

Staff. The needs and composition of the staff must be ascertained. Possible needs are tennis and squash courts, private gardens for resident medical staff and study gardens for resident student nurses. Hospitals with large grounds may require kitchen gardens for vegetables and cut flowers.

Access. Separate car parks are likely to be required for staff and visitors, the former probably including coaches. Separate access may be required for ambulances and mortuary vans.

Parks. An exact client's brief is essential in designing public parks. Their proposed use may range from the grounds of an old country house in the green belt intended only as a place for walks and views, to a multi-use park in a high density area, which will be subject to heavy use and required for a wide range of activity.

The essential of the plan in either case is to ensure that all the proposed activities will be welded into an overall landscape, with a maximum opportunity for pleasant walks and views. Generous provision should be made for car parking and included in the overall scheme. Otherwise the intention of the plan will be nullified by unplanned car parking. The car park may, however, be sited outside but adjacent to the park. Requirement for glasshouses, maintenance yards, access for lorries and lavatories must also be ascertained. Noisy activities should be segregated from quiet areas.

Educational buildings. The major land use around schools and colleges will be for recreation.

Many schools now use open-air class rooms. These require sheltered positions and insulation from noise, which may be provided by planting, by baffle walls or by ground shaping. For primary schools safe pedestrian access is essential. Colleges and universities should provide

Plate 1.6. A tree planted car park. Harlow Town Centre.

c

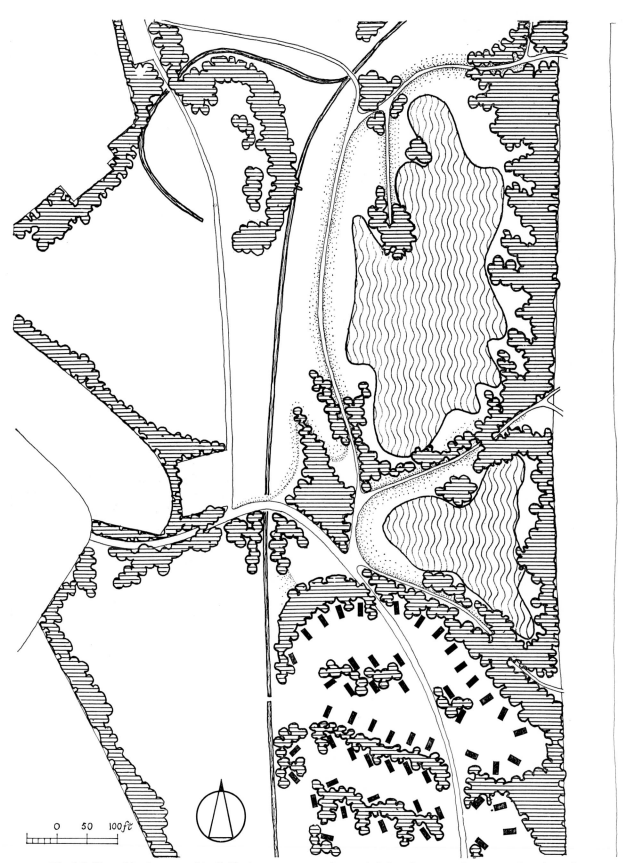

O 50 100ft

Fig. 1.3. Planted banks are used to divide the caravan camp into secluded enclosures, and to screen them from view.
Landscape Architect: Sylvia Crowe.

space for open-air study, opportunities for students to congregate and talk. It must be ascertained by consultations with the architects and clients whether the concept is to be that of a campus on the American pattern, where a large open space will cater for great numbers and for varied activities, or whether a more domestic scale is visualised. In any case the plan will need to cater for sports activities, spaces for open-air congregation, strolling and sitting, quiet areas for study, and fellows' or staff gardens. The two landscape elements of the plan will be the large area of the playing fields and the more intimate areas associated with the buildings. Car parks should be excluded from the internal landscape. Their siting, and that of the cycle parks, must be an early decision in evolving the plan. Collegiate discipline may make it possible to use grass as a ground covering under far higher density than would be possible in public schemes.

Industry.   The major function is always production —with this should be combined considerations for the surrounding landscape and good working conditions for the staff. To carry out the functions, good access, adequate storage space, and usually space for future development are essential.

Consideration for environment entails prevention of pollution or noise. While the care for this lies primarily within the industry, landscape treatment can help by planting wide tree screens and/or building baffles of spoil. Screening is always required for storage yards, car parks, etc. It may or may not be required for the main building. Expansion areas may also need grassing and screening.

Pleasant working conditions are primarily achieved by good appearance. In addition the following may be desirable:

Tree planting to give shade or shelter or to cut out noise.
Provision of out-door sitting areas. This is particularly appreciated by women workers.
Provision of recreation. Male workers appreciate a kick-about space.

There may in addition to these provisions for lunch-break, be wider sports facilities provided for after work and weekends.

Access will usually be required for staff and visitors' cars, workers' cars, works buses, bicycles, pedestrians and loading lorries. The various points of access, the expected volume and the required parking space for each must be ascertained or assessed.

Special requirements by different types of industry

Industrial estates. In these the individual requirements of each factory must be fitted into and reconciled with the overall landscape of the estate.

Space for large trees, which are the best foil for the

buildings, will have to be found either within the industrial sites, or on ground reserved to the estate as a whole. This point must be settled before the individual sites are let. A policy must also be agreed on fencing along road frontages, to ensure either a satisfactory type of fencing, or to reserve space for planting between boundary fences and frontages. Similarly a policy must be agreed for screening storage yards and for the treatment of areas for future expansion.

The estate may include common open space and recreational facilities, or individual firms may require their own. Convenient access by bus, car, cycle and foot will be required and separation of the foot and cycle from motor traffic is desirable. Foot and cycle tracks must be made direct and attractive if they are to be used.

Isolated industry and public utilities. Where siting requirements take certain undertakings out of industrial areas into the countryside, or into residential areas, the landscape architect will be chiefly concerned with making them acceptable in their surroundings, while maintaining their working efficiency.

To do this he must find out their essential working conditions, which may not always be the same as their traditional requirements. That is, the traditional solution to a certain problem may not be the best for the landscape. It is for the landscape architect to grasp the problem, and to think out afresh what the acceptable solution might

Plate 1.7. Trees give welcome shade in an otherwise open landscape.

be. Any fresh solution must however be carefully cleared with the technicians involved to make sure that there are no hidden snags.

Particular points on which the landscape architect should be able to contribute ideas are:
The disposal of waste and spoil.
Treatment of site boundaries (see p. 23, Chapter 1, and Chapter 6).
Multi-purpose use, such as recreation in conjunction with reservoirs.
Protection of surrounding country, visually and ecologically.

11

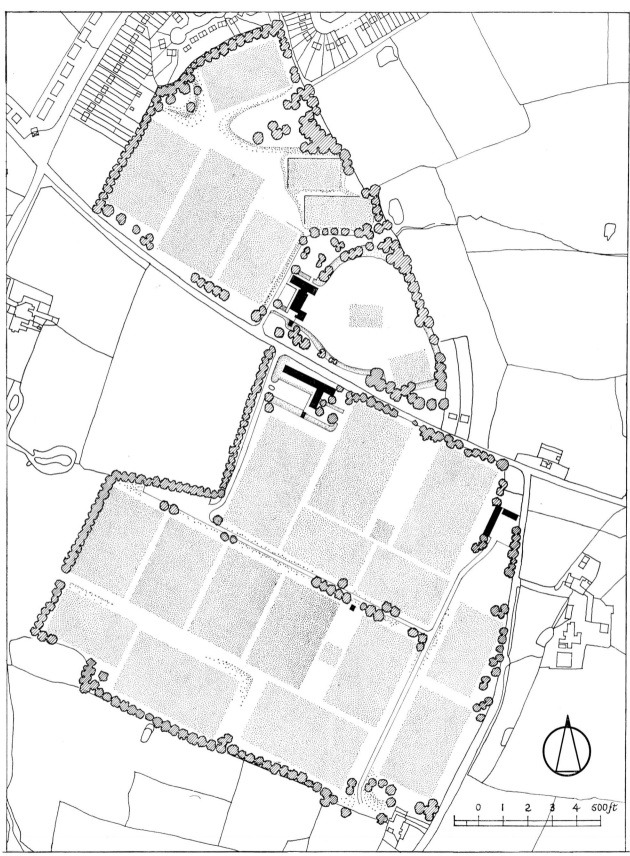

Fig. 1.4. Wast Hills Playing Fields, University of Birmingham, showing comprehensive arrangements for tree planting, car parking, Clubhouse and other facilities. Landscape Architect: R. Frank Marshall.

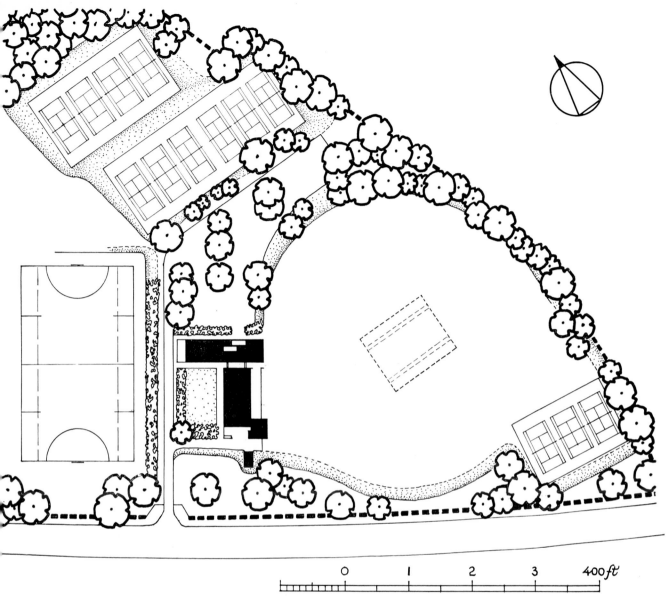

Fig. 1.5. Detail of Wast Hills Playing Fields, University of Birmingham. Landscape Architect: R. Frank Marshall.

Information which he will need will include:

Life and phasing of project, particularly relevant to mineral workings.
Amount, type and speed of accretion of waste materials, e.g. ash from power stations.
Amount and type of industrial material to be stored, e.g. coal for power stations.

Pollution—Fumes from chemical works or dust from quarries may inhibit plant growth, but planting may be needed to check dust or smell from causing annoyance outside the site. Amelioration by planting is usually only partially successful, and every possible step should be taken to ensure prevention of pollution at source. The landscape architect can contribute to this by foreseeing and pointing out the harmful effects on surroundings and vegetation and wild life.

Expected traffic—This will not only affect the amount of car parking and road use on site, but may necessitate road widening on site approaches.

Number of workers, and whether new housing will be required—A reservoir for instance may require on-site housing, and this must be integrated with the proposed multi-use of the site.

Degree of security necessary—This may often be exaggerated by clients, and tactful probing may be needed to find out the true position. This is very relevant where it is hoped to combine recreation with the primary site use.

Roads. Where the landscape architect is also qualified in road engineering, the aligning of roads and treatment of their boundaries and the intersections may be his responsibility solely. Where he is not so qualified, ideally

13

the should work in collaboration with the road engineers If his advice is sought at the earliest stages, his concern will be:

To bring full consideration of the landscape into the choice of route.

To ensure that in detail routeing the road preserves features of landscape value wherever possible.

To reconcile the grading required for traffic with the best interests of the landscape.

In cases where the route and gradient of the road is already settled, his contribution will be the grading of cuttings and embankments and roadside planting.

Information required for the compilation of road plans, includes:

Type and speed of traffic for which road is designed.
Sight lines.
Requirements for parking and lay-bys.

Landscape plans for roads must include sufficient widths of land beyond the road curtilage on each side to ensure that the road landscape relates to its surroundings. In some cases a small-scale plan will also be needed to show views to distant view points.

Recreation. Recreational requirements may be divided into informal pursuits which may function within an infinite variety of areas and types of landscape, and organised games which require specific sizes and conditions for their grounds.

Informal recreation

Water sports—Reservoirs and wet gravel pits are increasingly being used for water sports of various kinds. The possibility of catering for these sports should be considered wherever the opportunity arises. Decisions to be made are:

Which sports are compatible and which must be kept separate.
The effect of certain sports, e.g. water skiing and speed boats on bank erosion.
The suitability of the water for public access as regards purity and safety.
Any steps which must be taken to prevent bank erosion or water fouling caused by public access.

Caravanning and camping—Sites laid out as recognized camps require sanitation, water supply and usually a warden's accommodation (for space standards see p. 42). These are recognised as minimum space standards, but additional space for providing privacy for campers and screening from surroundings should be allowed (Fig. 1.3).

Fifty vans are usually the minimum required to justify the expenditure on water and sanitation. Firm standing for the vans and approach roads is required, but this need not entail exposed hard surface. Natural sharp drainage and shallow soil over make ideal site conditions. Wherever possible sites should be screened from surrounding view points. Thinned woodland forms one of the best sites. Safe access to the highway must be assured.

Riding, walking and cycling—All landscape planning projects should consider the needs of these users. Any or all of the three may follow the same general line, but cycles cannot share the same surface as the others. If walkers and riders share a ride, it must be wide and well drained enough to prevent winter ponding. All require separation from motor traffic, and a pleasant setting.

Organised games—Playing fields for football, cricket and hockey require large, level open spaces, and are therefore some of the first open-air users to be settled on the site plan. One in 40 is usually considered the maximum acceptable slope for football pitches (other than first-class pitches).

SITE PLANNING
Current minimum space requirements are:

	acres
Primary schools (excluding infants)	
Playing fields for up to 50 pupils	½
Secondary schools	
Boys only	
Playing fields for up to 150 pupils	4½
Girls only	
Playing fields for up to 150 pupils	4
Boys and girls	
Playing fields for up to 150 pupils	4½

(For detailed requirements relative to increased pupillage, see *Ministry of Education Regulations*, May 1959, No. 89).

Universities	
Playing fields for 5,000 students	150
Large towns	
Per 1,000 population	4

Additional land should always be allowed for tree planting, car parks, pavilions, etc. (Figs. 1.4 and 1.5).

The setting out of the pitches should give latitude to change the position of goalmouths, thus equalising wear. This means that for economy of space several pitches should be grouped together, on one level. For public recreation grounds minimum areas of 10 acres of grouped facilities are desirable; smaller areas tend to be uneconomic in upkeep.

There is a growing demand for a proportion of hard pitches for all-weather use. These must be visualised as interruptions to the green expanse traditionally formed by sports areas, and means devised of making them visually acceptable, or screening them on the same principle as car parks.

Public playing pitches can be left visually open, but private clubs usually require seclusion, and this again must be visualised as a break in the landscape. Unless the pitches are near a related building, a pavilion with changing accommodation is needed. This should be associated with the car park, and usually set in trees.

Sports stadia—These may be classed as buildings rather than open space. The requirement of a 'gate' means that they must be screened from their surroundings, and the stands, car parks and usually flood-lights, constitute a large urban unit. Their siting should therefore be regarded as a subtraction from and not an addition to, the visually open space system. The same applies to squash courts, indoor swimming pools, hard tennis courts and sports halls. All these uses, with their access roads and car parks, should be classed as urban buildings rather than landscape—although they may reasonably be sited in close relationship to open recreation areas or parks.

Children's playgrounds—The higher the density the more need for childrens' playgrounds. But even in country towns and villages they are needed, to deal with the present density of population and intensive agriculture which has reduced the areas of uncultivated land, once available for play.

The overall space allowance for childrens' playgrounds usually considered reasonable is ¾ to 1 acre per 1,000 population. More important than acreage is their siting, design and management. The different types needed are:

Under 5's. These must be sited very close to the child's home. Small, frequent provision is more useful than larger areas at a distance. These can be incorporated within the pedestrian system.

Nursery schools need attached playgrounds for the same age group.

Primary school age. One playground for this age should be sited within ¼ mile safe walk from all homes. They may usefully be grouped with primary schools, having interchangeable access from the school and from outside.

Over 11's. These require junior playing pitches and opportunities for adventure.

Constructional playgrounds (with play leader). Children's scramble courses, canoeing, camping, etc. These will serve all age groups (over 5) but particularly the over-10's.

1.6 Cost

Multiple use. This may mean that two or more functions are served by one feature, e.g. timber production and wind shelter, or it may mean that two or more functions are interwoven, e.g. when pedestrian ways are given their setting by passing beside sports fields. Both these forms of multiple use are desirable, and whatever may be the primary function of a site, its possible subsidiary functions should be considered in the site plan.

Both capital and maintenance costs are factors in design and their limitations must be considered throughout the development of the plan.

1.6.1 Overall rates per acre

At the time of first consultations with the client it is useful to be able to give a rough idea of the cost of different types of development. This will be based on an overall per acre rate.

Typical rates per acre (at 1966 prices) are:

Forestry according to size and fencing ratio *abt.* £150	
Parkland of grass and trees	£1,550
Rough grass	£950
Playing fields depending on cut and fill needed	£2,000–3,000
Garden or park with proportion of hard surface, walling, etc.	£2,000 to £4,000

1.6.2 Unit rates

In some cases it may be possible to estimate rates per unit of development, for example in residential areas cost may range from £15 to £40 per dwelling in the New Towns to £200 per dwelling for the more expensive schemes of private development. The figure is governed not only by the amount of open space but in particular by the amount of hard surface required and whether all the hard surface will be included in landscape costs or will be partly covered by architectural and engineering costs. The cost of landscape for high density housing may well cost more than for low density because a higher proportion of hard surface will be required. As densities increase, however, the high cost per acre will be shared among a larger number of dwellings and the cost per dwelling unit ceases to be such a reliable estimating guide.

1.6.3 Estimate of costs by elements

At an early stage in the development of the plan a rough cost check should be made to discover whether the figure originally mentioned is likely to remain accurate. In this check a rough break down of costs should be made listing such elements as:

Excavations.	Hard surfacing.
Grass.	Planting.

Special features, such as pools, walls and buildings.

A sum should be added for contract preliminaries and contingencies and to cover special site difficulties, such as inaccessibility, lack of topsoil or heavy excavation.

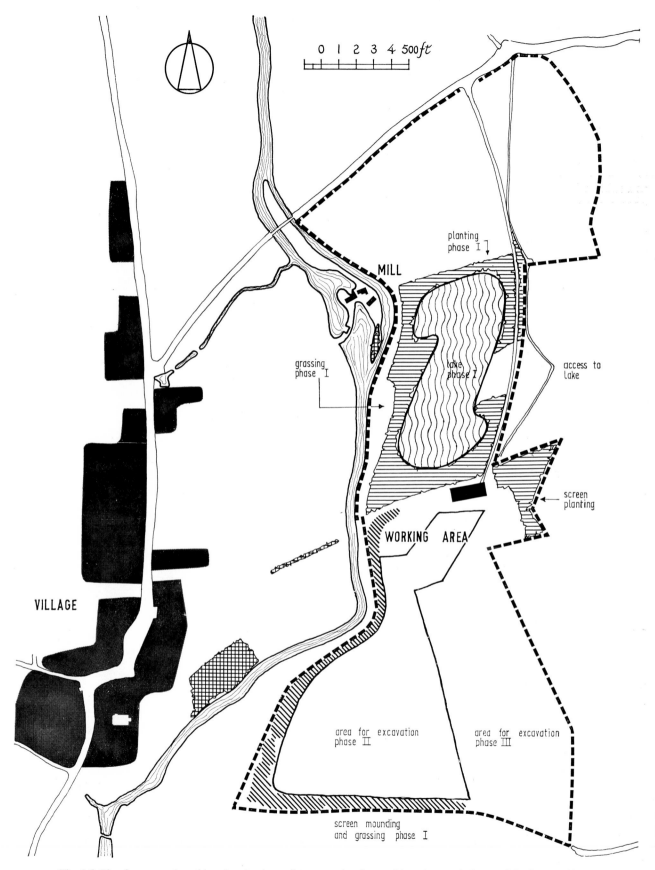

Fig. 1.6. Plan for a gravel working showing immediate screening for working plant and phases of further working.

Labels within the figure:

- 0 1 2 3 4 500 ft
- MILL
- planting phase I
- access to lake
- grassing phase I
- lake phase I
- screen planting
- WORKING AREA
- VILLAGE
- area for excavation phase II
- area for excavation phase III
- screen mounding and grassing phase I

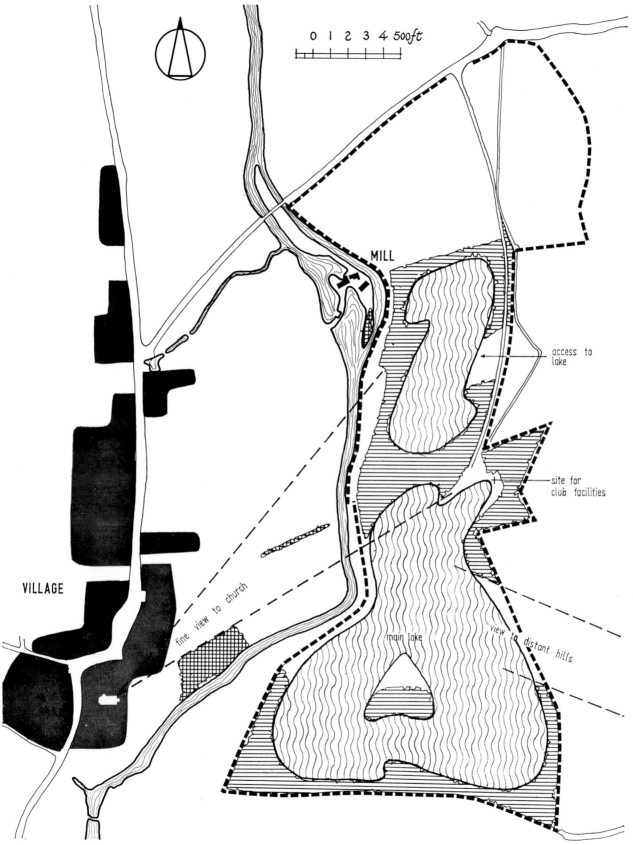

VILLAGE

MILL

access to
lake

site for
club facilities

fine view to church

main lake

view to distant hills

0 1 2 3 4 500ft

Fig. 1.7. Gravel working, progressive restoration completed to give final development of lake, related to the adjacent landscape.
Landscape Architect: Sylvia Crowe.

17

If the result of this check reveals that the final cost is at all likely to exceed the client's expectations, and cannot be reduced without jeopardising the plan, the client should be consulted before the plan is crystallised. More detailed costing will be applied when the plan is completed.

1.7 Maintenance

1.7.1 Standard of provision
The provision which will be available for maintenance is sometimes a difficult factor to ascertain, but unless it is foreseen and planned for, the plan is never likely to reach maturity in the form envisaged. Both the numbers and skill of the staff which is likely to be available must be discussed with the client. Possibilities of maintenance by contract must also be considered. The plan must be adapted to the degree of maintenance which can be foreseen. Instruction on maintenance should accompany site plans. (See also Chapter 12—Maintenance.)

1.7.2 Means of maintenance
The means of maintenance must also be foreseen, e.g. grass areas must either be mown or grazed. If mown they must be accessible and able to be cut; if grazed, protection of adjoining planting must be assured. The use of machinery must be allowed for on all but the smallest sites. Provision must always be made for access for maintenance. The requirements for this depend on the size and type of development and the type of machinery which is likely to be used. The following are typical examples of what may be necessary:

Access for gang mowers to large grass areas and sports fields.
Lorry and machine access to allotments or any large areas of cultivated ground.
Wheelbarrow access to small areas.
Access for lawn mowers to all grass areas however small.
Access for maintenance to patios, roof gardens and window boxes.

Water points must be provided for all areas needing irrigation. Tool sheds, maintenance yards and glasshouses must be planned for convenience of access and working.

1.8 Timing

1.8.1 Phasing
The landscape plan must often be developed in stages for the following reasons:

(a) Future extension of buildings may be planned. In this case temporary landscape may be carried out over the future extension.
(b) Finance may only allow the plan to be developed gradually.

In both (a) and (b) the plan must ensure a good appearance in the early stages, and a minimum of wasted cost.

(c) The project may change radically over the course of years. This is the case in mineral workings, where the site plan may comprise at least three stages:

Immediate action to screen or improve the appearance of plant and early workings.
A working programme of progressive reinstatement which will ensure the best appearance compatible with working requirements.
A final plan showing eventual reinstatement of the workings (Figs. 1.6 and 1.7).

The same type of problem applies to power stations where ash will gradually accumulate over the years.

1.8.2 Duration of project
Some projects have a foreseeably short life. The landscape plan for these should give the quickest effect possible, but it may still be worth planting trees for the future in the hope that they will be compatible with the succeeding land use.

1.8.3 Short- and long-term plans
It is often desirable to combine planting for quick effect and for long term. The plan should show clearly which trees are to be retained and which removed (Figs. 1.8 and 1.9).

1.9 Elements of the plan

1.9.1 Siting of structures
Landscape architects may be called upon to site structures in consultation with architects or engineers, or where they have a dual qualification may be solely responsible. The site plan must determine which elements are part of the landscape composition, and which are to be subordinate or completely screened. Examples of this principle are:

Power stations, where the main buildings will be dominant elements, but the many small ancillary buildings,

18

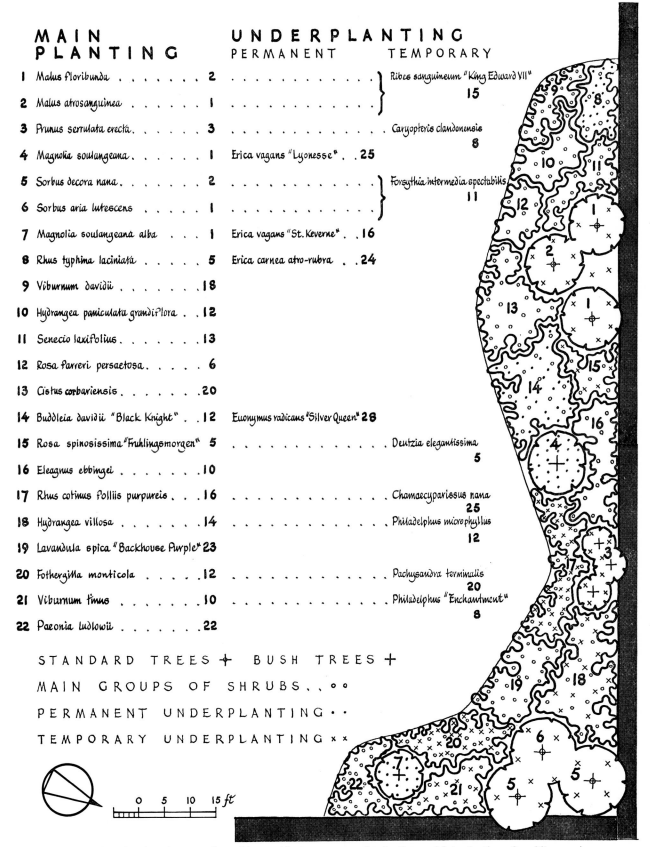

MAIN PLANTING

1	Malus floribunda	2
2	Malus atrosanguinea	1
3	Prunus serrulata erecta	3
4	Magnolia soulangeana	1
5	Sorbus decora nana	2
6	Sorbus aria lutescens	1
7	Magnolia soulangeana alba	1
8	Rhus typhina laciniata	5
9	Viburnum davidii	18
10	Hydrangea paniculata grandiflora	12
11	Senecio laxifolius	13
12	Rosa farreri persaetosa	6
13	Cistus corbariensis	20
14	Buddleia davidii "Black Knight"	12
15	Rosa spinosissima "Fruhlingsmorgen"	5
16	Eleagnus ebbingei	10
17	Rhus cotinus folliis purpureis	16
18	Hydrangea villosa	14
19	Lavandula spica "Backhouse Purple"	23
20	Fothergilla monticola	12
21	Viburnum tinus	10
22	Paeonia ludlowii	22

UNDERPLANTING

PERMANENT — TEMPORARY

Ribes sanguineum "King Edward VII" 15

Caryopteris clandonensis 8

Erica vagans "Lyonesse" 25

Forsythia intermedia spectabilis 11

Erica vagans "St. Keverne" 16

Erica carnea atro-rubra 24

Euonymus radicans "Silver Queen" 28

Deutzia elegantissima 5

Chamaecyparissus nana 25

Philadelphus microphyllus 12

Pachysandra terminalis 20

Philadelphus "Enchantment" 8

STANDARD TREES + BUSH TREES +

MAIN GROUPS OF SHRUBS.. ∘∘

PERMANENT UNDERPLANTING ··

TEMPORARY UNDERPLANTING ××

0 5 10 15 ft

Fig. 1.8. Plan showing slow growing subjects with permanent underplanting and interplanting of rapidly growing shrubs which will be removed as the permanent planting matures.

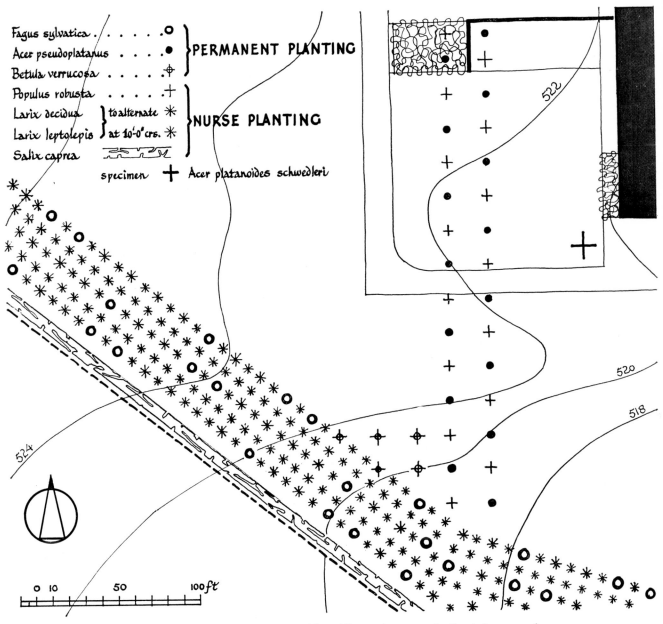

Fagus sylvatica . . . . ○
Acer pseudoplatanus . . . . . ● } PERMANENT PLANTING
Betula verrucosa . . . . . ⊕
Populus robusta . . . . . ╪
Larix decidua } to alternate ✳
Larix leptolepis } at 10'-0" crs. ✳ } NURSE PLANTING
Salix caprea ～～～
specimen ╋ Acer platanoides schwedleri

○ 10   50   100 ft

Fig. 1.9. Slow growing tree planting with rapidly growing nurse planting to be removed
as the permanent planting matures.

the fences, the sewage works, etc. will be played down
or concealed within the general landscape treatment. A
dam may be dominant, but the filter-beds concealed.

Distinction should be made between buildings mainly
occupied by people, such as schools, hospitals and dwellings, and buildings which are primarily cladding for
machines, such as factories and power stations. In the
former, views outwards and inwards are of equal importance, in the latter appearance from outside is paramount,
combined with working efficiency and consideration for
the staff.

All buildings, roads and car parks should be sited to
leave the maximum space available for other uses, e.g. a

dwelling should be sited to give the maximum space for
the enjoyment of the sunniest and most sheltered part of
the site. A south-west slope, sheltered from wind and free
of frost pockets, is the most favourable for a garden and
the building. The access road should be contrived so that
it does not cut through or overlook the most favourable
area (Fig. 1.11).

The same principle applies to hospitals, and to any
building whose inmates may wish to enjoy the grounds.
The siting of buildings, e.g. schools, requiring extensive
games facilities, will be governed by the availability of
sufficient level ground for playing fields.

In machine buildings any space not required for working purposes and traffic is likely to have a mainly visual

20

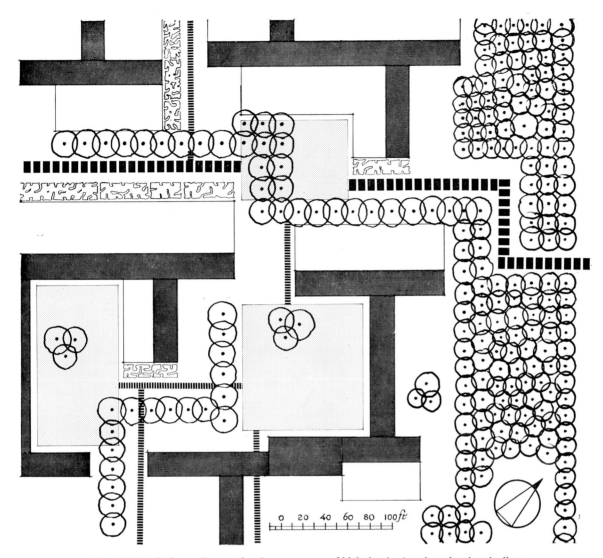

Fig. 1.10. Preliminary diagram for the open space of high density housing, showing the lines of movement and the static spaces.

function, and should be allocated where it will most help the surrounding views. For instance an adjustment of a few feet in siting the building in relation to a boundary may enable a screen or some large trees to be planted in a vital position.

Except in the case of a structure which it is intended to conceal, buildings should not be at the lowest point of the site for reasons of drainage. Only very rarely should they be at the highest. Even where it is intended that a building shall be in a commanding position, the brow of the hill is preferable to the actual summit (Fig. 1.12). Where it is desired to screen or partially screen the building and yet give it a good outlook, a position well below the brow is preferable (Fig. 1.13). In the case of a table-land, siting well back from the brow may give conceal-ment from surrounding lower land (Fig. 1.14). Such a position is however likely to be exposed.

Given good architecture, siting on steep ground is favourable to good landscape but both architecture and landscape will be more costly.

1.9.2 Siting the main plant masses

Tree planting. This may be required:

As protection against wind (see Fig. 1.17), noise or fumes.
To screen undesirable views into or out from the site.
To give privacy.
As a visual or ecological link with the surrounding landscape.
To frame views or form focal points.
To give shade.
To form space division (Figs. 1.17 and 1.18)

The general positions to serve these needs will make the skeleton of the planting—which may or may not be augmented in developing the plan.

21

Plate 1.8. Hedges above eye level help to create space division.
Rous Lench, Worcs.

The effects of leaf fall must be taken into account in the case of reservoirs, sewage works and roads. On the latter large leaves may cause skidding. Selection of correct species may often overcome the dangers. In siting trees the effect of their shadows on buildings, etc., must be recognised and the effect of their roots on structures (see Chapter 5).

Off-site planting. In dealing with large concerns such as power stations or oil installations, which will affect the surrounding countryside, the possibility of off-site planting should be considered. It is sometimes possible to arrange this with the local planning authority or with neighbouring land-owners.

Main hedge and shrub planting. These serve much the same purposes as tree planting but at a lower level. Where complete screening or shelter is required they should be combined with the tree planting. Visually hedges give space division. To register as more than a ground pattern they must be higher than eye level. Shrub planting gives the contrast of solid against the void of unplanted spaces (Plates 1.8 and 1.9). Shrub planting may also be required for ecological reasons, e.g. encouragement of wild life, the formation of game coverts and the amelioration of wet soil conditions. Any flower and colour effects should be considered within the context of the functional planting.

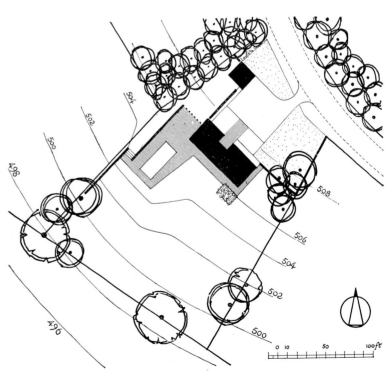

FIG. 1.11. House well sited for arrangement of a sheltered private garden and for pleasant views from principal rooms.

22

1.9.3 Contours

Much of the design potential of a site lies in its contours. They affect the siting of all construction. They can be used and manipulated to relate the site to its surroundings or to relate one element to another, e.g. a change of level can provide an access barrier without a visual barrier. If the change of level is sufficient, it can also provide a

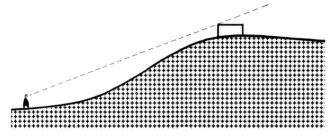

Fig. 1.12. A building in an exposed position, sited on the brow of a hill.

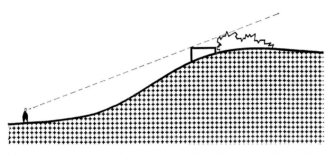

Fig. 1.13. A position below the brow allows both screening and a good outlook.

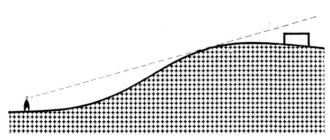

Fig. 1.14. Building on a table-land may be screened by the brow of the hill.

visual and sound barrier. This device can be used for such purposes as traffic separation, containing noise within a playground in residential areas, forming a noise baffle between heavy traffic roads and residential areas, and separating noisy activities from quiet areas in parks.

Changes of level are one of the most subtle means of creating the desired proportions between one space and another and of creating the element of surprise. Distances appear greater looking downhill, shorter looking up-hill. A very slight cross fall will be obvious seen against a building, while slight fall away from the building will be imperceptible.

Plate 1.9. Hedges below eye level form a ground pattern.

Most constructions produce surplus spoil from underground works. This must be planned for creatively in the site plan. It may be used either to unite the new construction with the existing landscape, or to contribute some new form to the landscape. Banks left at their angle of repose are rarely satisfactory unless used deliberately for a geometric effect. They are difficult to maintain. Any banks formed by the cut and fill of a levelled area must be dealt with in a positive way on the site plan and treated as part of the complete design. For details of ground modelling and related problems of drainage, etc. see Chapter 4—Earthworks.

1.9.4 Site boundaries (see also Chapter 6)

The site plan should always include enough of the surroundings to show their relationship to the site. In the case of a project having a wide field of influence a small-scale location plan is also needed. In this sense the site boundary must not form a mental barrier.

Plate 1.10. Shelter planting. Holland.

23

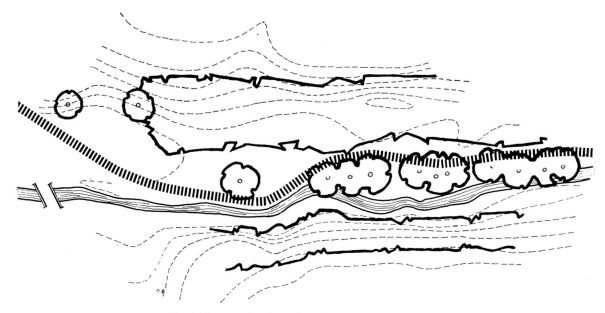

Fig. 1.15. PLAN showing valley siting of secluded footpath.

A physical barrier may be required for the following reasons:

> Legal definition.
> Prevention of trespass, safety barrier, stock and rabbit protection.
> Shelter.
> Delineation of land use.
> Visual sense of enclosure.
> A combination of these (Figs. 1.19, 1.20, 1.21, 1.22).

Types of boundary suitable for each purpose are considered in Chapter 6. The site plan should make clear the reason for and desirable characteristics of each boundary. A client requiring security fencing for certain parts of a site will usually assume that this security fence should follow the site boundary. But this is seldom either necessary or desirable. It will usually be found that a less drastic type of barrier can be used along at least part of the boundary, with the security fence sited back within the site, to protect whatever is vulnerable. This is particularly important where the boundary marches with a public road or footpath and the landscape architect should ascertain the genuine needs of the case.

1.9.5 Water (see also Chapter 8—Water)

If natural water is to be used, e.g. by the damming of a stream, the siting possibilities will be strictly limited, and therefore have priority of placing in building up the site plan. The possibility of using water should always be considered because of its unique value in a landscape. Where the possibility exists flooding will often be the best land-use for old workings or low-lying ground, owing to its value for fishing and recreation and the importance of water conservation for the landscape as a whole.

1.9.6 Street furniture (see also Chapter 7—Outdoor Furniture)

While the detailing of this will not appear in a site plan the positioning of the more important elements may do, and some reference to the type to be used may appear in the report. Items to be accommodated include shelters of various kinds, seats, litter bins, telephone kiosks and other Post Office fixtures, direction posts and notices. It may be impossible to site those items which are the responsibility of an authority other than the client, e.g. the Post Office fixtures. Constant review of site plans as development proceeds and consultation at the earliest

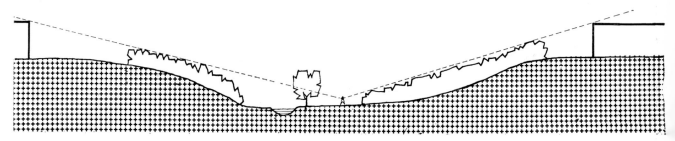

Fig. 1.16. SECTION showing footpath seclusion achieved by planting.

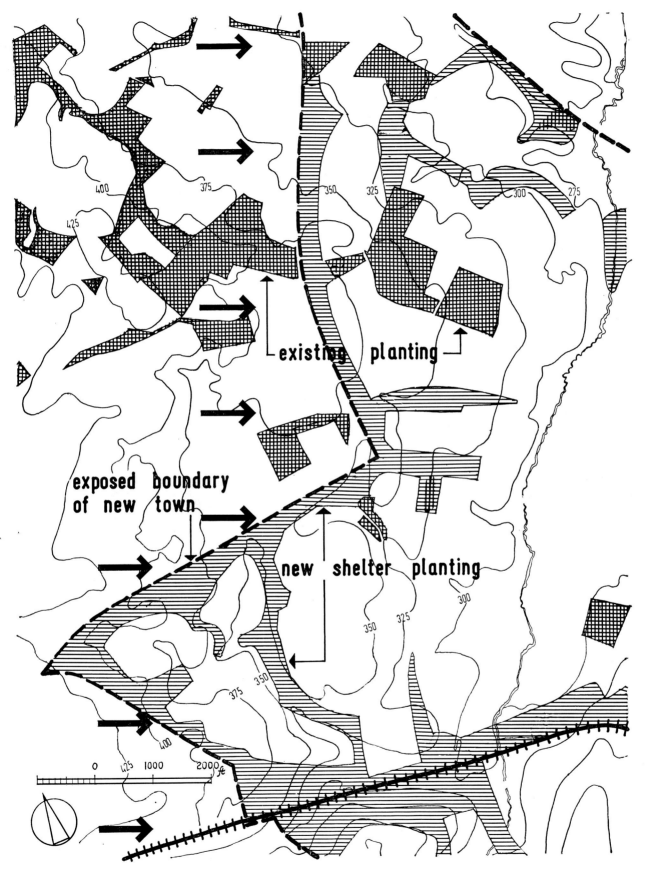

Fig. 1.17. Tree belts sheltering a New Town from prevailing winds.

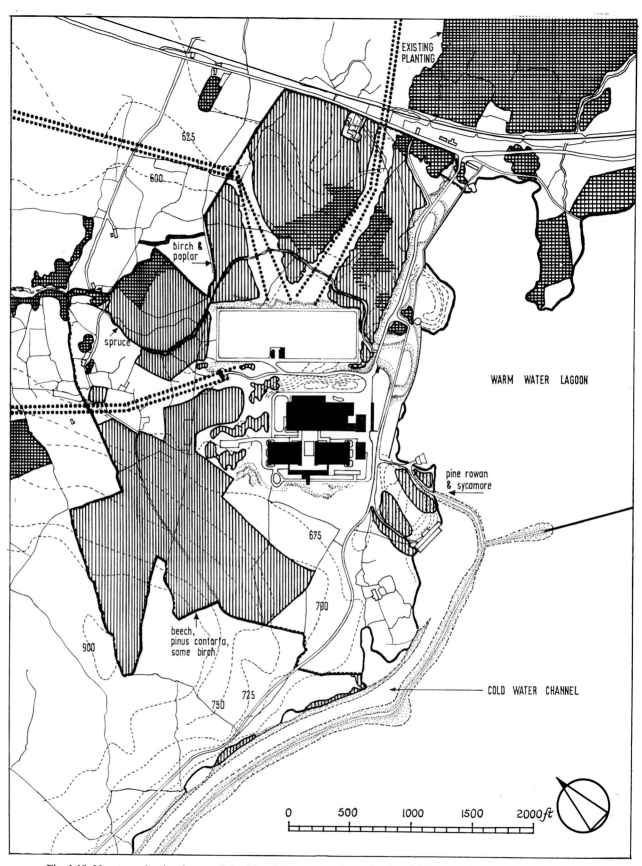

Labels on map:
EXISTING PLANTING

birch & poplar

spruce

WARM WATER LAGOON

pine rowan & sycamore

beech, pinus contorta, some birch

COLD WATER CHANNEL

625
600
675
700
800
900
750
725

0   500   1000   1500   2000ft

Fig. 1.18. New tree planting forms a link with existing scattered woodland and helps to unite a nuclear power station to its setting in the Welsh mountains.

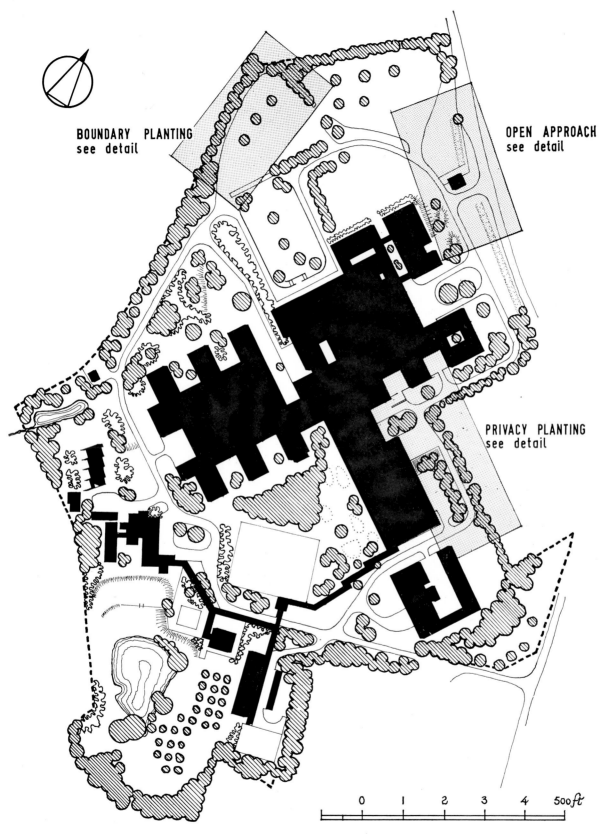

BOUNDARY PLANTING
see detail

OPEN APPROACH
see detail

PRIVACY PLANTING
see detail

0   1   2   3   4   500 ft

Fig. 1.19. A large hospital site where boundaries must be differently designed
according to need of security and privacy.

27

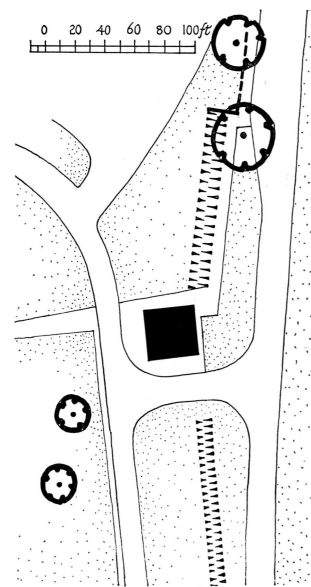

Fig. 1.20. Open approach detail. Ha-ha on boundary to preserve open views.

(e) floodlighting. In plans for projects which are to be kept subordinate to the surrounding landscape, the least conspicuous lighting fixtures are appropriate. But in public gardens the lighting may be displayed as part of the design. Early consultation with the lighting engineers is essential in all cases.

1.9.8 Drainage and underground services

The general configuration of the ground will govern the drainage plan. Undrainable areas on the site should be avoided if possible, but if they do occur must be foreseen and dealt with either by planting moisture-absorbing plants or some other means.

Drains and other services are often laid across the only spaces on a site which are large enough for trees. They

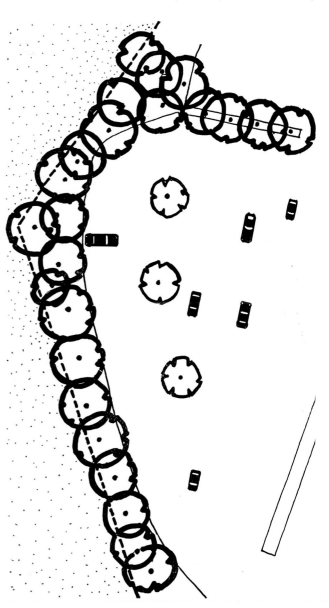

Fig. 1.21. Park railing defines boundary. Stock-proof but permits open view beneath tall trees.

opportunity, is the only method of dealing with these. Most public utility and other authorities in fact prove helpful if personal contact can be made with their representatives on the site and initiative is taken in offering alternative siting which meets their technical requirements.

1.9.7 Lighting (see also Chapter 7)

The general type of illumination, although not the details of lighting fitments should be included in a site plan. The alternatives are (a) column lighting. There are standard heights for different degrees of illumination. It is also possible to substitute a few very high columns for the regulation number of standard columns, (b) low level lighting, from bollards, hand rails, etc., (c) pavement lighting, (d) lighting fixtures incorporated in the buildings, should instead be laid compactly, preferably beside a path or fence line (Fig. 1.25). Early consultations on services are essential if the best use is to be made of the available space. Depth, vulnerability to root action and probable needs for access should be ascertained. The position and level of manholes should be agreed and incorporated into the plan.

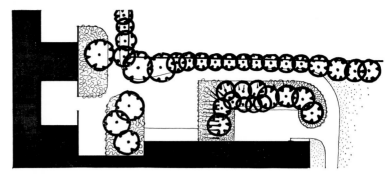

Fig. 1.22. Solid planting on the boundary to give complete screening for privacy.

1.10 Translation of basic information into landscape plan

The plan must be considered simultaneously as a contribution to the landscape as a whole and as a solution for the use requirements of the site. The first requirement is met by ensuring that the site will accord with, and contribute to, any pleasant character in its surroundings and will ameliorate any unpleasant character. Meeting the second requirement depends on the success with which the functions of the site are translated into an acceptable design form.

The site plan must not only present a solution which will work smoothly and efficiently, but must appear to do so—the most satisfying plans are those which look inevitable. A solution which appears forced or obviously clever is rarely the right one. The guiding principles of the plan will emerge from a study of the two sets of factors already considered (see pp. 3 and 4) but while they may often carry equal weight, and ideally may be synthesised into a new landscape, there are some cases where the site factors, and others where the use factors will dominate. For instance, when siting a camp in a National Park the site factors would have precedence, while in the design of an industrial site in an urban area, the use factors would predominate.

One of the first decisions should be how far the existing character of the site is to be preserved and how far modified. But whatever the decision, it must be realised that to some extent some adjustment is always necessary, since any change of land use or any introduced structure will make its mark on the site ecology and will need to be counteracted, while on the other hand, some of the original site conditions, such as climate and elevation will still be determining factors in the new landscape.

Certain elements of the plan will be seen to have priority in siting, e.g. function may decide the position of the access road or of structures. Site factors may make the siting of shelter-belts in certain positions essential, or the conservation of some particular feature, such as a skyline, a wood, or a view may be of paramount importance. These basic site factors must be grasped at the out-

set and a mental picture of the essential character of the site should be formed and adhered to, however much the details and arrangements of different elements may change during the evolution of the plan. The plan will evolve by manipulating all major elements into their optimum positions having regard to the site factors and then combining with them the smaller and more flexible elements.

It will usually be found that the functional elements tend to divide themselves into static spaces or rooms, and lines of movement or passages. The distinction and proper relationship between these elements is basic to the plan, and both by siting and treatment they should express repose and movement respectively. This principle applies even when the use of the static space is in itself active, as in a playing field, for it will still require to be offset from the lines of through movement. Equally, a path for strolling may be secluded and tranquil, but it still forms part of the pattern of movement (Fig. 1.10).

The most direct routes of access and communication between the various elements will form the basis of the movement pattern. But these direct routes may be modified in the interests of other aspects of the plan, such as the need for traffic separation, the need to keep certain static areas separated from movement and the general appearance and pleasantness of the site. A devious route may also be used for the sheer pleasure of wandering, but in this case its deviousness should never be apparent from any one point. In adjusting the various traffic flows, there will be priorities for destinations and types of traffic requiring direct routes, and tolerance for routes which can deviate without inconvenience.

The whole plan must be kept fluid until the essential elements have all been satisfactorily settled. Rigidity and premature detailing can cause mental barriers which prevent the emergence of the best solution.

Not only has every element of the plan a minimum size, but most have an optimum size, and it is equally important to allow ample space for those elements requiring it, and to scale down the space for elements requiring

29

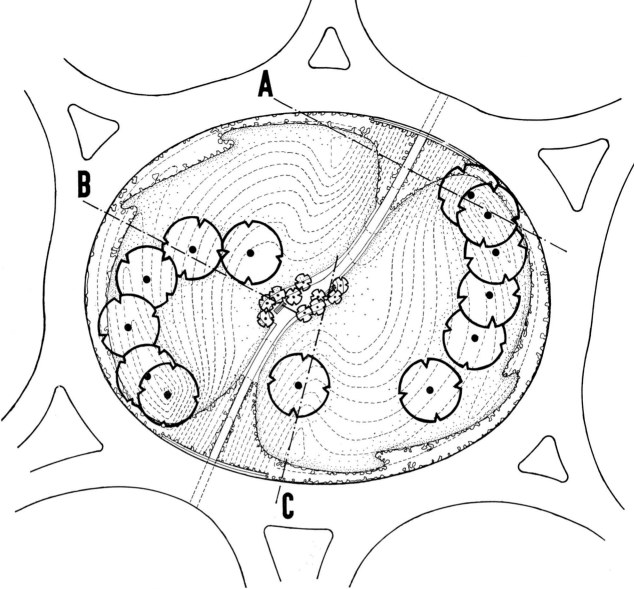

Fig. 1.23. Ground shaping to provide sound-baffle. Roundacre, Basildon. PLAN.

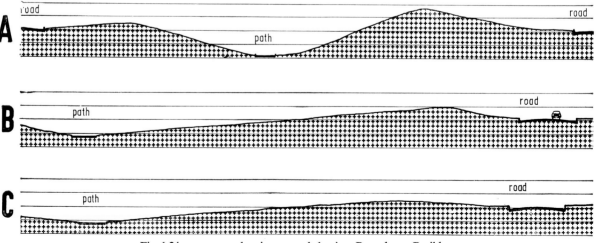

Fig. 1.24. SECTIONS showing ground shaping. Roundacre, Basildon.

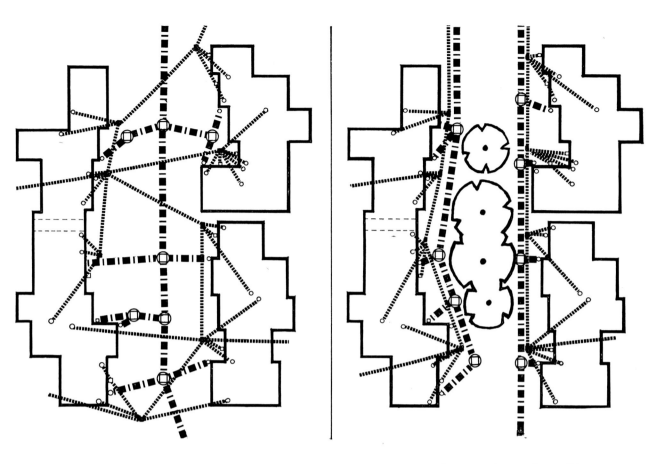

Fig. 1.25. Underground services cutting across a green may preclude tree planting. Rerouting may be possible.

a sense of enclosure and intimacy. For instance playing fields not only require a definite playing area (Fig. 1.4) but should also have space for trees, spectators and in many cases parking and car parks, while tree belts need sufficient space not only for the trees themselves but to give the necessary clearance for roots and shade. On the other hand, children's playgrounds and rest gardens need to be scaled down to give a feeling of seclusion and intimacy. These optimum sizes contribute to the variation in scale which is necessary to a successful plan.

At all stages of the plan up to the final dimensioned working drawings, some tolerance of spacing should be allowed to cover possible discrepancies in surveys, or in site constructions.

To summarise, the site plan should be coherent and well balanced, showing clearly its pattern of circulation, its areas for different uses and its structure of land-form and major planting. It should show its relationship to its surroundings and express the character of the site. It should enable the function of the site to operate efficiently remembering that pleasant living conditions and good appearance are part of that efficiency.

Bibliography

Landscape Architecture, John Ormsbee Simonds, Iliffe.
Site Planning, Kevin Lynch, M.I.T. Press, Cambridge, Massachusetts.
Playing Fields and Hard Surface Areas, Department of Education and Science, Building Bulletin 28, H.M.S.O., London.

2 Practice of Landscape Architecture

GEOFFREY COLLENS

2.1 The client

2.1.1 Different types of client

Although clients now include local authorities and government agencies there remain many private companies, organisations and individuals who seek landscape advice. After a decline in private garden design over a considerable period, there has been a certain revival in this type of commission in the last few years, together with the increase in larger scale work.

2.1.2 The main classification of clients

Private persons who wish to have gardens designed.

Local authorities who commission parks or reclamation schemes and seek advice on roads, siting of buildings and housing estates. The main types of local authorities are county councils, city, borough, urban district or rural district councils.

Government agencies such as the Ministry of Public Building and Works, the Forestry Commission and New Town Corporations.

Nationalised industries, national and local supply boards and their agencies, such as the Central Electricity Generating Board, local water boards and regional hospital boards.

Industrial concerns, private companies and developers who commission work concerned with commercial, industrial, reclamation, recreation and housing schemes.

Amenity societies who often ask for landscape advice in connection with their particular local problems.

Architects, engineers, town planners or members of other professional bodies who require the technical advice of a landscape architect and seek his collaboration as a consultant to themselves rather than to their client.

Some of the above clients may also need the advice of a landscape architect to help with planning inquiries at which he may be required to act as an expert witness to support their case or to oppose development proposals to which they object. In many cases the clients also employ landscape architects as members of their technical staff, sometimes using them as liaison officers between outside consultants and their employers. For example the Ministry of Public Building and Works, the Ministry of Transport, the Central Electricity Generating Board, the New Town Corporations, County Council Planning Departments, city authorities, and several local authority parks departments have their own staff of landscape architects.

2.1.3 Serving the client

A different response is needed for service to each type of client depending on the nature of the commission and the type of work required. Most private individuals like personal service with a minimum of letters and paper work and they often expect the advice of a landscape architect to include detailed explanations of schemes and of the plant material to be used. Committees and other similar clients often ask for more written material and regular reports but seldom require detailed explanations of projects once the basic designs have been agreed.

Private clients, both large and small, are usually in a hurry for a scheme to be produced and carried out. These clients sometimes include a small minority on whom pressure has been brought to bear, by planning authorities for example, to produce an acceptable development proposal which includes landscape treatment and who would not otherwise commission landscape designs.

Most local authorities and government agencies commission landscape architects in good time to work to a reasonable predetermined programme. However, there are still isolated cases where the landscape architect is brought in at the end of the planning stage and sometimes when the project is nearing completion, and is expected to finish off the job in a seemly manner. In these unfortunate cases it will often be found that financial provision for landscape work is inadequate. It should not be automatically assumed that work commissioned in conditions which are far from ideal will necessarily turn out unsatisfactorily and in the interests of good landscape the designer should attempt to do the best possible with limited time and resources.

2.1.4 Commissioning landscape work

In some local authorities the technical officer may have a complete say in the way the project is designed and handled with his responsibilities delegated to him by the relevant committee, but in some cases he is an intermediary and will have to submit all major issues to his committee for a final decision. He is usually an engineer but might be an architect, planner or an estates officer.

The technical officer may present consultant's schemes to the committee and it is quite usual for the consultant not to meet the committee members and to deal almost exclusively with the technical officer. But some direct contact with the committee is nearly always helpful. It is particularly desirable for the consultant to meet the committee when a scheme is presented for approval.

2.2 Briefing and conditions of engagement

2.2.1 The brief

The employer should start by setting out his requirements as a basis for discussion with the landscape architect who will refine these user requirements into a more explicit brief. The formulation of the programme is a two-way process, as the client does not always know exactly what he wants and needs to be guided by the landscape architect. The designer will find it almost impossible to produce a good scheme based upon a bad or confused brief, and it is essential that at this early stage the basic functional needs should be analysed and clarified so that time is not wasted in producing impractical sketch designs. A few large employers who commission schemes of a repetitive nature have evolved standard briefs and terms of reference within which a consultant can work.

2.2.2 I.L.A. conditions of engagement

The landscape architect is a skilled professional person qualified by examination before becoming a recognised practising member of the Institute of Landscape Architects. He works within a strict Code of Professional Conduct, but the Institute does not have a Royal Charter to give standing to its members as do the R.I.B.A. and T.P.I. Nor is there a Registration Act to restrict use of the professional title 'Landscape Architect' in the way, for example, the term 'Architect' is limited to those on a statutory register.

The landscape architect advises clients on all matters concerning the design and implementation of landscape work from the initial conception at sketch plan stage to the final certifying and checking of accounts on completion. He will advise on the approximate cost of the work, the most appropriate contract method, and the most suitable basis for assessing the fee. He is able to obtain and advise on estimates received from contractors and as to their suitability, as well as supervise the work during construction.

In the event of the client not knowing of a suitable landscape architect he may write to the Secretary of the Institute of Landscape Architects explaining the nature of the work and asking for suitable nominations.

2.2.3 I.L.A. nomination committee

The Secretary of the Institute will refer the client's enquiry to the Nomination Committee; this committee is composed of senior experienced members of the profession who are in no way concerned with private practice. Normally the prospective client would be sent a list of several names from which he can make his own final choice. When several landscape architects are being considered by a client for one particular project it is not ethical for any landscape architect to attempt to secure the work by any other means than by his own competence for the work in question.

2.2.4 I.L.A. scale of fees

There is a scale of fees prescribed by the Institute of Landscape Architects for most classes of work which is from time to time adjusted by the council as may be necessary. This scale (see *Conditions of Engagement and Scale of Professional Charges*, I.L.A., 1969) lays down the *minimum* fee which any member of the Institute will charge for his services. It is important for any client commissioning work to be certain that the landscape architect he appoints has the resources to cope with the scope of the work under consideration. It may well be that the fee required would be in excess of the prescribed minimum.

The Code of Practice does not permit members to charge less than minimum scale. This rules out attempts by clients to seek reduced fees and prevents undercutting of fees by members to secure the commission, and should there be any doubt as to the exact method of fixing the fees, members and clients are advised to contact the Secretary of the Institute who will obtain a ruling on the matter. There are many landscape works of a direct contract nature about which there need be little doubt in assessing the approximate final cost and the scale fee which would then be charged as percentage on the contract. This applies to sports grounds, public and private gardens, parks, etc.

Landscape architects by virtue of their own wide knowledge and design ability are more and more employed in a consultant capacity where there need be no contract work at the disposal of the landscape architect. This may apply to engineering, architectural, town planning and constructional developments carried out in association with other professions. In these and other similar cases the only reasonable method of fixing the fee is on a time basis, and the method of assessing this is clearly stated in the scale. As the time spent on schemes of this type can vary considerably according to the complexity and intricacy of the work it is generally not possible for the landscape architect to assess his total fee at the outset. The time-charge method has proved by usage and experience to be satisfactory and much work has been carried out for both government departments and local authorities who have been satisfied with the arrangement. If, however, for reasons of cost planning the client at the beginning would wish to exercise a more rigid control it is suggested that the work is programmed according to financial stages, and the landscape architect should inform the client when so much time has been spent, and the amount of fees due.

2.2.5 Formal agreement
In some instances a client will enter into a formal contract with the landscape architect and this will incorporate the fee basis to be adopted, together with the intervals at which payment will be made and other appropriate terms of reference. If the fee basis changes during the course of the contract a further written agreement will have to be signed by the client and the landscape architect to cover the amendment. In the absence of a signed contract the scale of fees should at least be confirmed in a letter before work commences.

2.3 Landscape reports

Reports are usually required only on larger schemes for local authorities or public bodies. Private clients do not often require reports of any size or frequency as they are usually keen to get on with the actual planning and construction work with a minimum of paper work beforehand. Reports for private clients are sometimes produced however where the employer wishes to carry out the work himself over a period of time.

2.3.1 Preliminary report
This will probably need to include most of the following items:

Assets of the site recorded (see also Chapter 3—Survey).
Special features influencing the design assessed, such as good vistas, worthwhile trees, existing streams and ponds and outcrops of rock.
Impact of buildings on their surroundings.
Change in natural landscape brought about by the development.
Description of existing site character.
Topography, climate, soil.
Maintenance problems.
Basic siting considerations.
Drawings, photographs, diagrams, montage presentation should also be included where appropriate to provide explicit information.

2.3.2 Main report
This will cover all aspects of the scheme starting from an analysis of user requirements (see also Chapter 1—Site Planning).

The main reasons for the landscape scheme will be described together with some details of the methods and programming of work by the landscape architect.

Descriptions of the type of planting and plant material will be needed.
Any off-site planting recommended should be the subject of a separate chapter.
A note on maintenance should give guidance to the client on this vital aspect.
The programming of work needs to be stated indicating the relationship to planting seasons.
If appropriate, recommendations should be made on immediate work to be undertaken, such as the establishment of tree nurseries.
Approximate cost figure for the total job must be given, together with any other statistics which are necessary.
Special details applicable to the site can be described and illustrated.
Perspectives should be included to illustrate the plans and to show the character being aimed at, and diagrams, site views and photographs of models are all helpful illustrative material.

It may be necessary to include details to specify amongst other things, surfaces, levels, grading, earth modelling, car park positions, rearrangement of roads and paths if desired, fencing recommendations, siting and design of external lighting.

2.3.3 Number of reports
The final report will contain many proposals which are subject to eventual modification and everything will be detailed more exactly in the working drawings which follow the production of the report. Where a report is required in quite a small scheme, this will be a single document which is simple and brief. A preliminary report followed by a final version are all that is required in normal circumstances and intermediate documents are only necessary when the programme is so long and

problems so complex that further reports covering special aspects are needed. Reports are favoured by all types of clients because they form an easy and attractive means of reference to the cardinal points of any project and can be referred to more quickly in a bound volume than in bundles of separate drawings.

2.4 Landscape drawings, specification and bill of quantities

All design work will be based directly on the site survey and an analysis of the client's requirements, and from this information working drawings will be made. There are advantages in preparing the design at the scale that will be used for working drawings, but in most cases this will involve more detail drawing than is necessary to indicate the suggested design, particularly if several alterations or amendments may be considered.

2.4.1 Working drawings

All working drawings should be set out direct from the original survey and grid and not from the sketch design drawings, to ensure a proper degree of accuracy. Working drawings for all constructional details should follow the current landscape and architectural practice of presentation and notation. Working drawings for large site work may have to follow civil engineering practice in showing sections and relating plans to grid or chainage lines.

For very large sites a map notation may be necessary and on most sites it will be essential to have a key master plan which indicates areas with special detailing set out separately on drawings at a larger scale.

Working drawings for planting plans must clearly show what is intended by containing a plant list on each planting plan. The scale of the plan should be large enough to show the actual names and positions of plants as this is the clearest system for a contractor to follow on site (see also Chapter 9—Planting). Alternatively a key system can be used with key numbers placed against each plant on plan. The plant list must be on the planting plan and not on a separate sheet and should be written like a bill of quantities containing the key number, the quantity, the Latin generic name, planting size and any special notes such as 'half standard, feathered, clean stem to 8 ft'. The common name may also be shown if the drawing is to be used by the client or others to whom this might be helpful. The plants listed should be varieties which are grown commercially and a requirement that stock should be from a nursery close to the site, although theoretically desirable, is often unreasonable in practice.

All working drawings should be fully dimensioned but the setting out of the plants might be made approximate, subject to staking out and checking on the site at the time of planting. If this is the case the procedure to be followed must be clearly defined in the specification so that the contractor fully appreciates that planting positions must be staked out for the landscape architect's approval before planting operations commence.

2.4.2 Bill of quantities

All except minor contracts should have a bill of quantities if put out to tender as this ensures that all tenderers bid on an equal basis and simplifies the making and pricing of amendments during the course of a contract. Part of the bill will consist of the plant schedule used on the planting plans. For substantial contracts a quantity surveyor should be engaged to prepare bills and to give a full service through to settlement of the final account.

Although there are many different ways of setting out the planting portion of the bill, there are some advantages in arranging for the price of each plant specified to include the complete cost of the planting operation. For example, for trees this will include the digging of the hole, providing topsoil to the tree pit, planting the tree, staking, tying and mulching. By ensuring that all these items of work are included in the one unit price a simpler method of pricing is obtained than when these items are broken down separately for pricing. Normal practice however is to itemise and price each labour separately and in this case variations are possible down to each item, for example, more excavation, extra ties, etc. Similarly it is sometimes advantageous to have a bill written in a manner which groups all the work related to one area e.g. 'north courtyard' or 'screen planting to car park') especially on large contracts. Major design alterations or omissions can then more readily be managed than if all paving and all planting is bulked together. Although this separation may be more difficult for the contractor to price, it does permit the use of special rates; these are reduced for bulk work in a simple area, and increased to cover difficulties of access to internal courtyards for example.

2.4.3 Specification

All contracts using a bill of quantities must also incorporate a specification. This is usually divided into main sections following a system of lettered and numbered clauses.

General Conditions

This covers the preliminary aspects of the contract and sets out all the items of administration and overheads which must be allowed for in the contract pricing.

Materials

All materials to be used and the appropriate suppliers are specified and standards are laid down including reference to British Standards where they are applicable. Materials will include a detailed description of paving, grass seed mixtures, fertilisers, tree stakes and ties, and all other supplies which are needed for the particular contract.

Workmanship
Here should be described the specific methods of construction, planting, turfing, etc., to be used on the contract.

Maintenance
This section will clarify the degree of maintenance to be included as part of the contract showing what work is expected in this respect both during and after the contract. It will also include clarification of the system of guarantees on materials and plants which may be written into the contract. The maintenance period may vary depending on the time of year the contract is done, but is seldom more than 9–12 months.

Bill of Quantities
As previously described, covering all items of materials and work.

Schedule of Rates, Materials and Labour.

The specification should cover all the necessary items as briefly as possible. Long and complex documents may confuse the contractor and probably add to the price of tenders received. This demands a proper blend of common sense and business management. An elaborate specification for a small or simple job will do nothing to secure the client's proper needs. On the other hand a large project for a public authority requires a systematic specification especially when work may extend over a long period.

2.5 Letting the contract

The two parties to the contract are the employer and the contractor and although the landscape architect will act as the agent of the client in all details and negotiations on the running of the contract, it is his clear duty to act fairly and impartially in enforcing reasonable standards of materials and workmanship, within the limits indicated in the contract. On difficult sites and in adverse weather conditions there may be occasions when he must exercise discretion and expect no more than is reasonable from this specialist contractor and here the landscape architect must be quite firm as the arbiter of what is reasonable even if the client has different views.

2.5.1 Negotiated contract
In some instances, depending on the type of work, it is possible to arrange for a tender to be negotiated with one selected landscape contractor without inviting competitive bids. This usually occurs for private clients only and generally on high class schemes where a first rate contractor is selected on the basis of other work he has undertaken of a similar nature. Even in these circumstances a bill of quantities and specification must be used so that a simple and effective method is obtained for running a contract and checking the value of the work.

2.5.2 Tenders
If competitive tenders are to be obtained a list of firms to be invited should be agreed with the client before the contractors are asked whether they wish to tender. Some authorities have approved lists of contractors or sub-contractors from which a selection can be made or agreed with the client. Most local authorities have standing orders which regulate invitation of tenders and sometimes it may be necessary to invite open tendering from all contractors who wish to submit a price. A firm indication of intention to tender should be obtained from each contractor on the agreed list before tender documents are despatched.

It is usual to obtain not less than three and not more than six competitive prices for a job, the latter number being on more important large contracts. Each tenderer will be sent a contract document in duplicate (at least) which will include the bill of quantities, and/or specification and working drawings. He will be asked to return one set of documents duly completed in a special envelope to be opened only at a specified date and time.

Some engineering consultants ask for several copies, triplicate or more, but this places an unreasonable administrative burden on the smaller contractor. Adequate time should be allowed for pricing; at least two full working weeks. Tenders are often opened in the presence of the client.

2.5.3 Contracts and sub-contracts
It is usual to arrange for the successful contractor and employer to enter into a formal agreement on a standard I.L.A. form of contract, but in many instances the employer (especially public bodies, corporations and large firms) has his own form of contract which would be used in place of the I.L.A. one.

In some cases the landscape work is a sub-contract to a building contract and in these circumstances the R.I.B.A. nominated sub-contractor standard form or similar will be used. This tender form indicates that prices must allow for the $2\frac{1}{2}\%$ discount which the general contractor is entitled to receive on the value of all sub-contracts. The landscape contractor will then be a 'nominated sub-contractor', that is to say his employment will not have been decided upon by the general contractor himself. Alternatively it is possible to measure landscape work in the main bill and allow the general contractor to sub-contract or otherwise arrange for the execution of the work. This is a reasonable method for landscape work which includes a high proportion of earth moving, paving and details of a constructional nature; all items which may be somewhat beyond the experience and equipment of the average landscape contractor. For planting work this method is not satisfactory and the general contractor should be required to have the work done by a specialist.

The advantage of having the landscape work as a sub-contract is that its programming and dovetailing with the building work is under the direction of the general contractor who organises all trades on the site. However, care must be taken to ensure that the general contractor fully accepts this responsibility. Given the opportunity, he may attempt to disclaim the specialist skill needed for general organisation of landscape work, and unreasonably pass the entire burden of supervision to the landscape architect.

One disadvantage of this method is that the settlement of the final account of the building contract has to be delayed until the maintenance period of the landscape sub-contract has expired which invariably is at a date much later than the end of the building maintenance period, although this can be an incentive for the general contractor to see that the work is properly programmed and completed on time. Problems can also arise over payment as this will come to the landscape contractor through the main contractor instead of direct from the employer. When the main contractor is behind schedule he must cooperate with the landscape sub-contractor whose work is partly seasonal and cannot be reprogrammed easily.

It should be clearly stated that the successful tenderer is not permitted to sub-let any part of the work without the prior written agreement of the landscape architect.

2.5.4 Acceptance of tenders

It is usual for the lowest tender to be accepted, but if good reasons exist it may be desirable in rare instances to appoint the second lowest and the right for the employer to choose other than the lowest tender should clearly be stated in the general conditions of the specification. Acceptance or rejection of tenders should be decided upon without delay and the unsuccessful tenderers informed accordingly, and a contract signed by the successful firm.

From time to time problems of contract procedure arise. These may be of a minor nature (incorrectly addressed tenders for example) and no more than commonsense and ordinary fairness is necessary. More serious problems can arise and the checking and advice of an experienced quantity surveyor is invaluable in these circumstances. Exceptionally, however, serious problems may arise which call for discretion, careful judgment and scrupulous fairness.

2.6 Consultations

2.6.1 Relationship with other professions

Although there are projects where the landscape architect is the only professional person employed, in most cases he is one of a team or group of consultants, such as town planners, architects, engineers, horticulturists, agriculturists and foresters. It is essential at the beginning of every project to ensure that the limits of responsibility are clearly defined. In some cases for instance the landscape architect will be responsible for all the space between buildings while on other occasions he may design the soft landscape work only with the hard landscaping detailed by architects or engineers.

From the outset the method of working between members of a group of consultants must be decided to ensure efficient design and running of the contract. All the operations on site and production of drawings should be agreed between consultants to avoid conflict or overlapping of responsibility on drawings or in specifications. As a general working rule, ultimate project responsibility should rest with only one supervisory architect, landscape architect, engineer or other consultant. Specialist advice, negotiations and sub-contracts must be dealt with to channel information and instructions through this principal. On large projects or in the case of teams experienced in working together, this central responsibility may be little more than nominal, but it should clearly exist to be used in cases of doubt and difficulty.

2.6.2 Meetings

In exclusively landscape contracts the landscape architect will initiate regular site meetings, but where the landscape work is included as a sub-contract, landscape problems will be dealt with during the course of normal site meetings dealing with the main contract. All those expected to be present at a meeting should receive notification, ideally 3–4 weeks in advance. Where regular meetings are held (often monthly), reminders should still be sent out. In all major contracts the principal or the landscape architect supervising the contract should attend such meetings and not send an assistant.

Minutes of all meetings should be taken, but must be brief and to the point, recording all decisions but omitting full reports of lengthy discussions. These must be circulated to all those present and to others who are involved. As a result of some important meetings a brief report may need to be made to the client or other interested party not normally present or represented at site meetings.

2.6.3 Advisory work

Many large developers of land now engage landscape architects as consultants to advise on general policy and to assist with particular projects. Many afforestation, conservation, coastal, reclamation, road development, national and regional park, power production and distribution problems are now being tackled by national agencies with the advantage of such advice. Executive authority is not vested in the landscape architect, in fact no actual landscape contract may arise out of consultations, but by a process of formulating agreed land use policies, major decisions of land acquisition, design and management can be made, with due consideration having been given to overall landscape needs.

In the case of particular projects, of power production, New Towns, etc., a landscape architect may also be retained as a consultant to advise on policy and special problems. The authority may carry out substantial landscape works under its own technical staff on the basis of advice accepted.

Consultation procedures must be devised to suit each particular client and problem. Site meetings and committee procedures can be extensive, but regular attendance and prompt submission of reports are essential to establish confidence and to give the client a landscape service which will be respected and acted upon. Personal qualities are of primary importance but they must be backed by efficient office routine geared to match the scale and pace of each project. If the authority employs its own landscape staff their ability to adopt proper landscape policies, secure adequate financial provisions, and carry out effective work will usually be reinforced by the assistance of the consultant. Close collaboration here can be readily established.

2.7 Contract management and supervision

2.7.1 Control of work in progress

Where the landscape architect is retained to give a full service, site visits will be required regularly during the course of the contract. Although impromptu visits have advantages at times, it is often advisable for site visits to be arranged for a specific time, with the contractor, so that he can be on hand to answer queries or raise points needing immediate site decisions. It is very desirable, especially on large schemes to have a competent clerk of works capable of supervising the landscape work. Unless this is the case the landscape architect is burdened with an unreasonable degree of day to day supervision.

Special arrangements must be made for landscape work which is a sub-contract. The landscape architect and the specialist contractor may have an informal working arrangement, acting directly and keeping the architect or general contractor fully informed. But formal contract responsibility for giving instructions will be that of the architect or engineer (on whose behalf the landscape architect is acting as a consultant). The formal instructions will be given direct to the general contractor who must then instruct his sub-contractor.

All site instructions should be confirmed in writing immediately on return to the office. It is an advantage to use some kind of standard instruction form so that all communications to the contractor during the course of the contract are in a file of quick reference sheets which eliminate the need for looking through a correspondence file for information.

It is possible to divide these forms into two categories:

Landscape architect's instructions which clarify a point or tell a contractor to proceed with some particular portion of the work, not involving any alteration in the contract.

Variation orders which instruct the contractor to make variations in the contract by omission, addition or substitution. The variations must refer where applicable to the original clause number in the bill of quantities. It is useful for office purposes to note the reason for the variation and whether the client needs to be informed. All changes in the plans or specification should be confirmed in a variation order issued by the landscape architect and the pricing of the additions or omissions should be agreed at the same time.

If the specification states that the employer is entitled to accept part or the whole of a tender there is a case for specifying the percentage latitude allowed in this possible variation, especially when applying to large quantities of plants, where a low unit rate is quoted because of the quantities involved. If additions are made which cannot be based on the unit price in the tender, a price must be obtained for the work from the contractor and approved by the client, if necessary, before an instruction is given to proceed with the extra. This avoids disputes on prices of new items at the final account stage.

2.7.2 Certifying payments

During the course of the job the contractor will submit statements for the value of work done and the landscape architect, if satisfied that this a correct assessment, will have made out a certificate for 90% of the amount (or 80% of materials on site), 10% being retained for the period of the contract.

The contract will normally state that the employer must honour the certificate by paying the contractor within 28 days of the certification. In most cases half of the 10% retention is released at the point of practical completion and half at the end of the maintenance period.

2.7.3 Hand-over of site
At the time of practical completion, the site should be offered for hand-over to the client or his representative, so that a clear understanding is reached on the terminating of the contractor's responsibility and the beginning of the client's for maintaining the scheme. The hand-over is most conveniently timed either in autumn or spring, owing to the seasonal nature of the work. However, on many sites it will be found that the hand-over is not a single clear-cut matter. The client, may for example, have to take over grassed areas after the contractor's first cuts, but will not necessarily take over planted areas at that time. This sort of arrangement should be avoided if at all possible. On large sites, particularly those associated with extensive building projects or housing schemes in which blocks are handed over stage by stage, there may be corresponding staged completions of landscape work. It is very important that all parties concerned, architect, general contractor, specialist contractor, client and his maintenance staff should be advised by the landscape architect, in writing, of the up-to-date division of maintenance responsibilities. In all cases the parcels for hand-over should be as large as possible and all elements of parcels should be complete.

A maintenance inspection must be held at the end of the maintenance period, at which point the contractor will be instructed to remedy the defects and replace dead plants where these failures are the result of his work. These remedial works and replacements will be done at the contractor's own expense and this fact must be clearly stated in the specification. Some additional replacements may be necessary at the client's expense, in certain circumstances. Once this work is done and the client has agreed to take over, all maintenance and replacement work is the sole responsibility of the owner, unless he retains the contractor on a separate maintenance contract, which is a course of action seldom taken. The need for good thorough maintenance and after-care is not always fully appreciated by clients. Their attention should be drawn to this important aspect to ensure that the newly-planted scheme does not suffer from neglect after completion, resulting in large numbers of plant casualties and the gradual disintegration of the design concept (see also Chapter 12—Administration and Maintenance).

2.7.4 Final account
If a file of variation orders has been kept carefully the final account will be a simple matter of pricing out the items on these forms. If it is a fixed priced contract, most of these items can be calculated by reference to the unit price and schedule of rates for materials and labour contained in the tender and contract documents. Settlement of the final account is made easier if the variations have been priced as the job proceeds and are not all left to the end of the contract. The contractor should be asked to sign the final account when it has been agreed.

2.8 Negotiations and legal aspects relevant to landscape architecture

2.8.1 Consultations with authorities
Consultations with statutory and local authorities are necessary on many jobs. On frequent occasions planning permission is granted for development subject to a satisfactory landscape scheme being submitted for approval.

Normally, provided the client agrees, this should be discussed with the planning department concerned before a formal submission is made, in order that the planting scheme takes into account the particular reason for the request for landscape work in the planning consent. With such a condition applied to a consent it is often essential for the landscape proposals to be prepared for approval before any building takes place on the site.

2.8.2 Town and Country Planning Act, 1962
This Act consolidates the Town and Country Planning Act, 1947 with its subsequent amending Acts.

The Act and its predecessor establishes a comprehensive control of land use in England and Wales. First, it provides that all development taking place on land after 1 July 1948, must have planning permission. 'Development' is defined as 'the carrying out of building, engineering, mining or other operations in, on, over or under land, or the making of any material change in the use of any building or other land'. Both in the Act and in delegated legislation under the Act certain exemptions are made in order to reduce the administrative burden of dealing with applications for all types of development which fall within the definition. Secondly the Act nominates county councils and county borough councils as local planning authorities with the functions of granting permissions, subject to permission for county councils to delegate this function to county district councils in certain circumstances. Thirdly, the Act makes the Minister of Housing and Local Government the chief policy maker for land use.

(Further amending legislation was enacted in 1968, but the principles described here remain.)

Accordingly in relation to landscape and site layout work the importance of the Act is that it requires planning permission to be obtained in all cases except where it is automatically granted under the Act or subordinate legislation. Of particular interest is the power contained in the Act to make Tree Preservation Orders, Building

Preservation Orders and orders to compel the proper maintenance of waste land.

By the Town and Country Planning (Landscape Areas Special Development) Order, 1950, the automatic planning permission granted by delegated legislation to enable agricultural and forestry building and works to be carried out is made subject to a condition that notification of such a development is to be made to the local planning authority, who have fourteen days in which to object after which time, if no such objection is made, the development can be carried out.

2.8.3 Tree Preservation Orders

A planning authority has statutory powers to place Tree Preservation Orders on individual trees or groups or woodlands which it considers worthy of preservation within the area of its jurisdiction. This most frequently happens in towns and suburbs well endowed with trees but subject to appreciable redevelopment where the planning authority wishes to ensure that redevelopment will not involve the loss of the best trees in the area. There are also powers for speedy emergency placing of Tree Preservation Orders under the Civic Amenities Act.

Once a Tree Preservation Order has been served on an owner of a property the specified trees normally may not be cut down without the prior consent of the planning authority. A fine can be, and often is, imposed for non-compliance with such an order.

If a landscape architect is involved in the planning of a scheme containing trees protected by a preservation order he will often find that a flexible attitude will be adopted by the planning authority and that some trees which inhibit the building layout can be removed if the final scheme proposes new trees sufficient in number and size to provide a degree of replacement for the loss.

The Tree Preservation Order should be applied to sites before planning applications are submitted as there is some doubt about the validity of placing such an order on a site where the planning permission granted implies the acceptance of the removal of existing trees.

2.8.4 Forestry Acts, 1919–51

The Forestry Act, 1919, established the Forestry Commission and charged them with the general duty of promoting the interests of forestry, the development of afforestation and the production and supply of timber in the United Kingdom. The Act empowers the Commissioners to make advances by way of grant or loan for the purpose of the afforestation or replanting of land, to establish or assist in the promotion of woodland industries, to collect and publish statistics relating to forestry, to promote and develop education in forestry, to carry out forestry research and experiments, and to make or aid in making such enquiries as they think neces-

sary for the purpose of securing an adequate supply of timber in the United Kingdom.

The Forestry Act, 1945, changed the constitutional status of the Forestry Commission. Forest policy became the direct responsibility of the Minister of Agriculture and Fisheries and the Secretary of State for Scotland acting jointly, and the exercise of the functions of the Commissioners became subject to the direction of those Ministers, the powers of the commissioners to acquire land being transferred to the Ministers. The land vested in the Commissioners, at the date of the Act, became vested in the Ministers, who manage and use, as they think fit, any land vested in or acquired by them which they have not placed at the disposal of the Commissioners for the purpose of the exercise of their functions. The land in the possession of the Commissioners at the date of the Act was deemed to have been placed at the disposal of the Commissioners until the Ministers otherwise direct. The Commissioners' powers under the Forestry Act, 1919, in respect of forestry operations, education, research and grants were unaffected.

The Forestry Act, 1947, provided for the dedication of land to forestry purposes, the enforcement of forestry dedication covenants (in England and Wales) and of dedication agreements (in Scotland), and empowered certain classes of owners to enter into such covenants or agreements.

The Forestry Act, 1951, made permanent the control by licensing of the felling of growing trees, previously operated as a temporary measure under *Defence Regulation No. 68*. The control was taken over from the Board of Trade by the Forestry Commissioners in January 1950.

The Forestry Act, 1967, consolidates the various Forestry Acts from 1919 to 1963. In 1965 the forestry functions of the Ministry of Agriculture in Wales were transferred to the Secretary of State for Wales. The Secretary of State for Scotland is still responsible for forestry in Scotland.

2.8.5 The woodland dedication scheme

This scheme has already been adopted by over 2,800 estates, involving over 850,000 acres of woodland, and provides the most comprehensive form of assistance available from the Forestry Commission. Briefly, the owner enters into a covenant or agreement with the Forestry Commission, under which he undertakes to manage his woodlands for the main purpose of timber production in accordance with an agreed plan of operations, and to ensure skilled supervision. In return he receives, under the Basis II provisions which have been most generally adopted:

Planting grant, currently £22 12s. per acre, for every acre satisfactorily planted, replanted, or otherwise restocked.

Annual management grant, in respect of all effectively managed woodlands, which for this purpose include those existing at the date of dedication, plus in most cases a further area determined by the agreed plan of operations, to cover replanting and extensions. The amount of grant is currently at the rates of 20s. 3d. per acre for the first 100 acres, 13s. 9d. for the second 100 acres, and 8s. 9d. for the remainder, on any one estate.

Alternatively, an owner may elect, at the outset, to receive assistance under the Basis I arrangement. He will then receive 25% of the approved net annual expenditure on the dedicated woodlands, until such time as they become self-supporting. If he adopts this basis, he must keep accounts in a prescribed form.

An owner who dedicates his woodlands binds himself, and his successors in title, not to use the lands so dedicated for any purposes other than forestry. Provision is however made for a relaxation of this requirement should exceptional circumstances arise. When a dedicated estate changes hands, the successor in title is invited to continue to manage the woods under the approved plan of operations, and if he undertakes to do so he becomes entitled to the appropriate grants.

2.8.6 The National Parks and Access to the Countryside Act, 1949

The Act established the National Parks Commission with powers to formulate proposals for the establishment of National Parks and advisory functions for the preservation and enhancement of natural beauty throughout England and Wales. There are no National Parks in Scotland. The recent Amenity Lands Act (Northern Ireland), 1965, makes legislative provision for National Parks there. Responsibility for each National Park rests with the County Council where the whole of the park is within one county. In other cases a planning board or a joint advisory committee is established. In the former case the board is the local planning authority for its area instead of the County Council. Fig. 2.1 shows the location of National Parks established under the National Parks and Access to Countryside Act, 1949.

Control of development is exercised under the general powers of the Town and Country Planning Acts as elsewhere, but the park authority is specifically instructed to have regard to the needs of agriculture and forestry. The park authorities have powers and may be assisted by government grants to provide accommodation, meals, camping sites and car parks. They may improve waterways for amenity, and restrict traffic on roads in conjunction with the Ministry of Transport. The authority may supply information about the park to the public by means of publications and information centres.

The Act enables the local planning authority in a National Park or elsewhere to enter into access agree-

Fig. 2.1. National Parks in England and Wales established under the National Parks and Access to the Countryside Act, 1949.

ments with owners of open country, or in default of agreement by Access Orders, to enable the public to enjoy these areas for recreation. A warden service may be established to assist visitors and to enforce bye-laws to ensure proper standards of behaviour. The Act provides other powers available throughout the country. These enable authorities to plant and improve areas of derelict land.

Areas not suitable for designation as National Parks may be designated as Areas of Outstanding Natural Beauty. The Act enables the Nature Conservancy to establish Nature Reserves and local authorities may also do this.

The Act provides for a survey of public rights of way,

for the settlement of disputes over such rights and for definitive maps of rights of way, subject to periodic revision. New rights of way may be created if necessary by compulsion. Paths may be diverted and obsolete paths closed. The National Parks Commission have powers to propose long-distance routes for walking or horse riding. If approved by the Minister* the local authorities are responsible for carrying out the work of creating new rights of way and for maintenance with the aid of government grants. In 1968 the Countryside Commission took over the powers and responsibilities of the National Parks Commission, and in addition is responsible for guiding the creation of Country Parks.

The National Parks Commission and the Nature Conservancy are required to prepare annual reports. These reports† are valuable accounts of progress in these fields.

2.8.7 Control of caravan and camp sites
Caravan sites are controlled under the Caravan Sites and Control of Development Act, 1960, and the Public Health Act, 1936. Camping sites for tents, etc., are controlled under the Town and Country Planning Acts. Generally, a person intending to operate a caravan site must obtain planning permission from the local planning authority and a site licence from the local authority. The licence must be prominently displayed on the site. Local authorities may themselves provide caravan sites.

Planning permission and a site licence are not required if the caravan is used in conjunction with a dwelling house, is on the site for less than 28 days in a year and used only casually, is under the auspicies of an approved recreational organisation, or is used in connection with building or agricultural operations or travelling showmen.

The Minister of Housing and Local Government is empowered to specify model standards‡ for caravan sites. The standards made in 1960 may be summarised as follows.

Permanent residential caravan sites
Caravans should be at least 20 ft apart and not less than 10 ft from a carriageway. The density should not exceed 20 caravans per acre.

Roads should be at least 13 ft wide (9 ft if part of a one way traffic system). Footpaths should be at least 2 ft 6 in wide.

* In England the Minister of Housing and Local Government In Wales the Secretary of State for Wales.
† *National Parks Commission and Nature Conservancy Annual Reports*, H.M.S.O. The Nature Conservancy Council now operates in conjunction with the Natural Environment Research Council and makes no separate reports (since 1 June 1965).
‡ *Model Standards for Caravan Sites*, H.M.S.O., 1960.

No caravan or toilet block should be more than 150 ft from a road. Each caravan should have a hard-standing.

Provision for fire-fighting equipment, water supply, drainage, sanitation and washing facilities are specified. Each caravan should have a refuse bin.

Lockable covered storage space, at least 30 sq ft per caravan, should be provided not less than 15 ft from any other caravan, but separate from the caravan served.

Properly surfaced parking space for a minimum of one car per three caravan standings is specified. Other spaces, not necessarily surfaced, should bring the provision up to one parking space per caravan.

An area equivalent to one-tenth of the site area should be devoted to recreational purposes.

Holiday caravan sites
(sites in regular use, except during the winter)

The density should not exceed 25 caravans per acre.

Standards for water supply, drainage, washing facilities, paving footpaths, storage facilities and hard standings are relaxed from those specified for residential sites.

Where densities are 12 to the acre or less, no standing should be more than 180 ft from a water stand pipe.

2.8.8 Agriculture Act, 1947
Under this legislation Agricultural Advisory Services were established which can supply technical advice and information which can be of considerable value to the landscape architect undertaking large scale landscape surveys and dealing with landscape and planning problems in the countryside.

Bibliography

Caravan Parks—Location, layout, landscape, H.M.S.O., 1962.
Elements of Quantity Surveying (5th Edition), Willis.
Handbook of Architectural Practice and Management, Royal Institute of British Architects.
Specification (section on Landscape), Architectural Press.
Specification Writing for Architects and Surveyors, Willis, Architectural Press.
Standard Method of Measurement, Royal Institution of Chartered Surveyors.
Standard Method of Measurement, Institution of Civil Engineers.

I.L.A. standard instruction/variation forms and certificates are available from the secretary of the I.L.A.

3 Site Survey and Appreciation

NORMAN CLARKE

3.1 Introduction

3.1.1 The need for a survey

A landscape survey is the collation of detailed information not only in respect of the physical characteristics of a site but of all relevant information and data on the factors and influences affecting the site and its development. It is the basis on which a landscape scheme is founded and the quality of the landscape architect's design will depend on the appraisal and use of the information obtained. This information comprises:

A survey of the physical characteristics of the area, its form and content and factors affecting its use and development for the purposes required.

The landscape architect's visual observations made on the site and the appreciation of the influence of the outer landscape on that of the site and *vice versa*.

The necessary research made into the various aspects of the problem.

These factors will all contribute to an intimate knowledge of the site and its possibilities in formulating a functional and effective scheme.

The recording of adequate and accurate information will be of prime importance not only during the preparation of a proposed scheme but also in the later preparation of the bills of quantities and contract documents.

3.1.2 The preliminary survey

The first informal reconnaissance must be a personal inspection by the landscape architect and cannot be delegated.

It starts as the site is approached, with an appreciation of the surrounding landscape for no region or site can be regarded as self-contained, except perhaps the small private garden.

An Ordnance Survey contoured map, $2\frac{1}{2}$ inches or 6 inches to the mile, according to the size of the area to be inspected, will be necessary together with a 1 : 2,500, 1 : 500 or 1/16th plan showing the basic features, buildings, boundaries, access, etc. A camera or sketchbook will also be useful for recording purposes.

A preliminary inspection of the topography, soil, vegetation, drainage, buildings and roads, and a visual appraisal of the views into and out from the site will provide a basic knowledge of the site's assets and liabilities, its character and its problems.

3.1.3 The detailed survey

The preliminary survey will be followed by the systematic collection of more detailed information, all of which must be recorded and indicated cartographically, diagrammatically or pictorially. This information may be obtained from published maps and data, some parts of it may be provided by the plans and drawings of the architect, engineer or others also engaged on the site, and some information may be provided by specialists such as meteorological consultants.

The following is a guide to the information required in a survey for most kinds of landscape development and the means of recording it. For smaller schemes it may not be necessary to investigate some of these aspects of a survey but even when such detailed information is not required an assessment of it will need to be made during the design process. For instance, whilst it may not be necessary to prepare detailed geological and ecological maps for a small project the landscape architect's brief observations of the nature of the ground and vegetation and his experience and knowledge of similar conditions will guide him in his planting proposals.

3.2 Information needed for the landscape survey

3.2.1 Topography

The topographical map is the basic plan of the area. It may be based on an Ordnance Survey map or a geometrical survey to a suitable scale and will show the shape and physical details, the ground form, boundaries and all existing natural features of the site. (Fig 3.1)

Scenery. The type and pattern of the immediate

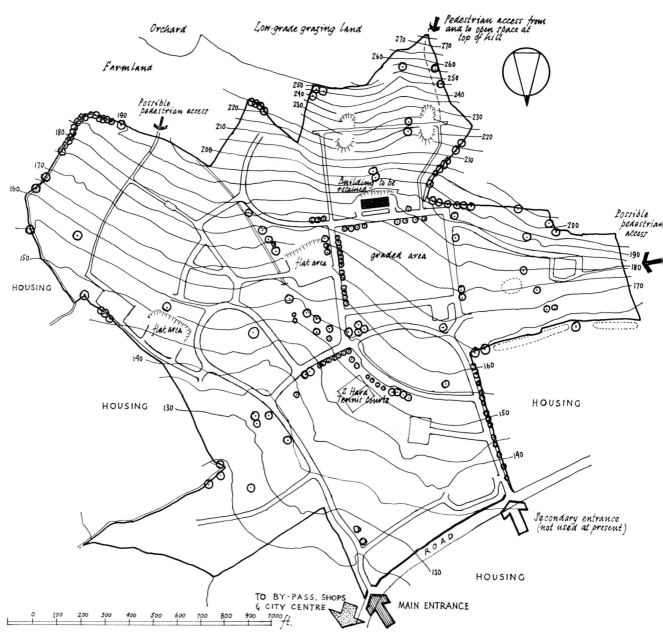

Fig. 3.1. TOPOGRAPHY—Survey plan showing topography and access.

and surrounding landscape should be recorded by camera, sketches or brief notes for reference during the preparation of the scheme.

Contour pattern. From contoured maps the relief and height of land, the shape and form of hills and valleys and the angles and directions of slopes can be obtained but these must be augmented for any areas which may receive detailed treatment, such as ground modelling and earthworks, by level surveys showing spot levels or contours at 1 ft or 5 ft intervals according to the type and scale of the proposed works. All levels shown must be related to an O.S. Bench Mark or other reliable and identifiable datum.

Detailed level surveys should also carry over site boundaries where possible in order that earthwork proposals may tie into the surrounding land forms.

Slope analysis. A slope analysis diagram may be prepared from the contour survey to show by various textural tints slopes of varying degree, e.g. steeper than 1 : 5, 1 : 10, 1 : 20, 1 : 50, and flatter than 1 : 50. This will enable usable flat areas, difficult slopes, etc. to be easily appreciated on a plan (Fig. 3.2).

44

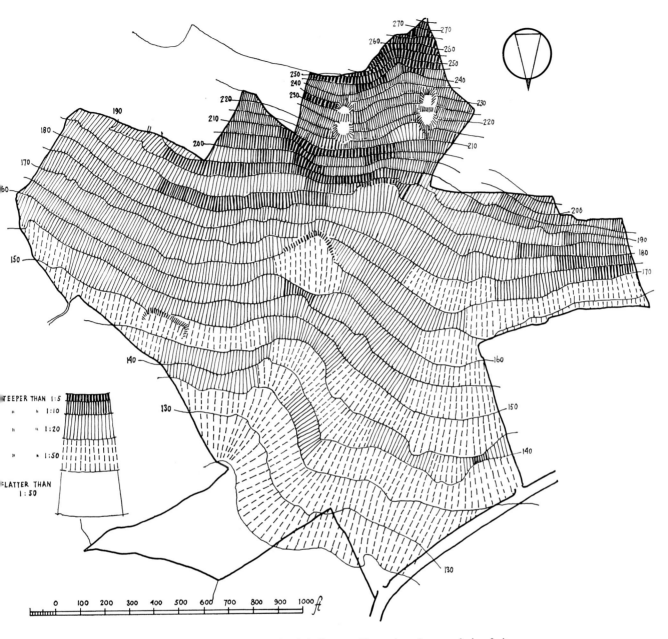

Fig. 3.2. SLOPE ANALYSIS—Shaded diagram illustrating slope analysis of site.

Access and communication. Information regarding road and footpath access into and around the site for vehicles and pedestrians, bus routes, desire lines to shops, points of entry and areas of difficult access may be indicated on the topographical plan or on a separate drawing. Future road proposals, highway widening lines and information on footpaths may be obtained from County or Local Authority Highways Departments, Redevelopment Plans, County Footpath Maps, etc.

3.2.2 Geology and soil

Geology. Solid (1 : 625,000) and drift (1 in to 1 mile) geological maps published by the Ordnance Survey on behalf of the Geological Survey of Great Britain provide the basic geological information. More detailed information of particular areas is available from the handbooks published by the Geological Survey. Notes on borings (often available from the engineer or architect for a project), trial holes or the observation of quarries, excavations and diggings in the area will give the required information on the nature of the subsoil or bedrock. Areas of outcrop rock should be carefully plotted and this information should also be transferred on to the topographical map (Fig. 3.3).

Soil. A physical examination of the topsoils to determine their classifications, depths, textures and chemical reactions should be made. Classification of soil

45

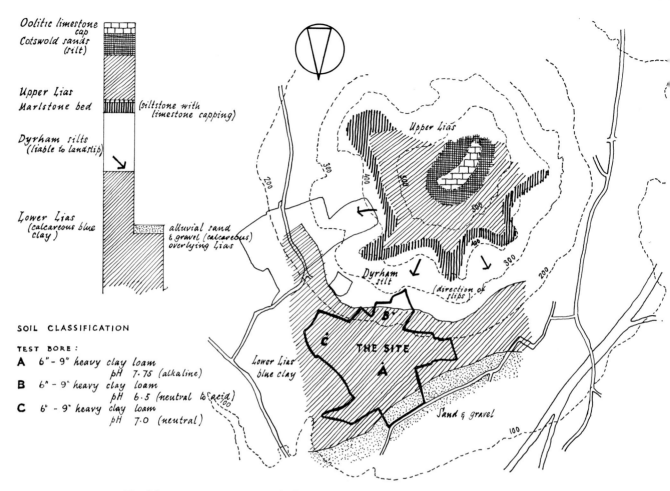

Geological column labels (left):

Oolitic limestone cap
Cotswold sands (silt)

Upper Lias
Marlstone bed — (siltstone with limestone capping)

Dyrham silts (liable to landslip)

Lower Lias (calcareous blue clay)

alluvial sand & gravel (calcareous) overlying Lias

Map labels:

Upper Lias
Dyrham silt
(direction of slips)
Lower Lias blue clay
THE SITE
Sand & gravel

SOIL CLASSIFICATION

TEST BORE :

A 6" – 9" heavy clay loam
        pH 7·75 (alkaline)
B 6" – 9" heavy clay loam
        pH 6·5 (neutral to acid)
C 6" – 9" heavy clay loam
        pH 7·0 (neutral)

Fig. 3.3. GEOLOGY AND SOIL—A simplified presentation of the geological map (drift) which includes information from soil test reports.

type, sands, loams, silts, clays, chalk and peat with finer distinctions where necessary, e.g., coarse sand, fine sand, sandy loam, medium loam, clay loam, etc., can be made by observation and handling. Depth of topsoil (the A, B and C horizons of a soil profile) can be seen in a trial pit or by using a hand auger. The presence of a hard pan below some sandy soils should be noted. Texture depends on the size of the soil particles from stones and gravel (over 2 mm in diameter) down to clay (particles below 0·002 mm in diameter). Flints or boulders may be present and the condition of the soil, its wetness or excessive dryness must be investigated (see also Chapter 10—Grass, section on soils, and Appendix, Soil Texture and Constituents).

Chemical reaction of a soil may be found by testing for soil alkalinity or acidity (the pH value) with a simple form of apparatus consisting of an indicator solution. Colour changes in the solution indicate the pH value (between pH 4·0 and pH 8·0). Greater accuracy within a range of pH 3·0 to pH 8·8 may be obtained by the use of special indicators with individual ranges of 1·6.

Further soil tests may be made in the laboratory and will provide information on the available potash and phosphates, the exchangeable calcium, the percentage of humus in a sample as well as other special concentrations such as toxic elements if this information is requested. County Agricultural and Horticultural Advisory Services, a few commercial seed firms, experimental stations and the Sports Turf Research Institute may be consulted on this. A general guide to soil conditions may also be obtained by the botanical identification of plant communities growing in the soil. These can indicate alkaline, acid, poor and barren, hot and dry, salty, marshy, wet or waterlogged soils. (See Appendix for plants which assist in indicating soil conditions.)

A study of this data will show the deficiencies of the soil and suggest means by which it can be ameliorated and fertilised to restore it to a well-balanced and workable material.

3.2.3. Climate

For the development of landscape over large areas such as New Towns, power stations, hydro-electric schemes, areas of regional planning, National Parks, etc., a knowledge of the climate of the area is of importance and drawings showing the climatic factors which will have an effect on the area may be necessary for the larger schemes.

Regional climate. General information on climatic zones, temperature, rainfall, direction of prevailing winds and wind velocities may be obtained from a climatological atlas or textbooks on the subject. Any additional information required for a particular area would need to be prepared by a meteorologist or specialist in this field. Data is collated on rainfall, temperature, sunshine and wind from the nearest weather stations at a similar altitude and exposure and these are adjusted to apply to the site in question if individual site data is not available.

Local climate. A study of the local climate and climatic factors is necessary if good living conditions for people and plant life are to be obtained. The topography of the site, its altitude and exposure or protection by neighbouring land forms or windbreaks will affect the temperature and wind velocities in the area. Proximity to coast or industry will affect the light factor and produce salinity or fog and air pollution. The seasonal variation of temperature and humidity of the air due to geographical position will affect the detail planning of a locality and even small areas within a locality such as parks and woodlands.

Micro-climate. A true micro-climate refers to a thin layer of air within a few feet of the ground over a relatively small area and for a short period of time but the term can also refer to the areas of space between buildings, valleys and sheltered hollows. Warm or cold slopes, free or impeded air drainage, heat reflection from hard surfaces, atmospheric pollution, exposed or sheltered areas, frost hollows and draught corridors will have an important bearing on the planning and landscape treatment of small areas such as gardens and courtyards and must be carefully considered.

Such information can be shown diagrammatically on a plan of the area with additional climatic graphs, wind roses if available.

3.2.4 Plant ecology and site vegetation

The scenic character of the site will have been noted on the topographical survey, e.g. high forest, woodland, heathland, downland, parkland, water meadow, etc. This is followed by an ecological survey in detail appropriate to the project. For some larger schemes a detailed survey of a wide area showing the ecological grouping and distribution of trees, shrubs, herbs and grasses plotted and indicated diagrammatically may be required. Often it will take the form of a plotted survey of the trees, hedgerows and other vegetation on the site.

Identification of species, height, spread, girth or diameter of the trunks of trees, height and spread of shrubs and hedgerows with notes on their condition, trees and

other vegetation worthy of retention as well as those which may or should be removed, will all be indicated. This latter information will be of use in the preparation of the contract bill of quantities.

The felling of trees is, with certain exceptions, subject to licences governed by the Forestry Act, 1951. Applications to fell should therefore be made to the Regional Conservator, Forestry Commission, for the area on form G.11 obtainable from that office. Applications to fell trees are usually forwarded to county planning authorities for information and action in the event of the need to protect the trees by the making of a Tree Preservation Order or the negotiation of replacement planting.

Tree Preservation Orders are made by county councils and local authorities and confirmed by the Minister of Housing and Local Government and complete records of such orders are maintained by the authority making the order. Owners of trees included in an Order are informed and consent to fell, top or lop such trees must be obtained from the authority making the Order through the Regional Forestry Commission Office also on form G.11.

3.2.5 Water and drainage

Water in the form of rivers, streams or lakes can be one of the greatest assets of a site but as floodwater, surface run-off or bad drainage it can be a liability if it is not controlled. The availability of water supplies in the vicinity of new developments of industry and housing may be a decisive factor in their location.

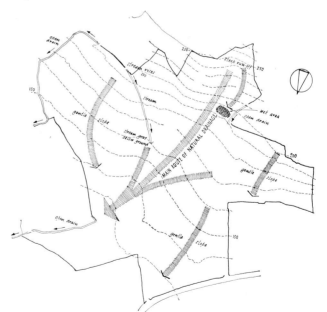

Fig. 3.4. DRAINAGE PATTERN—Broad indication of main lines of natural drainage.

Natural drainage pattern. A plan of the natural drainage of an area should be prepared to show all water courses, their directions and levels in summer and winters water gathering grounds, feeding reservoirs, rivers, stream,

47

or lakes, and perhaps underground supplies should all be delineated. This information may be included on the geological survey map or shown separately (Fig. 3.4).

Any use of water or alteration of drainage channels, both natural and piped, must be subject to the agreement and regulations of the Water Conservancy Board and main drainage authorities of the area who should be consulted at an early stage of the project.

Surface water. Areas of flooding and their frequency and depths, wet areas due to a high water table and other ground conditions of marsh, bog, or erosion due to water should be noted. The ecological survey will also have provided useful information on the water content of the soil by the identification of the flora and plant associations.

Surface water drainage. Ground water is derived from the water table which may be above, at or just below the soil surface. Such water may be held in the surface layers even of sand or gravel soils by an impermeable clay stratum to form a waterlogged soil but often the water table is so far below the surface that it has little or no effect on the surface soil which therefore depends on rainfall for its water content. After heavy rains however the water content is so increased in the top layers of some soils due to their slow permeability that it runs off the surface of sloping ground or stands as free water until it can percolate through to lower levels to run out as underground water into ditches and streams.

The landscape architect's survey must therefore include an investigation into the soil drainage and this should include the plotting of any artificial or piped drainage channels, french drains, mole drains and outfalls.

The need for further artificial drainage whether by agricultural land drains, mole or other forms of drains in order to reduce the water content of the soil or to lower the water table must also be assessed. In some podsolised soils bad drainage may be rectified by deep ploughing or sub-soiling which will break up the hard 'pan' which is found below the surface of such soils. Heavy clay and compacted soils which quickly become waterlogged may sometimes also be greatly improved by sub-soiling that breaks the surface crust so that artificial drainage is unnecessary (see also Chapter 4—Earthworks, Section on drainage).

Pools, lakes and canals. Water areas, natural or artificial should be plotted on plan, water levels taken, and their structure, the nature of the bed, banks, revettments or walls noted together with the means of water supply, drainage and overflows to outfalls. Drawings of constructional details will be necessary if existing features are to be retained or altered in the future scheme (see also Chapter 8—Water).

Water supply. The supply of natural water should be investigated for purity, quantity and flow, and in the case of piped water the size and positions of mains, location of stopcocks and meters should be plotted. This information is obtainable from the local authority or the main drainage authority.

3.2.6 Artifacts
The existence of engineering, architectural and other man-made works within the area should be accurately surveyed and plotted on the topographical map.

Buildings and enclosures. If these are to be retained or altered measured drawings may be necessary to a large scale ($\frac{1}{4}$ in or $\frac{1}{2}$ in to 1 foot). Such drawings should define the exterior finishes and materials, the bondings of brick and stone work, details of steps and copings, d.p.c. levels, floor levels and inverts of drainage systems, details of pavings, fences and walls, etc.

Roads and services. Roads and paths should be plotted and surfacings indicated, bridges, cuttings and embankments measured. Existing overhead and underground services should also be noted and plotted. Information on proposed electricity, water, gas, methane, oil and telephone cables and services is available from the appropriate authorities and county planning departments.

3.2.7. Land use
Significant and useful information for the larger scheme, may be obtained from a land use map. A composite maps

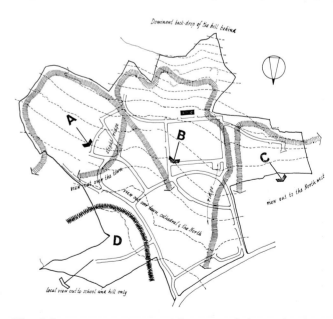

Fig. 3.5. VISUAL ANALYSIS—Diagram analysing main visual features within the site and indicating the main prospects afforded over the surrounding landscape.

well presented, can give an immediate impression of principal land uses, patterns of use, major functions of each locality and an intermingling of uses.

The regional pattern, farmland, industrial, housing, Green Belt, etc., and the local pattern, arable, grazing, parkland, woodland, public open spaces, etc., should be defined by the standard system of notation described in Appendix III, *Ministry of Town and Country Planning Circular 92* (1951) and could be further implemented by notation showing more detailed use of each area of the site, e.g. the type of crops, type of open space, etc. Information could also be included on the local materials used, e.g. stone, brick, flint, thatch, pavings, fencing etc.

County Development Plans define Areas of Great Landscape or Historic Value, Nature Reserves, Areas of Special Scientific Interest (botanical, ornithological and geological) and it is advisable to consult the plan where large areas are concerned.

3.2.8 Visual analysis

A diagram should also be prepared to show the visual limits of the site. Such limits may be within the boundary of the site as when buildings, woodlands, tall hedgerows, hills and ridges stop the view or they may be beyond the site to distant hills or the horizon. A diagrammatic plan either as a separate drawing or as an overlay to the topographical map should by broad tints indicate these visual barriers from selected viewpoints. It should also show the primary views into and out of the site which need to be preserved as well as views into or out of the site which need to be screened. Buildings of particular value in the landscape, focal points and other important features should all be included (Fig. 3.5).

3.2.9 Preliminary recommendations plan

After a study of the many factors and influences affecting the site and the appraisal of the assets and liabilities in relation to the use for which the site is to be put a plan showing the broad pattern of zoning and landscape should be prepared. This should not be a detailed drawing but should express the broad principles to be adopted and the major lines of the plan. It is the basis on which the master plan is built (Fig. 3.6).

It will show the distribution and balance of the various areas of differing use in the scheme, their setting within the landscape pattern and the linking of these areas by the lines of communication. Areas of existing planting to be preserved and new planting will be defined, the direc-

tion of important vistas, the siting of buildings and other major elements of the design will also be shown.

3.2.10 Landscape conservation

An aspect of development today which is assuming greater importance is landscape conservation and for the implementation of this the landscape survey for a project can be used to discern and define those features of a landscape which should be conserved or preserved, those which may need to be redesigned, remoulded or reinforced and those which cannot be conserved under the new land use conditions of the site. The landscape architect may be the only member of a development team who is competent to appreciate fully the effect that the development will have on the scenic value of the area and its effect on the ecological balance of the landscape under the altered conditions of development and he will need to advise on these aspects of the problem. Conservation of existing landscape may be more valuable than the creation of new landscape forms, for instance where the controversial siting of large works in the countryside is concerned and in such cases the landscape architect's contribution may be of prime importance both aesthetically and economically.

An existing ecological balance of an area can however only be preserved under reasonably static conditions and the alteration of these conditions in the process of artificial development such as happens when natural drainage or water tables are interfered with, alterations in temperature or exposure are made in areas of building, or when alterations in land usage, farming patterns or maintenance techniques are made, can result unwittingly in a changed landscape environment. The area which it is desired to keep as 'natural' as possible might need to be protected in part from the damage resultant upon large scale developments, by irrigation to conserve moisture for existing plant life, protective enclosure to prevent biotic changes, screen planting to improve any resulting creation of unfavourable climatic conditions, etc., and only a critical study of the landscape survey can provide informed knowledge and competent recommendations. In this connection scientific information and advice on conservation techniques may be sought if necessary from the regional organisations of the Nature Conservancy whose scientific officers are anxious to help in such matters. Also, most counties now have a County Trust for Nature Conservation, with a Scientific Committee whose members have specialised and intimate knowledge of the county, from whom advice may be obtained.

3.3 Co-ordination of survey information

The submission of survey drawings to accompany a report to support the reasoning of the landscape architect's intentions will be dictated by the nature of the

commission and the type of client or employer for whom the work is required (see Chapter 2—Practice of Landscape Architecture). Some clients, in particular the private

49

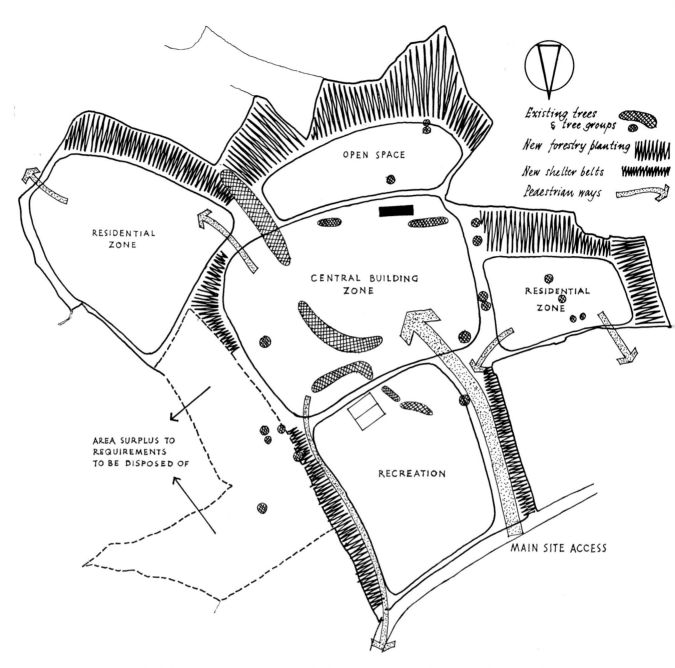

OPEN SPACE

RESIDENTIAL ZONE

CENTRAL BUILDING ZONE

RESIDENTIAL ZONE

AREA SURPLUS TO REQUIREMENTS TO BE DISPOSED OF

RECREATION

MAIN SITE ACCESS

Existing trees & tree groups

New forestry planting

New shelter belts

Pedestrian ways

Fig. 3.6. LANDSCAPE APPRAISAL—Preliminary recommendations and zoning expressing broad principles of design which arise out of analysis of the survey.

individual, will require only a detailed scheme showing the designer's proposals together with a short explanation of the intended scheme. Others, such as government agencies, nationalised industries and local authorities may expect a complete survey to be included with the report and master plan. It is necessary therefore that this information should be clearly and concisely presented, and it may be more convenient to the client if the survey information contained in the report could be classified and mapped under the headings of:

Natural factors (Fig. 3.7).
Land use characteristics (Fig. 3.8).

This is a first-stage analysis distinguishing between natural landscape matters which must be accepted or over which the designer has little control, and those which may be more freely modified in new development.

The 'natural factors' sub-division would include topography, geology and soils, climate and ecology, whilst

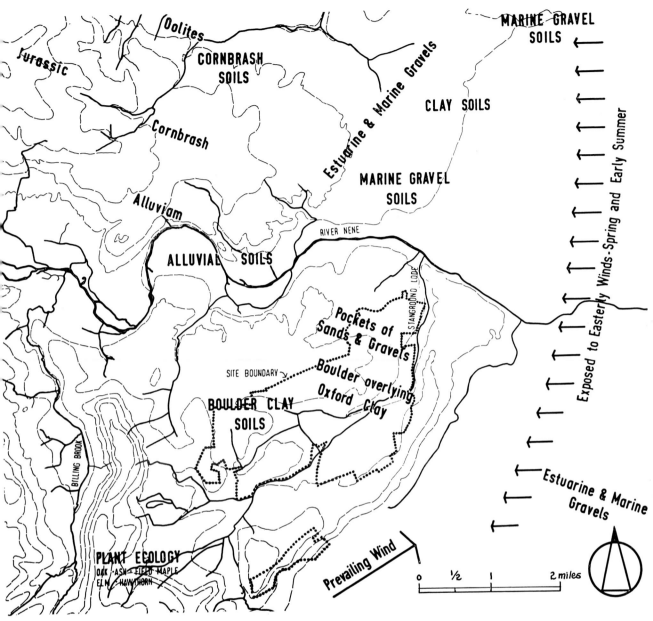

Fig. 3.7. LANDSCAPE SURVEY—NATURAL FACTORS.
A first-stage analysis picking out natural conditions over which the designer has little control.
Survey at Peterborough. Landscape Architect: A. E. Weddle.

'land use characteristics' would comprise the information on farming, planting and other uses of the land, drainage, access, etc.

If the drawings and maps are large they should preferably be presented on standard size sheets which may be bound into a folio or they may be photographically reduced in order to be reproduced on the same size of paper as the report. The latter will be useful where a large number of copies of a report are to be supplied. Loose or rolled drawings are inconvenient in most cases. It is also possible that good presentation can place two or more maps, diagrams or overlays in juxtaposition on the same sheet and if this can be done so that the in-

formation given is readily appreciated by laymen members of committees this will prove advantageous.

The following summary of survey drawings and the data provided and possible co-ordination of drawings is suggested.

3.3.1 Topographical map
The basic survey map of the site showing contours and/or levels, access and communications existing and proposed by local and statutory authorities.

Slope analysis diagram. This should include sectional drawings through the site. This may be a separate

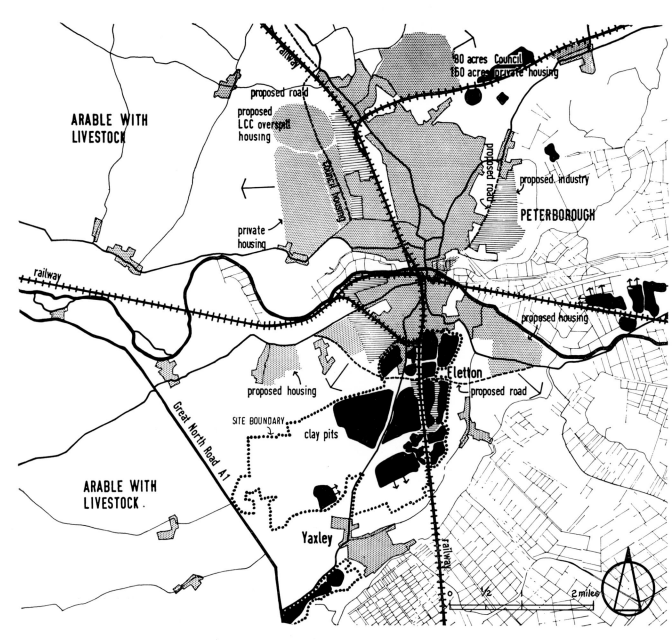

Fig. 3.8. LANDSCAPE SURVEY—LAND USE CHARACTERISTICS.
Diagram showing the complexity of land use which has contributed to the character and problems of the
existing landscape south of Peterborough. Landscape Architect: A. E. Weddle.

drawing or an overlay to the topographical map but is often only for the designer's use.

Visual analysis diagram. This shows the limits of vision, skylines and views into and out of the site and indicating zones for screening purposes. It may be a separate drawing or an overlay to the topographical map.

3.3.2 Geological map

This shows the solid and drift geology, soil classification and soil laboratory tests when they are available.

Drainage map. A map showing natural and artificial drainage water levels, areas of flooding, wet areas, etc. It may be a separate drawing or an overlay to the geological map.

Site strip diagram. This shows areas of soil stripping, filling or other earthworks. It is usually an overlay to the geological map.

3.3.3 Climatology map

This includes seasonal temperatures, rainfall, sunshine,

52

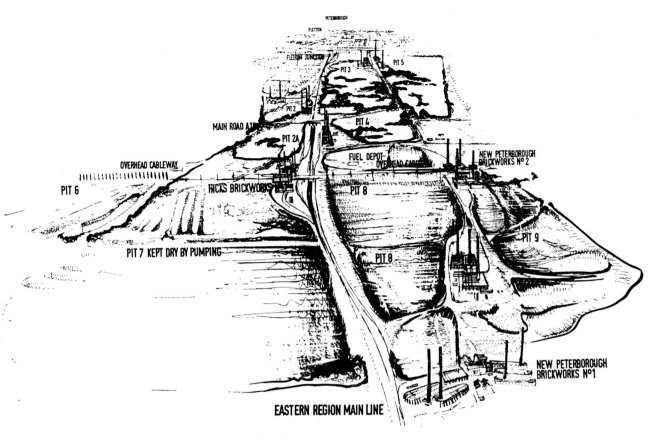

Fig. 3.9. LANDSCAPE SURVEY.
Pictorial illustration showing the visual character of the whole site. Reclamation
project at Peterborough. Landscape Architect: A. E. Weddle.

wind direction and velocity, areas of shelter and exposure, with zones for windbreaks and shelter planting.

3.3.4 Ecological map or tree survey
This is a survey of the distribution of plant communities, climax growth and detailed information of heights, spreads and condition of vegetation.

Tree preservation diagram. This shows trees to be retained, removed or transplanted. It may be a separate drawing or an overlay to the ecological map.

3.3.5 Artifacts plan
This is a plan of hard assets of engineering, architectural or man-made works, services and communications. It may be shown on the basic survey if it is not too detailed, e.g. housing layouts.

3.3.6 Land use map
This may be required for some projects, especially those of a planning nature, it should show the patterns of development and use with details of local building materials, etc.

3.4 The application of the survey

It must be stressed that the collation of survey material and the preparation of drawings showing this in visual terms are not end products but the fundamentals from which the designer can analyse the problem and assess the design potential inherent in the site.

Research will also be necessary to assist in solving many of the problems connected with present day landscape work and consultations with specialists in particular subjects will also call for adequate survey information to be available.

The landscape master plan for the redevelopment of a large scale project which may take many years to complete or even a plan for a smaller and simpler area should be accompanied by the landscape architect's report and this report should show how the survey information has been used as a design tool in producing the landscape scheme. It should interpret for the client the information given in survey drawings, charts, graphs and diagrams and explain how these have formulated the principles of the design and also the landscape policy of the project.

Finally the survey detail of the physical attributes of

53

the site will form the basis from which measurements and information are taken for the specification and bills of quantities for the constructional work.

Bibliography

Climates in Miniature, T. B. Franklin, Faber and Faber.

Climatology, W. G. Kendrew, Clarendon Press.

'Element design Guide', Clifford Tandy, *Architects Journal*, 25 October 1961.

Field Drainage, H. H. Nicholson, Cambridge University Press.

Forestry Practice, Bulletin No. 14, Forestry Commission, H.M.S.O.

Geology and Scenery, A. E. Trueman, Penguin Books.

Good Soil, S. G. Brade-Birks, English Universities Press.

Introduction to Plant Ecology, A. G. Tansley, Allen and Unwin.

Practical Surveying, Usill and Hearn, Technical Press.

Shelter Belts and Microclimate, J. M. Caborn, Bulletin No. 29, Forestry Commission, H.M.S.O.

Survey for Town and Country Planning, J. N. Jackson, Hutchinson.

Tomorrow's Landscape, Sylvia Crowe, Architectural Press.

4 Earthworks and Ground Modelling

BRIAN HACKETT

4.1 Survey (see also Chapter 3—Site Survey and Appreciation)

4.1.1 Clearing

Earthworks and ground modelling operations will involve on many sites the clearance of vegetation, and this may constitute an element in the total cost. If the site is well covered with trees, a record should be made of the number per acre, whether they have any value for timber purposes, or whether the tree debris must be disposed of by burning. Also a record should be made of the ground level around trees to be retained. Information should also be obtained on the extent of the operations necessary to remove the root system of the trees.

General clearance of tree-covered areas with negligible timber value can be achieved by two tractors moving in parallel and dragging a heavy chain between them. There are also special fitments which can be mounted on tractors for this purpose. These methods may also uproot the root system, but where this does not happen or the stumps of felled trees remain, there are other attachments which are usually effective.

4.1.2 Surveying and levelling

The provision of an accurate record of the dimensions and position of the different surface elements of the site is essential, and the degree of detail to which this should be carried out will be dependent on the scale and nature of the proposed earthworks and ground modelling operations. The objective of levelling operations should be the preparation of a contour plan of the site related to a reliable datum, preferably an O.S. bench mark. The contour intervals will again depend upon the proposals and on the existing topography of the site, but 1 ft intervals

are necessary to the designing of playing field and other 'level' surfaces for surface drainage considerations, and 5 ft intervals are the maximum for large scale operations requiring a reasonable degree of accuracy.

It is very important that the survey should carry over the site boundaries in order that earthwork proposals may tie in to the surrounding land form.

4.1.3 Water bodies, etc.

The levels of the water in pools and streams during drought, normal and high rainfall periods is desirable, also the contouring of the pool or stream bed if filling is envisaged. In any event, the maximum depth of water should be recorded. It is also very desirable that the water table levels under different conditions should be noted, and this may require the excavation of several trial pits; in fact, the more information that can be obtained on underground water and springs, the better.

4.1.4 Soil and subsoil

The depths and nature of the topsoil and the subsoil should be noted, and this information should be related to the latest information available from the Geological Survey. Where rock is suspected, it is important that a geological investigation is made.

4.1.5 Access

Information on the accessibility of the site to earth-moving machines and on the room available for manoeuvring is necessary at the design stage.

4.2 Soil and subsoil characteristics

Earthworks and ground modelling operations are concerned with the physical nature of the material moved, rather than its ability to support vegetation. But the design of new land forms must relate to matters like aspect, run-off, drainage and water table, all of which are significant in the development of vegetation. Also, the need to conserve the topsoil should be borne in mind and especially in relation to the new land form design when

considering positions for the temporary mounds of topsoil while the earthwork and ground modelling operations are proceeding.

4.2.1 Soil types

The major soil types which are likely to be encountered are gravels and gravel soils (e.g. with sand mixtures, clay mixtures, or both), sands and sandy soils (e.g. with

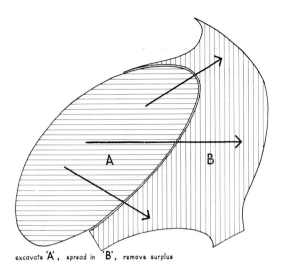

excavate 'A', spread in 'B', remove surplus

Fig. 4.1. DRAFTING METHODS OF SHOWING EARTHWORKS. A. Movement of material from areas of excavation to areas of fill. Supplemented by site directions.

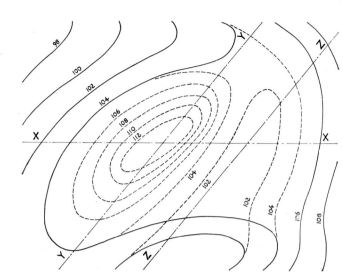

Fig. 4.3. DRAFTING METHODS OF SHOWING EARTHWORKS. C. Areas of excavation and fill shown by contour lines indicating existing and proposed grades.

gravel mixtures, clay mixtures or both), fine grained soils (e.g. silts and clays of various kinds), and fibrous soils (e.g. peat).

The characteristics of soils in so far as movement by mechanical equipment is concerned are as follows:

Sandy gravels, shales, hardpan shale and ripped rock (decomposed or weathered granite, gneiss, etc.)—these present loading problems and cause considerable wear and tear on equipment.

Sands are 'dead' and hard to load and transport, unless carried over a maintained road. Spreading and compacting depends on fill maintenance to prevent wind and other types of erosion as the work progresses.

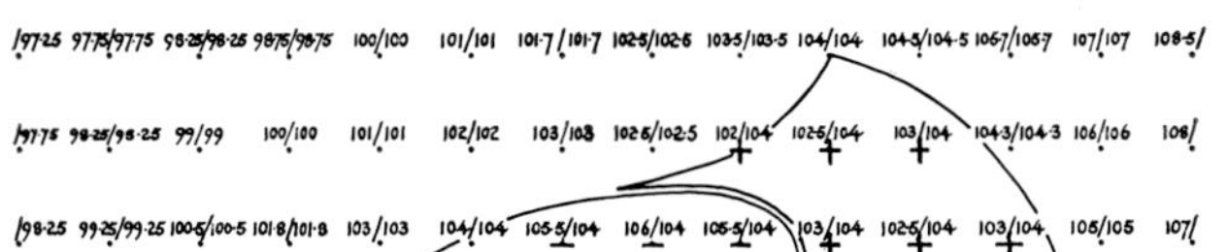

Clays, silts, loams and variations such as sandy clays, silty clays, etc.—easy to load, spread and compact (excepting excessive moisture in mud).

Fibrous soils—of little use for earthwork formation.

4.2.2 Angle of repose

While the surface covering of vegetation or paving can help to stabilise slopes in soils, each soil has its own particular angle of repose or stability, which may vary with the amount of moisture in the soil. For earthworks which consist of mounds of transported material raised above the original level, the angles of repose will be around the following:

Very wet clay and silt	1 : 3
Wet clay and silt	1 : 2
Dry sand and gravel	1 : 1¾
Dry clay	1 : 1½
Moist sand	1 : 1¼

These should not be regarded as finished slopes, which will normally be somewhat flatter. Precise gradients will depend on many factors, including bearing capacity of substrata, loading above the slope, surface treatment, as well as the precise nature of particular clays, sands, etc.

4.2.3 Bearing capacity

Whilst the bearing capacity of soils is likely to require investigation for building and engineering works rather than for landscape development, different soils and other materials are likely to give bearing capacities approximating to the following:

OLD LEVEL/NEW LEVEL   OLD LEVEL REDUCED   OLD LEVEL RAISED

Fig. 4.2. DRAFTING METHODS OF SHOWING EARTHWORKS. B. Areas of excavation shown by old spot levels reduced to new: areas of fill shown by old spot levels raised to new.

56

Sandy, sandy-clay and firm clay soils—1 to 4 tons per sq ft.
Consolidated clay—5 tons per sq ft.
Gravel and sandy gravel—6 tons per sq ft.
Compact sandy gravel and soft rock—8 to 10 tons per sq ft.
Rocks—40 to 60 tons per sq ft.

But, owing to the variation in surface and sub-surface material, proper loading tests should be carried out where weights above the customary use of landscape may be experienced.

Moisture content is closely allied to the bearing capacity of soils and subsoils, and at its optimum (usually given as a percentage of the dry weight) the particular soil is at its maximum compaction state. The maintenance of the moisture content at the level to achieve maximum compaction is sometimes a difficult process under the varying weather conditions and the juxta-position of excavated or fill material with the undisturbed material behind and under the cut.

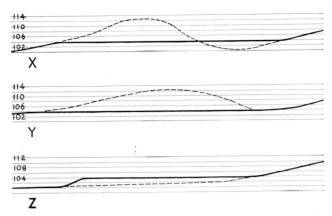

Fig. 4.4. DRAFTING METHODS OF SHOWING EARTHWORKS.
D. The use of cross-sections to show the new formation, and the cut and fill.

4.3 Ground shapes

The principles which lie behind the design of a particular land form can be grouped under a number of headings.

4.3.1 Limitations imposed by material and machines
Some of these matters have been referred to under the notes on the angles of slopes at which stability is likely to be achieved. Perhaps the first principle in this group is the difference in volume between soils and subsoils in their original state and during and after removal to a new situation. The design may have to make allowance for 15% and sometimes 25% more cut than fill, but if compaction takes place, the design may have to make

Machine	Rating	Min Curve Radii	Max Machine Slope Angles Longitudinal	Horizontal
Power shovels	(Capacity) ½ cu yd	21 ft	—	—
	5 cu yd	38 ft	—	—
Dragline	½ cu yd	43 ft	—	—
	5 cu yd	85 ft	—	—
Wheel type tractor dozer	(Horsepower) 34	15 ft	45°	25°
Track type tractor dozer	65	12 ft	40°	40°
ditto	93	15 ft 7 in	45°	45°
ditto	140	20 ft 9 in	30°	15°
ditto	235	20 ft 5 in	41°	41°
Track type tractor scraper	93	22 ft	45°	45°
ditto	140	25 ft	45°	45°
ditto	235	29 ft	45°	45°
Wheel type tractor scraper with 235 H.P. push tractor	225	30 ft	30°	15°
ditto	345	36–38 ft	30°	15°
with 345 H.P. push tractor	345	36–38 ft	30°	15°

F

allowance for 5% to 10% less fill than cut. The new land forms must also relate to the matter of drainage; for example, cuts or excavations may lead to situations below the surrounding water table or to pits in which the drainage may be trapped, and they should, therefore, be designed so that the flow of surface and underground water can be maintained. Also the direction of slopes of the new landforms may lead to a disproportionate discharge of water in particular areas—either the design should be modified or adequate drainage arrangements made.

In designing the curves in plan of new land forms, it is wise to relate these to the minimum turning circles of the machines to be used. Also, the areas within new land forms (i.e. small valleys and concave forms) should be adequate to allow the machines to manoeuvre. The turning circles vary with the type and make of machine, but the table on p. 57 gives an approximate indication of the minimum curve radii.

The angle of slope of the land forms is more likely to be controlled by the machine's lubrication requirements than by the centre of gravity of the machine, but some machines, like the power shovel, the dragline and the backhoe, can handle slopes well beyond the angle of repose of the excavated material. Limiting slope angles in relation to different machines are given in the table above.

4.3.2 Factors influencing costs
The major factors which influence the cost of earthworks operations are:

- (a) The location of the site.
- (b) Access into the site and manoeuvring room within it.
- (c) Availability of the most suitable equipment.
- (d) The nature of the material excavated and moved.
- (e) Water table and other site conditions.
- (f) Separation or otherwise of the topsoil from the subsoil.
- (g) Weather conditions.
- (h) Time set for completion.
- (i) Skill of the machine operator.
- (j) Length of haul from cut to fill positions, and the ease with which the cut can be moved to the fill positions. At one time 500 linear yards was regarded as the economical haul maximum for large machines, but this factor has decreased in importance.

It has also been shown that there are real cost differences arising from the *type* of design, even when all of the above ten factors are the same as between one design and another. For example, the following design variations do affect cost, provided contractors when estimating take them into account:

- (a) Designs of a 'hill and valley' or 'undulating' type are less expensive to grade than designs of a 'terracing' type. They are also as visually effective with smaller volumes of earth moved.
- (b) On sites up to one quarter of an acre in area, the cost differences between one design and another are insignificant. At 5 acres, the nature of the design is a significant cost factor, but with one exception when the design is such that it can be graded by operations taking place independently within each of say twenty '1 quarter acres' areas within the major area. Thus, somewhere between an area of $\frac{1}{4}$–5 acres lies an area at which the designer should carefully review his design in relation to economy.
- (c) Designs which allow circumferential and parallel movement lines of the machines as they load and unload material, and within reasonable distances of 500 yards or less, are likely to lead to savings.
- (d) Designs which restrict cut and fill operations within separate areas, as opposed to a balance over the whole site, are economical.
- (e) Although possibly monotonous, the subdivision of a land form design into roughly equal elements, e.g. the volume of each mound being more or less similar is likely to be a cost reducing factor.
- (f) In comparing (1) flat terraces, (2) sloping terraces, (3) undulating topography and (4) hills and valleys formed in a concave basin, the last proves to be the most economical.

4.3.3 Functional aspect of land use
The functional aspect is obviously important in its influence upon the design of earthworks, and has a long historical background ranging from the rice terraces of the Far East and the mound type fortified villages of the Ancient Britons, through the star-like fortifications around cities of the artillery age and the hidden barrier of the 'ha ha' between the cattle and the eighteenth century parkland of England, to the cutting of platforms for contemporary houses on steep sites and the grading around major road flyover junctions.

The situation at the present time errs on the side of the customary arrangement of land uses dominating the land form design, for example, sites are completely levelled by a cut and fill operation in order to allow the floor levels of the different factory processes to remain the same. Often, the different processes can equally well take place at different levels, resulting in a more interesting land form design.

Certain land uses present basically uninteresting land forms, especially playing fields with their extensive nearly level areas, though in flat countryside this is acceptable visually. But in sloping or undulating situations, terracing and spectator embankments can be designed to create

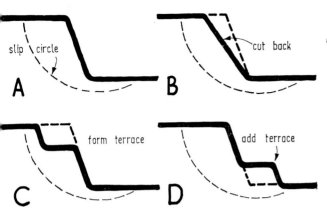

Fig. 4.5. FORMATION OF SLOPES IN CUT.
A. If the slope is too steep there is risk of slip.
B. Risk of slip can be reduced by cutting back slope.
C. Risk may also be reduced by cutting out a terrace or berm.
D. An added terrace will give a counter-balance to check slip.

interest; artificial mounds and hollows may be required, however, to marry up the extensive level areas with the existing topography in a satisfactory manner.

4.3.4 Site physiology

In addition to the function of the land use, the physiology of the landscape (which can be explained by the inter-relationship of the land, the water and the atmosphere, and the flora and fauna arising therefrom) constitutes a functional influence upon land form design, because a changed land form can evolve new ratios in the inter-relationship, even to the extent of creating a situation which can never be a stable one. Some of the matters which will need investigation in this respect are:

The water table. Excavation below the water table can lead to flooding or to seepage at the level of the water-

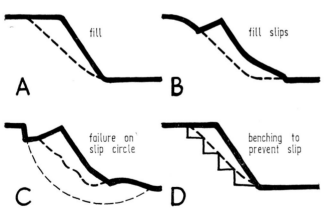

Fig. 4.6. FORMATION OF SLOPES WITH FILL.
A. Incorrect formation of slope. Weight of fill material, probably increased by absorption of heavy rain, may cause slip.
B. Slip of fill material along original formation.
C. Movement, along slip surface of the original formation.
D. Correct procedure, benching cut into original slope to prevent failure shown in B.

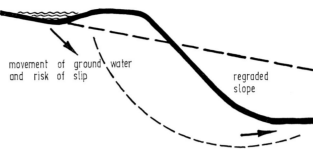

Fig. 4.7. Undrained areas behind new fill may lead to movement of ground water, excessive loading on regraded slopes and consequent slip.
   If this kind of fill is necessary, provision should be made for drainage at the top and bottom of slope.

table and below, necessitating the provision of drainage arrangements.

Angle of slopes. The angle of slopes should relate to the ability of the soil, with or without vegetation cover as the case may be, to withstand the erosive effect of the run-off of surface water. This is not directly connected with the slope angles limited by the angle of repose of the material. It is virtually impossible to lay down an accurate picture of erosion resistant slope angles for different soils, because of the great variation in weather conditions. A low, but concentrated, rainfall in an area with a loose soil cover will do more damage than a heavy rainfall spread over the whole year. In the former cases when the vegetation cover has been well nigh lost, slopes as low as 1 in 50 can be eroded by surface run-off of storm water. In this matter of surface water run-off, the arrangement of the land forms should be such that the run-off is well distributed and is not concentrated in one valley, unless special provision is made for this. The analogy of the streams leading to the tributaries and then to the river is a helpful one in this respect.

4.3.5 Maintenance of vegetation

The future maintenance of the vegetation cover on the slope. There are no precise rules about this aspect, but the following constitute a guide to the designer:

Close mown grass surfaces—angle controlled by the powered mowing machine, maximum 1 in 3. Hand mower can operate on this slope for small areas. For steeper slopes, hand scything of high quality is possible, but few gardeners are now equipped in this technique although the Flymo mower is a substitute.

Power scythed grass surfaces—sometimes called 'rough grass' surfaces. Some manufacturers of powered scythes

59

claim 1 in 1 as a maximum slope, but 1 in 2½ is a more realistic angle.

Groundcover plants—plants like ivy (Hedera) can survive and assist in stabilising very steep slopes. The maximum angle is likely to be determined by a combination of the possibility of preventing slip and erosion while the plants are established, and the problem of access for weeding and firming-in during establishment. Anything much steeper than 1 in 1 will be difficult.

Wild type shrub and tree cover—if pockets or small areas of terracing can be arranged, very steep slopes are possible provided slip and erosion can be controlled initially.

Fig. 4.8. Subsidence resulting from fine material being (indicated by arrows) carried away by the flow of ground water due to modified water table resulting from excavation.
Interceptor drains needed at top and foot of slope.

4.4 Grading principles and methods

After the decision has been made to alter the formation of the ground surface of a site, there are certain principles involved in the grading operations which need to be observed. These are listed below.

4.4.1 Stripping topsoil
The stripping of the topsoil after site clearance operations and removing it from the site for use elsewhere as a contribution to the 'national soil bank', or alternatively stacking it in temporary heaps for respreading after grading and building operations, where one or both apply.

4.4.2 Siting topsoil storage
The siting of temporary topsoil and subsoil heaps from the points of view of the site works, building operations

and the planning of the grading operations. Also in relation to impeding or facilitating the flow of surface water drainage during the site operations.

4.4.3 Planning grading operations
Planning the grading operations in harmony with the building operations, and also to avoid excessive surface compaction by machines concentrating on one area or route, also the mingling of topsoil and subsoil due to the rutting of the wheels and tracks.

4.4.4 Filling
A decision whether the filled areas must hold true to level or whether on a large project having artificial mounds or

Plate 4.1. Left, DW 21 Tractor with No. 470 Scraper. Right. D7 Tractor with No. 75 Bulldozer pulling a sheepsfoot roller.

Plate 4.2. Caterpillar DW 21-470 Tractor–Scraper combination. Push-load operation is assisted by a D8 Tractor working on wet silt-clay.

hills, some settlement can be accepted. In the former case, depositing fill in horizontal layers, with separate compaction operations for each layer may be necessary. In the latter case, a distinction should be made between (1) 'dumped fill' in which the excavated material is dumped without selection as it comes from the excavation, (2) 'end dumping' in which the excavated material is pushed over the edge of a valley and (3) 'selected fill' in which the excavated material is segregated for different levels and tasks in the filling operations.

4.4.5 Weather conditions
Planning the grading operations in relation to the likely weather conditions prevailing in the different seasons of the year. Long, comparatively dry spells, are likely to simplify the operations and thus reduce costs.

4.4.6 Water table
The effect of the grading operations on the existing water table. For example, where an excavation cuts across the water table, attention should be given to an adequate method of drainage at this point. Where mounds are formed above the normal land surface, the likely effect of these upon the water table should be considered in relation to the supply of water to any vegetation proposed on the mound; in this respect, the creation of an artificially elevated water table by means of flat saucers formed in an impervious topping to the basic grading (underlying the topsoil) is a solution.

4.4.7 Phasing topsoil replacements
The phasing of topsoil replacement operations to avoid

leaving the topsoil longer than necessary in the temporary heaps, and also to prevent it from suffering compaction of the respread topsoil by contractors' equipment which may be still operating on the site.

Plate 4.3. Motor grader carrying out precision bladework grading.

61

4.4.8 Preparation before topsoiling

Ploughing or otherwise breaking up the surface of areas which have been excavated into heavy or impervious subsoils before respreading the topsoil in order to improve the soil drainage in those areas.

4.5 Earthmoving methods

The types of machine used for earthmoving are basically divided into fixed and moving machines.

4.5.1 Machines fixed in position when operating

The dragline. This is normally used for large cuts or channels excavated below the level on which the machine is located. It can be used for shaping existing mounds, excavating valleys, and forming embankments and slopes. Whilst standing at a point of operation, the

Plate 4.4. The ability of modern earth moving equipment to undertake large alterations to land form is shown in this illustration of a track-type tractor-dozer at work.

size of the excavation depends on the length of the boom from the end of which an excavating bucket is dragged through the material to be excavated. Machines vary in size with boom lengths normally in the 25–85 ft range for machines moving on tracks, and up to 300 ft for walking draglines. The excavated material is usually dumped behind or at one side or other of the machine.

The power shovel. The power shovel also has a boom or jib, but very much shorter than that of the dragline and usually within the range 12–95 ft long. The bucket operates along the boom instead of along a cable as with the dragline, and it is thus more suitable for working in hard rock which has been broken up first by blasting. The power shovel is very suitable for loading into dumpers and lorries, but only those machines with long booms are likely to be of much use in building up mounds from excavation. Variants of

the power shovel are the trencher with an extension arm for deeper excavation, and the skimmer for surface stripping.

4.5.2 Machines mobile when operating

The tractor. This is a basic unit for pushing or pulling earthmoving equipment, and models are available with tracks for slow speeds under bad site conditions, or with wheels for faster speeds and better site conditions.

Tractor attachments. Several types of equipment can be attached to the tractor and these fall into two groups. First, the 'allied equipment' actually mounted on the tractor; for example, bulldozers, angledozers, winches, pipe laying booms, excavator attachments, earth augers. Second, 'towed equipment'; for example, scrapers, rippers, graders, sheepsfoot tamping rollers, scarifiers and rippers (sometimes also mounted). A wide range of horsepower in the power units is available, usually within the 35–235 hp range.

The cubic yards of earth movable in an 8 hour day vary from approximately 360 for a small unit on a 5 yd journey from point of excavation to point of deposition and back again, to 1,400 for a large unit of 130 hp.

Bulldozers are particularly suitable for forming plateaux and embankments. Scrapers can make shallow cuts, and

Plate 4.5. TRAXCAVATOR. Progress in the design of earth moving equipment will lead to greater flexibility in land form design. The Traxcavator, illustrated here, has increased the possibilities in excavation work for projects akin to basements and swimming pools. The bucket has extending arms which can dispose of the excavated material at a level above the floor of the excavation.

Plate 4.6. A wheel-type tractor scraper engaged on earth moving operations for highway construction. One of many types of machine now available.

have the advantage of being able to transport large loads over considerable distances. They operate most efficiently in soils lying between the extremes of dry sand and wet clay.

Other machines. There are also several machines which do not precisely fall into either of these two cate-

gories. The motor scraper in the smaller horsepower range is particularly suitable for small projects. The loading shovel is useful for moving earth from heaps into lorries. The motor grader is useful for grading roads, forming drainage channels and for trimming work. Several types of transporting equipment are available as lorries, dumper wagons, etc.

4.6 Compaction

4.6.1 Degree of compaction required
The consolidation of the material moved in earthworks and ground modelling is a matter of achieving a balance between a sufficient compaction to give a settlement-free surface, and the avoidance of excessive compaction which may prevent good local drainage within the soil. The most satisfactory solution is likely to be achieved when the fill material is deposited in layers about 6 in thick, each layer being compacted in moderation. Such a solution is not, however, realistic when large depths are to be filled, but good results can often be attained by mass compaction of the lower part, and adopting the layering technique coupled with land drainage in the upper part.

The moisture content of the fill is an important factor in compaction, and the ideal situation occurs when there is sufficient moisture to enable the grains to slide into stable positions without completely filling the voids between the grains. This ideal situation is known as the optimum moisture content and is expressed as a percentage of the dry weight of the fill. The method for ascertaining this is known as the Proctor test.

4.6.2 Achieving compaction
The various ways in which compaction is achieved can be related to types of equipment (see below).

The smooth-wheeled roller. This is available in many different weights with ballast from approximately 1½ tons to 18 tons. Compaction is normally achieved up to thicknesses of 9 in per layer, and is unlikely to become greater after about eight runs over any one area. This type of equipment is best suited to materials like hardcore and crushed stone, and soils with gravel, sand and clay mixtures.

Pneumatic-tyre rollers. These with ballast are available from about 9 tons to 50 tons. Compaction can be achieved up to 18 in layers, and almost any type of soil will respond, though sands and other granular soils are most responsive.

The sheepsfoot roller. This has projecting feet or spikes mounted on it, consequently it overcomes the problem of crust formation in the top layer of cohesive clays and silts, but it is not very suitable for sandy soils. Compaction can be achieved up to 9 in thickness, and up to twenty runs over any one area may be required. Various sizes are available from about 2 to 20 tons.

The vibrating roller. This is similar to the tandem type smooth-wheeled roller, but with a device for vibrating the roller. Its greatest value is with granular soils, such as sandy ones, which achieve their greatest consolidation through the particles being shaken into stable positions relative to one another.

Hand and the pneumatic tampers. These are used for very small areas, such as for filling in narrow trenches.

4.6.3 Avoiding compaction
In addition to the technique for achieving compaction in a satisfactory manner, the problem of improper compaction frequently arises in contracts. This often occurs when the landscape architect is commissioned at a late stage of a contract or when his authority to control site operations is limited.

A frequent situation is that of unnecessary surface compaction by building contractors' equipment of a ground level, which is to remain unaltered. A wise procedure is to specify that, where topsoil is to be removed and replaced at a later date, the subsoil should be ploughed up and roughly chain harrowed before the topsoil is replaced. This procedure will improve surface

Plate 4.8. FACESHOVEL. A medium-size N.C.K. Rapier 305 faceshovel loading rock with a $\frac{7}{8}$ cu yd heavy duty bucket.

Plate. 4.7. FACESHOVEL. A small N.C.K. Rapier 205 faceshovel working against a rock face with $\frac{1}{2}$ cu yd bucket.

drainage and add to the effectiveness of a land drainage system if installed.

It is also advantageous to limit the areas of operation for the building and/or civil engineering contractor by a clearly worded and enforceable clause in the specification, including also the provision of temporary fencing to protect certain areas.

The specification or bill of quantities can also with advantage, allow for a degree of flexibility in the final situation. This is especially important where small slopes, curves and mounds are included, and an assessment of the visual result on the site may suggest slight modifications.

4.7 Filling materials

4.7.1 Waste materials
Many earthwork and ground-modelling projects require working in waste material of one kind or another, and special problems frequently arise. For example, in the reshaping of a coal mine waste heap material may be met which is still in a state of combustion, or has burnt to a congealed mass which cannot be handled as a normal earth-moving operation. Waste material from electricity power stations can create dust problems which become more than usually serious when earthwork operations disturb the material.

Each of these problems is likely to require a special technique, varying from the conventional methods. Material which has an offensive smell, is likely to break down under weathering into fine dust, or may react chemically in the weathering process, is best handled in the same way that certain local authorities dispose of their refuse—by tipping over a moving slope at the edge of a fill, and then covering the fill after each tipping operation with non-active material, such as excavated subsoil, and finally adding a layer of topsoil.

4.7.2 Water-borne soil transportation

In certain circumstances, large-scale earthworks can be carried out by water transportation. This includes the operations of dredging from a river, lake or sea bed, and

Plate 4.9. FACESHOVEL. A large faceshovel. N.C.K. Rapier 1405 with a 3½ cu yd bucket.

transporting the material by ship for discharge elsewhere under water or for offloading on to vehicles. The transportation of soils by washing through pipelines is, however, an operation closer to the customary earthwork operations likely to be met in landscape design.

The use of pipes for soil transportation can take place over both land and water, steel-drum pontoons being used in the latter case for supporting the pipes. The material excavated is removed by a cutterhead dredge and suction is used to draw back soil and water in the ratio of about 1 to 5 by volume. Several discharge points

can be arranged by introducing junctions into the pipelines. The extent of this operation is indicated by the statement that, for a static position of a discharge point, an accumulated fill 5 ft deep will slope down at a gradient of about 1:15 for a radius of about 75 ft. Skilful control of the operation can lead to successful layering of the fill as part of compaction procedure.

4.7.3 Mechanical handling

Reference is also made to other special techniques, usually associated with the deposit of waste material, like the conveyor belt, the overhead cable and buckets, and the tramline for small trucks depositing at the top of an incline. If the landscape designer is faced with a situation where these special techniques are to be used, economies will result from the design being attuned to the technique, its limitations and possibilities.

Plate 4.10. DRAGLINE. The N.C.K. 205 illustrated is a smaller size dragline machine operating with buckets up to ⅝ cu yd and booms up to 50 ft length.

4.8 Calculation of cut and fill

4.8.1 Mensuration

The methods of calculating volumes of earth moved are those used in the normal processes of mensuration, such as the areas on triangulation of irregular shapes on plan multiplied by the average height of a series of spot levels giving the difference between the old and new levels at regular intervals on a grid, and the division of volume of cut into a number of sections whose volume can be found. A longer process is involved when it is necessary to achieve an exact balance between material cut and material filled. One method is to design the earthworks in a sand tray model, and by resisting the temptation to increase or decrease the amount of sand as the designer carries out his adjustment to the sand tray model in its

original form as a miniature of the site, the result must be an exact cut and fill, and the new levels can be plotted on a drawing which can then be subjected to a more accurate check. Finally, adjustment must be made for the change in volume, which is to be allowed as between cut and filled material, if the proposed method of compaction leaves the fill material in its deposited position at a different density than in its original position from which the cut was made.

4.8.2 Visual approximation

The design of a cut and fill balanced operation over and within a site can also be achieved by a two stage method

Plate 4.11. DRAGLINE. An N.C.K. Rapier 1405 dragline with bucket capacity up to 4 cu yd.

in which the new grades are adjusted by a visual approximation on several cross sections through the site. Then, the existing spot levels are totalled and divided by the number of positions to give an average level; this existing average is compared with the new average. In this method, it is unlikely that the two averages will equal one another at the first attempt, but it is usually possible to achieve comparability within a reasonable degree of accuracy after two or three further adjustments to the figures. The use of an adding machine will save much time and effort in making refinements to a design for the purpose of achieving a balanced cut and fill result. Also, techniques have been evolved which make use of a computer, for example, through a series of calculations along section lines, running parallel across the area over which the land form design is being developed.

Plate 4.12. DRAGLINE. The N.C.K. Rapier 1405 dragline. The boom length can vary from 60 to 120 ft with the use of 10 ft and 20 ft extension inserts.

4.8.3 Mass diagram

A method for calculating cut and fill operations which is used for long and narrow earthworks, like roads and railways, is the mass diagram. This is useful for determining the haul distances from points of cut to points of fill, the position and volume of excavations, the situation when

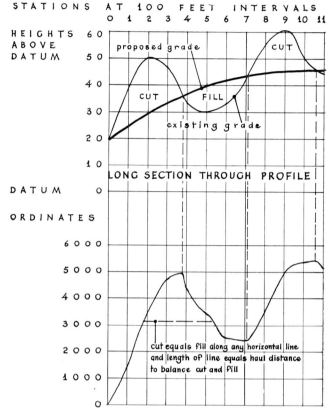

MASS DIAGRAM COMPUTATION			
STATION	THEORETICAL VOLUME		ORDINATE
	CUT	FILL	
0			0
1	+ 1 4 0 0		1 4 0 0
2	+ 2 0 0 0		3 4 0 0
3	+ 1 3 0 0		4 7 0 0
4		− 2 8 0	4 4 2 0
5		− 1 0 0 0	3 4 2 0
6		− 9 0 0	2 5 2 0
7		− 1 5 0	2 3 7 0
8	+ 1 1 0 0		3 4 7 0
9	+ 1 5 0 0		4 9 7 0
10	+ 4 2 0		5 3 9 0
11		− 2 0 0	5 1 9 0

Fig. 4.9. THE MASS DIAGRAM for computing cut and fill operations on long and narrow earthworks. Allowances can be made if necessary to the ordinates for shrinkage of the fill material.

it may be more practical to borrow material from a borrow pit, and the type of equipment.

The mass diagram (see Fig. 4.9) consists of a long section through the narrow site of the earthworks. This section is divided into a number of equal stations which are assumed to be the centre of gravity of the volume of earth extending 50 ft in both directions along the section.

At each station, the cut is designated as a plus (+) volume, and the fill as a minus (−) volume. In the computation, the ordinates are cumulative algebraic sums from the first station. These ordinates are plotted on the mass diagram below the profile, and the high and low points of the resulting curve represent the places of no cut and no fill. Also, any horizontal line drawn across the resulting curve represents the length within which a balanced cut and fill operation can take place for the length of haul represented by the line.

4.8.4 Allowance for bulking and compaction
Measurement of earth excavated and deposited is made on the assumption that the earth is 'in the bank', that is in its original state. After excavation the volume can increase up to 45% during handling, but can also decrease to less than its 'in the bank' volume on compaction. Obviously, an earthworks design which relies on an exact balance of cut and fill must specify that the compaction process brings the soil which is moved back to its original density. It is, however, wise to include a margin of at least 5% for soil to be brought in to the site, and this allowance can also cover the reverse situation in which it may be found necessary to remove soil from the site.

4.8.5 Quantities
In the calculations of soil moved and in bill of quantities descriptions a distinction between 'major' grading by large machines and in bulk, and 'minor' grading by hand or very small machines is helpful to an estimator and to the efficient administration of a contract. Reference should also be made to the recommendations covering the procedure for measuring and recording excavation in the Standard Methods of Measurement of the Royal Institution of Chartered Surveyors and of the Institution of Civil Engineers.

4.8.6 Roadworks
Earthworks in connection with road embankments and cuttings require not only attention to the balance of cut and fill within reasonable lengths from the points of view of economy and fitting the road to the landscape, but also special attention to the points of change from one curve to another in plan and section. Embankments and cuttings are improved in appearance when the top and the toe are rounded or easily graded into the existing land form. Also, the steepness of the slope should be varied to grade it into the changing topography along the line of the road.

The combination of a long curve in plan with a short vertical curve in the profile of a road grading design between two major slopes can lead to an abrupt modulation in the new topography created by the road grading. If the length of road over which the vertical curve occurs can be lengthened to coincide with the length over which the long curve in plan occurs, the result seen in three dimensions is greatly improved.

Plate 4.13. WALKING DRAGLINE. On large minerals sites very large draglines can be used. The N.C.K. Rapier W.1400 illustrated carries a 20 cu yd bucket on a boom 282 ft long.

Plate 4.14. WALKING DRAGLINE.
The N.C.K. Rapier W.1800 dragline illustrated carries a 40 cu yd bucket on a boom 247 ft long.

4.9 Drainage

Drainage is concerned with the removal of surplus water from agricultural and urban land. All such water derives initially from precipitation. This may have been directly on the area considered or on an adjacent area from which it has then moved by surface flow or subsurface percolation.

4.9.1 The soil and drainage

The structure of the soil and its mineral composition are intimately concerned with the behaviour of ground water. The soil may have been produced *in situ* or deposited after glacial transport. However, as all soil is derived from the chemical and physical breakdown of rock material the soil characteristics are related to the parent rock minerals. In transported soils mixing of different rock types has taken place and this has produced a wider variety of soils than parent rock material. Soils are not normally homogeneous. Soils may be generally classified according to the sizes of the particles of which they are made according to an internationally agreed scale.

A soil profile normally shows well-defined regions of topsoil and subsoil and, in some cases, of parent rock material in varying degrees of breakdown.

The soil itself consists of solid particles and a fluid

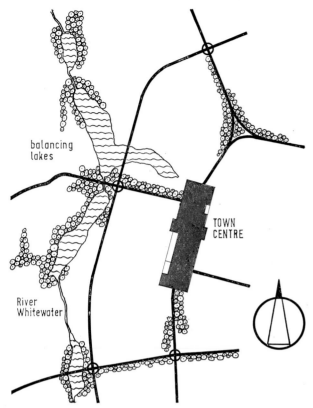

Fig. 4.10. THE HOOK PROJECT—balancing lakes used along the River Whitewater.

medium composed of gaseous air and liquid water. The soil porosity is a measure of the total soil volume not occupied by solid particles, and is usually expressed as a percentage pore space, i.e. the ratio of the volume of fluid to the total volume $\times 100$. The value of soil porosity gives an indication of its water holding capacity. Generally the coarser the particles in a soil and the greater the mixture of different sizes the lower the porosity.

Type of Soil	Average Percentage Pore Space
Coarse sand	28
Sandy loam	37
Silt loam	45
Clay	55

More important than the pore space are the sizes of the interconnecting channels between the pores which will determine the rate of water movement. Water will flow through the soil in response to an applied force. This may be gravity, causing a downward percolation, or a hydraulic potential, causing a flow in the direction of decreasing hydraulic gradient. Those soils with the smaller channels will exhibit the lower rates of flow. Coarse sands have a low value of porosity but drain

rapidly while clays have a greater pore space, but drain very slowly.

The water table in a soil is the upper limit of the pores which are completely filled with water. It thus separates the saturated region below from the unsaturated region above. In a waterlogged soil the water table is at or very near the soil surface. Water will drain from such a soil until that soil reaches field capacity. Further water can only be removed from the soil by evapo-transpiration. Most agricultural crops grow best in soils that have a water content slightly less than that at field capacity.

The rate of water movement through soil is measured by its permeability in units of in/hr. Some typical values are:

Soil Type	Permeability (in/hr)
Coarse sandy	18·7
Sandy loam	0·12
Silt loam	0·043
Clay	0·006

Actual soil profiles show varying permeability with depth. Three general cases exist:

(a) Increasing permeability with depth, e.g. loam soil overlying chalk—no drainage problem.
(b) Decreasing permeability with depth, e.g. a worked clay loam overlying a clay subsoil.
(c) Variable permeability with depth, e.g. boulder clays with perched beds of sand and gravel.

The maximum flow rate through a soil is fixed by the layer with the lowest permeability through which the water has to pass.

Rainfall rates in excess of the minimum permeability will cause water to accumulate in the soil or on the surface giving flood conditions on level ground and surface run-off on sloping ground. If the speed of surface run-off is excessive soil structure is destroyed and soil particles are transported giving rise to soil erosion.

Drainage is concerned with the removal of water in order to restore a soil to field capacity or to remove surface water which would accumulate on sites of low permeability.

4.9.2 Run-off and soil erosion

Rational formula. A rational calculation may be made of the amount of run-off from a site if it is assumed that all the precipitation leaves the site as surface water. A rainfall intensity of 1 inch per hour lasting for 1 hour would provide 1 acre inch or 3,622 ft³ of water. If this water were to flow off the site at a uniform rate it would be at a rate of 1·008 ft³/sec. By adding to the relationships so developed a factor C to account for the variation of peak run-off rates with intensities in different areas and under different surface conditions the rational formula for surface run-off becomes

$$Q = CiA \text{ ft}^3/\text{sec}$$

where Q is the peak run-off rate (ft³/sec), i the intensity of rainfall (in/hr) lasting for the time of concentration of the water shed, A the area of catchment (acres) and C the run-off coefficient.

Criticisms of rational equation.   The rational formula, while useful in giving some guidance, is now generally considered to be over-simplified and difficult to use. The main difficulty lies in choosing a suitable value for the expected intensity of rainfall. The British Standard Code of Practice 303:1952 suggests a modified form of the rational formula.

$$Q = 60 \cdot 5 \, APR$$

where Q is the run-off in ft³/min, A the watershed area in acres, P the permeability factor, and R the rainfall intensity in in/hr; with the following values of P for England:

Roofed buildings $P = 0 \cdot 95$
Roads $\qquad\qquad P = 0 \cdot 75/0 \cdot 90$
Paths $\qquad\qquad P = 0 \cdot 50/0 \cdot 75$
Gardens, lawns
and wooded areas $P = 0 \cdot 10$

Design formulae for predicting peak run-off rates.   The design of structures to deal with surface run-off is now generally based on information obtained from use of Bilhams formula for accepted recurrence intervals and duration of rain.

4.9.3 Ground modelling to control run-off

Reducing the peak intensity of run-off.   The maximum peak rate of run-off from a site is directly proportional to the maximum intensity of rainfall expected for the time of concentration and within the recurrence interval selected.

An increase in the time of concentration enables a lower value of rainfall intensity to be selected in predicting the peak run-off rate. This can be achieved by delaying the discharge of surface water from an area being developed by constructing impounding or diversion dams or ponds. These smooth out the main fluctuating discharge from the watershed to a low safe rate of water release to the main channel.

Decreasing size of watershed.   A decrease in the size of the collecting area will also reduce the peak intensity of run-off but will also lead to a greater number of structures to deal with the total run-off from an area

although the dimensions of each structure may be reduced.

Grass lined waterways.   The time of concentration may also be increased by impeding the surface flow of water as for instance by a grass sward in established waterways. This is an important method in controlling run-off from agricultural land because, in addition to the peak intensity, it also produces a more stable soil surface capable of withstanding higher water velocities.

4.9.4 Piped run-off of surface water

This may be achieved by structures offering less resistance to surface flow than that occurring naturally. In such cases open channels or, in extreme cases, underground pipes, of suitable dimensions to deal with the predicted run-off are used. Attention should be paid to the final discharge point. Such pipes rarely flow full and may be considered as special cases of open channels.

4.9.5 Piped drainage of underground water

Conditions requiring piped under drainage.   In soils with a low inherent permeability or with small slopes or low lying land, natural drainage is a slow process because of the small size of pore interconnecting channels. Porous pipes laid with a grade in such a soil will receive water from the surrounding soil by virtue of the hydraulic gradient existing between the pipe (which is in connection with the atmosphere at its outlet) and the soil water adjacent to it. Such water can then be discharged from the pipe to an adjoining ditch easily and speedily.

The usual type of such underground drains is the 'clay tile drain' made in unglazed baked clay in 12 in lengths and various diameters between $1\frac{1}{2}$ in and 8 in. The more usual diameters employed are 3 in for laterals and 4 in or 6 in for main lines. These tiles are laid end to end in a hand or machine dug trench with a specially formed base to locate the tile accurately and ensure accurate butting. Water enters these drains mainly through the small gaps between each 12 in length. Concrete land drainage pipes are also used but are more costly, partly by reason of their shortened life compared with clay tiles in soils having marked acidity or alkalinity and partly because of their material cost. Attempts have been made to lay such pipes automatically by injecting liquid or semi-liquid concrete behind a tine working to the required depth and then forming the concrete drain *in situ*. This requires a more expensive machine but economises in the cost of trenching.

New materials.   Many new materials are now becoming available for land under-drainage in the form of plastic pipes produced from special grades of polyethylene. Water enters the pipe in the soil through specially cut slots $1\frac{1}{4}$ in long at 2 in intervals and the pipe is currently available in 20 ft lengths and 400 ft coils.

Slightly more expensive in initial cost, savings can be made in transport and laying cost because of its light weight and applicability to machine laying. A porous backfill is normally used with the pipe to increase the hydraulic gradient in the soil surrounding the pipe and to equalise vertical and horizontal pressures on the pipe during soil settlement after laying.

Some specialist machines are also available which form a circular cross-section drain pipe on a former pulled through the soil from a continuous sheet of plastic foil material. The flat sheet is passed down the leg of the implement, is turned through a right angle, formed into a tube and the slotted edges latched together. These drains do not require trenches to be cut.

Mole drains. In pure clay soils a drainage channel can be formed *in situ* by drawing a cylindrical plug through the soil. If done under moist conditions a water carrying channel is produced with an average life of about 3–5 years. The gradient of the mole drains should be between 1 in 300 and 1 in 100 in most cases, these extremes being dictated by the need to avoid silting up on the one hand and washing on the other. Decreases of grade should also be avoided.

4.9.6 Patterns of laying drainage pipes

(a) In 'thorough' drainage a herringbone or straight pattern of laterals is laid which lead into main drains which in turn discharge into ditches or watercourses. A 3 in lateral size is standard with a 4 in or 6 in main line.

(b) In 'natural' drainage a single line of drains is laid along the natural lines of water discharge. This is specially applicable to the drainage of isolated wet areas in an otherwise dry location.

(c) 'Interceptor' drainage is practised to control the lateral movement of subsurface water. Interceptor drains laid on a suitable grade to obtain effective discharge are laid across the land slope and just above the seepage line. In this way the water is trapped and discharged before reaching the surface at the spring line.

Depth and spacing of tile drains. Empirical methods

Soil Type	Spacing (yd)	Depth (ft)
Clay	4–7	2–$2\frac{1}{2}$
Loam	8–12	$2\frac{1}{2}$–3
Sand	12–22	3–4

are at present used to establish the spacing and depth of drain tiles.

The greater the clay content of the soil the shallower and closer should be the drain tiles. Water will not reach deep drain tiles in an impermeable soil which, after heavy rain, may be observed to have a waterlogged surface without any discharge from the drain ends.

Laying of tile drains. The trench should only be excavated to the required depth. The depth and grade may be obtained by using boning rods and two sight rails previously levelled to the required grade. The base of the trench should be rounded to fit the tile surface. In a soil with a high silt fraction the surface sod and top soil should be placed in the drain before the rest of the backfill. In certain parts of the country a porous backfill is used. The gradient of the laterals should be greater than 1 in 250 or 3 in per chain and the gradient of the mains will suit the level of the discharge point and the designed carrying capacity. Junctions between mains and sub-mains and between sub-mains and laterals should be carefully made. Any junction at which a change in rate of flow is expected should have a silt trap with a removable inspection cover.

Protection of end of main. The point of discharge of the main line into a watercourse or ditch should be protected against the ingress of vermin and should be in glazed pipe to resist frost action. A hard surface to receive the discharge water is essential to prevent wash and the ditch side should be stone or brick faced around the discharging main. A main line should not pass within 6 yd of a hedgerow unless made of glazed pipe laid with sealed joints to prevent blockage by plant roots.

4.9.7 Ditches and French drains

Ditches. Important in controlling the level of the water table in the adjacent soil profile and in removing large volumes of water collected by tile drainage systems. They suffer from the disadvantage of restricting the movement of surface vehicles. The size and shape of a ditch will largely be governed by conditions at the site but as a general rule in a well-proportioned ditch the top width will be equal to the bottom width plus depth with the sides sloped at 45°. This may be varied according to the soil conditions. The gradient of a ditch will largely depend on the discharge level required, variations for different rates of discharge being taken into account in the cross-sectional dimensions of the ditch.

French drains. A ditch not full of water will control the water table in the adjacent soil. To improve the accessibility of areas interlaced by such channels, to ease maintenance and prevent land slip into the ditch a steeper sided trench may be used which is then filled with coarse stone or gravel to provide a French drain. These are always used in preference to open ditches on the sides of roads and railway cuttings to control the seepage which would otherwise occur on such slopes.

4.9.8 Machines for land drainage

Trenching machinery. A wide selection of machines for digging straight sided trenches are currently available. These fall into two main categories (*a*) the continuous rotary or endless-bucket trenchers, and (*b*) the single-bucket diggers. Group (*a*) tend to be more expensive, but achieve a higher rate of work in rock-free soils while group (*b*) are cheaper and with a slower rate of work can deal with soil with rock obstructions. They may also be fitted with special buckets for digging trenches of different widths and to a uniform depth. Both are used for trenching operations in conjunction with laying underground drains but the latter group may also be used for ditch construction although specialist side-arm dragline machines are preferred for this purpose.

Machinery for the automatic laying of drainage pipes. The rotary bucket trenching machines are particularly adaptable to the automatic laying of drainage pipes because of their steady continuous operation. For clay tiles a platform for storing tiles is required in addition to a chute on to which the pipes are placed end to end to travel down into the trench behind the machine. For plastic pipe a carrying rack for the 20 ft lengths is necessary and again a chute into which the pipe lengths are introduced by an operator on the machine. Special devices are required to maintain the true and correct grade so important in this work.

4.9.9 Disposal of run-off

Artificial drainage increases the volume of water which the rivers have to carry unless special provision is made to delay the flow of water to the rivers in times of heavy rainfall. An example of this is the provision of balancing ponds and lakes along the watercourse as in the L.C.C. New Town Project at Hook (Fig. 4.10). Without such provision artificial drainage tends to increase the risk of flooding from the overflow of rivers and streams.

Riverboard and internal drainage boards. The catchment areas of the principal rivers in England and Wales are covered by thirty-two river boards, together with the Thames and Lee Conservancies, and they are generally responsible for supervising land drainage within their catchment area, although only empowered to carry out maintenance or improvement work on the 'main river'. Internal drainage boards within the river board areas are responsible for the maintenance of streams feeding the main rivers in lowland areas.

Farm ditches and intermediate watercourses. Farm ditches are the responsibility of the farmer and in lowland areas will discharge directly into streams maintained by an internal drainage board. In upland areas there exist many miles of 'intermediate watercourses' linking the two which have recently received special attention by river boards.

Legislation. A considerable volume of legislation relates to the problems of the disposal of run-off, including the following:

H.M.S.O. *Land Drainage Act*, 1938, 20 and 21 Geo. 5, Ch. 94.

H.M.S.O. *River Boards Act*, 1948, 11 and 12 Geo. 6, Ch. 32.

H.M.S.O. *Land Drainage Act*, 1961, 9 and 10 Eliz. 2, Ch. 48.

see also

H.M.S.O. *Land Drainage in England and Wales*, Min. Ag. Fish. & Food, 1951.

H.M.S.O. *Land Drainage in England and Wales*, Cmnd. 916, December 1959.

Bibliography

'Basic design in land form', Brian Hackett, *I.L.A. Journal*, February 1960.

Data Book for Civil Engineers, vols. 1, 2 and 3, E. E. Seelye, John Wiley.

Field Drainage, M. C. Livesley, E. and F. N. Spon.

General Excavation Methods, A. Brinton Carson, F. W. Dodge Corporation, New York.

'Ground Modelling'. David Thirkettle, *I.L.A. Journal*, February 1961.

'Land form design and cost factors', Brian Hackett, *Landscape Architecture, U.S.A.*, July 1964.

Land Modelling, Brian Hackett, Public Works and Municipal Services Congress 1964: Final Report.

Soil and Water Conservation Engineering, R. K. Frevert, G. O. Schwab, T. H. Edminster and K. K. Barnes, John Wiley, New York.

Soil Mechanics, Foundations and Earth Structures, G. P. Tschebotarioff, McGraw-Hill, New York.

Soil Physics, L. D. Baver, Chapman and Hall.

Plate 5.1. WOODSTOCK, OXFORD—A classic example of paving for function and delight where each bend and kink of the path has a purpose. Stone setts channel the rainwater to and past the trees on the left.

5 Hard Surfaces

TIMOTHY COCHRANE

5.1 Introduction

Hard surfaces are important elements in landscape design especially in our increasingly urbanised civilisation. This chapter gives a general coverage of the major points to be considered in paving schemes, with references as necessary for more detailed information. The emphasis is on *paving for pedestrians* in courtyards and squares rather than on footpaths. Vehicular and sports surfaces are only briefly mentioned being well covered by many publications. *It is important to realise that what is said in this chapter must be related to differing local conditions.*

5.1.1 Function of pavings

The first function of any paved surface is to provide a hard, dry, non-slip surface which will carry the required load for pedestrian or vehicular traffic. It may also have other functions: it may indicate:

Direction—which can be suggested by the use of smoother flags on which people naturally walk to lead them across a grassed or gravelled courtyard, or by use of cobbles to deter people from wandering off route (Plate 5.1).

Hazard—Where vehicles cross a pedestrian path a change in the paving material for either or both routes will indicate change of function. A change in paving material is sometimes useful to draw attention to changes of level negotiated by steps or ramps.

Repose—Paving patterns can subtly indicate focal points where people pause in a paved area.

Ownership—Change of level or material or both (e.g. spaces beside public pavements outside hotels, shops, etc.).

G

5.1.2 Choice of pavings

With function decided upon it is possible to consider the available materials and to assess them on grounds of cost, appearance, etc. The following list should assist in selecting an appropriate paving:

Cost and availability—Is the material one with a high first cost matched by low maintenance costs, or *vice versa*? Has it durability, freedom from cracking and other failures, matched to the life expectation of the project, and is it readily available?

Appearance, weathering, cleaning—Textural range, colour suitability for plain or patterned work should be considered, not only when first laid, but also when weathered. In this respect, natural materials tend to weather unevenly, but in doing so usually become more attractive. It may however be necessary to select materials which can be cleaned down by washing and hosing; or if by mechanical vacuuming or sweeping, design should be of a structural strength to carry at least light machines. In some locations a dark and heavily patterned material such as setts may be used to conceal oil stains which cannot be readily cleaned off any surface.

Safety, noise, light reflectivity—Is the area one affected by liability of local authorities, or otherwise affecting public safety, and do conditions suggest selection of non-slip materials? Softer and coarser paving textures may cause less impact noise at source and provide absorption for other sounds. In some cases, light reflection, causing glare around buildings may be a consideration.

Subsoil, drainage, services—Do subsoil conditions suggest the use of an impervious surface, with full drainage, or can the paving be chosen to absorb rainfall? Must underground services be accommodated and what are their access needs, by means of manholes, etc., or by occasional excavation? *In situ* materials should not be used where they may be dug-up frequently, instead manhole covers can be integrated into a paved scheme.

Comparative cost of surfacing materials—Costs are very much affected by local conditions, soil structure, labour and transport costs, availability of materials (including wastes) and on the size of the contract. The local council engineer or surveyor could help here with local knowledge, but it must be remembered that his experience may be related more to roads than pedestrian surfaces. Table 5.1 gives a rough and ready comparative guide to some of the most common materials in use.

5.1.3 Patterns

After years of neglect paving design has only recently come into its own in this country. As Elisabeth Beazley comments, 'Good paving is nearly always the background of a scheme and should reinforce the character of the design as a whole; it might be deemed equally unsuccessful if attention is drawn to it either by its monotony (i.e. being out of scale with its surroundings), ingenuity or colour. Rare exceptions, e.g. mosaic pavings are not considered here. If a pattern is wanted, and it may be necessary to reduce scale, it is best introduced by a material already in use in other parts of the scheme (e.g. in the buildings or screen walls) or by varying the shade but not the actual colour of the material. Otherwise acceptable schemes (e.g. of precast concrete slabs) are often made garish by the use of two colours. Drainage channels can be most useful in giving scale.'

Technical aspects—See sections 5.4.1 and 5.4.2 for notes on trim, setts, bricks, etc. In addition concrete offers an infinite range of finishes and patterns due to the many ways in which its jointing can be designed. For flexible materials, only use as dividers those materials which will withstand rolling (e.g. setts, not concrete or stone). Costs can go up steeply when paving materials are mixed, and to avoid extra screeding costs it is as well to consider using materials of similar depth together (e.g. 2 in paviors with 2 in flags or 2 in flags with cobbles in 3 in concrete; while 1 in hot asphalt on concrete fill can be used as infills to 2 in flags). Jointing patterns can be varied widely but note that herringbone patterns need elaborate setting out and constant checking as against straightforward coursing.*

5.1.4 Paving for vehicles

Common surfacing materials are concrete, bitumen macadam, tarmacadam, cold and hot asphalts, sealed and unsealed gravel. Increasing the thickness of the sub-base and base or the addition of 4–6 in concrete will render many of the materials in this chapter usable for light vehicular traffic. This can be especially important at vehicle crossings, hard-standings and corners of pavements.

For detailed consideration of vehicular pavement design, consult the following publications:

Cochrane, Timothy. Element Design Guide Sfb Ba4(14) 'Roads and Pavings', *Architects Journal*, 9 November 1966 *et seq*. Comprehensive coverage regarding layout and constructional design of roads, with references to relevant publications.

Ministry of Transport, Road Research Laboratory, Crowthorne, Berks. *Road Notes* cover all aspects of roads; obtainable from H.M.S.O. *Road Note No. 29* is the key one covering design of flexible and rigid pavings together with M.O.T. *Specification for Road and Bridge Works*, H.M.S.O., 1963.

* *Paving patterns and their uses,* Cement and Concrete Association.
Architectural Review, April, 1957, R. Maguire.

Cement & Concrete Association, 52 Grosvenor Gardens, London, S.W.1, and Federation of Coated Macadam Industries, 37 Chester Square, London, S.W.1.

These produce various publications on materials for estate and minor roads.

5.1.5 Pavings for recreation

These include pavings for athletics: running tracks, field events, jump approaches, throwing circles and steeple-chase tracks; and all ball-games. (Rugby football is the only one which cannot be played on a hard surface.) There are three main paving types. First, concrete which is hard, non-resilient, but is long-lasting and requires little or no maintenance. Tarmacadam, asphalt and bitu-men macadam are more resilient and costly and need some maintenance, for example, surface dressing with bitumen emulsion. Ash, shale and proprietary mixes such as 'Redgra' are porous surfaces more nearly approaching grass in resilience and ease of play but which require regular maintenance of brushing, watering and rolling. Drainage is needed for surfaces particularly in the first two groups. Falls are specified in the literature on each sport.

Many proprietary materials utilising rubber and plastic are under development which will give resilience with the low maintenance advantages of hard pavings. Costs are still high. It is important to consider each sport separately due to different requirements. Up-to-date references are essential and the National Playing Fields Association,

TABLE 5.1: PAVINGS AND PAVING COSTS

Rates ruling at the end of 1966 in London, areas of 500 square yards; pavings forming part of a building contract value in excess of £10,000 tendered for in limited competition. The cost of insurance, supervision and the like are included. The rates stated are per square yard and include in each case the value of the concrete and/or hardcore base indicated.

FLEXIBLE SURFACES	Cost £ s. d.	to	£ s. d.	UNIT PAVINGS	Cost £ s. d.	to	£ s. d.
Gravel 3 in two-course gravel on 4 in rolled hardcore	13 9	to	16 9	2 in *Precast concrete flags*, B.S. sizes, natural colour, the makers' texture or no texture, spot-bedded on 4 in blinded and rolled hardcore	1 7 0	to	1 15 0
Tarmacadam 2 in two-course bitumen macadam, the top course red pigmented and finished with limestone chippings on 4 in blinded and rolled hardcore	19 0	to	1 1 0	2 in *Precast concrete flags*, on 4 in concrete and 4 in hardcore	1 19 6	to	2 10 0
Asphalt 1 in red pigmented hot-rolled asphalt on 4 in concrete and 4 in hardcore	1 6 3	to	1 11 6	Extra over precast concrete flags for coloured	3 0	to	4 0
RIGID PAVEMENTS				2 in *Proprietary coloured cement slabs*—with pointed joints on 4 in concrete and 4 in hardcore	2 5 6	to	2 18 0
Concrete 4 in concrete on rolled formation with an isolating layer of polythene-coated paper, including expansion joints at 40 ft intervals	18 6	to	1 0 0	*Brick paving*—of second quality engineering bricks set on edge on 4 in concrete and 4 in hardcore and pointed	3 15 6	to	4 6 0
4 in concrete as last but on 4 in hardcore, no paper	1 0 6	to	1 4 6	Brick paving of 2 in blue paviors bedded and pointed on 4 in concrete and 4 in hardcore	4 3 6	to	4 15 0
Extra for each additional inch of concrete	3 0	to	4 0	*Tiles*			
Extra for treating surface of concrete with a studded roller	2 6	to	5 9	6 in × 6 in *Red quarry tiles* with close joints on 4 in concrete and 4 in hardcore	3 5 6	to	3 15 0
Extra for reinforcing concrete with one layer of Ref. 125 fabric	5 0	to	5 6	Extra on quarry tiles if screeded bed required to form graded falls or to produce a particularly true surface	9 0	to	11 0
Pavings–2 in *New yorkstone* on courses one way, p.c. 45s. per sq yd spot-bedded on 4 in blinded and rolled hardcore	6 6 0	to	7 18 0	*Setts* 4 in *secondhand granite setts* set in mortar on 4 in concrete and 4 in hardcore	5 9 6	to	6 13 0
2½–3 in *Secondhand* rectangular *yorkstone*, p.c. 34s. per sq yd spot-bedded on 4 in blinded and rolled hardcore	5 6 0	to	6 8 0	*Cobbles* *Flint cobbles* set close in mortar on 2 in concrete and 4 in hardcore	3 16 0	to	4 18 0

Note—Combination of two or more types of paving in a pattern will increase cost by anything from 25% to 100% depending on intricacy of pattern.

Cost notes by Ernest Pasterfield and Partners, Chartered Quantity Surveyors.

57B Catherine Place, S.W.1, should be consulted as to the latest literature available. In addition to N.P.F.A. publications, the following are useful references:

Federation of Coated Macadam Industries and the Cement & Concrete Association, which issue specifications for the appropriate uses of coated macadam and concrete respectively.

Tandy, C. V. R., *Element Design Guide*, Sfb Ac6(15), 'Landscape, play spaces, etc.', *Architects Journal*, 26 September 1962. (Now under revision).

Smith, P. F., *The Planning, Construction and Maintenance of Playing Fields*, 1950, 30s. Covers all forms of hard surfaces for sports and play areas, with specifications. Some information now superseded by later publications.

Manufacturers of some specialised surfaces include:

Thomas Roberts (Westminster) Ltd.—'Redgra'.
En-tout-Cas Co. Ltd., Syston, Leicester.
United Reclaim Ltd., Speke, Liverpool.
Limmer & Trinidad Ltd., London.
Rub-Kor U.K. Ltd., Cheadle, Cheshire.
The Ruberoid Co. Ltd., London.

Playgrounds.　　　Much of the foregoing information is applicable also to playgrounds. Generally, softer materials are used throughout, with concrete or paving slabs and other hard materials at major pieces of equipment or access points. Experiments are being made with plastic and bitumen seals for gravel. Additional references include:

Allen of Hurtwood, Lady Marjorie, *Design for Play . . . the Youngest Children*, 1962. Section on paving materials for toddlers playgrounds.

New Playgrounds 1964, 7s. 6d. Use of concrete setts on sloping surfaces. List of rubber surface manufacturers. (Both by Housing Centre Trust).

Playgrounds for Blocks of Flats—Notes on Use and Surfacing, N.P.F.A., 1954, 2s. 6d.

5.1.6 Roofs

Roofed or decked areas are likely to be increasingly used in urban areas. They require special consideration and various treatments are possible. These include light decking, more heavily modelled sculptural shapes in reinforced concrete, or a treatment which gives an illusion of normal ground by superimposing a naturalistic garden design.

Waterproofing is necessary—the best way is tanking with $1\frac{1}{8}$ in asphalt. There must be adequate provision for rainwater disposal.

Lightweight screeds (for example vermiculite) can be used with cobbles, etc. set directly into them. Patent surfaces for roofs include 12 in × 12 in × $\frac{5}{16}$ in asbestos-cement tiles, 24 in × 24 in × 1 in cement-grano paving laid *in situ*; both laid on bituminous sheet membranes. Use can also be made of lightweight timber deckings laid

duckboard style on rot-proofed battens over the membrane. Care is needed with soil for planting on roofs, while water supply and drainage are necessary.

5.1.7 Foundations

The function of the pavement is to distribute point loads over the soil itself. Macadam pointed out that 'it is the native soil which really supports the weight of traffic, and that while that soil is in a dry state, it will carry any weight without sinking' (see Fig. 5.1 for terms used in paved surfaces).

Subsoil—Gault clay, heavy clay and peat give rise to difficulties and are especially susceptible to uneven movement. Lighter clays, silts, sands and gravels may be taken as more normal, but some, such as sand are only stable when contained. Rock and compacted gravels give good foundations. Excess water in the subgrade reduces bearing capacity and can also give rise to frost heave. This can be controlled by waterproof surfacing and adequate falls which restrict rain penetration. Ditches and land drains can be used to control ground water.

Preparation—Organic topsoil must be removed and any fill should be a suitable base material well compacted in 6–9 in layers. The formation should be rolled and compacted to required falls and cambers. On difficult soils likely to be affected by rain penetration during construction it is possible to apply a sprayed bituminous binder at the rate of 1 gal to 5 sq yd. For gravel and other flexible pavements, the formation should be treated with a weedkiller applied in accordance with the manufacturer's instructions. Sodium chlorate is effective at the rate of 12 lb to 10 gal of water applied to each 100 sq yd. This is however toxic to tree roots and where these are present, use may be made of simazine (Geigy) at the rate of 1 lb to 100 gal of water applied to each 500 sq yd, or of one of the other monoglycomates which fix in the surface and do not travel down.

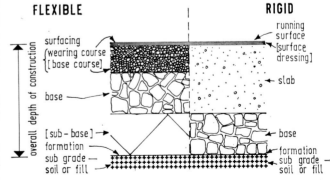

Fig. 5.1. PAVED SURFACES—DEFINITIONS—This covers the standard terminology of most types of paving. Items in brackets are those not always used, while 'formation' denotes the top of the subgrade.

Base—In flexible pavements the base is the main load distributing layer. It may be any material with an 80% CBR* when compacted, and which remains stable in water and is resistant to frost. Well-graded gravel, sands, hard core, hard clinker or slag will generally be suitable, but ashes are likely to be unstable when wet. With rigid pavements the loading is transmitted by the slab and the base would only be necessary to protect a poor subgrade from frost or to provide a suitable working surface.

5.2 Types of hard surface

5.2.1 Flexible surfacings

These are layers of compacted materials with no tensile strength and which spread the load directly over the soil and can be surfaced to keep water and frost from the subsoil. The material may be laid loose or incorporate a binder.

Gravel paving. If laid loose consists of a base and sub-base as needed laid directly on formation level without binding materials. The base is usually 4 in clinker or hardcore.

If left unsealed gravel has a precinctual and informal character and is, of course, useful around trees as it allows their roots to breathe, and avoids rigid paving lines round the trunks. It is cheap and suitable for occasional car parking. Treatment with weedkiller is necessary in spring (see section 5.1.7). Granite dust and pea shingle may also be used though the latter tends to be slippery.

Some self-binding gravels are available which lightly cement together after watering and compaction. They must be laid to falls. Colours vary according to the locality of source. Some include dust from lead and copper mines which has the additional merit of inhibiting weed growth. One type is hoggin, a gravel/sand/clay mix.

Construction—Heavy rolling at all stages is essential (8–10 tons for drives, but a 10–15 cwt hand roller may suffice for paths). Specifications vary greatly with subsoils and loads, but the following is fairly general (all are finished thicknesses): Sub-base as necessary, 4 in base of hardcore, clinker, etc. 2 in gravel (2 in mesh), 1 in fine gravel with some hoggin as binder, and finished with $\frac{3}{4}$ in fine gravel, fine grit, shell or stone chippings ($\frac{3}{4}$ in mesh) spread and rolled.

Ashes or cinders as a surfacing are suitable only for rough paths and running tracks. More than any other material construction varies with local conditions. Graded mixes (3 : 1 household/hard fine ash) can be compacted and rolled to total thickness of 5 in on 5 in base.

Loose cobbles. When laid directly on soil or hard-core loose cobbles provide an excellent hazard and are good by trees especially where the ground level by trees has to be raised. They can be used also as recessed trim between dissimilar materials, but give rise to cleaning difficulties. Sizes, $1\frac{1}{4}$ in to 5 in diameter. Real cobbles should be oval and waterworn or regularly pitted. Other so-called 'cobbles' are often split rather than waterworn, e.g. ballast, which is rougher than cobbles but can be used in similar ways. For reasonable economy it is essential to investigate local sources of supply. Indiscriminate digging from beaches and rivers is not permitted but some firms have rights over defined areas. Colours may vary, ranging from fawn to grey. Flint gravel rejects may be available from local gravel pits, and cement manufacturers using chalk as a raw material often have cobbles available as waste. Colours are in the darker blue and grey range. Wash mill flints are available from potteries. Cobbles are also imported from Normandy. They are well graded for size and the colours are pleasant medium to light greys.

Plate 5.2. Stone setts form a pleasantly informal trim at the junction of grass and gravel.

* Californian bearing ratio—A measure of the bearing capacity of soils, commonly used for vehicle roads—see *Road Note 29*, Ministry of Transport, H.M.S.O., for design guides.

Bound surfaces (with waterproofing binders and/or surfacings). Surfacing varies from open-textured coated macadams to the smooth and more expensive black toppings of the hot and cold asphalts. Although open texture looks better they are more vulnerable to weathering processes and are therefore not as durable. Non-slip qualities and appearance depend largely on the aggregate chosen and black tops can in fact be lightened by their use.

Surface dressings for both old and new pavements utilise hot tar or bitumen (also available in emulsion form). Wearing courses are provided for waterproof and non-skid surfaces, while the base course protects the base from traffic load (see Fig. 5.1).

Construction of flexible toppings. Thickness $1\frac{1}{2}$–$4\frac{1}{2}$ in depending on the traffic and the texture required. The Federation of Coated Macadam Industries recommends 2 in for foot traffic, though $1\frac{1}{2}$ in has been used. The minimum for vehicles is $2\frac{1}{2}$ in laid in one or two courses. *Road Note No. 29* gives design charts.

Compaction is achieved by 1–3 ton roller for playgrounds, up to 6–9 tons for roads, but use 10 cwt hand roller round manholes and awkward spots.

Stabilised soil base. This is best described as a weak, flexible but cheap concrete of cement mixed with earth,* which needs surfacing. It can be used for roads, car parks, cycle tracks, playgrounds, etc. It is only applicable where the ground is suitable (gravels, coarse sands, but not organic soils, while clay needs special processing), and where the contract is big enough to justify soil tests, expert advice, and careful supervision.

5.2.2 Rigid pavings

Rigid paving structures are those which utilise the tensile strength of the construction to transmit loads to the soil, as in the case of concrete slabs for roads or pavements. The most common is *in situ* concrete which is cheap, easy to use and popular, but it is important that the surface should be finished correctly and carefully with imaginative use of jointing and textured finishes. Even with the extra cost of these finishes and joints it is still far cheaper than many other materials. It is at its best combined with

Plate 5.3. GARDEN, HAMBURG—This composition of exposed aggregate and smooth concrete slabs with its water channels shows an imaginative treatment of the material.

other surfaces or trim, and good detailing and workmanship are vital. Concrete is chosen for its finish, use on bad soil (if local materials available), or its combination with other materials as it obviates rolling.

Minimum thicknesses are 3 in unreinforced for pedestrian traffic, 6 in unreinforced for vehicular traffic, or 4 in reinforced, with the addition of 1 in to each for vehicles over 30 cwt.

Normal mix is 1:2:4. For pedestrian surfaces reinforcement would normally only be used for crack control (square mesh about 2 in from top) increasing the spacing of joints needed from every 15 ft if unreinforced to 40 ft with mesh reinforcement approximately $4\frac{1}{2}$ lb/sq yd. Bad subgrades, embankments over 4 ft high, or paving over high water tables may also require reinforcement. Expansion joints need special construction detailing (Fig. 5.2). (See *Road Note No. 29* for design chart).

Various finishes can be employed. Those which are untextured rely on coloured cements and jointing for effect. These are not always satisfactory as the coloured concrete can look crude and artificial. Textured surfaces offer a much better choice of finish. They rely on exposure of the aggregate by brushing while still damp, spraying or using retarders or by mechanical means (crimping rollers, board patterns or even by bush-hammering and grit-blasting). A wide range of aggregates is available, in whites, pinks, greys, blues, greens, browns and blacks while colour of cement should be carefully chosen either to harmonise with, or to set off the chosen aggregates.† (Plate 5.3.)

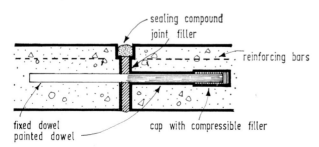

Fig. 5.2. CONCRETE SLABS—EXPANSION JOINTS—Reinforcement is stopped as shown and joint filler and sealing compound fills the gap. Where heavy traffic is expected dowels are used to transmit load.

* *Soil-cement roads*, W. P. Andrews, Cement and Concrete Association.
  'Soil-cement roads', *Fixed equipment of the farm*, Leaflet 19, Ministry of Agriculture Fisheries and Food.
  Road Note No. 15, Specification for the construction of housing estate roads using soil-cement, Road Research Laboratory.
  † Sources of aggregate (D.S.I.R.), H.M.S.O., 1s. 3d.

5.2.3 Unit pavings

Bases for pedestrian traffic, use 3 in well-consolidated good hardcore or sand-blinded clinker (well-burnt) rolled to paving falls. For occasional vehicular traffic add 4 in 1:3:6 concrete slab (1½ in aggregate) laid directly on formation or 3 in base.

Large units (flags). These may be laid in several ways:

Set on 1 in sand bed. Traditional. Satisfactory where sand cannot be washed out at edges or through open joints.

Bedded and jointed with mortar. The mix should be suited to the slab. Useful for wheeled traffic but not over services due to lifting difficulties.

Laid on five mortar dots at corners and at centre (1:5 mix)—easy to lift, and to level the slabs. Good if pavior is skilled, also gives easier access to services.

Joints—Butt joints are best for normal pavings and formal effects, as they keep water from the base and discourage weeds. Grout joints or brush in dry mix (5:1). Where plants are needed—spread sand on foundation, lay slabs with ½ in joints, fill with fine soil and top up for the first few weeks.

Stepping stones—Flags laid at 2 ft 6 in centres and 1½ in below grass level. Can also be laid *in situ* in grass but this is not easy. Cut out turf and lay 3 in concrete (1:2:4) on sanded clinker.

Materials—*Precast concrete* is the most common material, in sizes 1 ft 6 in to 3 ft × 2 ft. Normally made 2 in thickness for pedestrian traffic but a 2½ in slab is sometimes used where occasional light vehicle traffic will be met—garage crossings for example and in towns where service

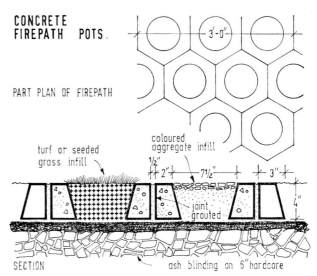

Fig. 5.4. CONCRETE FIREPOTS—Useful where a fire appliance access must be routed through a grassed area. (Acknowledgement: Wettern Bros.)

vehicles may mount the pavement from time to time. The most common slab is mass-produced and made to a dense, high quality, by hydraulic pressing in steel moulds (B.S. 368). It normally has a smooth creamy finish, but can be coloured or have the aggregate exposed by acid washing. Open mould casting is also done and at a much higher cost this opens up a variety of finishes including exposed coarse aggregates, textures impressed by rubber mats, and non-slip inserts of rubber or carborundum. Slabs which are not hydraulically pressed lack very high density and strength, but vibration can be used to produce a sound and durable concrete.

There have been many attempts to improve the somewhat dull appearance of concrete slab pavings, but discretion is needed. Various colours—greys, green, buff, red can be used, separately or in colour combinations. Shapes are available including L shapes and hexagons, but they need very careful detailing to avoid awkward junctions (Fig. 5.3).

Precast stone—This is dearer than precast concrete, yet much cheaper than stone slabs. Almost any stone can be 'reconstructed'.

Natural stone and slate—These are relatively costly, quarried in small quantities, but still most durable and pleasant materials. Slight irregularities and more organic weathering provides a welcome relief from that of manufactured materials. If locally obtained, secondhand stones are much cheaper. Being already weathered, they can look better, but cost more to lay. (Usually yorkstone from broken-up pavements.)

Laying—consult quarries as to sizes and adjust design to suit seams being cut.

Granite—Very hard and durable but expensive and rarely found in large slabs.

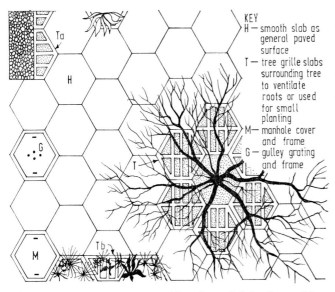

Fig. 5.3. HEXAGONAL PAVING—Note the varied details possible; tree grids (*Ta* + *Tb*) and gully grating covers *G* while manhole covers *M* are also integrated into the pattern. (Acknowledgement: Wettern Bros.)

KEY
H — smooth slab as general paved surface
T — tree grille slabs surrounding tree to ventilate roots or used for small planting
M — manhole cover and frame
G — gulley grating and frame

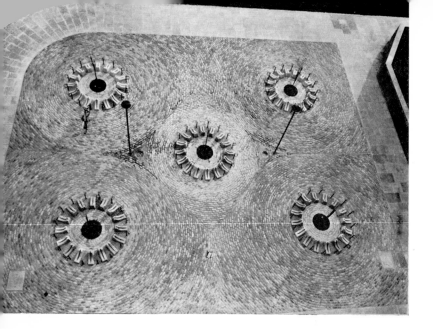

Plate 5.4. CYCLE PARKING AREA, CAMBRIDGE—The swirling circles of setts combine to present an interesting pattern. Drainage is to gullies by the lamp posts while gravel and setts laid in sand around trunks provide water and air to the trees.

Yorkshire—Best known is sandstone, buff-brown, also bluish. Riven faced, rubbed finish is more expensive. Similar stones from Lancashire and the Forest of Dean. Slabs $1\frac{1}{2}$–$2\frac{1}{2}$ in.

Portland Stone from Purbeck and Portland are soft grey/ whites. Slabs 2–$2\frac{1}{2}$ in.

Other stones are generally not robust enough for external pavings.

Slate is good but expensive. Lancashire, Westmorland and Cornwall—green, browns and Welsh slates—purplish, grey-black, are usually split to natural riven face. Sanded and rubbed finishes are available at greater expense. Thickness $\frac{3}{4}$ in to $1\frac{1}{4}$ in.

Small units. These are particularly useful for small-scale patterns (as in domestic work) or where a change of scale is needed inside a larger area.

Bricks—Many hard, well-burnt, non-dusting bricks *can* be suitable for use, but they must be chosen with care to resist frost and sulphate attack. If anything they should be slightly over-burnt. Usually they are attractively well-textured and therefore non-slip. Colours—dark blues, plums, reds.

Engineering pavers—Wirecuts and pressed. Sizes are usually as for other bricks but $1\frac{1}{2}$ in to $2\frac{7}{8}$ in thick. They are tough, with hard smooth surfaces, and also have non-slip patterned faces. Colours—red (south) and blue (north).

Laying—Many permutations are possible, on edge or face, herringbone, stretcher or basketweave bonds, etc.

An adequate camber or fall is essential to facilitate drainage and avoid slipperiness. Laid on sand or sand-lime (1 : 4) bed, or on a mortar bed. Colour and type

of jointing is an important factor in the overall appearance. Ordinary bricks have grouted $\frac{3}{8}$–$\frac{3}{4}$ in joints while engineering bricks are butt jointed.

Tiles and mosaics—These are usually limited to small areas of special emphasis. A large variety of sizes, shapes and colours is available; clay quarries—browns, reds; semi- and fully-vitrified tiles or mosaics—wide colour range. Pattern-making tiles (as quarries but in interlocking shapes) are available in great variety from U.K. and continental sources. Only a few clay tiles are frostproof.

Laying—Tiles $\frac{5}{8}$–$1\frac{1}{4}$ in thick, laid on 4 in concrete (1 : 2 : 4) with $\frac{3}{4}$ in cement/sand screed (1 : 3) and $\frac{3}{16}$ in joints of cement/sand (1 : 2). Mosaics $\frac{1}{8}$ in–$\frac{3}{16}$ in thick—Various proprietary methods of laying, utilising latex cements.

Setts—Granite, the hardest wearing surface of all, is the most common, but limestone and whinstone setts are also made. From 2 in and 4 in cube up to larger and rectangular blocks, they can be obtained new (very expensively) or secondhand. They are laid either with a fairly flush surface, or a rough surface to discourage access; used to create bold patterns (Plate 5.4), or as scaling-down trim (Plate 5.2). Its ability to stand rolling makes it suitable as a permanent shuttering to other materials, such as tarmac.

Laying—On 1 in sand bed, rammed $\frac{3}{8}$ in joints grouted after racking with chippings. Alternatively butted tight and laid on 1 in cement/sand (1 : 3) with joints brushed in with dry cement/sand (1 : 6).

Cobbles—see section 5.2.1. There are many ways in which cobbles can be used; random, roughly coursed, or laid in patterns; either flush or proud of the surface to give differing degrees of pedestrian control.

Laying—On 2 in compacted sand lay 2 in concrete (1 : 2 : 4) and place cobbles as required in this base. Other methods: lay dry and water with watering can. (Use concrete base for vehicles.)

Timber—Formerly used as tarred road setts, it is possible to exploit the qualities of timber as a paving material on terraces and patios, and especially on roofed areas where its resilience, lightness and smooth surface drainage can

Plate 5.5. GRANITE SETTS AND TIMBER DECKING —The jutting mound contrasts pleasantly with the smooth sophistication of the open timber decking.

be utilised. Durable hardwoods or treated softwoods can be laid with $\frac{1}{2}$–1 in gaps. A well-trafficked area with coarse-textured timber, adequate falls and good ventilation and drainage should be really non-slip, and would offer a welcome change from many of the other heavier paving materials used (Plate 5.5).

Precast concrete firepath pots—$11\frac{1}{2} \times 4$ in deep hexagonal precast concrete 'pots' in which the hollows are filled with grass or soft paving materials. Bedded and jointed on ash on a porous hardcore base these will support fire appliances in case of emergency, though normally giving the appearance of a lawn (Fig. 5.4).

5.3 Drainage and services

5.3.1 Surface water drainage
The aim of drainage is to get the water off the impermeable surface quickly by means of cambers or falls through gutters, channels or gullies to the disposal system. It can either be handled unobtrusively or designed as an attractive element of the paving pattern. Cross falls and cambers have generally replaced older methods of 'dishing' to separate gullies. In handling falls it is necessary to be bold. Quite steep falls (within limits as shown) have been used in traditional work and can be very effective, but it may be necessary to counteract any visual 'sliding' by using central channels in narrow places. Suggested falls are shown in Fig. 5.5, but it is always as well to check on local practice. Around buildings the paving should fall away at 1 : 50 minimum for about 10 ft to avoid 'splash-back' from rain.

5.3.2 Surface water disposal
Calculation of water run-off is usually by means of the 'rational' (Lloyd-Davies) formula. The Road Research Laboratory hydrograph method is only used in really large schemes, anything requiring a 24 in sewer or bigger (see Chapter 4—Section on Drainage, for formulae).

For paved areas and roads generally the permissible fall in channels or pavings (see section 5.3.1) governs spacing of gullies. As a rough guide on so-called flat roads anything from 60–180 ft spacing between gratings is usual, and standard large 18 in × 36 in gullies will drain 2,000 sq ft of road. When sizing gullies allow for 1 sq ft of grating area to 15 cu ft per min flow (plus factor of safety for obstruction by leaves, overrun, etc.).

Disposal may be to combined surface and foul water or to separate surface water systems (check with local authority). Soakaways must be used if there is no sewer. Several small ones are better than one large one. Storage chambers should hold $\frac{1}{2}$ in rainfall over area × impermeability coefficient, and should penetrate at least 2 ft into permeable strata.*

5.3.3 Surface items
Collection points for drainage, and points of access to underground services, appear on the surface in ways which must be carefully considered and if possible co-ordinated in their overall design. Drainage and service lines can be routed or rerouted within reasonably defined limits. Gullies and covers can be selected from standard ranges and be specially designed. Finally paving types can be selected bearing in mind particular needs to

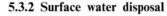

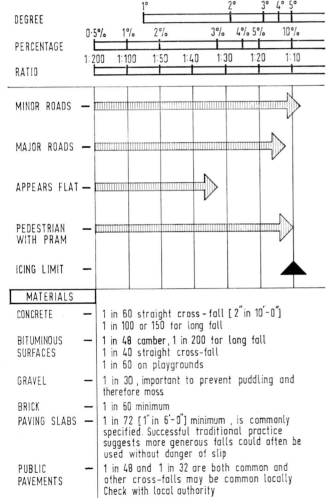

DEGREE	1°		2°	3° 4° 5°
PERCENTAGE	0·5%	1%	2%	3% 4% 5% 10%
RATIO	1:200	1:100	1:50 1:40	1:30 1:20 1:10

MINOR ROADS

MAJOR ROADS

APPEARS FLAT

PEDESTRIAN WITH PRAM

ICING LIMIT

MATERIALS

CONCRETE —	1 in 60 straight cross-fall [2″ in 10′-0″] 1 in 100 or 150 for long fall
BITUMINOUS SURFACES —	1 in 48 camber, 1 in 200 for long fall 1 in 40 straight cross-fall 1 in 60 on playgrounds
GRAVEL —	1 in 30, important to prevent puddling and therefore moss
BRICK —	1 in 60 minimum
PAVING SLABS —	1 in 72 [1″ in 6′-0″] minimum, is commonly specified. Successful traditional practice suggests more generous falls could often be used without danger of slip
PUBLIC PAVEMENTS —	1 in 48 and 1 in 32 are both common and other cross-falls may be common locally Check with local authority

Fig. 5.5. FALLS TABLE— A comparative table showing falls in varying conditions. Note that minimum falls increase with surface roughness.

* *Civil Engineering Code of Practice No. 5*, Drainage, B.S. Code of Practice 303, *and Road Note No. 35.*

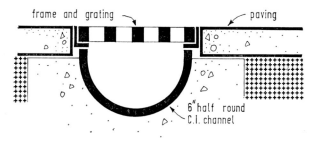

Fig. 5.6. CHANNEL—Shows half-round channel with grating cover.

Plate 5.7. A straightforward grille detail draining an area of exposed aggregate paving.

accommodate known drainage and service requirements. Efforts to hide or camouflage are seldom successful, but tidily ordered elements become relatively unobtrusive. In this respect rectangular covers should fit squarely into the paving pattern. If this is not possible circular gratings and covers present an acceptable alternative.

Gullies and gratings. Back inlet gullies provide the neatest system for rainwater downpipes. Other gullies which are open to receive direct discharge from rainwater pipes or to collect water from channels have grating covers to check entry of leaves and litter. They are removeable to give access for cleaning. For gratings cast iron is almost universal. Steel is sometimes used for its high strength to weight ratio. These notes refer to cast iron but also apply to steel except in that the gradings ABC operate in the reverse order.

B.S. 497 gives three grades:

A. Heavy duty—for main roads and service roads for heavy vehicles.
B. Medium duty—light traffic roads, but use A where oil-tanker traffic is expected.
C. Kerb type—for footpaths and verges.

Many sizes and patterns are available including those with hinges and which can be locked in position.

Common types include straight bar double triangular, plain square grating, storm gully grating, and kerb weir,

which are also available with anti-flood deflectors and gully covers and frames (Fig. 5.7).

Channel gratings fit block or half-round channels 4–12 in wide for most types of traffic (Plate 5.7 and Fig. 5.6).

Channels. These are used where hard surfaces meet kerbs and where two falls intersect. As well as channelling water run-off they also act as trim, especially useful on rolled surfaces where the roller cannot get up to the edge.

Materials may be *in situ* concrete, precast concrete to B.S. 340 or granite and whinstone, in various dressings to B.S. 435.

Sandstone is seldom used but traditional setts are useful for texture change. Cobbles also give texture change but their rough surface slows the flow of water. Hot asphalt can be ruled as a smooth margin to otherwise textured asphalt paving. Cast iron, in half round sections may suit special cases. Surrounding surfaces should be dished to channels; alternatively the channels themselves can be dished at higher cost. Some can be covered with iron gratings or grilles.

Plate 5.6. Dished and perforated stone gully set in brick paving.

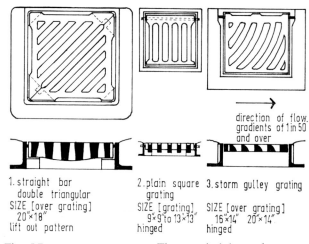

1. straight bar double triangular
SIZE [over grating]
20"×18"
lift out pattern

2. plain square grating
SIZE [grating]
9"×9" to 13"×13"
hinged

3. storm gulley grating
SIZE [over grating]
16"×14" 20"×14"
hinged

direction of flow.
gradients of 1 in 50 and over

Fig. 5.7. GULLY GRATINGS—Three typical heavy-duty types.

Manhole covers. There are many good traditional patterns available in cast iron in circular, rectangular, square, double triangular and single triangular shapes. Non-rocking covers should be specified. Gradings are as for cast iron gratings. Steel is also used; it is stronger and more expensive but rusts more quickly. Recessed covers, medium and light grades only, can be filled with paving material to match that of the surroundings. They are not always a perfect solution but are excellent with cobbles.

Setting of manhole covers is all-important and these points should be covered in the specification. Covers should always be parallel to the overall pattern and set well within the paving to obviate the untidy sight of manhole walls projecting and manholes astride two materials. Also keep the covers parallel to sloping surfaces. Round covers fit better into *in situ* pavings.

Concealed covers; this is sometimes done with service manholes, and the G.P.O. use a small triangular marker plate usually at the corner of a paving slab to indicate the presence of a concealed junction cover. Simply, the manhole is terminated with a cover below paving level and the paving (slabs on dots) or gravel, loose cobbles, etc. is continued over it. Other covers include those for all the major services, including hydrants, air valves, meter boxes, sluice valves and stopcocks. All are available in square or rectangular shapes from 4 in × 4 in to about 2 ft × 1 ft 3 in.

5.3.4 Public utilities

The report of the Joint Committee on the Location of Underground Services (1963) gives suggested spacing and depths for services below a 6 ft or preferably 10 ft 6 in footpath. From this it is possible to develop a reasonable system for fitting services into paved areas. In complicated cases, three-dimensional checks are useful especially for crossings (Fig. 5.8).

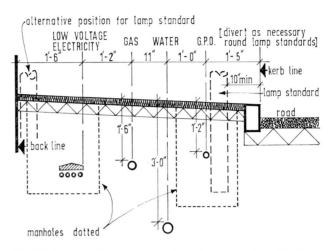

Fig. 5.8. Suggested arrangement of services under 6 ft wide footway, as recommended by the Joint Committee on the Location of Underground Services. Sewers are not shown as they are separately laid to independent falls.

TABLE 5.2

Services	Materials and Access Needs	Minimum cover
Water mains	Mainly 4 in dia. C.I., steel or asbestos (3–12 in dia. common; largest is 132 in dia)	3 ft 0 in depth (up to 12 in dia.) 3 ft 6 in depth (up to 24 in dia.)
branches	½ in–2 in dia. Manholes for stop valves and branches also access for bursts and new connections. Polythene useful, unaffected by soils or frost. Not always allowed for drinking water due to risk of gas absorption	2 ft 6 in depth

Gas mains
  service
  branches
	4 in dia. min., C.I. or steel
	1 in dia. min. W.I. steel
	¼ in dia. min. Fall to main (condensation). Access rarely required. Valves, pumps and vents needed for condensation
		24 in–30 in
		18 in–24 in

Electricity mains (H.V.)	Low voltage is wasteful on long runs, so street lights run off spurs from main below. Laid direct in ground or drawn through 4 in earthenware ducts in busy areas. Underground link disconnecting boxes 30 × 24 in m.h.'s at street intersections	18 in or by agreement with highway authority
feeders (L.V.) (to lights, kiosks etc.)	400 ft length usual maximum. Armoured cable with tile covers	Just below paving
G.P.O. telephone	Polythene cables in ground or in ducts. 2–3½ in asbestos and p.v.c. ducts encased in concrete. 170 yds max. between surface junction boxes.	9 in (protected cable), 14 in (steel or self-aligning duct) 18 in (3⅝ in earthenware ducts with 1,2,4,6 and 9 ways)

There is now more co-operation between authorities, and gas and water mains are sometimes laid in the same trench; but varying depths and falls of services limit the number of joint trenches possible. Certain technical as well as administrative difficulties also tend to the separation of services, e.g. water-breakage due to frost; damage due to traffic and subsequent contamination from sewers; absorption of gas; short circuits from electric cables; risk of gas-leaks and consequent explosions. Normally services are laid below footpaths, verges and paved areas to minimise disturbance to traffic. When below paving, services should be laid below small-scale paving units rather than below *in situ* paving, to obviate patchy making good after repairs or additional connections. Access boxes and markers are also easier to fit in. Table 5.2 covers some basic information on the various services. Hydraulic mains, district heating lines, and land drains are also met with. Fire hydrants and sluice valves are usually 900/1,000 ft apart and if possible kept at least 25 ft from buildings so that they will be usable in an emergency.

5.3.5 Trenches and ducts
The biggest source of paving failure is faulty compaction of trenches. They should be filled in 9 in layers with approved granular material. If of inferior quality, add 5% cement. Flooding during backfilling should *not* be permitted. The soil should be spread and compacted at its natural or optimum moisture content. Compaction is best done by power-driven rammers. Trenches for service pipes often become water traps. If so, surrounding saturated ground should be excavated and replaced with well-consolidated good subsoil or a suitable base material. Trenches should be routed as far away as possible from

trees with at least 4 ft clearance. If necessary pipes can be tunnelled under large roots while small cut roots should be trimmed square and tarred. Drying movements in heavy shrinkable clays can cause damage down to 5 ft deep to pipes and drains and where fast growing thirsty and suckering trees such as the poplar, elm or willow are used, damage can extend down to 10 ft below the surface. The only solution is to avoid these trees on such soils.

Ducts are used where ready and frequent access is needed, or to carry services through a concrete road, bridge or foundation. They vary from multiway earthenware tubes as used by the G.P.O., tubes in concrete formed by inflatable rubber/plastic tubing, through the usual 9 in or so ducts, to large crawlways with services hooked on to built-in lugs at the sides. Progress towards integrated ducting of public utility services has however been slow even in new towns, shopping centres and other 'comprehensive' developments.

5.3.6 Heating of paved areas
This is installed mainly to prevent ice formation and also to thaw snow. Radiant heating in slabs is now used for roads and shopping precincts. It can also be used to provide greater comfort conditions in spring and summer evenings and is particularly effective in sheltered areas with 'ceilings' of trees or awnings overhead. It is not so effective in windswept locations. The Road Research Laboratory have advised on pioneer schemes in this country. The usual method is to have embedded electrical coils. These may be at mains voltage with insulation cable, or at low voltage with uninsulated conductors. Hot water coils are also a possibility, but for pedestrian areas rather than for roads.

5.4 Trim and changes of level

Nothing can enhance or destroy the character of a paved area so much as its 'trim' or edge detailing. Trim should therefore be carefully chosen to accord with the character of pavings and their surroundings, urban, suburban or rural. Far too many inappropriate details appear especially in the use of heavy 'town' kerbs in village roads.

5.4.1 Functions of trim
Kerbs and edgings are needed to prevent lateral spread of flexible paving. They denote changes of level and can provide hazards, physical and psychological—especially to indicate segregation of pedestrians and vehicles. Boundary definition may be required. It need not be continuous, but act as a reminder especially under water or snow. Surface water drainage is often taken to margins and these are clearly visible either as raised kerbs or depressed channels. Mowing margins below grass level are provided as an aid to easy maintenance (Fig. 5.9). Junctions of

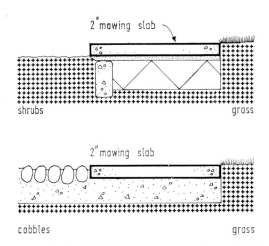

Fig. 5.9. MOWING STRIPS—Necessary at edges of paved areas and desirable against walls. Slabs can be of stone or concrete.

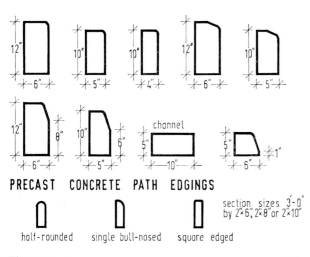

PRECAST CONCRETE PATH EDGINGS

half-rounded single bull-nosed square edged

section sizes 3'-0"
by 2"×6", 2"×8" or 2"×10"

Fig. 5.10. STANDARD KERBS AND CHANNELS TO B.S. 340

materials generally are best detailed by inclusion of a joining or insulating strip or 'trim'.

5.4.2 Types of trim

The many types of trim include those proud of surface, flush or depressed and may be continuous or intermittent. Materials must be durable for all purposes: granite, sandstone, precast concrete (heavy or thin), brick. For kerbs only: timber edging, metal trim, stone slabs on edge, stones and boulders for intermittent spacing. For flush and depressed trim only: various stones, slabs, setts, cobbles, asphalt, concrete and loose materials including gravel, cobbles, ballast. Other forms of trim include: low walls, fences or rails (see Chapter 6—Enclosure).

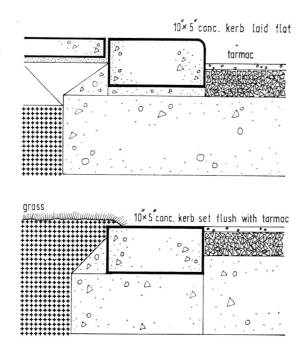

Fig. 5.11. FLUSH KERB—Contains the flexible surfacing while the grass provides an informal edging.

Plate 5.8. STREET PAVING, BASILDON—Cobbled cycle areas and tree grids combine to form an excellent articulation to this pavement separated from the shopping parade by a neat channel grille (see Fig. 5.15 for detail of tree grid design).

Raised kerbs are used mainly for roads, but elsewhere as character dictates. *Granite and whinstone* (B.S. 435) are good and really tough, but can cost three times as much as precast concrete, so are now used only in special circumstances. Finishes range from fine to rough, in rectangular sections of minimum length 1 ft 9 in, 4 in to 12 in width × 6 in to 12 in depth. *Sandstone* (B.S. 706) sizes generally as granite, but longer sections are more readily available. *Precast concrete* (B.S. 340) is popular and relatively cheap. It has a natural finish, smooth and creamy, which can be improved and still be much cheaper than granite. Square and splayed sections in 3 ft lengths, 4 in to 6 in × 5 in to 12 in depth (Fig. 5.10). Reconstructed granite kerb made of granite aggregate and tooled to resemble the natural material is available at half the price of granite. Flush kerbs (Fig. 5.11) to roads and driveways give a much better appearance, and are available in the above materials and lengths. Precast concrete edging, 6 in × 2 in on 3 ft lengths (B.S. 340) is used as edging to contain gravel and tarmac paths and their bases (Fig. 5.12).

85

5.4.3 Changes of level

The potentialities of exploiting changes of level are limitless; steeply sloping steps—wide sweeping stairs with spacious landings—gently curving ramps, and these in various combinations. Due to the greatly increased sense of scale outdoors, widths and goings must be as large as possible in the context of the adjoining landscape, especially so where overhanging or encroaching planting is envisaged.

Steps. These can be solid, sculptural, floating or cantilevered; or be in the form of a plinth. Domestic scales for the angle of descent are generally inappropriate though a really steep flight can have a character of its own. Favourite formulae are $R \times$ Tread $= 75$ in, and $2R +$ Tread $= 27$ in—in both cases with a riser height of 3 in to $6\frac{1}{2}$ in. A tread of 17 in and a $4\frac{1}{2}$ in riser are suggested for a leisurely ascent, while a 12 in tread is a normal minimum for external use. It is generally accepted that three steps are the minimum for a flight but innumerable examples of safe single steps exist in obvious places at changes in paving functions as at road kerbs. Long flights of steps should be broken up into flights of say 10–14 steps, with generous landings.

Construction can be of reinforced or mass concrete (stiff broom or hand tamper finish for slip resistance), concrete slabs on brick or concrete risers, or of tarmac and kindred surfaces with timber risers. Treads can be of concrete, concrete paving slabs, setts, stone, brick, slate or even timber. Materials should be chosen with care as steps are a hard test for any material. Of stones, york-

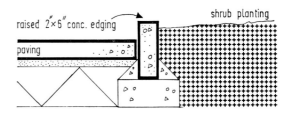
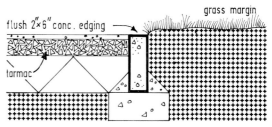

Fig. 5.12. TRIM—Standard 2′ 6″ edging. The details show an up-stand kerb to retain planting and a flush kerb recessed below grass border.

stone is probably the best for the purpose. Non-slip inserts of carborundum can improve the slip resistance of concrete steps. Projections and depths of nosings or overhangs should be generous (Fig. 5.13).

Ramped steps. These have never really been common in Britain but can be useful on a long slope as they enable a steady ascent. Allow for three paces to each tread while risers and nosings should be clearly marked.

Ramps. An angle of 1:10 is the usual maximum up which prams or wheelchairs can be pushed, although

Plate 5.9. TOR GARDENS, KENSINGTON—A cheap and effective method of paving with alternate panels of precast slabs and *in-situ* concrete contrasting with cobbled areas, irises and low shrubby planting.

1:12 is preferable. It is also the critical limit for reasonable safety in icy conditions though electric heating may be used in important locations and a gradient of 1:7 is negotiable for very short stretches. Many methods are available for non-slip surfaces; ruled, gridded or other patterns in concrete, crimping roller for concrete and tarmac, and special non-slip pavings. Drainage is vital and any pattern should shed water gently to recessed gutters for collection in channel gratings or gullies. Ramps may also be placed alongside short easy flights of steps.

5.5 Planting in paved areas

5.5.1 Selection of planting positions

The check list in Table 5.3 covers some general points to note in selecting and designing planting positions in paved areas. Some solutions to overcome local difficulties are suggested.

5.5.2 Trees

Existing trees. Many established trees still continue to collect nourishment from underground water from other catchment areas percolating through the subsoil. Otherwise they would not survive without irrigation. Where paving is lower than the tree allow ample room for roots, with good irrigation; where paving is raised make up level with washed gravel or with vertical drains round it to original level.

Young and 'semi-mature' trees. For these adequate watering, staking and tree guards are essential, while tree trunks should be wrapped with water-miscible plastic to prevent excess transpiration due to reflected heat from paving.

Choice of trees for paved areas. Names are listed in reputable catalogues and other books under headings for 'Town and smoky localities', 'Street trees', 'Plants for shady places' but note that these lists are only a guide to be interpreted with great care and discretion taking full account of local conditions. Lists commonly err towards normal town conditions and seldom deal with

TABLE 5.3.

Problem	Solution
Frost pockets these occur in low areas without air drainage.	Leave gaps in enclosing walls.
Draught funnels—common amongst tall buildings.	Use wind hardy plants and avoid north east draughts.
Waterlogged areas—often in clay or peaty areas.	Provide drainage or use raised beds.
Vandalism—this is normally experienced in towns and can be acute in housing areas.	Use grouped planting away from access points, tough, spiny plants, and semi-mature trees rather than saplings. Good staking and tree guards will help.
Excessive drying out—Urban areas are usually warmer than country. Intensified by heat storage and reflective qualities of paving. Isolated trees dry out quicker; growth is advanced and more exposed to damage by spring winds or frost.	Seek or provide shelter. Protective wrappings for delicate plants and young tree trunks. Transpiration retarders, spraying and irrigation are needed during the establishment period.
Overshadowing by buildings	Use shade bearing plants.
Atmospheric pollution—direct by solids and sulphur, also diesel and petrol fumes, and indirect by light restriction.	Use plants which are known for their resistance to urban conditions. Avoid conifers.
Run-off pollution from paved areas—salt, petrol, oil, tar, soapy water, etc.	Use kerbs, and provide proper traps if used for irrigation.
Drip from overhead cables—copper wires.	Avoid these positions.
Gas main leaks—even a small one caused by traffic vibrations can be harmful.	
Animals—Urination, scratching and digging.	
Root restriction and amputation—due to hard pavings and excavations for trenches, services and buildings.	Careful planning of pipes and planting. Leave ventilation spaces in paving.

adverse conditions found in dense urban areas, of heavily industrialised towns for example. Better than the textbook list, examine any available site evidence which shows what is already growing there, and note whether it is thriving, growing, or just struggling. Do not select those trees with

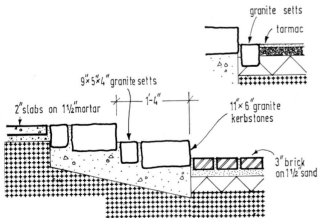

Fig. 5.13. STEPS—Secondhand materials, including those found on site, can often be incorporated in constructional detailing. The example shows steps formed from granite setts and road kerbs.

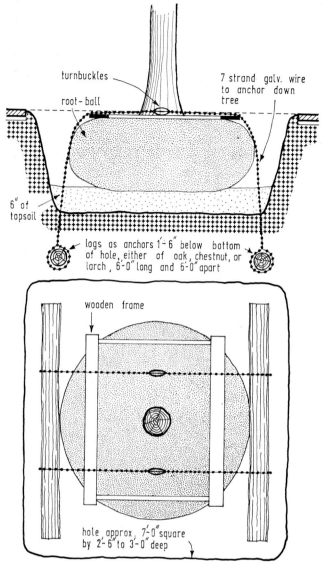

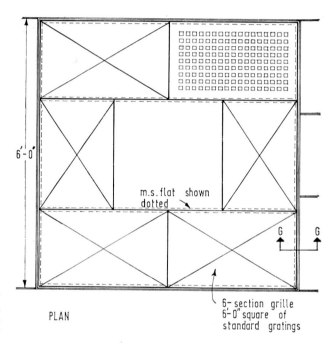

planting at paving level, in raised beds, in plant boxes or containers with a minimum height of 6–9 in. Care is needed in positioning, and in particular avoid north-east winds. Flush planting is easily introduced into path edges, crevices in steps, etc., but raised beds with kerbs are much less vulnerable to damage and litter. With ground cover alpine plants, the kerb height should be sufficient to allow for plant overhang. For dwarf shrubs and conifers, excavate plant holes to a depth of 18–24 in and backfill with good soil, giving each plant a 2 ft square station, then lay paving with 9–12 in apertures at the plant positions. This allows room for plant feeding below the paving.

5.5.4 Drainage and irrigation
A correct water balance is vital for plants. In paving, planting is unnaturally constricted and artificial methods are necessary to ensure sound growth. Ideally water

Fig. 5.14. CONCEALED GUYING OF LARGE TREE IN PAVED AREA
After tree is positioned 6 ft × 6 in logs are dug in about 18 in below bottom of hole. Wires are fixed by splicing and stapling. Earth is rammed and wood frame fixed over root-ball before turnbuckles are spliced and tightened. They can be adjusted periodically to counter settlement. Another method utilises driven stakes.

excessive leaf fall, branch shedding characteristics, such as elms and, in clay soils, those with voracious rooting and suckering systems such as poplars and willows. Soils have a marked influence on selection. They vary from shrinkable clays, where planting should be kept clear of buildings and pavings where drainage pockets can be troublesome, to the other extreme of light sandy soils where trees can be placed close to pavings and services but will need extra irrigation to counteract rapid drainage.

5.5.3 Shrubs and ground cover planting
Artificial soil conditions are easily provided for smaller

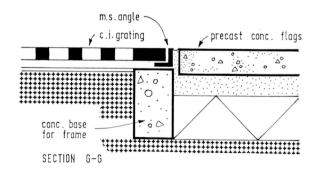

Fig. 5.15. CAST IRON TREE GRILLE (See Plate 5.8)—This large grille is made up of six standard gratings. Sections are small enough to lift for maintenance. Other designs (square and circular) have removable inner sections to allow for tree growth.

88

should stay long enough in the root area to nourish the roots before percolating slowly into the subsoil. Where conditions do not allow this, drainage is necessary to prevent 'ponding' of stagnant water. In impervious clay subsoil further excavation and filling with washed ballast may be necessary. Always dish bottoms to fall to land drains laid around the circumference with vertical drains or outlets to catchment areas; there must be adequate safeguards against poisonous substances (see section 5.5.1).

Natural water supply.   Extra run-off from paving can be channelled to planting areas, while unsealed gravel forms an excellent paving around trees. Treated with non-penetrative weedkiller it is neat and simple and allows air and water to penetrate. Trees, in fact, offer a difficult problem as their catchment area extends around the perimeter of their spreads. Open joints can be left in paving or filled with weak mortar or sand. But slight frost heave may result with minor undulations appearing. In impervious pavings, use tree grids, or precast concrete gratings laid flush with the surrounding paving (Fig. 5.15). These can be linked by open or storm drains to even out water intake. Paving slabs with holes or grilles are useful around tree perimeters where the roots get their nourishment.

Artificial water supply.   This is often necessary especially due to excessive evaporation and overheating of tree roots through shallow pavings. Comprehensive irrigation schemes for planting would include time-controlled sprinklers for small planting and outlets for shrubs and trees. At the other end of the scale a tree grid can be lifted out, a shallow saucer scooped out in the soil and 20–40 gallons of water run slowly in. For smaller plants adequate water is necessary for the first year after planting but after establishment in suitable conditions, most alpines and conifers will thrive quite happily with only occasional watering.

Bibliography

Civil Engineers Data Book, E. E. Seelye, John Wiley.
Design and Detail of Space Between Buildings, Elisabeth Beazley, Architectural Press.
'Element Design Guides', *Architects Journal*, Sfb(15) 25 October 1961; AC6 4 December 1963, C. V. R, Tandy (currently under revision)
Sfb(14) 9 November 1966 *et seq*. Timothy Cochrane.
'External pavings', Robert Maguire, *Architectural Review*, February and April 1957.
Landscaping for Flats, Design Bulletin No. 5, Ministry of Housing and Local Government, H.M.S.O.
'Paving patterns and their uses', Cement and Concrete Association.
Specification, Sections on Roads, Landscape and Floors, Architectural Press.
Trees in Towns, R. J. Morling, Estates Gazette Press.
Trees in Town and City, Ministry of Housing and Local Government, H.M.S.O.

Plate 5.10. COURTYARD, COVENTRY—The strong brick grid well contains a medley of different types in this outdoor building exhibition of paving materials.

6 Enclosure

FREDERICK GIBBERD

6.1 Need for enclosure

6.1.1 Function and materials

Enclosure means to shut in and the technical need for it is to give security, privacy or shelter. These functions are provided by a physical barrier, a visual barrier, or both. It is important to recognise that there can be a fundamental difference between visual and physical barriers. With the former the object is to conceal the view; it is a process of space-defining and therefore a raw material of the art of landscape design. With the latter, the problem is the relatively simple one of providing a physical obstruction. Shelter from the elements is a by-product of visual barriers but it also exists in its own right, as in tree planting for a wind break.

There are two broad groups of materials, plants and man-made structures. Plants, being organic, provide enclosure which is constantly changing in form, colour and texture; with artifacts, there is no modification of form and the only changes that may take place are surface ones of texture and colour, through processes of weathering or the application of colour. Plants cannot be left unattended and if their form has been shaped, as in a hedge, there must be periodic attention by clipping, pruning or training but man-made structures can require very little maintenance—granite bollards, a brick wall. Plants are most often chosen for their aesthetic effect, or for man's innate love of growing things but for a whole range of man-made structures, like fences, are used solely for functional reasons—which is not to say that they must not be beautiful objects in themselves. As barriers formed by natural materials may take some time to establish, the two groups are sometimes combined, as when a hedge is planted against a chain link fence. The design choice for either of these two groups is determined, in the first place, by considering the functional requirements—what is required of the barrier and what its life should be—the amount of money available for the job and the maintenance necessary which has, of course, to be balanced against the initial cost. Since man is conscious of the appearance of things, the functional solution needs also to be considered in terms of appearance, both of the object itself and the object in relationship to the environment as a whole. This aesthetic choice is largely based on intuition and experience but unfortunately trained designers are seldom involved. In the past, with its limited range of materials and craft techniques, this did not matter, but today, the complexities of materials and construction make it imperative that the trained designer should be involved in choosing or designing the method of enclosure; that he is seldom so involved largely accounts for the chaotic appearance of the visual scene.

6.1.2 Physical enclosure

The design basis for a physical barrier is its function and the objective must be to perform it with the least possible material. It is necessary, therefore, to be quite clear what kind, or kinds of access it is being erected to prevent—if, for example, a barrier is to be erected to prevent a car running off a carriageway, must it also exclude dogs? The answers to these questions can produce such widely different solutions as a bollard or tubular steel rails filled with chain-link. Whilst the function of barriers is to prevent access, they are also used to delineate property ownership and, as such, are debased structures. The Englishman's over-developed sense of privacy and sense of personal property has given him a passion for enclosure and the scene suffers from a superfluity of barriers. In addition, design is often over-emphatic or over-elaborate, thereby causing unnecessary disturbance to the view. It is not always appreciated that physical barriers are possible as minor incidents such as bollards, or with no disturbance at all, such as the ha-ha.

6.1.3 Visual enclosure

Visual barriers have the simple functional use of concealing the view of an object, either to give privacy or to hide the object from the scene but they have a much wider and more fundamental use which is that of space defining. Visual barriers can enclose spaces for particular functions and make of them particular places in a far greater degree than can a physical barrier—thus, a fence round a bowling green will keep people off it but a hedge, by visual enclosure, makes it an environment, a room, with its own identity. In their wider use as space-defining objects, visual barriers are one of the raw materials of landscape design. As such, they have an unlimited range of application from large-scale landscape design, where trees can be combined with land forms to make broad spatial compositions; through urban design, where visual barriers can be an extension of architecture to create the different space zones of a town; to the formation of small-scale intimate local spaces, as in garden design.

6.2 Plants for enclosure

6.2.1 Types and qualities

Plants are primarily used for visual enclosure and for shelter; as physical barriers they are limited to hedges, used as an alternative to fences or walls. Their choice over artifacts is because of their association with other organic material (field hedges), because of the desire to obtain contrast between the works of man and nature (a tree screen behind architecture), or simply because of man's love of natural things. Being organic, plants present the problems of growth and time; the time interval before they are either effective visual or physical barriers and the limited length of life before they need to be replanted. They may, in some instances, involve considerable maintenance costs, as their form is only constant when clipped, pruned or trained. Of the two broad groups, evergreen and deciduous, the choice, planting conditions being similar, is primarily aesthetic. Evergreen plants give the most complete visual enclosure, except in broad-scale or dense planting, such as wood or copse. Deciduous plants provide complete changes of form, colour and texture over the seasons; they are often abhorred by those responsible for the upkeep of the urban scene because falling leaves have to be disposed of; but this is no reason for depriving the townsman of his right to enjoy one of nature's most remarkable gifts. Evergreen and deciduous plants used for enclosure can be placed in three broad groups; trees, shrubs and hedges; and there is a vast range of material to choose from. The first selective processes are ecological ones, as set out in Chapter 9—General Planting, section 9.2.2. Beyond this, limiting the species to those that are indigenous to the district will preserve the character of the environment. If new species are required, the selection will be based on those that give the most effective enclosure; functional expression is the objective. Beyond this it is largely a matter of the composition of the landscape; should the hedge unobtrusively follow the contours of the landscape?—may a tree screen break the silhouette?—and so on. Each design poses its own particular set of problems and only by asking the most searching questions will the pitfalls of decoration be avoided.

6.2.2 Trees

The use of trees for enclosure falls into three broad groups: space defining, screening against view and screening against wind. Space-defining is the art of landscape

Plate 6.1. A hedge clipped to take on the architectural character of a wall.

enclosure, and trees combined with land form, are its raw materials. The subject is dealt with elsewhere in this book (Chapter 1—Site Planning, and Chapter 11—Tree Planting) and mention must be made of an admirable book, *Trees for Town and Country* (Lund Humphries). Tree screening to hide ugly structures of disfigured landscape, like planting for visual enclosure, is primarily an aesthetic problem and little need be said here, except to mention that there are many alternatives to the common technique of masking the object with a row of fast-growing trees, like Lombardy poplars, close against the boundary. Thus trees may be used to distract attention from the unpleasant view; they may be planted close to the view point, to cut out the prospect—the nearer the trees are to the view point, the greater will be the effect—and the species can be selected to have a formal relationship to the object to be obscured. Shelter belts or wind breaks are formed by belts of trees singly or in systems or by small blocks of trees of various shapes. The effect of the wind break is to reduce the surface wind velocity to the leeward of the belt and partly to the windward. The barrier deflects the on-coming air stream upwards and accelerates it somewhat but eventually the original pattern of wind velocity is re-established at ground level, at a distance of about thirty times the height of the barrier. If the barrier is solid, air currents from the main flow may be drawn downwards to cause vigorous eddies within 10 to 15 ft of the barrier; on the other hand, if some wind can penetrate the shelter belt, it will reduce the turbulence and the airstream deflected over the top will re-establish itself more gradually. The degree of permeability which achieves optimum shelter has been established at about 40%. With agricultural land the shelter falls into three broad categories: arable areas, upland pastures and exposed grazing. Each type has its own problems and reference should be made to *Shelter Belts for Farmland* (Leaflet 15, Ministry of Agriculture, Fisheries and Food) which deals most thoroughly with the subject.

6.2.3 Hedges
Hedges are the alternative to fences for physical enclosure and to walls for both physical and visual enclosure. As wind breaks they are more effective than draught walls because they are permeable. Hedges are the complement of trees and land shaping in the art of landscape enclosure; they largely provide the English agricultural field pattern resulting from the Enclosure Acts of the seventeenth and eighteenth centuries; in town design they define space for different functional uses—such as playing fields and in gardens they provide the partitions and dividing screens which give the design structure. As with trees, the choice is a very wide one indeed and is based on the considerations outlined elsewhere (see Chapter 9—General Planting). Hedges that are to provide a physical barrier are generally strong-growing plants with thorns, those that

are to form a visual screen tend to be evergreens; and those that are to be windbreaks are sturdy and dense in growth. It is of importance to consider the appearance of the hedge as a whole rather than as a series of individual plants—a beech hedge is a very different thing from a beech tree and, as with the grouping of different species of trees in a clump, hedging plants may be combined to give variety in colour and texture throughout the year—tapestry hedges. Thus beech, combined with holly and yew, will have contrast between the three different species and the contrast will differ in the winter from the summer, when the beech leaves turn brown. J. L. Beddall has made a useful study of hedging, *Hedges for Farm and Garden*, (Faber and Faber). The following are the more common types.

6.2.4 Evergreen hedges
Yew (*Taxus baccata*), 'the aristocrat of hedging plants'. Strong, compact growth and dense texture make possible shaping into precise forms that may, on the one hand, take on the architectural character of walls or, on the other, the exuberance of topiary work (Plate 6.1). Its sombre dark colour makes a beautiful contrast with ground covers such as grass and pavings and a fine background for flowers. The disadvantages are cost and slow growth, 3 ft in five years: the latter may be overcome by double planting with a cheap, quick-growing hedge such as *Lonicera nitida*, which is subsequently grubbed up. Holly (*Ilex aquifolium*), has characteristics of yew of close texture, slow compact growth and high cost and it forms an excellent alternative. It is not so dense and has the particular qualities of a shiny, light-reflecting leaf and, due to the leaf spikes, greater resistance to animals Box (*Buxus sempervirens*), may be bracketed with yew and holly for its excellence but it has neither the sombre, light-absorbing qualities of yew, nor the shine of holly. Compact but slow growth makes it an expensive but excellent visual barrier. Privet (*Ligustrum ovalifolium*), makes a good barrier up to 10 ft in exposed places but it is often considered to be less attractive than the previous examples, possibly because of its suburban associations: growth is moderate and it is a gross feeder; cost is reasonable. *Lonicera nitida* is characterised by its small-scale form, tiny leaves and rapid growth, 5 ft in five years; it tends to straggle and become top-heavy, limiting its use to comparatively low hedges and, being both cheap in cost and fast in growth, it is useful for rapid effects. Of the many other types, *Cupressus macrocarpa* and *Escallonia macrantha* may be mentioned for their resistance to wind on the south coast but are not hardy in the north.

6.2.5 Deciduous hedges
Quickthorn (*Crataegus oxycantha*), said to be introduced by the Romans, provides a tough, impenetrable fence for field enclosure and is an integral part of the English

agricultural scene. Large scale, mechanised farming and the high cost of maintenance is resulting in many miles being grubbed up with loss of shelter for crops, animals and wild life. Two deciduous species of particular value as visual screens, because they retain their leaves in winter, are beech (*Fagus sylvatica*) and hornbeam (*Carpinus betulus*). Both are slow starters but make a fine hedge up to 20 ft. Of similar appearance, the winter leaves of beech give a warmer brown colour. Beech does well on light and chalky soils and hornbeam will often succeed where the former is unsatisfactory, as on heavy clay.

6.2.6 Decorative hedges

A very wide choice of plants for decorative hedges can be found under the broad headings: coloured stems for winter effect; leaf colour; autumn foliage; berries and fruiting; and flower colour. J. L. Beddall again gives a wealth of advice in *Colour in Hedges* (Faber and Faber). Most of the plants are more closely associated with garden rather than landscape design. Typical evergreen decorative hedges are laurustinus (*Viburnum tinus*), with attractive winter flowers; barberry (*Berberis stenophylla*) for a dense informal hedge up to 10 ft with yellow flowers in spring; *Cotoneaster salicifolia* for a good tall hedge with

Plate 6.3. A coursed stone retaining wall surmounted by a hedge.

red berries in autumn. Of the deciduous types, *Cotoneaster simonsii* can be trimmed to narrow width, has tinted foliage and vermilion berries in autumn; *Philadelphus* has single or double white flowers, for informal hedges; and a whole range of roses, the more robust of which, such as *Hugonis,* *Canina,* musks and rugosas will withstand children and dogs.

6.3 Walls for enclosure

6.3.1 Types and functions

Walls for enclosure have the characteristic that they can form complete physical and visual barriers of very long life. They are an essential part of urban and village design but in open landscape they are only used as an alternative to fences and hedges in those districts where stone is found in abundance. The most impressive historic use for walls is for defence; not only is the fortified wall a splendid thing in itself but it draws a sharp distinction between town and countryside which subsequent generations have so far failed to achieve by mere legal definition. Walls for

Plate 6.2. A random rubble retaining wall.

enclosure may be divided roughly into four main types: (1) Walls higher than eye level, used to form a complete physical and visual barrier: they are often associated with architecture such as screen walls linking dwellings together and giving continuity of facade. (2) Walls for partial enclosure, below eye level in height but still providing visual obstruction, generally used as an alternative to hedges or fences, such as the eighteenth and nineteenth century rear garden wall. (3) Dwarf walls, where a strong physical barrier of architectural qualities is required as an alternative to trip fences or low hedging; they are often associated in design with pavings or combined with other barriers—a metal fence over a dwarf wall. (4) Retaining walls, used to form changes in level, either for formal reasons, as an alternative to land shaping, or for functional purposes, such as a cutting. The subject is a large one and those not familiar with building construction might consult Davies and Petty or W. B. McKay, for general information (see bibliography at end of chapter).

6.3.2 Rubble walling

Rubble walls, used as boundary fences, are a characteristic of those areas of the countryside where timber is scarce and stone readily available. There is a shortage of masons and stone walling is expensive but those who do use local stone have the satisfaction of making a construction that looks inevitable and one that will outlast

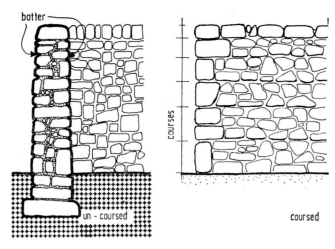

Fig. 6.1. RUBBLE WALL—Random and random coursed, showing batter and capping detail.

by many years all other alternatives. It is encouraging that some authorities, like the Central Electricity Generating Board, advise their consultants that the question of cost should not preclude stone being considered where it is the obvious answer. Stone walling should never be imported for decorative purposes in an environment foreign to it—Cotswold stone for raised traffic islands or flower beds is a nauseating sentimentality. As the kinds of stone vary enormously (gritstones and shales of the north and Wales, the limestones of the Peaks and the Cotswolds, sandstones of the Midlands, granites of Cornwall) there are many different local building techniques. The general

principles that apply to almost all of them are: that the walls are always built with a batter, or inward slope, of about $1\frac{1}{2}$ in in each 12 in of height; the foundations and courses are horizontal but a wall built on the slope is finished at the top to follow the contour of the land and care is taken to break the vertical joints. The core of the wall is generally packed with small stones, stone chippings and sometimes earth and long stones are used as ties across the wall. The bond is either random rubble, or random coursed, with some stones selected or roughly dressed into shape to allow coursing. The traditional dry wall is being largely replaced by mortar-jointed walling, as less skill and less stone are required. Rubble walling is built of stones, either irregular in shape or squared but not dressed to the same degree as ashlar and having comparatively thick joints. The subject is well described and illustrated in a British Standard Code of Practice (C.P. 121 : 101 (1951) Masonry-rubble walls). (Fig. 6.1.)

6.3.3 Brick walls

Brick walls are covered by a Code of Practice (C.P. 121 : 101 (1951) Brickwork). Being composed of small prefabricated units laid in horizontal courses, they are less flexible in form than stone. In particular, they cannot take up changes in level without stepping the top of the wall which means they cannot 'flow' with the land form, as can stone walls or hedges and so, apart from their association with farm buildings, they are an urban building form. The appearance of a brick wall is dependent on the colour and texture of the brick

FREE-STANDING BRICK WALLS: CONSTRUCTIONAL DETAILS

	Thickness (in)	Max. Height (ft)	Piers		Expansion Joints		Mass Concrete Founds		Notes
			Size (in)	Spacing (ft)	Preferred Spacing (ft)	Max. Spacing (ft)	Min. Width (in)	Min. Depth (in)	
1	$4\frac{1}{2}$	4	$9 \times 4\frac{1}{2}$	15	30	30	$13\frac{1}{2}$	6	Expansion joint at every second pier position $\frac{1}{2}$ in joint between 2 No. 9 in × $4\frac{1}{2}$ in piers
2	$4\frac{1}{2}$	6	$13\frac{1}{2} \times 9$	$13\frac{1}{4}$	$26\frac{1}{2}$	30	$13\frac{1}{2}$	6	Expansion joint at every second pier position; $\frac{1}{2}$ in joint between 2 No. 9 in × 9 in piers
3	$4\frac{1}{2}$	8	$13\frac{1}{2} \times 9$	$8\frac{1}{2}$	$25\frac{1}{2}$	30	$13\frac{1}{2}$	6	Expansion joint at every third pier position; $\frac{1}{2}$ in joint between 2 No. 9 in × 9 in piers
4	9	6	—	—	20	30	27	9	London County Council permitted max. height of 9 ft if wall built in cement mortar
5	$13\frac{1}{2}$	9	—	—	20	30	$40\frac{1}{2}$	$13\frac{1}{2}$	London County Council permitted max. height of 13 ft 6 in if wall built in cement mortar

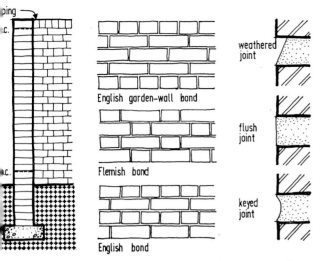

Fig. 6.2. BRICK WALL—Various bonds and jointing details are shown, together with capping, foundation and d.p.c. details.

English garden–wall bond

Flemish bond

English bond

weathered joint

flush joint

keyed joint

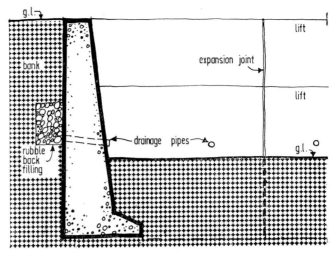

Fig. 6.3. MASS CONCRETE RETAINING WALL—Note the rubble back-fill and provision of drainage pipes.

g.l.

bank

rubble back filling

drainage pipes

expansion joint

lift

lift

g.l.

itself, the type of mortar joint and the bond. The days when it was impossible to use an ugly brick are over and very great care is needed in the choice of modern machine-made varieties, as eccentric textures, unpleasant arrises and fierce colours are common. If costs are so tight that a reasonable brick cannot be specified, it is better to turn to some other material. The aim in design should be to get a direct and simple expression. Joints should preferably be in lime–cement mortar as there is a wider colour range and less shrinkage and cracking than with cement alone; the finish can be with a bucket handle or wiped over with a rag; pointing, or special architectural effects, such as raking out the horizontal joints for emphasis, will seldom tell in a landscape scene. Similarly, with bonding, complicated patterns are seldom worth the trouble and expense. Flemish bond, with headers and stretchers alternating in each course, is generally less monotonous in appearance than the alternating courses of headers and stretchers of English bond; an alternative is English garden wall bond, where a course of headers alternates with two to five courses of stretchers. The table opposite sets out construction detail for free-standing brick walls under normal conditions. The foundations sizes are the minimum small concrete footings as previously required by the L.C.C. by-laws; other local authorities may allow smaller footings and the appropriate by-laws or Building Regulations should be consulted. The expansion joint referred to is a continuous vertical joint filled with a material like bitumenised cane-fibre to allow compression and decompression without permanent deformation. A damp-proof course (B.S. 743: 1951) must be provided at a minimum of 6 in above ground level and one is advisable immediately beneath the coping (Fig. 6.2).

6.3.4 Concrete walls

Concrete walls can be divided into two broad groups:

in situ and block. *In situ* walls seldom occur in landscape design except as retaining walls, owing to the comparatively high cost of shuttering. Block walls are of three main varieties: (1) plain blocks (B.S. 2028:1953), which have a comparatively smooth grey concrete surface, suitable for use in open countryside (say, farm buildings); (2) profiled blocks, in which the block is cast in a mould to give it an irregular surface, either to a geometric pattern or one reminiscent of natural materials, 'rock-face'— their advantage over plain blocks is that marking from atmospheric pollution is not so visible; (3) exposed aggregate blocks composed of aggregates chosen for their colour and texture which are exposed by removing the cement skin—their advantage over the two previous types is that as the greater part of the surface is of a natural material, the block weathers well, the blocks are normally only faced on one side, their chief use being in cavity wall construction or as permanent shuttering to *in situ* concrete walls. Plain concrete blocks are normally 18 in × 9 in × 4 in, 6 in or 8 in thick but profiled and exposed aggregate blocks vary in size with different manufacturers.

6.3.5 Retaining walls

Retaining walls set the following problems: the construction of the wall itself to withstand the earth pressure, the expansion of the wall along its length, and the drainage of moisture from the retained earth. Most forms of block construction are suitable for retaining walls but where there is considerable earth pressure (as in a cutting), concrete either *in situ* or reinforced, is tending to supersede traditional materials like blue brick or granite blocks, because of the cost. In all but the simplest structures, the advice of a consulting engineer should be sought on design. As a rough guide for a simple retaining wall, say 6 ft high, the wall in reinforced concrete will not be less than 6 in thick and in mass concrete 12 in thick. Walls of

95

any length will require expansion joints whatever the material, e.g. a 12 in thick reinforced concrete wall 6 ft high will require expansion joints at approximately 15 ft centres. Drainage at the foot of the wall is normally achieved by back-filling with hardcore and providing weep holes through the wall—3 in or 6 in pots are a usual device (Fig. 6.3). Of considerable importance is the texture, uniformity and finish of the exposed wall. In a tall wall the design should recognise that there are horizontal junctions between lifts, otherwise there will be unsatisfactory making good and rubbing down. A textured surface will help to take up inconsistencies in construction and in weathering and so the use of rough board formwork shuttering, such as flat sawn Douglas fir, should be considered (see reference, end of chapter). The illustration (Plate 6.6) shows a retaining wall in engineering bricks with its expansion joint and clay drainage pot and a hard surface at the foot, to keep the design precise.

6.3.6 The ha-ha

The ha-ha, that unexpected ditch by which the eighteenth century landscape architect was enabled to tear down the enclosing wall or hedge to let the garden extend into the countryside, is virtually a retaining wall sunk into the ground. It is not, as is generally supposed, an English invention but was devised by the French as a means of obtaining a *claire voie* of open countryside at the end of formal alleys.

The ditch is about 4 ft deep with the wall on the garden side and the ground on the open side sloping down to its foot. The ground slope should not be more than 1 in 3 for ease of maintenance and the wall is to normal retaining wall construction described in the previous section. The illustration (Plate 6.5) shows a 4 ft deep ha-ha constructed from standard concrete blocks with alternating headers and stretchers laid to a slight batter, with the interstices filled with soil.

The ha-ha has been little used during the last century but the revival of large scale landscape design, coupled

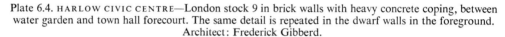

Plate 6.4. HARLOW CIVIC CENTRE—London stock 9 in brick walls with heavy concrete coping, between water garden and town hall forecourt. The same detail is repeated in the dwarf walls in the foreground.
Architect: Frederick Gibberd.

with the modern inventions of muck-shifting machinery
and ready-mixed concrete, make it a practical method of
enclosure without visual obstruction.

6.3.7 Copings

The purpose of a coping is to finish the top of a wall and
exclude water from penetrating to the walling below.
There are marked differences between copings used for
the free-standing walls of enclosure and those used in
buildings; the latter are designed to throw the water clear
of the wall surface and are backed up by a waterproof
membrane as no water can be allowed to penetrate the
wall into the rooms of the building but neither of these
factors is of great importance in, for instance, a garden wall.

Furthermore, as a wall is a simple and bold structure
compared with a building, its coping needs to be simple
and bold. If the coping as a design component can be
omitted altogether, then so much the better; thus, random
rubble stone walls look far more convincing when finished
with the traditional methods of a top course of stones on
edge, or stones roughly shaped to a batter. Similarly,
brick walls can be finished with a course of brick on edge
or the standard saddle-back or bull-nose brick, all of
which will preserve the brick-like quality of the wall. Thin
concrete copings generally look out of scale on most
walls, unless they are in architectural context. Concrete
copings can be satisfactory on low walls but if they project beyond the wall face they can easily be displaced and
when thin tend to look mean; 3 in is probably the minimum thickness but there are many instances where a

Plate 6.5. Ha-ha wall being constructed of standard concrete blocks
with alternating headers and stretchers laid to a slight batter.

really robust section with a bold weathering will be far
more in scale with the scene. The picture (Plate 6.7) shows
a bold triangular-section pre-cast concrete coping to a
dwarf wall enclosing a car park.

6.4 Fences and railings

6.4.1 Types and choice

Fences and railings are used for so many different functions, they have defied classification. Their prime use is

Plate 6.6. Retaining wall in engineering brick, with expansion joint,
drainage and hard surface at the foot of the wall.

as a barrier, either an actual physical one or a deterrent
to access; only a few types of fence, such as close-board-
ing, provide visual screening. There are three main groups,
as follows: (1) unclimbable fences, generally vertical bar
types, 4 ft to 6 ft high, which are difficult to get over;
(2) boundary fences, the most common being post and
wire and post and rail fences, seldom more than 4 ft
high, which form a barrier to animals and generally discourage access, mainly a rural type; (3) trip fences or
rails which can be stepped over but which discourage
access simply because they are there. Types of fences with
special functions are traffic barriers, temporary fences,
security fences and screens. The first question to be asked
in considering the type of fence and rail to be used is
whether it is necessary at all. There is a great deal of quite
unnecessary fencing in the scene, for the following reasons:
the responsibilities that rest on local officials for public
safety; the desire of lawyers and owners to have properties emphatically defined; and the dislike of the divided
responsibility for the maintenance of fences that are
jointly owned. These, together with the Englishman's

Plate 6.7. A bold triangular-section pre-cast concrete coping to a dwarf wall enclosing a car park.

passion for fencing for its own sake, are responsible for the kind of visual disorder that is illustrated in Plate 6.10—this, it is to be noted, is in a new town where a positive attempt was made to prevent multiplication. Fences are largely standardised articles, prefabricated in sections or lengths and they are all the better for that; personal expression with secondary elements seldom helps the scene. The choice of fence is considered in the first place in terms of function, cost and maintenance. Particular aesthetic questions that need asking are—is it well-proportioned, is it simple and unfussy, will it fit happily into the ground shape, will its direction look inevitable, will its forms confuse the prospect and is it in character with the *genius loci*?

6.4.2 Strained wire or strained line wire

Strained wire fences (B.S. 1722: Part 3), are most commonly used in agriculture as a barrier against farm animals; as an urban form, they are limited to temporary fencing, generally associated with a hedge—as between rear gardens. The structural principle is to stretch wire between posts of wood, metal or concrete. There are innumerable ways of doing this, from wires fixed to rough and ready wood posts, to prefabricated proprietary systems where the materials are reduced to the minimum; but in all cases they depend for their efficiency on the tautness of the wire. With all post and wire fences the critical visual element is the post, for the wire is hardly seen and so, by comparison, throws the former into prominence. Heavy posts, or light-coloured posts, such as concrete, can cause great disturbance to a rural scene and thin timber or black-painted metal sections are preferable. The object in design is to reduce the structural members to the absolute minimum section compatible with keeping the wires taut; the lighter they are, the cheaper the cost and the better the appearance. Thus, instead of a fence with post of equal thickness, there can be two sizes: main posts or straining posts, between which the wire is stretched and which are braced; and intermediate posts which keep the wires the right distance apart. A typical timber line wire farm fence (Fig. 6.4) will be 4ft high and have 6in × 6in straining post braced by 4in × 4in, with 3in intermediate posts at 9ft centres. The wire is fixed by adjustable hook or eye bolts to the straining posts and by staples to the intermediate ones. Full constructional details of this and other types of farm fence are contained in the Ministry of Agriculture's admirable leaflets, *Permanent Farm Fences*, Ministry of Agriculture, Fisheries and Food, Leaflet No. 5. A further saving of material and labour can be effected by substituting droppers for some of the intermediate posts: these are light bars which are suspended between the wires to keep them apart without giving physical support. The droppers are light timber or metal sections and most proprietary line wire fencing systems adopt them. A development of the use of droppers is the 'spring dropper fence' (Fig. 6.5). Here the posts are placed as widely apart as possible (55yd is generally taken as the maximum) and the droppers are placed between them at 11ft centres. Such a fence is elastic and it is an ideal form for farm use as animals dislike anything which springs

Fig. 6.4. STRAINED WIRE FENCE—Braced timber straining and intermediate posts; plain wire topped by barbed wire.

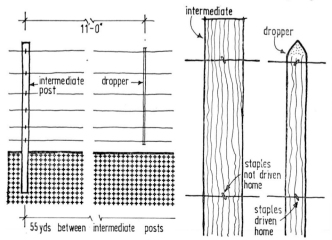

Fig. 6.5. SPRING DROPPER FENCE—This construction of wire fencing permits wide spacing between intermediate posts.

back when pushed or lifted and it has the additional advantage that the farm worker can pass under it anywhere on its length—squeezing through line wires makes them sag in time.

6.4.3 Woven wire fences

Woven wire is a rectangular wire mesh in which the vertical wires act as droppers: in other words, it is a prefabricated strained wire fence (Fig. 6.6). The posts are the same as for line wire fences. So that the horizontal wires are all equally tight and the verticals perpendicular, they are attached to a metal stretcher bar, which is itself bolted to the straining post. The wires are so widely spaced that the fence looks light and open and has none of the mesh-like quality of chicken wire. It is not to be confused with the heavy diamond mesh of the chain link fence, to which it should be used in preference for all normal agricultural purposes. The fence is covered by B.S. 1722, Part 2.

6.4.4 Chain link fences

Woven chain link diamond mesh wire is the strongest and heaviest post and wire fence and the most objectional in appearance. The height is from 4 ft to 6 ft and it is essentially a barrier fence because it is so difficult to scale. The structural system (B.S. 1722: Part 1) is similar to woven wire fences excepting that line wires are required to support the mesh. Posts are in metal or reinforced concrete,

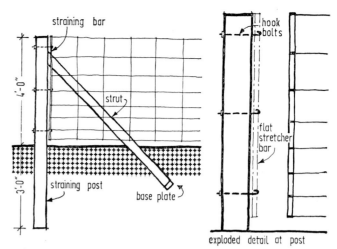

Fig. 6.6. WOVEN WIRE FENCE—A rectangular wire mesh fence.

the latter being most clumsy, particularly the straining post. Chain link is seldom necessary for agricultural use but it has become a familiar part of the suburban or urban scene, as a cheap substitute for metal or wood barrier fences. It is one of the ugliest of modern inventions and, if it must be used, then it may be planted up with a hedge which will, in time, obscure the rusty mesh. There is a case for chain link as a security fence, because other alternatives are so costly. When used as such, the posts may be rolled mild steel angles or T's which, when painted black, make a lighter and more homogeneous fence than

Plate 6.8. Continuous metal bar estate fencing in a rural setting.

99

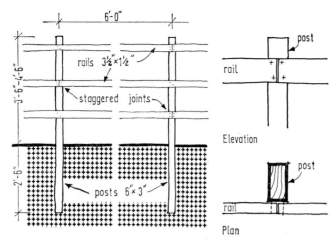

Fig. 6.7. WOOD POST AND RAIL FENCE.

concrete posts and rust stains will not be so visible. As an alternative, rectangular-section hollow tubes, with welded top caps, make a neat and tidy job. The mesh is normally galvanised mild steel which has a limited life (corrosion sets in, under most conditions, between 5 and 7 years), and for a more permanent job aluminium alloy, stainless steel or plastic-coated mild steel may be considered.

6.4.5 Wood post and rail

Posts and rails, 3 ft to 4 ft 6 in high, of wood or metal, make a more permanent fence than posts and wire. They are a physical barrier against animals but the rails provide a convenient foothold for trespassers. Both wood and metal are used extensively in rural areas as boundary fencing and look an inevitable part of the scene (Plates 6.8 and 6.9), but neither is normally associated with urban building. The fences have a strong horizontal direction and it is important that the rails should follow the contours of the land. The traditional wood types have two or three horizontal rails supported by vertical posts sunk in the ground and projecting above the top rail (Fig. 6.7).

The Ministry of Agriculture Leaflet No. 5 again gives valuable data and the construction is covered by a B.S. 1722: Part 7. Timbers which can be left in their natural state for posts in the ground are oak, larch and Spanish chestnut. Softwoods, such as Douglas fir and spruce, require preservatives. There is a variety of fixing methods, the simplest being nailing and, perhaps the most durable and best-looking, mortising; a compromise between the two is widely-spaced mortised posts with one or two lighter section nailed posts, 'prick posts', between them (Fig. 6.8). Metal straps, brackets or bolts for fixing tend to make the joint look over-elaborate and clumsy.

6.4.6 Metal continuous bar

Metal post and rail, or continuous bar fencing (B.S. 1722: Part 8) is an alternative to wood for boundary fencing in rural or open areas. It provides a much lighter and less obtrusive fence than wood with predominantly horizontal lines which reflect the shape of the land. The traditional type is of mild steel or wrought iron with round bars threaded through flat section standards. The commonest type today is prefabricated in 15 ft lengths with joiner standards at each end and intermediate standards at 3 ft centres, the top rail is round or square section and the lower rails flat, making a much stiffer structure than with round rails. Where greater strength is required the flat standards are replaced by T or H sections (Fig. 6.9).

6.4.7 Vertical bar railing

Vertical bar railings are panels of closely-spaced vertical mild steel bars held at the top and bottom by a flat rail; the panels are supported by standards at a maximum of 9 ft centres. Heights are from 4 ft to 7 ft and the absence of horizontals for a foothold puts the fence into the category of unclimbable. The fences are covered by B.S. 1722: Part 9, with the laborious title of *Mild Steel or Wrought Iron Inclimbable Fences with Round or Square*

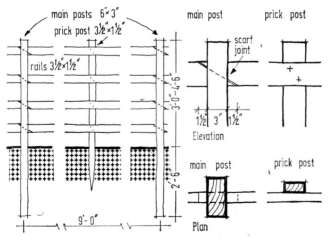

Fig. 6.8. WOOD POSTS WITH MORTISED RAILS.

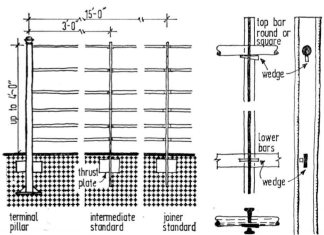

Fig. 6.9. METAL CONTINUOUS BAR FENCE—A light horizontal bar fence.

Plate 6.9. Timber post and rail fence.

Verticals and Flat Standards and Horizontals. The normal vertical bar fence is self-adjusting; that is, the bars are slotted through the horizontals, enabling the fence to follow the angle of the ground to a maximum gradient of 1:6. The fence is primarily urban in character and has its antecedents in the wrought iron railings of large towns and country houses—public gardens or playing fields are typical modern usages. In the countryside it is seldom functionally necessary and when it is used it tends to look foreign because of its strong verticality. There is a wide variety of design but the bars are generally at 5 in centres, of square or round section. Decorative effects are obtained by treatment of the top of the bar; this is normally passed through the top rail and finished with a spike but blunt top bars are common (Fig. 6.10); a less effective but more friendly type has the bars bent over in semi-circular form, like a hairpin. Vertical bar fences are also made as rigid fences with the bars welded or riveted to the rails. They have to be manufactured to specified levels and are a less flexible and more 'architectural' fence—a common usage is over dwarf walls.

6.4.8 Palisade fences

The traditional palisade fence is of wood and consists of closely spaced flat vertical sections spiked to top and bottom rails, supported by posts at about 6 ft centres. It is a greater barrier than timber post and rail because there is little foothold and the projecting tops of the pales make it difficult to scale. Although coming into the category of an unclimbable fence, it is not as efficient as iron post and bar, as it is less strong and the spikes are not so formidable. The palisades vary from 4 in × 1 in to 3 in × 1 in and are generally spaced with the gaps slightly wider than the pales. The ease with which the tops can be shaped has resulted in all kinds of designs from rounded to spiked forms and this, together with the bold and rhythmical

Plate 6.10. A multiplication of fencing leading to visual disorder.

101

Plate 6.11. Metal rod fence and gate.

silhouette, gives the fence its decorative qualities. The fence is covered by B.S. 1722: Part 6 and, as it is difficult to produce a bad design, there are many satisfactory proprietary makes. The fence is essentially one of country associations and one of the many charms of the English village is the white-painted palisade fence made by local craftsmen (see Plates 6.14, 6.17, 6.18); whilst permissible in a suburban environment, it usually looks out of place in the town. The most satisfactory finish is white paint; green merges with the background and the rhythm and precision are lost; black looks heavy in large areas; and

other colours tend to look 'arty'. Where a stronger palisade and one with less maintenance is required, proprietary concrete palisade fences are sometimes substituted—happily less frequently than in France, where some quite astounding patterns have been produced. It generally looks out of place in the countryside and in urban areas is a heavy substitute for iron vertical bar railings.

6.4.9 Trip fences and guard rails

The normal purpose of trip fences and guard rails is to protect grass or planted areas from being trodden on. As they are not more than about 2 ft high, they are a visual rather than physical deterrent. Whenever possible they should be used in preference to boundary fencing, as they are so much more inconspicuous. When the fences are set in the edge of pavings the standards need relating to the joints and, when in grass, they should be set in a concrete mowing strip, to avoid trimming by hand. Trip fences are usually of mild steel and there is a variety of proprietary designs based on hoops and pales, most of which are cut-down versions of standard boundary fencing. Mild steel posts and rails are superseding fences because they are less conspicuous, will take curves more easily and are cheaper. The rail is generally 1 ft above ground and the standards or posts are between 3 ft and 4 ft 6 in centres, depending on the strength of the rail and the rigidity required. The posts are split at the foot and set in concrete and finishes are either galvanising or painting, which must have a corrosion-inhibiting primer. Traditional and standard designs are usually based on $\frac{7}{8}$ in diameter rails passing through standards but rails can be square and standards **I** section. As an alternative, round or square section tubes can look equally simple and efficient, providing the joints are the sleeve variety, but they cannot so easily take up curvatures. Concrete is sometimes used for the posts instead of metal but they look clumsy as the posts appear out of scale with the rails. When a strong rail is required, such as a

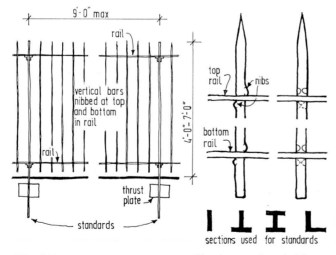

Fig. 6.10. VERTICAL BAR RAILING—Closely spaced vertical bars held at top and bottom by a flat rail.

Plate 6.12. Vertical bar railing and gate.

Plate 6.13. Formal 'architectural' fencing surmounting a brick wall.

Plate 6.14. Example of timber palisade fencing.

barrier to motorcars, timber posts and rails are a possible alternative to dwarf walls or bollards. The rail should be a heavy section (6 in × 2 in, 7 in × 1½ in), with half-lapped joints over stout posts (say, 4 in × 3 in) chamfered on top. Such a rail is not to be confused with traffic barriers, used to prevent vehicles running off a carriageway, where corrugated or trough section metal is bolted to heavy wood posts for greater strength and ease of replacement.

6.5 Bollards

6.5.1 Types and functions

Bollards are vertical barriers which, being free-standing objects, are one of the most unobtrusive ways of preventing access; they have no great height and no horizontal line is drawn across the scene. Their common use is to prevent motor cars encroaching on pedestrian areas by narrowing a space. Other uses are the sub-division of paved areas to direct the flow of traffic, the marking of property boundaries and the protection of property—such as the corners of buildings from casual traffic. There are a variety of bollards for special purposes, such as illuminated types for traffic direction, removable tubular steel bollards for cases where very occasional access is required and hinged tubular steel bollards for reserving

Plate 6.15. Example of timber palisade fencing.

Plate 6.16. Example of timber palisade fencing.

103

Plate 6.17. A row of stone bollards marking off the edge of the carriageway.

individual parking spaces. Traditional bollards are of natural stone, such as granite, and cast iron and some very beautiful designs are still to be seen. Both types are rapidly being superseded by reinforced concrete owing to cost but a revived interest in cast iron might encourage

alternative designs [support centres vary]

4'-6" max

7/8" dia. m.s.rail

1¾" × ½" standard

mowing strip

concrete base

Fig. 6.11. TRIP FENCE—A low fence to protect grass or planted areas.

manufacturers not to destroy all their old moulds. Although reinforced concrete is used for all kinds of conditions, wood (not less than 4 in × 4 in) is satisfactory for pedestrian control and mild steel tubes are sometimes substituted. Neither of the latter materials has the strong and robust appearance of the traditional bollard and

they have closer affinities to post and rail fences—the introduction of a horizontal rail makes them a fence, which it can never do when between bollards.

6.5.2 Concrete bollards

With the increasing practice of pedestrian/vehicular segregation, concrete bollards are becoming a familiar part of the urban scene. They are favoured because they provide a strong, reasonably cheap barrier with its own decisive character which causes few of the disturbances to the floorscape that occur with kerb, wall or rail. The materials used are Portland cement, concrete aggregate from natural sources and rolled steel bars. The form should be robust and simple; thin or over-elaborate shapes do not express strength. There is a variety of pleasant proprietary designs on the market, obtainable in different finishes, such as white concrete, bush-hammered granite, lightly exposed, crushed gravel and reconstructed stone: over-complicated textures detract from the character of robustness. As a barrier to vehicles, the bollards are placed with 5 ft clear between them. Their total height varies from 3 ft to 5 ft and they are set 12 in to 18 in in the ground, on a 4 in concrete base. When set in pavings, the bollards may be surrounded by cobbles, shingle or some similar material to avoid cutting the slabs.

Plate 6.18. A metal bollard protecting the corner of a pavement.

Bibliography

Brick Information Sheets, Nos. 7, 8, and 12, National Federation of Brick Industries.

Building Construction, vol. 1, W. B. McKay, Longmans Green.

Building Elements, Davies and Petty, Architectural Press.

Colour in Hedges, J. L. Bedall, Faber and Faber.

Hedges for Farm and Garden, J. L. Bedall, Faber and Faber.

Permanent Farm Fences, Leaflet No. 5, Ministry of Agriculture, Fisheries and Food, H.M.S.O.

Shelter Belts for Farmland, Leaflet No. 15, Ministry of Agriculture, Fisheries and Food, H.M.S.O.

Shelter Belts and Windbreaks, J. M. Caborn, Faber and Faber.

The Small Garden, C. E. Lucas Phillips, Heinemann and Pan.

Trees for Town and Country, Brenda Colvin and S. R. Badmin, Lund Humphries.

7 Outdoor Fittings and Furniture

IAN PURDY

7.1 Seats and sitting areas

7.1.1 Description, principles and uses

Simplicity of form and detail, ease of maintenance, cost, durability, finish and resistance to vandalism are all important factors guiding selection of seats.

In considering the basic requirements of a comfortable seat it should be borne in mind that the seat height should be low enough for the body's weight to be borne by the feet so that there is no pressure on the thighs. If the seat is higher than the length of the sitter's lower leg some thigh pressure is unavoidable. Also the depth of seat should not be so long that the edge of the seat causes pressure behind the knees. Work carried out for the design of seats for offices suggests certain essential dimensions which are shown in Fig. 7.2.

The type of seat to be used in any particular area is dependent on its siting. In metropolitan areas the seats should be monumental in character, the design forming part of the urban landscape; in the country they should be rough and workmanlike, the key quality being simplicity, often emphasised by using the local material such as stone, slate or timber, but care must be taken to avoid false rusticity. Scale is important and materials should be in character with the surroundings. In small spaces the simplicity of bench or chair is essential and the attempt to attract attention by an overdressed design or intricacy of finish merely looks silly. Visually it is better to have seats designed as benches without backs, a form which is least obtrusive in the landscape, but seating in public

Plate 7.1. Teak seats, lighting fittings and plant holders forming part of the courtyard of the Derby and District College of Art and Technology. Architects: Building Design Partnership.

106

PRINCIPLES
BENCHES and SEATS should be simple in design.

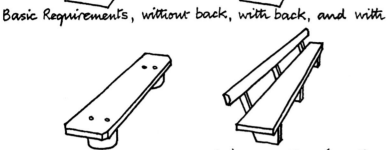

Basic Requirements, without back, with back, and with back and arms.

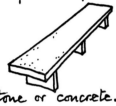

Simplest interpretations are of timber, thus (seats & backs are as far as possible of one piece..

or of stone or concrete.

False rusticity is unnecessary and quite often ugly.

Where surfaces are made up of units, e.g. timber slats or battens, it is desirable for them to follow the 'direction' of the seat; as shown.

SHAPES:

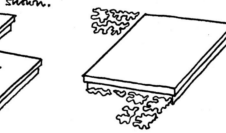

e.g. as part of landscaping..

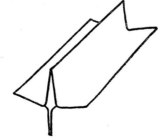

back to back..

making use of a tree.

Fig. 7.1. Design principles for seats.

places must take into account requirements of old people and other users who will require seats with arms and backs. Seats as an element of design need a background, whether this consists of planting, walls or trees and they should be related to other objects in the landscape and should be co-ordinated wherever possible with other street furniture (Fig. 7.1).

Urban seating may be back to back, continuous, pedestal or wall mounted. In some cases *in situ* seats cantilevered from walls can be used or retaining walls can be wide enough to act as a bench; circular or multi-sided seats may be useful around trees or other features. If seats or benches are to be used as a permanent fixture it is preferable for them to be open underneath, particularly where a feeling of lightness is desired or where a line of vision should not be stopped. This is especially important where paving or grass continues beyond the seat.

Stacking or removable chairs are suitable for private gardens, open spaces and public parks which are adequately controlled or policed. In areas which are not policed seats should be fixed either to the ground, walls or other suitable points. Supports and fixing must be of a form which will resist easy removal. Seat bolts should be countersunk and nuts riveted to discourage removal. Where supports are carried below ground level to form a foundation the depth should not be less than 2 ft.

7.1.2 Sitting areas

The location of seats and sitting areas must take into account climatic conditions; some should be in the shade, some in the sun, but all should be sheltered from wind or draughts. It is important to ensure that people sitting in seats close to footpaths do not impede pedestrian movement along them. Generally seating should be situated a minimum of 6 ft back from pathways, and it is preferable that seats are placed to give a view of the landscape rather than sited to look at areas of pedestrian movement.

Seats should be well away from children's play spaces, but in playgrounds seats are an important factor in ensuring the maximum use of the playground. Mothers do not wish to stand up when supervising their children and ample seating accommodation, sheltered from the wind but sited to catch sunshine, should be provided. Seats are also an essential part of any playing field equipment and adequate numbers should be provided particularly near facilities such as tennis courts, bowling greens, etc.

The ground surface around sitting areas receiving intensive use needs careful consideration. Where the surface is grass the turf very quickly becomes worn and patchy and is always damp in wet weather. In designing and laying out sitting areas durability and hard wearing surfaces with adequate drainage are required. The materials used around the seat should also be related to, and in keeping with, the surrounding ground surfaces.

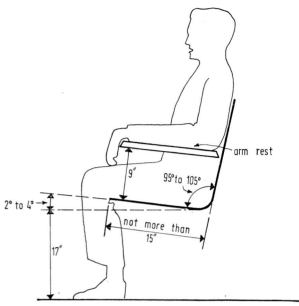

Fig. 7.2. Guide to seat dimensions.

7.1.3 Costs

Some types of seat available and comparative costs are summarised in Table 7.1 below.

TABLE 7.1: COMPARATIVE COSTS FOR SEATS

Materials	Cost*	Notes
Teak or other suitable hardwood	£18–£35	Curved seats are available from some manufacturers. Seats in other hardwoods some 10–15% cheaper in cost
Cast iron legs and frames with hardwood slats	£12–£20	Slats or plank form of seats available
Aluminium alloy frames, hardwood slats	£20–£27	Enamelled steel slats also available from some manufacturers
Concrete frames or supports, hardwood slats	£10–£20	Depending on aggregates and finishes required
Tubular or square steel frames, hardwood slats	£11–£22	

* Prices are for comparative purposes only based on single seats at 1966 prices. Reductions are available for quantities. Detailed information and costs should be obtained from manufacturers.

7.1.4 Materials

Points to be remembered when considering the various materials available include:

Timber—Probably most durable when constructed in Burma teak (*Tectona grandis*) but other suitable woods

108

include afrormosia, oak, iroko, keruing, agba, afzelia, African mahogany, African walnut, utile.

Concrete—This is mainly used in the form of a composite construction in conjunction with timber seats or backs, but simple benches consisting of slabs and supports can be pre-cast. Usually the slabs are of a steel-trowelled finish with supports having a smooth or textured exposed aggregate finish. Other alternatives include reconstructed stone—finishes available include Hams Hill (warm buff), Doulty (cream) and Portland stone (greyish white). Where exposed aggregate finishes are used heavily textured surfaces should be avoided and the careful choice of the grading of aggregate with the right degree of exposure is important. Aggregate faced finishes include shingle, Cornish granite, grey or black granite and pink limestone.

Metal—Bench or park seats are made with enamelled or painted cast iron and in square or round section mild steel tube. Aluminium alloy frames and rustproof steel slats enamelled in a choice of colours are also available.

Where aluminium is used care must be taken with the fixing to avoid corrosion through galvanic action. Also when salt is present in the atmosphere moisture corrosion is accelerated, and for this reason the direct contact of aluminium and other metals in marine atmospheres should be avoided. Where steel bolts are used for fixing they should be galvanised. Certain timbers, such as oak and chestnut amongst the hardwoods, liberate organic acids in damp environments and when the timber is unseasoned. This may cause severe corrosion of aluminium and it is wise to treat any timber, which comes into contact with it, with a suitable wood preservative, followed by the use of an aluminium or bituminous paint.

7.2 Plant containers

7.2.1 Function

Containers can be used to provide vegetation in urban areas or used architecturally to emphasise spaces, pedestrian ways or as an element of building design. They may act as a barrier separating or articulating the spaces between buildings, defining areas available for pedestrians and vehicles, identifying and indicating changes in ground level and they can give 'scale' to the street scene, particularly as their proportions can be related to the human figure. Plant containers should not be used where it is possible to grow plants naturally in the ground. Normally containers should be grouped, the number

Plate 7.2. Wall seat in precast concrete and teak, litter bin at Queen's Gardens and College of Technology, Kingston-upon-Hull. Architects: Frederick Gibberd, C.B.E., A.R.A

109

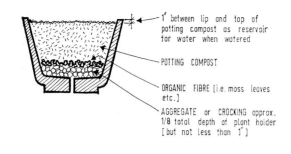

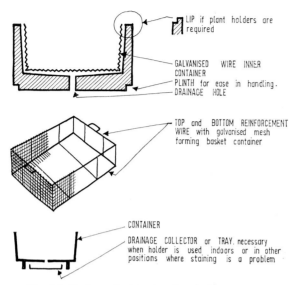

Fig. 7.3. Design principles for plant holders.

1″ between lip and top of potting compost as reservoir for water when watered

POTTING COMPOST

ORGANIC FIBRE [i.e. moss leaves etc.]

AGGREGATE or CROCKING approx. 1/8 total depth of plant holder [but not less than 1″]

LIP if plant holders are required

GALVANISED WIRE INNER CONTAINER

PLINTH for ease in handling.

DRAINAGE HOLE

TOP and BOTTOM REINFORCEMENT WIRE with galvanised mesh forming basket container

CONTAINER

DRAINAGE COLLECTOR or TRAY. necessary when holder is used indoors or in other positions where staining is a problem

being dependent on the design requirements. Single plant holders, other than those used as window boxes, should be avoided.

7.2.2 Siting
The first consideration for deciding the siting of any sort of plant container must be the welfare and success of the plants themselves.

In congested urban areas light is the most vital factor and this must be considered in a photographic sense, the requirement is not sunshine but adequate light. All flowering plants and most foliage plants need uninterrupted top light and care must be taken in siting them to avoid overhanging balconies, canopies, etc. Other conditions to avoid include traffic fumes, smoke, winds and draughts. Particular care must be taken to avoid unnecessary draught conditions in passage ways, doorways and entrances.

7.2.3 Principles of design
Plant holders should contain sufficient body of soil for the plants' nutrition, have adequate water retaining capacity, be provided with adequate drainage and be capable of easy maintenance; portability may also be a requirement (Fig. 7.3).

7.2.4 Sizes
Generally the maximum volume of soil which two men can handle without mechanical assistance is approximately 2 ft × 2 ft × 1 ft. Sizes of plant holders will, however, be dependent on the design and type of use. Their depth, however, should never be less than 12 in to ensure an adequate amount of growing medium. If trees are intended to be used in containers the minimum depth should be increased to 2 ft.

7.2.5 Drainage
Holders should contain sufficient broken material of a large aggregate at the bottom to allow water to pass through. Drainage itself can be provided by a simple hole in the bottom, but care must be taken to avoid external staining from the drainage holes.

7.2.6 Growing media
Growing media can be soil or inorganic materials, e.g. vermiculite or water. Vermiculite has the advantages of lightness and cleanness and is very suitable for use on roofs or indoors; but as a growing medium it does not retain, unlike soil, the plants' nutritional requirements. Care must be taken therefore to ensure that adequate nutrient is provided. Composite mixes normally used in plant holders consist of 3:2:1 loam, peat and sand or 6:4:1 loam, peat and sand, the growing medium normally being dependent on the plants to be used. The use of organic fertilisers may be required as a reinforcement to the growing medium dependent on particular conditions.

7.2.7 Maintenance
Plants will be put in containers either on a permanent or temporary basis. Where they are temporary they can

Plate 7.3. Double seat in Burma Teak for Loughborough College of Technology. Architects: Richard Shepphard, Robson and Partners.

110

be lifted either individually or collectively, but it is preferable if the plant container has an inner wire basket which may be lifted out and the plants removed. The wire basket should be of galvanised wire and the sides packed with polythene or sphagnum moss.

7.2.8. Materials and types available
Plant holders can be square, circular, rectangular or triangular in plan with parallel or tapering sides, traditional or special shapes also being available. Materials used are stone, concrete, clay, terracotta, metal, timber, glass fibre and asbestos cement.

Plate 7.4. Reinforced concrete frame exposed aggregate finished aformosia seat designed by L. Berger A.R.I.B.A., Borough Architect, Southampton. Made by Southern Stone and Concrete Limited.

Stone—Stone containers are usually traditional in form, heavy in weight and most appropriate for permanent planting. Types of stone used include York, Portland stone, various granites and marbles.

Designs should provide for adequate drainage since, owing to the thickness of the material, the amount of porosity is very limited through the sides of the container.

Concrete—Normally light reinforcement is used in the concrete but the extent of this depends on design of the plant holder. Exposed aggregate finishes can give a wide variety of colour and texture but care is necessary to ensure that the simplicity of form is not destroyed by exaggerated exposure of the aggregate. Surface finishes include brushing, bush hammering, and rubbing; and the use of textured or corrugated formwork should be considered. Glass smooth surfaces can be obtained by casting concrete against formwork lined with plastic sheet.

Shapes available include conical, tubular, hexagonal, rectangular and curved. These are usually manufactured in white or grey concrete. The walls of the containers vary between $1\frac{1}{2}$ in and 2 in thick and some types are

available without bases for deep-rooted plants. Hexagonal and timber plant kerbs are also produced which can be built up into tiers of any required height. Reconstructed stone holders are made in the form of square tubs, vase and bowl shapes.

Clay or terracotta—Porosity of the surfaces is important. There is a tendency for these materials to harbour disease in the pores of the walls. Care must be taken to wash the pots, especially when new, but also when any replanting takes place. Terracotta is used for the production of various traditional forms of holder—mainly conical in shape but also as pots or large vases.

Timber—Where timber is used a waterproof lining should always be provided. In some cases it may have advantages because of the insulation it gives to the roots against sudden temperature changes. Where timber is painted, care must be taken to ensure that non-toxic paints, stains

Plate 7.5. Plant crater constructed in granite setts with a brick lining at the Owen's Park Student Village, University of Manchester. Architects: G. Grenfell, Baines of Building Design Partnership.

or preservatives are used. Round and square tubs, rectangular boxes and barrel tubs are available from a number of manufacturers. Timbers used include Burma teak, iroko and oak.

Fibre glass—Mainly used at present to manufacture various forms of reproduction antique urns or tubs; the possible application for other shapes should be discussed with the manufacturers.

Asbestos cement—Conical, rectangular and curved moulded units are manufactured in natural grey asbestos

111

or various coloured finishes. Interlocking rectangular trays which can be built up to various heights are available.

Metal—When any form of metal is used care must be taken lest it comes into contact with the planting media. Metal should always be protected or coated, generally with a bitumastic paint to avoid the toxic effects of metallic salts on the plants. In hot weather there is a tendency for the temperature rise in the holder to cause rapid drying out of the planting material and consideration should be given to the use of a suitable insulating barrier between the outside container and the growing medium. Possible insulating materials include polystyrene or Asbestolux.

Metal in the form of lead, painted galvanised iron, zinc or aluminium is principally confined to special designs and most often used for window boxes.

7.3 Lamps and lighting

7.3.1 Lighting requirements
The optical requirements of outdoor lighting resolve into three principal types:

(*a*) Lighting for carriageways.
(*b*) Pedestrian or amenity lighting.
(*c*) Lighting of a decorative nature suitable for gardens, illumination of plants, statuary or buildings.

Street lighting is of a complex technical nature and normally the landscape architect's responsibilities would be confined to lighting which is of a decorative nature or only suitable for pedestrian ways. The Code of Practice C.P. 1004: Part II: 1956 'Street Lighting, Roads other than Traffic Routes' (at present under revision) may be taken as a guide to the general lighting requirements needed in pedestrian areas. When applied to lighting columns and lanterns it recommends a height of 15 ft (tolerance +1–2 ft), a spacing of 100 ft with a normal maximum of 120 ft between columns and an absolute maximum of 150 ft. The usual amount of light to be 600–2,500 lumens per 100 ft length of road. Of equal importance to the quantity of light required is that of colour and the daylight appearance of the lamp post and lantern. Details of well-designed modern lighting fittings can be found in the Council of Industrial Design Index.

TABLE 7.2

	Tungsten	Mercury/Fluorescent	Sodium	Fluorescent	Tungsten Halogen
Colour	Yellow/white	Green/white	Yellow (monochromatic)	White	White
Colour rendering	Very good	Good	Poor	Very good	Very good
Lamp wattage range	40–1,500	50–2,000	45–200	40–125	750–1,500†
Normal life (hr)	1,000	5,000	4,000	5,000	2,000
Lamp dimensions	Normal domestic size approx 7 in long	Similar to tungsten	Approx. 12 in long	Sizes vary from 1–8 ft, circular and bulk-head fitting available	Between approx. 2–10 in in length, diameter of only approx $\frac{1}{2}$–$\frac{3}{4}$ in
Lantern types	All types	Similar to tungsten, choke and capacitator usually housed in column base	Medium size lantern	Large lantern	Small flood lighting lantern
Cost of typical 15 ft column and lantern‡	£15–£17	£15–£20	£20–£25	£25–£30	—

† Lower wattages for special applications.
‡ Cost of electric service will be dependent on site conditions and availability of existing supply.
The figures given in this table only outline the principal characteristics of various lighting sources; detailed information is available from manufacturers.

Important points to remember in the choice of fittings are the relationship between lamp post and lantern, the structural requirements of the column, the provision to be made for terminating the main supply, control gear, fuses, time switches and ancillary equipment required by the lantern (Fig. 7.4).

7.3.2 Light source

The design of the lantern itself relates to the type of lighting source and Table 7.2 sets out in outline the characteristics of light sources generally used for street or amenity lighting.

Generally gas discharge and tungsten lamps are compact in size and light source, but require accurate optical control to distribute the light properly and avoid glare. Fluorescent lamps are popular with some authorities because of the advantages of the natural colouring, the low intensity at the light source and the long lamp life. A disadvantage is the size of lantern required which, when related to the lamp posts, often results in a clumsy design and unfortunate daylight appearance.

7.3.3 Amenity lighting

This can be defined as lighting suitable for the illumination of areas such as pedestrian walks, squares, parks or the forecourts of buildings where vehicular traffic is not normally found. Its function is also connected with the adequate policing and security of areas and 'morality'

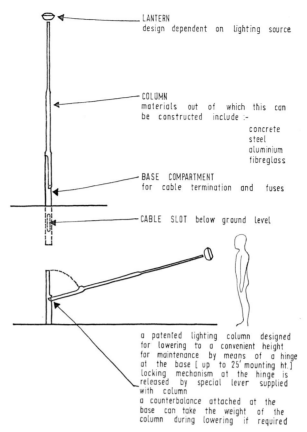

LANTERN
design dependent on lighting source

COLUMN
materials out of which this can be constructed include :-
concrete
steel
aluminium
fibreglass

BASE COMPARTMENT
for cable termination and fuses

CABLE SLOT below ground level

a patented lighting column designed for lowering to a convenient height for maintenance by means of a hinge at the base [up to 25' mounting ht.] locking mechanism at the hinge is released by special lever supplied with column
a counterbalance attached at the base can take the weight of the column during lowering if required

Fig. 7.4. Lighting columns: components.

Plate 7.6. Precast concrete plant holders, Stevenage Town Centre. Architect: L. G. Vincent C.B.E., F.R.I.B.A., consultant Architect and Planner to the Stevenage Development Corporation. Landscape Architect: Gordon Patterson.

lighting. As the requirements for amenity lighting are less stringent, more use can be made of the decorative effects of both fittings and illumination.

Bulkhead fittings can illuminate steps, wall fittings, pathways and passages; floodlights playgrounds or large pedestrian spaces.

In siting lighting fittings consideration must be given not only to the functional requirements but also to the relationships with other street furniture, buildings, trees or planting and must take into account such points as the annoyance caused by lighting falling on bedroom windows of houses, etc. Fittings used should be robust in construction and of a type suitable for their particular siting. Vandalism can be a considerable problem and must be borne in mind when deciding on the design of lantern to be used, the biggest danger being the destruction of the lantern glass. Glassfibre lanterns are proving successful against vandalism and are increasingly used.

7.3.4 Decorative lighting

Decorative or garden lighting can be used in three principal forms:

(a) To illuminate paths, walks, steps, living areas for use at night.
(b) To illuminate and dramatise plant material.
(c) As another decorative element in the garden—in fact, gardening with light.

Lighting can either be direct light where the illumination is from the source directly to the tree, flowers, plants, pools, etc. and where in all cases the source of light should be hidden or, alternatively, indirect light where a reflecting surface directs the illumination to the area or object to be lighted (Fig. 7.5).

The use of glow light as a major element of the landscape design should also be considered. In this case the light itself becomes the object to be seen and is not intended to have any great illumination value. This is illustrated by the classical Japanese use of stone and paper lanterns which were often placed where paths cross or in the middle of a shrubbery or on the banks of a lake. Trees or a bush were planted close by the lantern so that the leaves partially concealed the lighting but gave the light a shimmering appearance (Fig. 7.6).

The final arrangement of night lighting is best done by trial on the site, but it is important in all cases (except where glow light is used) to avoid excessively harsh lighting effects and generally it is preferable to baffle the source of light.

The hue of light can be chosen either to give a reasonably favourable rendering of the colours (incandescen-lamps or tungsten halogen lamps) or alternatively to int tensify or change the colour of the foliage. The blue light from mercury vapour lamps intensifies the colour foliage of conifers, cedars, thuyas. Sodium vapour lighting can be used for leaves yellowed by the Autumn, red light can emphasise the colour of copper beeches.

The use of fluorescent tubes for the lighting of trees and shrubbery has become very popular in this country primarily because the fluorescent tube is considerably

Plate 7.7. Tubular plant bowls, in the town garden at Cement and Concrete Association, Wrexham Springs.

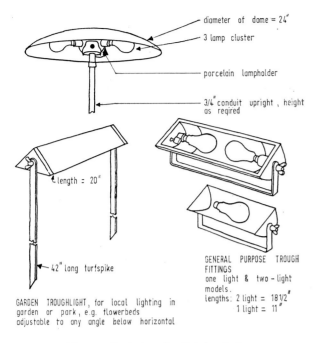

GARDEN TROUGHLIGHT, for local lighting in garden or park, e.g. flowerbeds adjustable to any angle below horizontal

GENERAL PURPOSE TROUGH FITTINGS
one light & two – light models.
lengths: 2 light = 18 1/2"
1 light = 11"

Fig. 7.5. Typical garden lighting fittings.

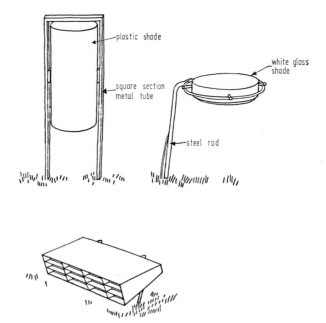

low level fitting with light baffle

Fig. 7.6. Continental examples of low level lighting fittings.

more efficient than incandescent lamps with colour filters and, because the electrical load is very much reduced.

Coloured tubes are manufactured in pink, blue, green or gold and in lengths from 2 ft to 5 ft.

The green colour tube can be used for the lighting of dense shrubbery and, particularly, evergreens. Gold or pink tubes have been used for the lighting of tree trunks and branches and pink, in particular, for the lighting of copper beeches. The initial cost is much less than that of sodium or mercury vapour lamps and with weatherproof control gear installation it becomes relatively simple. Automatic colour change dimmers are available for hire or direct purchase if required.

7.3.5 Lighting equipment

Permanent outdoor lighting must be weatherproof. The need is for small, easily adjustable units which can be either spiked direct into the ground or provided with suitable base plates. Types available include, downward lighting fittings for illumination of flower beds or other planting, either in the form of dome lights (Fig. 7.5) approximately 2 ft in diameter for use with incandescent lamps (the outside of the dome available in various colours) or, alternatively, trough lights with incandescent or fluorescent lamps, fitted with turf spikes adjustable to different angles and suitable for general illumination (Fig. 7.8). General purpose trough fittings for highlighting features, fitted with glass panel front covers, are also available and these are often suitable for ground lighting where a wide beam of light is required. For

Plate 7.8. Bollard lighting unit designed and manufactured by Atlas Lighting Limited.

115

Plate 7.9. 15 foot steel column and lantern with provision for litter bin fixing. Commended entry in Council of Industrial Design. Lamp-post and Lantern Competition. Designed by R. Steven, P. Rodd and J. Barnes. Made by Atlas Lighting Limited.

Plate 7.10. Lighting column with fluorescent fittings. Stevenage Town Centre. Architect: L. G. Vincent, C.B.E., F.R.I.B.A., consultant Architect and Planner to the Stevenage Development Corporation. Landscape Architect: Gordon Patterson.

isolated trees, thickets and statuary some form of directional floodlighting may be necessary. Small and large projectors are produced with narrow or broad angle lighting beams. Small low wattage sealed beam reflector lamps are also available which can be used with simple weatherproof housings, illuminating objects 15–20 ft away. Projection floodlights are available from a number of manufacturers with turf spike mounting bases as an alternative to normal bases.

7.3.6 Cables and wiring

Cables and wiring for street lighting would not normally come within the scope of the landscape architect's responsibilities, but he will be concerned with requirements for decorative lighting.

Where decorative lighting is used it may be an advantage to return to store during the winter the lighting fittings, conduit and other equipment. There is, therefore,

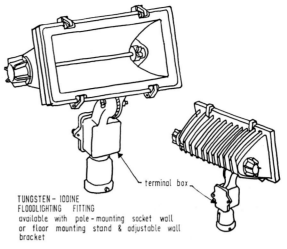

diameter of reflector = 13½"
overall height of unit
[less base = 26½"]

LONG RANGE
FLOODLIGHT
PROJECTOR
throwing a narrow beam

screwholes

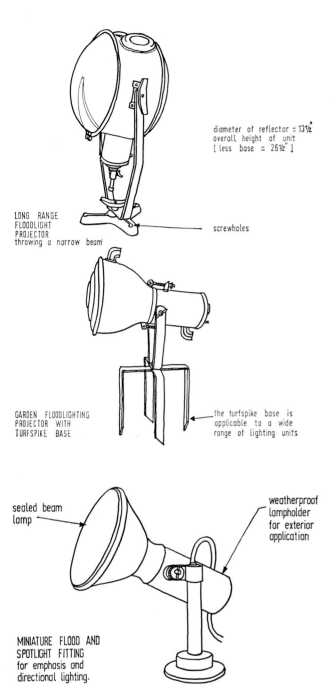

GARDEN FLOODLIGHTING
PROJECTOR WITH
TURFSPIKE BASE

the turfspike base is
applicable to a wide
range of lighting units

sealed beam
lamp

weatherproof
lampholder
for exterior
application

MINIATURE FLOOD AND
SPOTLIGHT FITTING
for emphasis and
directional lighting.

Fig. 7.7. Typical floodlight projectors

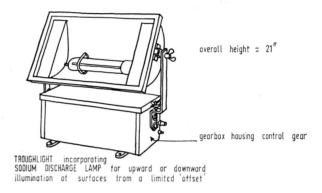

terminal box

TUNGSTEN – IODINE
FLOODLIGHTING FITTING
available with pole – mounting socket wall
or floor mounting stand & adjustable wall
bracket

overall height = 21"

gearbox housing control gear

TROUGHLIGHT incorporating
SODIUM DISCHARGE LAMP for upward or downward
illumination of surfaces from a limited 'offset'

Fig. 7.8. Typical floodlight projectors.

It is considered good practice to lay a tile on top of the cable wherever required for protection.

P.V.C. cable with an earth continuity conductor—This cable will require laying in a conduit and must be properly protected wherever it is used.

P.V.C. sheathed armoured cable—Armoured cable must always be used and specified when running connections directly on the ground and for all temporary installations where mechanical damage may occur to cables at ground level.

In all cases cables must be terminated in weather proof outlet boxes. All lighting fittings and switches must be weatherproof and it is essential that all lamp fittings should be efficiently earthed. Where cables are permanently installed trenches should be dug and the cables buried at least 18 in below ground level. If it is necessary to place cables at shallower depths they must be protected and protection must always be provided where they enter or leave the ground.

an advantage in making and using temporary installations or, alternatively, incorporating a permanent 'ring main' system through which temporary installations and surface cables can be connected. The cables likely to be used for temporary or permanent decorative lighting or floodlighting are:

Pyrotenax cable—This form of cable can be laid directly in the ground, but to ensure protection from any corrosive elements in the soil it should be sheathed in P.V.C.

117

7.4 Litter Bins

7.4.1 Principles and uses

Litter bins should be simple in character, robust and easy to maintain, easy to empty and handle. There are advantages in having separate wire or metal baskets inside the main container because there is then less danger of damage when being emptied. A good bin should not only hold litter but should, as far as possible, conceal the litter it holds. Containers should be as indestructible as possible and preferably fireproof (Fig. 7.9).

In urban settings there is a need for co-ordination with other street furniture. It is preferable for containers to form part of other elements in the street. They should relate to such items as lighting columns, shelters, seats or walls. In a more diverse landscape such as parks, public gardens, rural areas, etc., containers should be sited adjacent to the main circulation areas or routes and

to prevent litter blowing about and to discourage foraging by animals or birds. Special types are available for temporary use and for outdoor functions such as race meetings, fairs, etc., but care must be taken to see that the design of the container used does not itself form an element of litter in the landscape.

The act of emptying a bin will vary from tipping a small container into a handcart to shovelling quantities of a wide variety of rubbish by hand into a lorry. The cleansing of containers varies from practically nothing to laborious burning and scrubbing out. It must be borne in mind that the term 'litter' embraces a strange assortment of objects and substances particularly in overcrowded areas. Similarly vandalism varies from being almost non-existent through various stages of occasional bonfires and minor damage, to that of almost complete demolition. It is not unknown for a concrete bin to be completely shattered by children, and insecurely fixed containers may be thrown about or stolen. Factors other than human ones have to be contended with and squirrels and birds may be a problem in one place, and deer or ponies may

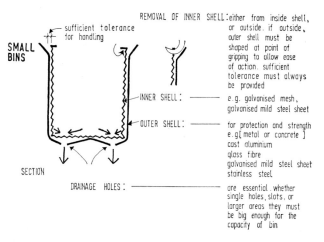

Fig. 7.9. LITTER BINS. Diagram showing main requirements.

should be immediately available for use and be easily seen and identified.

Although litter bins should be related to other street furniture and are often required close to seats in public parks, gardens or other open spaces, the problem of unpleasant odours must be remembered. In some areas, such as holiday resorts, bins quickly become full, particularly at the height of the season and in hot weather they can become so offensive that would-be sitters are discouraged. In cases where this may happen litter bins with lids, possibly worked by foot pedals, may be advantageous.

When they are placed adjacent to roads or lay-bys where infrequent servicing is likely, containers must be large enough to hold considerable quantities of waste and be designed to be weatherproof with some form of cover

Plate 7.11. Wall- or column-mounted litter bin in sheet metal
Designed by John and Sylvia Reid A/A.R.I.B.A.

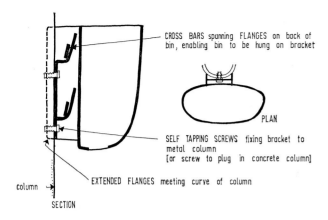

CROSS BARS spanning FLANGES on back of bin, enabling bin to be hung on bracket

PLAN

SELF TAPPING SCREWS fixing bracket to metal column
[or screw to plug in concrete column]

EXTENDED FLANGES meeting curve of column

column

SECTION

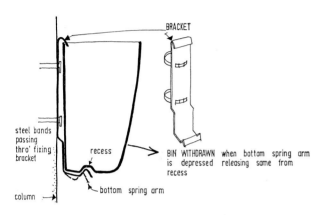

BRACKET

steel bands passing thro' fixing bracket

recess

bottom spring arm

column

BIN WITHDRAWN when bottom spring arm is depressed releasing same from recess

Fig. 7.10. LITTER BINS: Fixing to columns

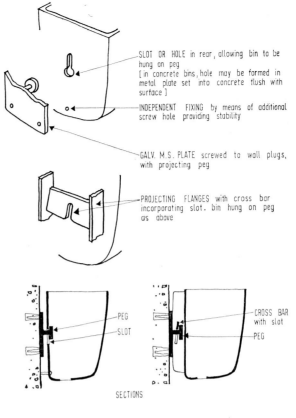

SLOT OR HOLE in rear, allowing bin to be hung on peg
[in concrete bins, hole may be formed in metal plate set into concrete flush with surface]

INDEPENDENT FIXING by means of additional screw hole providing stability

GALV. M.S. PLATE screwed to wall plugs, with projecting peg

PROJECTING FLANGES with cross bar incorporating slot. bin hung on peg as above

PEG
SLOT

CROSS BAR with slot
PEG

SECTIONS

EXAMPLES taken from a typical manufacturers product

Fig. 7.11. LITTER BINS: Fixing to walls.

pose an entirely different one elsewhere. Where consideration is given to hooded or protected bins care must be taken that the mechanical function does not lead to excessive wear and tear, accidental damage or difficulties in emptying. Generally the public are reluctant to push a dirty or sticky flap to dispose of their rubbish and the advocates of an open-mouthed container that 'invites' litter may well be correct in their arguments. Hygiene is important and must be coupled with good design.

7.4.2 Types of litter bin

There are five principal types of container. These are:

(a) Containers for mounting on lighting columns or poles (Fig. 7.10).
(b) Wall-mounted types or types for fixing to vertical surfaces (Fig. 7.11).
(c) Free-standing litter bins (Fig. 7.12).
(d) Large capacity bins or containers for public spaces or sites adjoining roads.
(e) Movable containers for temporary use.

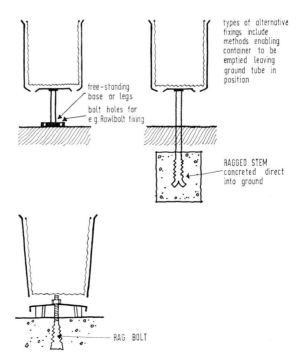

types of alternative fixings include methods enabling container to be emptied leaving ground tube in position

free-standing base or legs
bolt holes for e.g. Rawlbolt fixing

RAGGED STEM concreted direct into ground

RAG BOLT

Fig. 7.12. LITTER BINS: Fixing to ground—freestanding.

119

Plate 7.12. Large free-standing litter bin of perforated metal with removable inner wire baskets. Designed by D. Goad and J. Ricks of Donald Forrest, A.R.I.B.A.

The list of approved designs for street furniture prepared by the Council of Industrial Design includes all the types mentioned above and a British Standard for litter bins is also in the course of preparation.

7.4.3 Materials

The choice of litter bin to be used will be dependent on its siting, its relationship to other street furniture, its capacity and its method of emptying. Materials available include:

Sheet Metals—Galvanised sheet metal with a galvanised wire removable inner container forms the traditional type of litter bin. The metal is normally galvanised or lead coated steel sheet and is usually available in any British Standard colour either stove-enamelled or spray painted. Perforated metal sheet is also available and plastic coated steel is offered by some manufacturers.

Aluminium—Cast aluminium is used for some litter bins generally cast in one piece with flanges, slots and drain holes; primed ready for painting as required on site. Removable wire baskets are provided either in galvanised mild steel wire or coated in plastic to any required colour. Care must be taken when using aluminium that fixings or any other adjacent metals are protected to ensure that no galvanic action takes place with the aluminium.

Timber—Various designs of litter bins are produced in oak or oiled teakwood slats mounted on galvanised steel strip. Inner baskets are either galvanised or of stove-enamelled sheet steel, or of a heavy gauge wire mesh.

Glass Fibre—Resin impregnated reinforced glass fibre or press-moulded containers are increasingly being used by local authorities. The glass fibre is self-coloured with smooth wall finishes on both surfaces and often fitted with a removable galvanised sheet metal inner container or alternatively a wire mesh basket.

Concrete—A number of containers are available constructed with a cast concrete outer shell; these are usually cast in one piece with fixing plates and holes. Generally

Plate 7.13. Free standing litter bin made of steel and stove enamel. Designed by Design Research Unit.

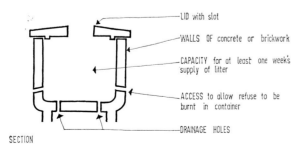

LID with slot
WALLS OF concrete or brickwork
CAPACITY for at least one week's supply of litter
ACCESS to allow refuse to be burnt in container
DRAINAGE HOLES

SECTION

Fig. 7.13. Large capacity bins.

TABLE 7.3: COMPARATIVE COSTS OF LITTER BINS

Materials	Cost*	Notes
FREE-STANDING BINS		
Timber slatted	£3 15s.–£6	Depends on size, design and timber used. Available on pole or mounted on legs
Galvanised steel sheet	£4 15s.–£8	Depending on finish and design
	£10–£28	For large capacity bins
Concrete	£6–£12	The higher price ranges are for large capacity bins
Cast aluminium	£9–£12	
Galvanised wire	£1–£4	Price depending on type of frame and does not include for inner containers
POLE- AND WALL-MOUNTED BINS		
Timber slatted	£3 15s.–£5 5s.	Depending on size and design
Steel, metal either galvanised, painted or plastic coated	£2–£4 10s.	Depending on size and design
Concrete	£6–£12	Depending on size and design
Fabricated and cast aluminium	£2 10s.–£13	Fabricated aluminium bins generally cheaper than cast aluminium
Fibre glass	£2 10s.–£4 10s.	Material used self-coloured to standard colours
Galvanised wire	18s. 6d.–25s.	Does not include inner container

* Prices shown are for comparative purposes only and are based on supply of 25 fittings at average 1966 figures. Prices include inner containers in either galvanised sheet metal or galvanised wire, except where stated. Detailed information should be obtained from manufacturers.

the thickness of the shell varies from $1\frac{1}{4}$ to $2\frac{3}{8}$ in and normally the finish is smooth grey, using granite based aggregates, but alternative aggregates can be provided if an alternative finish is required. Removable internal wire baskets are provided in galvanised mild steel wire.

7.4.4 Costs
Table 7.3 sets out some comparative costs and materials available for pole-mounted, wall-mounted and free-standing litter bins.

7.4.5 Large capacity bins
These may often be designed as specific pieces of street

Plate 7.14. Column-or pole-mounted litter bin with a glass-fibre container with removable sheet metal interior. Designed by John and Sylvia Reid, A/A.R.I.B.A.

furniture for urban or rural use. Where this type of container is used the design must take into account the infrequent servicing. Covers or lids are preferable; adequate self-drainage is needed and there are advantages with very large containers if arrangements can be made to burn the refuse whilst still in the container. Fig. 7.13 illustrates certain of the principles of this type of design. Standard designs are available in concrete, perforated metal and glass fibre, though the very large containers are usually specifically designed for their particular site.

7.4.6 Movable containers
The problems of litter disposal for functions of a temporary nature such as fairs, race meetings, processions, etc., have been considerably eased with the development of movable containers using disposable paper sacks. These consist of free-standing containers with metal supports holding paper bags. The holders are galvanised or plastic coated and have either open tops or rubber or plastic lids. The paper sack (of a high wet strength) is clipped to the top of the holder and is designed to be dismantled easily. Wire protectors for the sacks are now available against vermin attack. Stands can be in concrete or metal with wheels or legs and in some cases can be provided with pedal-operated lids. Wall-mounted types are also produced and further refinements in the design of the sacks include the introduction of polythene which is available in black or dark green.

Plate 7.15. Directional signs in the new Number 3 Passenger Building at London Airport.
Commissioned by the Architect Frederick Gibberd and designed by
Colin Forbes of Fletcher, Forbes and Gill Limited.

7.5 Signs and signboards

7.5.1 Design principles

Signs should be designed to ensure instant recognition by the clarity of the message. Uniformity of appearance, consistent application of symbols in preference to text, standard support structures, colour and type face, and uniform positioning of signs are essential aids to legibility. The more detailed the information the weaker is the impact of the message or its 'retention value'. Signs should be as few in number as possible and not add to the visual clutter; frequently too many signs only impede and confuse the public seeking information. This is particularly important for car drivers. Multiplicity of diverse signs defeats its own object and only produces visual chaos.

Where possible, therefore, signs should be mounted together and should be as small as compatible with their function and effectiveness. Motorway signs are very large; they are designed to be read from a great distance to give the driver travelling at speed adequate information in time; correspondingly sign areas can be reduced and become quite small where they are intended for pedestrians, provided they are not dwarfed by adjacent advertising or other messages.

Care should be taken that signs are not sited so as to be obscured by structures or growing trees or hedges. They should easily be seen both by day and night, and the design must take into account the problems of illumination or the use of reflective materials.

In order to reduce the number of obstructions on the footpath, signs should be fixed to walls and other suitable structures where at all possible, but careful consideration should be given to their mounting height. The eye level of a driver in a car is substantially below that of a pedestrian; signs for vehicular traffic should not be more than 3 ft 6 in to 4 ft measured from the ground to the bottom edge of the sign. Consistency of mounting height is most important since it will avoid unnecessary searching for vital information.

7.5.2 Types of signs

Signs fall into three types:

(a) Signs giving definite instructions
   (1) Mandatory.
   (2) Prohibitory.
(b) Warning signs.
(c) Information signs.

Internationally understood pictorial symbols were proposed at a United Nations Conference in Geneva in 1949 and have been adopted by most European countries. The acceptance of the recommendations embodied in the Report of the Traffic Signs Committee (Worboys Committee) prepared for the Ministry of Transport at last brings British road signs into line with the signs and symbols adopted by the rest of Europe. Furthermore, use of standard traffic sign materials and structures can provide a reasonable level of uniformity.

These signs define symbols and colours to distinguish the various types of information or instruction (see Fig. 7.14). As important as the face of the sign is the rear and support structure which should be as inconspicuous as possible so as not to detract the attention of drivers or pedestrians travelling in the opposite direction. In practice these are usually coloured black or dark grey.

7.5.3 Methods of sign manufacture
These include:

Silk screen reproduction. Modern screen printing is largely based on the use of stencils made from drawn or painted originals. A very wide range of materials can be printed, wood, metal, glass, fabrics, etc. The process is economic for small numbers.

Transfer lettering. This consists of printing on a thin film with either water or spirit soluble gum so that the layer of paint or ink forming the lettering or symbol can be slid off the face of the temporary carrier and stuck on to the permanent surface. It is possible to transfer complete notices in one operation.

Scotchlite and Scotchcal reproduction. A patented process, using a heat–vacuum application which causes a printed adhesive coating of Scotchcal or films of Scotchlite reflective sheetings to bond permanently on to a suitable backing, and enables superimposed lettering and emblems in these materials to become integrated with the backing material. The resulting sign should have a very much longer life than ordinary painted notices.

Photographic reproduction. Photographic prints of type setting are often used for temporary applications such as exhibitions, but can also be incorporated in a laminated plastic which provides weather resistance. Because of cost, signs are largely confined to black and white. In spite of the laminated protective coating it is likely that colour photographs would fade under ultra-violet light (sunlight).

Bold	*Classical*
VERTICAL **New Haas Grotesque**	VERTICAL New Clarendon
ITALIC *Doric Italic*	ITALIC *Ultra Bodoni*
CONDENSED **Playbill**	CONDENSED Roman Compressed
EXPANDED **Egyptian Expanded**	EXPANDED **Wide Latin**

Fig. 7.14. The examples illustrate some of the wide range of type faces available for signs and signboards.

123

Three-dimensional signs. Formed by incised or raised lettering of many types. Materials used in the manufacture of solid letters and signs vary widely, e.g. they can be cut out of sheet plastic, sheet metal, cast in aluminium, engraved on plastics or metals or fabricated from wood. The choice depends on a number of factors and consultation with an expert sign-maker is advisable.

Painted signs. In spite of the methods for fabricated signs set out above painted signs are invaluable

Plate 7.17. Directional signs in the new Number 3 Passenger Building at London Airport. Commissioned by the Architect Frederick Gibberd and designed by Colin Forbes of Fletcher, Forbes and Gill Limited.

Plate 7.16. Directional signs in the new Number 3 Passenger Building at London Airport. Commissioned by the Architect Frederick Gibberd and designed by Colin Forbes of Fletcher, Forbes and Gill Limited.

where only a few are required and renovation presents no problem. The success of a painted sign depends invariably on the skill of the craftsman signwriter. Control of painted signs is difficult since invariably a signwriter will have his own method and 'preferred alphabet'. A full size template is invaluable in ensuring that the design is faithfully executed by the craftsman.

Carved or sculptured signs. In small park settings carved and painted timber signs are frequently quite appropriate and can enhance the character of the setting. Other suitable materials include stone, slate or concrete.

7.5.4 Materials for construction of signs
Signs can be made from non-ferrous materials such as aluminium or aluminium alloy which are reasonable in

cost, resist corrosion, are light in weight and can be embossed when in sheet form.

Vitreous enamel on a steel base is often used and has the advantage of colour fastness and long life (e.g. signs on railway stations and Underground stations), but it is liable to 'starring' from flying stones, etc. which can then destroy the finish. Enamelling can also suffer if any distortion occurs to the steel base and care must be taken in the fixing of the sign to its supports. Plastic signs usually of acrylic sheet are used either solid or transparent and illuminated from behind (e.g. petrol stations). If the number is large enough master moulds (which are expensive) will justify a three-dimensional treatment. Acrylic signs are particularly suitable in corrosive atmospheres and situations where the minimum of maintenance is required. Here again expert advice from the sign maker is essential at an early stage.

Other materials include Melamine faced plastic laminates, P.V.C. or aluminium, bonded to plywood backings. Weaknesses can occur at the edges and in most cases protective framing or lipping is required to keep the weather out.

7.5.5 Lettering
Lettering should be bold and simple. Sans serif lettering

Plate 7.18. Standard entrance sign for the Milan Underground.

in upper and lower case is now used on traffic signs and the spacing of the letters has been rationalised in the Worboys Committee Report. This can well serve as a guide for many types of signs on which a landscape architect may be asked to advise. Where it is proposed to use type faces which are designed for printed text care should be taken not to misunderstand the nature of the type design. Type faces are designed flat compared with signs or lettering which are two- or three-dimensional. They are intended to be seen at a certain distance and the subtleties of detail identifying the particular type face are only valid for these distances. They may diminish or become very obtrusive outside a limited range of sizes. The truly functional type face is the one that properly spaced makes its message clear from the distance from which it is intended to be read.

When considering the selection of lettering for signs it should be confined to as few type faces as possible and it must be decided if a classical or bold type is required; also whether an expanded or condensed type face is best suited to the particular layout or sign. Fig. 7.14 indicates some differences between bold and classical letter types.

The degree of clarity and legibility of any lettering is

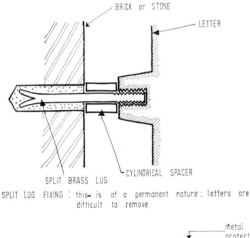

SPLIT LUG FIXING : this is of a permanent nature : letters are difficult to remove

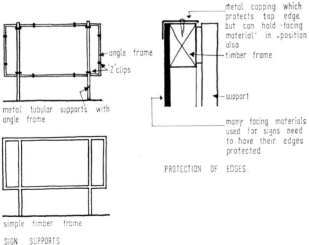

Fig. 7.15. Fixing methods for signs.

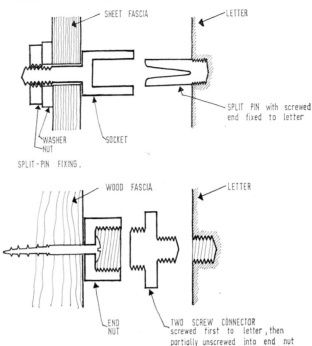

Fig. 7.16. Fixing of letters.

not only determined by the size of the letters themselves but it should be borne in mind that the pleasing appearance of lettering depends as much on the spacing between the letters as upon their shape. A type face should be selected that offers freedom of space and if special titling of descriptive material is required the use of lower case letters may prove helpful.

7.5.6 Fixings

Where signs are free-standing a simple supporting frame should be made up using either timber, tubular steel or square section steel posts. There are advantages in using steel uprights as they combine strength with a relatively small cross-section. Fig. 7.15 illustrates various forms of fixing for different types of signs. Where applied letters are used the most satisfactory type of fixing, in most cases, is a locator which provides the letters with a stand-off from the fascia. This eliminates the risk of weather staining and also allows the letter to be easily removed or replaced (Fig. 7.16).

Bibliography

Better litter bins, Design, December 1960.
Floodlighting of Buildings, Technical Report No. 6, Illuminating Engineering Society.
Flower boxes and architecture, W. R. Watson-Smyth, *Architect and Building News,* 22 May 1952.

Lettering on Buildings, Nicholete Gray, Architectural Press.

Lettering for Architects and Designers, Milner Gray and Ronald Armstrong, Batsford.

'Lighting of parks, statues and water displays', L. Gaymond, *A.P.L.E. Conference Report*, 1963.

Street Furniture, List of Approved Designs, Council of Industrial Design.

Traffic Signs, Report of Committee on Traffic Signs for All-Purpose Roads, H.M.S.O.

8 Water

G. A. JELLICOE

8.1 General information

8.1.1 Introduction

No water scheme should be designed without prior knowledge of an assured water supply; a guaranteed method of retention, artificial or natural; means to keep the water fresh; and a system of overflow and drainage.

8.1.2 Water supply

Natural. Running water from spring or stream is usually very fertile. Make sure that supply does not dry up in summer. The use of any water from a stream or river requires the permission of the River Conservancy Board. Usually there is no charge.

Piped water. This provides a guaranteed supply and can be obtained from the local water board with a payment according to the requirements; because of cost the water is usually recirculated, and topped up to make good evaporation losses, etc. Piped water has been filtered and is infertile.

8.1.3 Water retention

Methods of water retention are as follows:

Natural—If there is any doubt whatsoever, the holding capacity for ponds, lakes, etc., must be tested with trial sumps, when necessary over a period of weeks. Water can be lost by continuous seepage at the sides, or more alarmingly through a flaw in an apparently impenetrable clay overlying a porous ground such as chalk. Usually saturation at the lake side accounts for an apparent loss of water for a few days after filling, but thereafter is stabilised. Experience may also show that water which carries sediment will in time create a protective layer irrespective of the nature of the original bottom. (e.g. streams on chalk). Care must be taken about alterations to existing earth dams, which can easily become porous if disturbed.

Puddle clay—This is traditional material for canals and lakes. It should be 6–9 in thick, properly laid and consolidated. It is the cheapest of all methods, but difficult to keep clean. It cracks when exposed, but soon closes on being re-covered with water. Its main use today is to cover hard materials as an added precaution against seepage.

Mass concrete—A good quality mass concrete is waterproof although cracking may occur if there is no reinforcement; a backing of puddle clay is advisable and a waterproof cement or rendering to the inside face is an advantage.

Bricks—These give a special texture and become saturated. They are not normally waterproof (engineering bricks with waterproof mortar excepted) and require puddle clay or special asphalt tanking.

Reinforced concrete—This is the material favoured by engineers for most works. It can be guaranteed permanent and if vibrated a 6 in thickness is impervious. Generally it is safer to specify a waterproof cement.

Timber for sides—A traditional material for canals, but lately has been superseded by reinforced concrete; but it is less costly and more agreeable to the landscape. Elm, teak or greenheart are used, the size, etc., being dependent on the position (Fig. 8.1). Though not waterproof it can be backed with puddle clay if it is desirable to prevent seepage. The probable life is not less than 60 years.

Sheet piling—This is used in heavy engineering works; in many situations the vertical sheeting can look agreeable in itself, or it can be topped or concealed in combination with another material where visible.

Polythene—This has only recently been introduced and its permanent properties are not yet known. It has been used primarily to make reservoirs on sand. The recently made lake of the University of Birmingham is completely lined with Visqueen 1,000 gauge black polythene sheeting. Prefabricated sheets, the largest of which were 60 by 24 yd, were made up and heat-sealed on site to form a complete membrane. Immediately after laying, dumper trucks drove on to the film and deposited loads of gravel subsoil. This was spread by hand over the flat bottom to a depth of 4–6 in, with a 12 in layer of backfill on the sloping sides (Fig. 8.2).

127

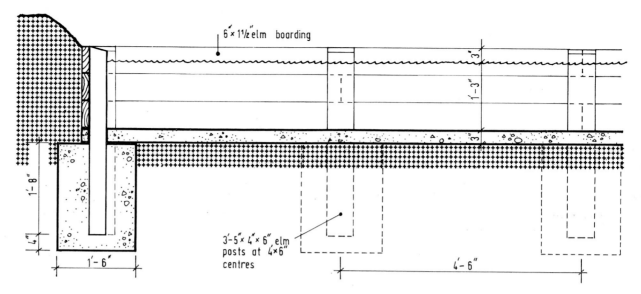

Fig. 8.1. Detail of timber sides to a canal.

8.1.4 Water freshness

It is paramount that water should not become stagnant, and so become unsightly and a possible danger to health. There are four main methods of keeping the water fresh.

Consistent flow of natural running water—A very small but *continuous* supply of stream water can sustain a great volume (e.g. Blenheim Palace Lake). It is always advisable to provide a catch pit between stream and the lake to stop sediment, weeds and floating substances generally. The natural bottomed lake will have to be cleaned out once or twice a year probably by a rake operated from a barge, but the relative cost of maintenance of water against mown grass is in favour of water. Fish and ducks are added cleansers (see section 8.5.2 below). Hard finished surfaces present no serious problem of cleansing.

Biological treatment—Experiments have recently indicated that it is possible to keep static water fresh by promoting biological balance and some artificial topping up. Each situation calls for a different specification, but a standard one (provided by Frances Perry) is as follows:

As a general rule, fish and aquatic plants require water which is neutral or slightly alkaline. One with a pH value about 8 is ideal; below 6·5 or above 8·5 causes discoloration and complications.

Clear natural water has a slightly greenish tint, due to the presence of minute forms of algae. Organic matter in the pond ultimately releases mineral salts into the water; bacteria are the agents and oxygen renders them innocuous.

Oxygen comes from two sources; the air (and the tower the temperature of water the more surface oxygen is absorbed) and submerged aquatic plants. These through the process of photosynthesis and in the presence of light use carbon-dioxide to make their food and release oxygen into the water. Oxygen is extremely important in relation to water clarity and may be introduced by movement as in streams, waterfalls, fountains, etc. or through the presence of abundant submerged vegetation.

In the case of static water the last is highly important. Underwater oxygenators provide a balance to animal life and by virtue of competition tend to starve out the lower plants such as algae.

Some oxygenators are naturally more efficient than others, notably Elodeas, Callitriche, Myriophyllums and *Lagarosiphon major*. Floating plants create natural shade and are useful in the early stages of a water garden (until the lily leaves and other aquatic foliage develops). Some however spread too quickly and one would only advocate the use of frogbit (*Hydrocharis morsus-ranae*) or water soldier (*Stratiotes aloides*) for this purpose. Marginal aquatics and water-lilies have an aesthetic value and also provide hiding places for small creatures which ultimately become fish food. Fish in turn fertilise the plants with their excreta, keep down pests and provide some of the carbon dioxide for photosynthesis. Avoid the 'mud bottom' types like tench and mirror carp as these constantly agitate the water. Goldfish and golden orfe keep near the surface and are easily seen in clear water.

Recirculation—It is possible to re-use water and help ensure freshness by means of pumps. The capital cost is not large, and is spent on the pump itself, the pump chamber, and the pipe runs. The running costs are small (for more details see section 8.3).

Chemical treatment—This is also possible.

128

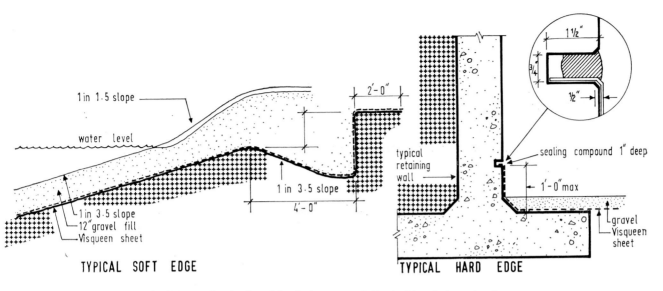

Fig. 8.2. Details of soft and hard edges to pools lined with polythene sheeting.

8.2 Tranquil water

8.2.1 Natural rivers, lakes and pools

Where it is desirable to create an informal or apparently natural sheet of water, the treatment of the banks is of paramount importance. The problem is to create artificially a system of defence against water that would take a long time to evolve naturally. There are two main methods of dealing with the effects of scour water in motion; that of following the *natural way*, which with an existing hard material such as rock depends upon the nature of the rock itself, and care in choosing a line which will expose the right shape and amount of rock. Careful stripping to cleavage and bedding planes will allow a more ready weathering and help to avoid a long period of rawness if the rock is one which normally weathers reasonably rapidly. With soft soil it may be possible to establish a vegetation margin, which if temporarily protected during early stages, will become sufficiently durable as a 'natural' bank. It is a method that has been studied over a long period in Germany under Professor Seifert, but because of the discouraging time factor there is little experience in this country. The other way is the *artificial way* where the visual effect is informal but not necessarily naturalistic. In certain stone counties such as Oxfordshire it is still economic to use the traditional method of random stones deposited dry against the bank, and generally used at the bend of rivers. If a formal surface such as timber or concrete is used, it must finish as close as reasonable to the water surface, with the soil and plants so disposed as to conceal the edge.

If the water is fertile the natural bottom of pools presents no problem of aesthetics, however difficult may be that of cleaning (see section 8.1.4).

8.2.2 Artificial canals, lakes and pools

Depth. Care should be taken to decide the correct depth, which depends upon the purpose. Paddling pools are described below, but non-paddling pools in public places should be not less than 21 in deep in order to discourage children but not too deep for safety. A water lily pool may vary from 9 to 18 in or more, depending upon the variety of plant. A reflecting pool, giving the same effect as a puddle, may be as shallow as is practicable taking evaporation loss into account. A fish pool can be deeper, and should provide also for privacy. Boating and amusement lakes need to be deep enough for rowing, but for safety and economy should not exceed this depth. Unless the designer has other good reasons, it is an axiom in pool design that the water level be as close to the rim as is consistent with wind disturbance; a pool is most convivial when it is abundantly full and 'winking at the brim'.

Floors. Although reflections are the main pleasure of static water, the eye penetrates the surface especially when looking down from above as from a bridge or an upper window. For this reason it is wise to design the bottom to give added interest remembering that it is to be seen through water and consequently the view is confused by light refraction. The following are a few of the examples that are within range of decorative design:

A surface of rough stones set in concrete: these will collect plants and will soon be transformed into a green bottom of great charm. The following for infertile water only: a pattern of circles or other designs of movement

129

incised in the surface concrete before it has set; painted surfaces of all kinds; large pebbles spread loose upon the surface, chosen and disposed for their colour pattern; if in a public place these should only be used where there is proper supervision. In a public garden a rough surface uncomfortable to the bare feet discourages paddling.

Weirs. In any large scheme it is essential that levels over the whole area be taken exactly, for an opportunity

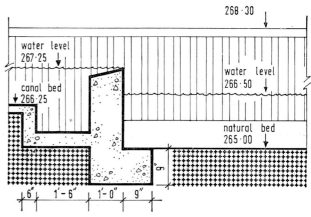

Fig. 8.3. Section through concrete weir, Hemel Hempstead.

Plate 8.1. Detail of concrete weirs, timber, sides, and pebble floor, Hemel Hempstead Canal.

may arise for making weirs and cascades even on apparently level sites. Where there is an abundance of water, there should be a lip so that water falls clear of the vertical. The specification must state that this lip is to be exactly level, and no approval should be given until the first water test has been made. As the water course may

need to be drained off, a pipe or similar opening should be provided through the bottom of the weir wall which can be opened when required. If the water flow is small or likely to be so in dry weather, it is advisable to assist the effect of falling water by an illusion such as channelling the water into vertical grooves in the face (Fig. 8.3 and 8.4).

Overflows and drainage. The overflow should be inconspicuous unless developed as a feature such as a cascade; its level should be determined exactly beforehand, and not an approximation. For emptying purposes the floors of all artificial pools, etc. should fall to a drainage outlet (Figs. 8.5 and 8.6). Small pools can be satisfactory without any plumbing. Unnecessary equipment is to be avoided in such cases. Filling can be by hosepipe, and emptying by portable pump or syphon. The overflow may irrigate bog plants; alternatively a soakaway can be arranged under a pebbled area.

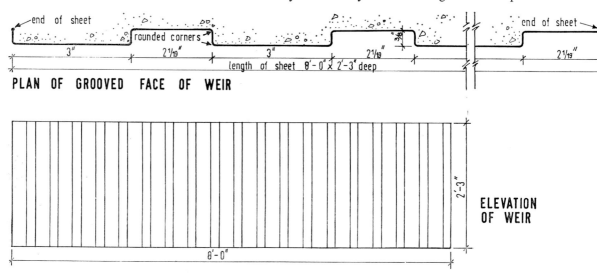

Fig. 8.4. Detail of vertical grooves on weir to break falling water.

130

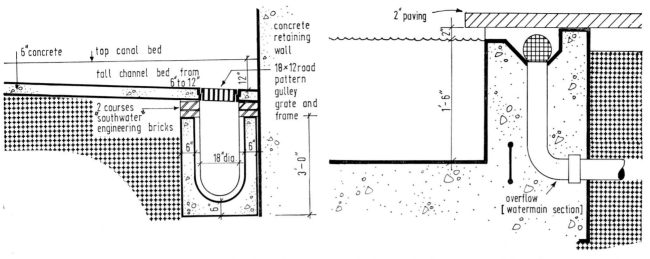

Fig. 8.5. Section through a typical cleaning channel.

Fig. 8.6. Section through concealed overflow, garden pool.

Reservoirs. These pose the problem of the shore at low water, which usually coincides with the summer holiday season. In tropical countries it is possible to grow a crop, but as yet no general solution to overcome unseemliness has been found in Great Britain. The most satisfactory so far is dry stone laid on a steep angle (as at Tryweryn, by Frederick Gibberd). As to planting, conifers are favoured because their needles fall vertically; but trees such as willows that themselves drink a great deal of water, are specially to be avoided.

8.2.3 The diversion of running water during progress of works

It is imperative that during the preparation of the designs a phasing plan be drawn up to indicate how the contractors can divert a stream or river upon which the landscape architect has set a new design. This problem may sometimes determine the actual design; in any case diversion may be costly. To make the canal dry for the contractors at Hemel Hempstead, the river was let into a new but unused sewer and pumped out to rejoin the old bed down-stream.

8.2.4 Construction of a large pool

The services of an engineer are advisable. The following is a description of a typical construction:

The foundation naturally depends on site conditions, but in general a 6 in minimum thickness of well-consolidated hardcore, with 2 in of blinding concrete is required, any soft spots being excavated and filled with hardcore. It is desirable to cover the blinding concrete with a layer of waterproof paper or plastic sheeting to enable the structural bed to move freely and so permit any movement to occur at predetermined joints (Fig. 8.7).

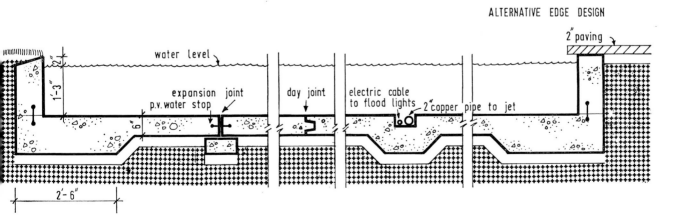

Fig. 8.7. Section showing jointing details and alternative edge designs for a reinforced concrete pool.

131

Plate 8.2. Brick lends itself to curved forms. Detail from island at Hemel Hempstead.

The design of the structural bed depends on the depth of the pool and the site conditions. For deep pools constructed on sites with high water table levels, consideration must be given to the pressure of water acting under the pool. This pressure not only affects the strength of the bed, but it can also lift the whole pool should it be emptied for cleaning or other purposes. The slab may have to be increased to provide dead weight, and specially reinforced to resist outside pressure when empty.

In general the minimum thickness of the structural bed should be 6 in of vibrated reinforced concrete of 1:2:4 mix with $\frac{3}{4}$ in maximum sized aggregate. Precautions must be taken to prevent shrinkage cracks which occur when concrete dries out. This can be achieved by dividing the bed into a number of bays not exceeding 225 sq ft. Individual bays are then cast and isolated from the adjoining bays by 18 in gaps, the edges of the bays being shuttered to form continuous grooves or rebates. After 2 or 3 days, when each bay has dried out and shrunk the gaps are carefully filled in. It should be noted that the reinforcement must be continued across the joints.

Expansion joints are also required to allow for movement which may occur in the concrete bed due to temperature changes. The joints should divide the bed into bays not exceeding 30 ft in width or 900 sq ft in area and where they terminate at the edge of the pool they must continue up and into the wall. The joint is constructed by casting a water stop into the edges of two slabs which are 1 in or so apart, the gap being filled with a flexible filling to within 1 in of the top and later completely sealed with mastic. The water stop is a strip of P.V.C. or rubber

6–9 in wide and shaped rather like a dumbell in section. It should be noted that, unlike the day joint, the reinforcement must not continue over the gap. Because of this the two slab edges should be supported on a continuous concrete strip beam.

The wall of the pool will naturally vary in thickness according to the depth of water retained and the amount of reinforcement employed, but in general 8 in should be adequate for most pools. The wall should be cast in maximum lengths of 20 ft with joints similar to those used in the bottom slab. Expansion joints as previously mentioned should be a continuation of the joints used in the bed. The wall is usually shuttered on top of the edge of the structural slab and as there will be a horizontal joint at this point, a continuous water stop should be used.

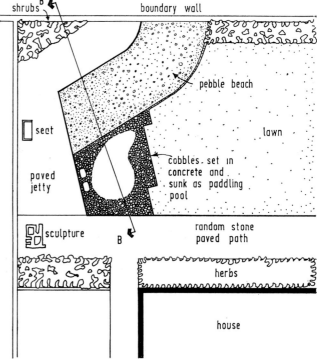

GARDEN PLAY AREA

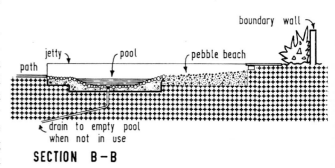

SECTION B–B

Fig. 8.8. Paddling pool, with associated detailing.

132

Plate 8.3. Paddle Pool, Elm Tree Road, London (see Fig. 8.8).

Alternatively a continuous groove or rebate can be cast into the top of the slab at this point and after the surface has been thoroughly roughened by hacking, the wall can be shuttered and cast on.

As an indication of the amount of reinforcement required, a shallow pool built on good ground with the described foundation should require one layer of HT mesh B.S. 126–3·54 lb/sq yd placed 1 in from the surface in the slab bed, and HT mesh 106–7·88 lb/sq yd placed centrally in the walls. All mesh sheets overlapping by 1 ft.

8.2.5 Construction of small pools
Any variation from the rectangle or straight line will affect the material used. Curved shuttering to concrete is expensive and usually beyond the capacity of a small contractor; small units such as bricks are more flexible and familiar. Fibreglass in one piece is now used for very small pools; the designer should acquaint himself with its properties.

8.2.6 Swimming pools
Location.   This must be sunny and protected from wind. Pools need a supply of water and electricity, and enough space to contain the chlorinating plant, which is not easily concealed. Siting should be not too close to trees, because of falling leaves. The immediate surroundings must include sufficient hard surface as durable margins and for sunbathing.

Construction and equipment.   In principle the construction is similar to that of a large pool, but because of the technical complexities such as that of the chlorinating plant, the heating plant, if there is one, cleanliness generally, and safety precautions, it is advisable to take expert advice from the many firms who now specialise in standard construction and equipment. If the pool is tiled

special attention should be given to the expansion joints of the concrete; tiles have been known to buckle in an empty pool twenty years after completion. It is often desirable to depart from a standard design, but the landscape architect must thoroughly understand the constructional principles which are usually established by long experience.

The effect of chlorinating plant.   The water is defertilised and is therefore manifestly artificial. The usual commercial colour of light blue is given by chlorinated rubber enamel, but this can be obtained in alternative tones, such as pure white which tends to emphasise the colour of the water itself. In small private pools the inflow of the circulating water is usually invisible, but in larger pools and lidos this can be a considerable feature as a cascade.

Plate 8.4. Cooling water for industry used as decoration, Sylvania Thorn Colour Television Laboratories, Enfield.

133

Natural heating. It is now possible to cover small pools with polythene, which collects the sun's heat and raises the temperature. In practice it is troublesome to cover and uncover, and looks disagreeable in the landscape.

Wave machines. The imaginative possibilities of the artificial wave have not yet been fully explored, and the breaking of waves upon a sloping plane might still further simulate the sea shore.

8.2.7 Paddling pools
The isolated paddling pool recalls natural conditions and therefore should have a shelving beach of a material, such as smooth pebbles, associated with nature. The floor under the water should be enjoyable to the soles of the feet. It should not be so deep as to cover children's knees. It must be able to be easily cleaned (Fig. 8.8, Plate 8.3).

Facilities for children paddling are becoming a feature in rivers and lakes in urban areas. Care must be given to the problems of scouring, cleanliness, and the safety of those who adventure into deeper water.

8.2.8 Water barriers
The modern water barrier corresponds to the eighteenth century ha-ha, for its purpose is to provide a fence which, though not itself invisible, nevertheless conceals its true purpose. Like a normal so-called unclimbable fence, its intention is not to keep out the determined attack but rather the casual. It should be more than jumping width and too deep for paddling; its water must be fresh under one of the systems described above; it should be decorative in appearance. Its traditional forbear

Plate 8.5. Water barrier between factory and public highway, Cadbury Bros., Moreton, Cheshire.

in England is the cattle moat round a manor house, rather than the impregnable castle moat (Plate 8.5).

8.2.9 Water and industry
Modern industry needs huge volumes of water for cooling. This water may be recirculated together with additional make-up water, or cooled and returned to the river. In either case a considerable structure is called for, and the opportunity of creating a landscape asset should be seized wherever possible. For instance, there is in the central area of St. Helen's, Lancashire, a display of cooling fountains probably unequalled anywhere and yet

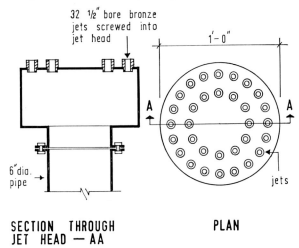

32 ½" bore bronze jets screwed into jet head

1'-0"

6" dia. pipe

A — A

jets

SECTION THROUGH JET HEAD — AA   PLAN

Fig. 8.9. Jet head detail, fountains at Hemel Hempstead.

not recognised for more general application of their spectacular potential.

It must be accepted that there is at present no more efficient way of cooling water than the enclosed vertical cooling tower which creates a forced upward draught. But where circumstances allow, there is opportunity for the cooling lake and fountains (Plate 8.5). The use of tepid water for fish farming or for stocking with tropical fish has still to be explored.

8.2.10 Drainage as a landscape feature
In flat land storm water drainage may often be turned from a scar to an asset. The banks can be remodelled and planted. The drainage authority must be consulted. The main problem is the rise and fall of water with the consequent changing exposure of banks. Weirs to stabilise the height of water are not normally permitted, anything added to impede the flow being unacceptable. There are cases however where flood control measures may permit the use of balancing ponds (see Chapter 4, section 9.9).

8.3 Turbulent water

8.3.1 Fountains in water
Apart from conveying water irrationally and delightfully from one spot to another, fountains can also have

functional purposes, for example to cleanse the surface of the water by spraying; to cool it for industry or to discourage paddling.

Originally fountain design was governed by gravity supply of water. Fountains have never been so popular in England as in the hot countries, probably wholly because of climatic conditions; they should therefore be used with discretion since in wet weather they add to the sense of gloom and dampness. Partly for this reason, the study of fountain design in this country has lagged behind that of the continent; we are almost entirely inexperienced in not only what effect we want, but how to get it. The circulating and pressure pump has overcome difficulties of supply and head, and the appropriate power can be calculated by the manufacturer when he knows the total number of jets and their sizes and the height of throw required.

Location. In principle the jets should come at some time between the spectators and the sun, since the jet of water is most spectacular when it appears luminous. Fountains should not be in too enclosed a space, for climatic reasons. The distance from any public path should be at least three times the height of the jet owing to wind gusts; this may be modified if height can be controlled by valves (Plate 8.6).

Design. Unless the landscape architect is thoroughly experienced in fountain design, he will find it impossible on the drawing board to reach anything other than a first approximation of design. Probably the most technically proficient of all fountains are those at Versailles, where experience was gained continuously over a number of years. The problem in Britain is that the demand for original fountains is small and the expenditure on each is so modest that neither professional nor contractor can afford to spend a great deal of time in

Plate 8.6. Fountain and Lake, Hemel Hempstead (see Fig. 8.9).

experimenting. But it is important that a contingency is included in the estimate for rearranging nozzles on site, adjusting some to new design arrangements, and if necessary changing them. Generally it is possible to fix on paper the placing of nozzles, but it is not possible (without great experience) to foresee the exact arcs and interlacing lines of the jets themselves (Fig. 8.9).

Pipe sizing and power. These requirements vary according to the design, and early advice should be

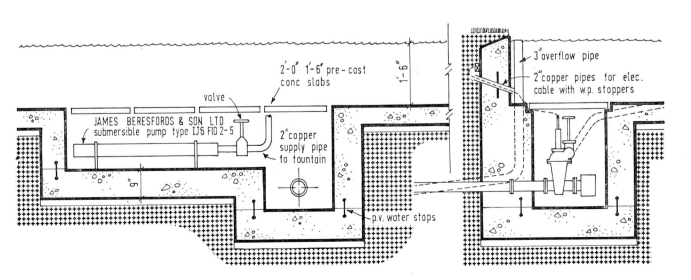

Fig. 8.10. Section through concealed sump housing submersible pump and drain valve.

135

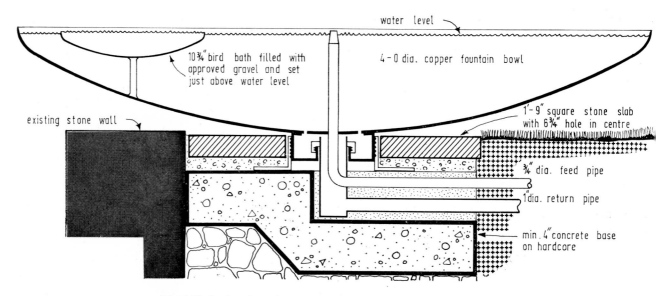

Fig. 8.11. Section through copper basin. Foundation and copper bird bath.

taken from the manufacturers. An example is as follows: Tall fountain, Hemel Hempstead:

(*a*) Number of jets: 32 each $\frac{1}{2}$ in diameter
(*b*) Pipe size: 6 in internal diameter
(*c*) Height of throw: 20 ft
(*d*) Power of pump: $12\frac{1}{2}$ hp
(*e*) Size of pump chamber:
        6 ft 6 in × 6 ft 6 in × 6 ft 6 in
(*f*) Distance of fountain from chamber: 100 ft
(Fig. 8.10)

Precautions must be taken, especially where there are leaves, that the return flow is protected by a wire basket (or something similar) to prevent blockage.

Pipe lines. The simplest method is to run the pipes along a groove or chase in the surface of the bottom of the pool or basin and fill in with a weak mortar. This can easily be removed should repairs be required. Normal materials are copper and iron and where they pass through a concrete wall or bed, a puddle or otherwise waterproofed flange must be fitted and cast in with the concrete wall.

Plastic pipes are also suitable and are sometimes claimed to be invisible, although in practice this is not the case.

Height of nozzles. These should normally be concealed, but when projecting above the surface of the water should do so to the minimum height consistent with efficiency.

8.3.2 Fountains in basins, bowls and birdbaths

Fountain basins traditionally were of rich material such as bronze but owing to the high cost alternative materials

have been employed. The most practical appears to be fibreglass that can emulate the sensitivity of metal at less than half the cost; its detail is determined by what can be moulded. It is beautifully translucent but the bowl must be kept clean, otherwise the result is commonplace. Timber bowls which are used by the Swedes would be very costly in England, which has no such timber tradition. Stone bowls can only be used on a small scale, for example for birdbaths, and the material thus used seems to be debased.

The variations on the fountain and bowl theme are endless. Reinforced concrete is satisfactory, but difficult to bring to a refined finish. The following description of a recently completed bowl at an Oxford college is included as one example only of a multi-purpose use; it had to be of good scale as a memorial bowl of water, contain a fountain, act as a bird bath and to cost no more than

Plate 8.7. Copper Memorial Basin, fountain and submerged bird bath, Oxford (see Fig. 8.11).

Plate 8.8. Trevi Fountain, Rome. Probably the most masterly work in existence combining sculpture, water and rock form. (Designed after Bornini.)

Plate 8.9. Bubble fountains, West Germany Pavilion, Brussels Exhibition, 1958.

£125. The solution of bird and human scale lay in one small bowl floating within a larger bowl; the two bowls are standard copper cylinder ends, the curves being functionally correct and therefore aesthetically agreeable. The jet height is about 9 in, and the falling spray disturbs the surface into wavelets which keep the bird bath fresh. The bird bath is popular. The pipe size to the jet is $\frac{3}{4}$ in diameter and the pump is $\frac{1}{4}$ hp in a concealed chamber 14 ft away. The return pipe is virtually concealed. The bowl can be dismantled from its base. The wind tends to blow wavelets over the edge, and the sound has proved disturbing at night (Fig. 8.11).

8.3.3 Fountains and sculpture

In design it must be decided whether the water or sculpture motif is to predominate. In practice the sculpture should be wholly wet or wholly dry, unless it has been previously planned otherwise as in many compositions on a grand scale e.g. Trevi fountain, Rome (Plate 8.8).

8.3.4 Bubble fountains

These are an interpretation of a natural spring. Their purpose is to keep adjoining material damp; they should be used in conjunction with materials such as the English marbles, which best display their quality when wet. A recent design from Germany is to be seen in Russell Square where the bubble emerges from the hole in the centre of a stone; clearly care must be taken to ensure evenness of distribution, and an agreeable surrounding overflow such as through pebbles (Plate 8.9).

8.3.5 Secret fountains

These were used historically to surprise and wet visitors in a hot dry climate. Their use in England is restricted, but at Ditchley Park in Oxfordshire a concealed line let into pebble paving was able before the war to throw up a water curtain to screen bathers from the house. Technically there is no problem, for provided there is sufficient power the nozzles are self-cleansing; the water should fall back upon the pebble paving and drain away from the pool.

8.3.6 Waterfalls and cascades

The natural cascade. The technique of design does not necessarily mean a copy of nature, but is rather an abstract form. The finest classical rock and water forms are probably Bernini's Trevi fountain in Rome. As yet there is no modern counterpart in the way of abstract design, although there are in England a number of cascades, such as High Force in the County of Durham, that should be a source of inspiration. Unless a cascade is made in a setting where such a feature would have been a reasonable possibility, the 'natural' cascade dependent upon recirculated water can look unconvincing. The following is a description of a natural cascade of rocks as might appear in the highlands of Scotland.

To make a waterfall look natural one must first study nature. What happens? Soft underlying rock is eroded from under a hard stratum. The hard stratum overlap need not be prominent but, unless there is a big rush of water, it must have a pronounced lip. A rounded lip

L

137

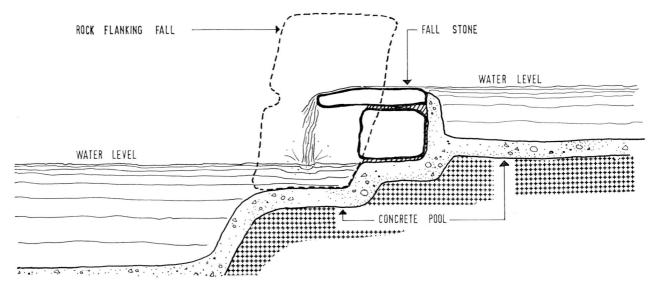

ROCK FLANKING FALL

FALL STONE

WATER LEVEL

WATER LEVEL

CONCRETE POOL

Fig. 8.12. Section of a 'natural cascade'.

means a slobber and no waterfall. Again, the lip must have a face absolutely horizonta (by spirit level) for a short distance back or the water channels into one corner. As a variation a broken fall can be made by means of a series of irregular steps at different levels laid on the same principle as the one broad fall. One need not fear a touch of mortar here and there to correct levels, as these do not show under the water. Lastly the sides of the pool behind must be at least $1\frac{1}{2}$ in above the level of the fall. It is surprising how the water level rises before it goes over the fall (Figs 8.12 and 8.13).

Artificial cascades. The water is normally re-circulated, in restricted supply, and therefore the maximum effect must be obtained by the minimum material. The most difficult problem and probably the most spectacular is to organise the water so that it falls over the lip in a single sheet like glass. This requires great accuracy of finish to the lip. Alternatively the lip may break up the water flow into different forms designed to catch the light. Because the cascade is not inherently an English art, experience in design now made possible by the circulating pump, is very slight. Design should allow for adjustments on site.

8.4 Miscellaneous

8.4.1 Roof gardens

It is not generally realised that water is an excellent permanent material on a flat roof, which is already protected against storm water and which is normally liable to movement of expansion and contraction. The water is a natural insulator. Nevertheless public opinion is such that it has not yet overcome the feeling that it is dangerous to put water overhead, and that it might penetrate the structure. The following is a description of the roof garden at Messrs. Harvey's at Guildford, in use since 1958 (Fig. 8.14, Plate 8.10).

No additional strength was needed for the main building structure. Normal weight asphalt covering was used in double thickness, and all roof garden material was laid direct on this without penetration (an exception being the supports for the wind screens, over which special precautions were taken). The depth of water is 9 to 12 in. One section (planned in relation to what lay in the building underneath) being deeper to accom-

modate larger water lilies. The bottom was laid with loose shingle varying in tone from yellow to purple, suggesting a change from shallow to deep water. Island curbs made from precast standard quadrants, which are not water-proof, were used to keep the island soil permanently

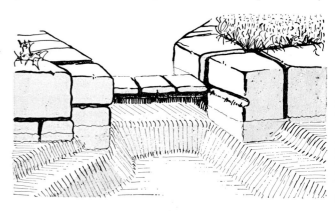

Fig. 8.13. Sketch of a 'natural cascade'.

138

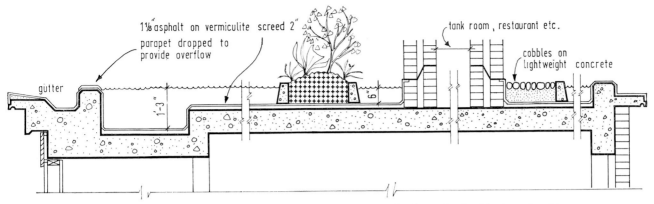

Fig. 8.14. Section through water roof garden (Harvey's, Guildford). Shows details of kerbs and tanking.

saturated for water plants. The water face of curbs was slightly inclined to allow ice to expand. Water circulates from a pump in the adjoining lift and tank structure through fibreglass fountain basins; there is one 'balancing' tank. Loss of water through evaporation is very high since the island soil and plant consumption is added to that of the surface of the water itself. Pipes are plastic, laid diagonally on the surface, and even though confused with pebbles are disagreeably visible. Water contains its right number of fish to maintain biological balance, but these were invisible to curious visitors and a gross of goldfish were added for effect. The garden is closed in winter and the water drained, the fish being accommodated elsewhere in winter quarters. Techniques of illusion include the level of water and rim of the building being so close as to suggest the water passing out of the picture and joining with the sky, and the appearance that the stepping stones are floating on the surface of the water; this is obtained by painting the supports of the stone under the water in black, the whole shape being economically precast and placed direct on the asphalt.

8.4.2 Underwater illumination
There is no technical problem. The essence of this is the capacity of water to become illuminated by refraction, unlike other materials. Fountain jets, for instance, become columns of light from one lamp only. Advice should be sought from manufacturers of standard equipment.

8.5 Biological

8.5.1 Water plants
Whenever water and plant beds adjoin care must be taken that while water can enter the adjoining soil, the soil itself cannot seep back into the clean water. The best method is to build the edging in a porous material such as bricks as for the islands at Hemel Hempstead (Plate 8.2). The depth of the pools for plants such as lilies in the pool itself depend upon choice of plants; here again there must be plant baskets or other protective measures to retain the soil.

8.5.2 Wild life
It is becoming apparent that the designs of modern water schemes are no longer confined to the study of the action of the water alone, but include all the organic happenings related to water the life of which depend upon its

Plate 8.10. Water roof garden, Harvey's, Guildford (see Fig. 8.14).

Plate 8.11. Duck Island, Stevenage.

139

presence. The English lake and tree plantings attracted to themselves automatically all the wild life that is guaranteed by the processes of nature. It is the concern of the landscape architect today to help generate such processes for normally confined areas and it should be remembered that an excess of people tend to drive wild life away.

The following notes are an introduction only:

Water that is filtered but not chlorinated is rich in potential, and quickly promotes its own wild life if encouraged to do so. For instance, a textured bottom will catch seeds and allow them to grow; these in turn provide food for fish; fish require privacy as well as food, and therefore either require further and larger plants or caves and crevices, to give the necessary cover. The cycle of nature that has provided underwater plants and fish now attracts birds and wild fowl. Ducks particularly help to keep water plants in check, although it is as decoration that we most admire them. The traditional island in the public park lake is to meet the needs of ducks; their protection from people is essential.

The following is a description of the duck 'island' at Stevenage New Town (Plate 8.11):

The principal purpose of the 'island' at Stevenage is that of a refuge for the duck. The pond in which it is situated is relatively small, and the water fowl are,

from time to time, worried by dogs and cats. The island can also be filled with brushwood, which serves as a nesting ground during the laying season. It also helps as 'ice-breaker' during the winter time.

The island is formed of 4 in × 4 in × 4 ft wrought heart oak posts, each driven into the bed of the pond. The posts are set at 12 in centres. The construction was set out by means of a full-size wooden template of wire mounted upon a lattice raft which was then floated on to the pond.

The most stately and spectacular of the water fowl is, of course, the swan, which requires not only a large sheet of water but a considerable area of protected island or foreshore where it can nest. A swan at nesting time is dangerous to the public as well as to fellow fowls.

In addition to water fowl the surface of water can be enriched by adjoining bird life and for this there must be plenty of tree and ground cover; probably on an island or a sanctuary. No lake design today can be considered comprehensive in the landscape unless it includes all the features and sanctuaries required by nature for the normally indigenous wild animals. Such wild life can be inspected at close quarters from bridges and so forth, the principles of design being similar to those employed in the modern zoological garden where the tendency is to provide near to natural conditions for animals and cage off the human spectator in elevated viewing positions.

8.6 Exhibitions

8.6.1 Water design for exhibitions

This subject is outside the scope of this handbook. It is dependent for its effect upon the highly keyed spectacle and upon the impact of the moment. To be successful each item is designed specifically for an original purpose. Nevertheless, just as in architecture, the stimulus of ex-

hibition landscape is such that it has a profound effect upon contemporary design and elements of it soon become the vernacular. Many original *ideas* have emerged from international exhibitions over the past few years (Plate 8.12).

8.7 Humphry Repton on optics, illusion and emotion

Although closely allied, these two sciences are separate in so much that illusion is concerned with the mind, and optics with understanding the vehicle, the eye, which may itself create deceptions. Illusion is wholly concerned with emphasising the effect in reality that has already been created in the designer's mind. The actual technique is largely a matter of common observation and thereafter of deduction. For instance, distance in a canal can be increased or decreased by adjusting the apparently parallel lines of perspective. Size can be increased by adjusting architectural details such as the handrails of bridges whose normal height is familiar. Distance can be increased by eliminating boundaries; or making lakes into rivers by concealing the ends; or suggesting mysteries behind islands.

All design is ultimately poetry rather than reality, and it is appropriate to complete this section by quoting at some length from Humphry Repton, who is not only a master of the technical aspect of his subject, but never lets the reader forget that above all he is concerned with art and emotion. (From *Observations on the Theory and Practice of Landscape Gardening*, by H. Repton, Esq. (1803).)

The reflections. The reflection of objects in water are no less dependent on the laws of perspective, or of vision, than the instances already enumerated.

If the water be raised to the level of the ground beyond it, we lose all advantage of reflection from the distant ground, or trees; this is the case with pieces of water near

140

the house, in many places, for all ponds, on high ground, present a constant glare of light from the sky; but the trees beyond can never be reflected on the surface, because the angle of incidence and the angle of reflection are always equal; and the surface of the water will always be a perfect horizontal plane. This I shall farther explain by the following lines (Fig. 8.15).

The spectator at a, in looking on the upper water, will see only sky; because the angle of incidence b, and that of reflection c being equal, the latter passes over the top of the trees d, on the lower ground; but the same spectator a, in looking on the lower water, will see the trees e reflected on its surface, because the line of reflection passes through them, and not over them, as in the first instance.

There are other circumstances belonging to reflection on the surface of water, which deserve attention, and of which the landscape gardener should avail himself in the exercise of his art. Water in motion, whether agitated by wind or by its natural current, produces little or no reflection; but in artificial rivers, the quiet surface doubles every object on its shores, and for this reason, I have frequently found that the surface could be increased in appearance by its sloping banks; not only that which actually concealed part of the water, but also the opposite bank; because it increased the quantity of sky reflected on the surface.

Example. The spectator at A, sees the sky reflected only from B to C, while the opposite bank is round; but if sloped to the shaded line, less of the bank will be reflected in the water, and the quantity of sky seen in the water, will be from B to D; and as the brilliancy of still water depends on the sky reflected on its surface, the quantity of water will be apparently increased.

As properly belonging to this chapter, may be mentioned a curious observation, which occurred in the view of the Thames, from Purley. In the morning, when the sun was in the East, the landscape appeared to consist of wood, water, and distant country, with few artificial accompaniments; but in the evening, when the sun was in

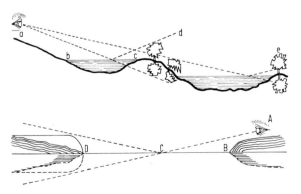

Fig. 8.15. Optical diagram, Humphry Repton.

Plate 8.12. Fountains and Cascades, Horticultural Exhibition, Hamburg, 1963.

the West, objects presented themselves which were in the morning, scarcely visible. In the first instance, the wood was in a solemn repose of shade, the water, reflecting a clear sky, was so brilliantly illuminated, that I could trace the whole course of the river; the dark trees were strongly contrasted by the vivid green of the meadow, and the outline of distant hills was distinctly marked by the brightness of the atmosphere. I could scarcely distinguish any other objects; but these formed a pleasing landscape, from the breadth or contrast of light and shade.

In the evening the scene was changed; dark clouds reflected in the water rendered it almost invisible, the opposite hanging wood presented one glare of rich foliage; not so beautiful in the painter's eye, as when the top of each tree was relieved by small catching lights; but the most prominent features were the buildings, the boat, the path, the pales, and even the distant town of Reading, now strongly gilded by the opposite sun.

On comparing this effect with others, which I have frequently observed since, I draw this conclusion: that certain objects appear best with the sun behind them, and others with the sun full upon them; and it is rather singular, that to the former belong all the *natural* objects, such as woods, trees, lawn, water and distant mountains; while to the latter belong all *artificial* objects, such as houses, bridges, roads, boats, arable fields and distant towns or villages.

The rippling motion. The rippling motion of water is a circumstance to which improvers have seldom paid sufficient attention. They generously aim at a broad expanse and depth, not considering that a narrow shallow

141

brook in motion, over a gravelly bottom, is not less an object of beauty and worthy of imitation; the deep dell, betwixt the boathouse and the bridge, might be rendered very interesting, by bringing a lively brook along the valley; the embouchure of this brook should be laid with gravel, to induce cattle to form themselves in groups at the edge of the water, which is one of the most pleasing circumstances of natural landscape. It sometimes happens near large rivers, that a clear spring bubbles from a fountain, and pours its waters rapidly into the neighbouring stream; this is always considered a delightful object in nature, yet I do not recollect it has ever been imitated by art; it would be very easy to produce it in this instance, by leading water in a channel from the upper pool, and after passing underground by tubes, for a few yards, let it suddenly burst through a bed of sand and stones, and being thus *filtered by ascent,* it would ripple along the valley till it joined the great water. Milton was aware of

this contrast between the river and the rill, where he mentions, amongst the scenery of his Allegro,

'Shallow brooks and rivers wide'.

Bibliography

Although water-design both ancient and modern has been illustrated as much as any other element in landscape design, there appear to be few, if any, works devoted wholly to technique. The information in this chapter has in the main been based on the author's own limited experience. He wishes however to acknowledge in particular the following:

Terrace and Courtyard Gardens (Chapters 19–21), A. D. B. Wood, Collingridge.
Water Gardening, Frances Perry, *Country Life*.

9 General Planting

PATRICIA BOOTH

9.1 General

Plants are the most vulnerable of the materials that a designer can use in the landscape and it is essential that arrangements for future maintenance be made before planting is included in any scheme. It is not enough to have money available, there must be suitable trained labour and supervision to give plants the care they need. When this has been assured, successful planting can be achieved by attention to detail at every stage:

(a) Appreciation of site conditions and the requirements of the client.
(b) Choice of material to suit these conditions and selection of good strong plants.
(c) Thorough preparation of the ground.
(d) Careful planting at suitable times.
(e) Regular aftercare to establish the plants.
(f) Maintenance to maturity in accordance with the intentions of the designer.

Before planning with plants it is helpful to remember that any area which has been cultivated will become colonised by plants suited to its particular conditions, and if left undisturbed the area will eventually reach the climax vegetation associated with that habitat. Therefore, in any habitat, the amount of maintenance will be minimised and the best possible growth ensured when the designer follows the pattern of the vegetation that would grow naturally by using native plants or associated species and cultivars. This principle can be applied to most landscape planting. It is only in special areas under the care of skilled gardeners, that more contrived patterns, using a wider range of plants, may be appropriate.

This chapter outlines general planting methods which can be used on most sites; special techniques for planting and establishment (e.g. hydroseeding, natural regeneration) may have to be devised for use in difficult conditions. The same principles of plant selection and the use of ecological studies as a basis for design apply to any planting problem.

9.2 Planting design

9.2.1 Introduction
From the very wide range of plants that will grow in the British Isles it should be possible to find a species to suit any design requirement. Site conditions will limit the choice considerably and must be the main factor in plant selection for landscape work. Then from the material that can grow on the site the designer has to choose species which will give the effect required. This choice may be further limited by the availability of the plants in the numbers and sizes required and at a reasonable cost.

9.2.2 Influence of site conditions on choice of plants and planting

Climate. *Wind*—In very windy situations special attention should be paid to site preparation, particularly on shallow soils, since it is essential that plants should quickly obtain a good roothold. It is also important to plant young specimens, especially of conifers, to avoid root damage. Plants should be spaced closer than normal to give mutual protection and some form of shelter may be advisable to assist establishment, e.g. coir matting or wind-permeable fencing. Once quick growing species have become established to provide windbreaks, less wind-tolerant species can be introduced in the shelter provided. In seaside areas winds may be salt laden and plants should be chosen from salt-resistant varieties.

Frost—Plants are very variable in their resistance to frost; this resistance also varies with the age of the plant. Existing vegetation is the best guide for new planting and the main structure of any planting scheme should be formed from plants known to be hardy on the site. Plants of doubtful hardiness should not be chosen unless particularly required, and then only in small numbers to avoid large gaps occurring after a hard winter.

Shade—This may vary from complete lack of sunlight at all times to shade at certain times of the day or seasons of the year. The plants that can be grown will also depend on other associated factors that may limit growth. Lack of water is likely to be a problem in most shady places and larger plants may affect plants growing in their shade by the competition of their roots for nutrients and moisture and by water drip from their branches. Given sufficient moisture most evergreens and plants with green leaves except conifers will grow in shade; plants with grey or golden leaves require plenty of light if they are to thrive. Variegated plants are often chosen to lighten dark areas; those with silver variegations will usually do better than golden varieties. Flowering plants which are shade tolerant tend to produce more foliage and fewer flowers when light is restricted.

Atmospheric pollution—Industrial atmospheric pollution may affect plants in several ways; it can restrict the light available, form choking deposits on the leaves, deposit detrimental substances on the soil, or weaken the plant with poisonous gases. Plants vary in their resistance to different sorts of pollution, and the source and type of pollution will give some guide to the choice of plants. Most conifers and evergreens are intolerant of pollution (there are exceptions); plants which are in leaf only for a short period of the year are usually resistant. In any area it is wise to plant a mixture of species since it is difficult to be sure which will survive best in any particular conditions.

Soils   (see also Chapter 10—Grass, section on soils). Soils may be loosely grouped according to the dominant constituent which affects their characteristics and the type of plants which will grow on them. Plants will be further limited according to the degree of alkalinity or acidity and to the amount of water available, and this may outweigh other considerations in excessively wet

Plate 9.1. Ground cover planting of mixed evergreens and greys. Leaf form and texture are contrasted as well. Designed by Peter Youngman, P.P.I.L.A.

or dry places. The reaction of a soil may be expressed using a scale measured by the hydrogen ion concentration; the numbers on this scale are called pH. A soil at pH 7·0 is neutral and will suit most plants, less than pH 6·0 is acid, and more than pH 7·5 alkaline (calcareous). While calcifuge plants will grow on a soil of pH 4·0–6·0, this pH value will not suit other plants and where it is wished to grow these, especially in heavy clay, an application of lime will be beneficial.

Loams—These are the ideal soil for most plants and provide few problems in choice of plants or cultivation.

Sandy soils—If these have a high proportion of relatively large particles they may be very liable to drought since they cannot retain water. It is easy to establish plants in sandy soil provided that sufficient water and nutrients are made available; organic manures are preferable since these will retain moisture as well as provide plant foods. Sandy soils should not be left bare for any length of time because they are liable to erosion, nutrients are quickly leached out and weeds soon become established. When acceptable it is better to plant small plants, preferably out of pots, or to sow seeds *in situ* since these will become established more quickly.

Clay soils—These contain a high proportion of very small particles which retain moisture and nutrients and impede water movement. They are very sticky when wet and set very hard when dry, making cultivation difficult. Heavy soils should not be worked when wet to avoid compaction by treading or machinery. Clay is best cultivated roughly in autumn and left to be broken down by frost action before planting in spring. Drainage is important otherwise root systems will not be able to penetrate because of the lack of air. Clay soils are rich in nutrients and suitable plants will grow vigorously when care is taken with the initial cultivations.

Chalk soils—Such soils are those where an excess of calcium carbonate gives a soil-character which outweighs the effect of texture. They are usually light shallow loams and are liable to drought because of the porous nature of the underlying chalk. Before planting the subsoil should be broken up to allow roots to penetrate and organic matter should be added to the top soil to help retain moisture. Chalk soils tend to puff up in frosty weather so that new plantings may be forced out of the ground and will need treading-in. It is not advisable to try to acidify chalky soil; the effect of attempts to do this tend to be very temporary. Plants should be chosen from those that will thrive in an alkaline soil.

Peat soils—These have a high proportion of organic matter and consequently a high water-holding capacity. Alkaline peats make excellent soils once they have been drained, but acid peat occurs in regions of higher rainfall, is difficult to drain and will support only a limited range of plants.

Protection from people and animals. Young plants in rural areas will require protection from livestock and wild animals, mainly rabbits (see Chapter 10—Tree Planting).

In urban areas domestic animals may be a nuisance but people are likely to do the most damage, by trespass or deliberate vandalism. Losses in newly planted areas are decreased when they are surrounded by chestnut paling until the plants are established; where this is not feasible it is essential that an area should be completely planted-up as thickly as possible, before the public is allowed near it. Planting in slightly raised beds or in containers helps to prevent trespass, and larger-sized plants tend to deter vandals. Plants with built-in deterrents of thorns or prickles are useful to protect more vulnerable species, but they should not be used where they might catch passers-by or in play areas for children. Plants with single stems should be avoided in preference to those which produce several shoots from below ground level and quickly regenerate when broken down.

9.2.3 Choice of plants to suit design requirements

To choose exactly the right plant for a given design it is necessary to be clear about the role it is to play, so that a species can be selected which will not only fulfil its function but will express the intentions of the designer. This involves a detailed knowledge of the visual characteristics of a plant and of how these change through the seasons and through its life. Basically, plants should be chosen to grow naturally into the mass and disposition required, without constant pruning or training. The mass may be achieved by using a single plant or more often groups of the same species which will grow together to form larger masses similar in outline to the single plant. Planting in groups not only helps to unify a design but there is evidence that many plants grow better in association. After defining the mass required, the forms composing it can be considered and the designer's idea amplified by choosing plants of suitable colour and texture.

Form—This is determined by the way in which the main stems or branches grow. This is easier to see in winter but it is also expressed by the internal shadows of summer foliage or of evergreens. It is this form which gives a plant its character and personality. Too many different forms in one group of plants can give a very restless effect. It is usually preferable to limit variety and to use very strong forms as focal points. It is especially important to choose suitable forms for planting in restricted areas, so that the character of a spreading or arching plant, for example, is not later destroyed by the need for drastic pruning.

Plate 9.2. The speckled stems of a grove of silver birch make a point of interest in an otherwise brown winter landscape.

Colour of foliage—This is more important than flowers or fruits which are usually only of interest during a comparatively short period of the year. In the soft light of the British countryside the more subdued colours seen against a background of restful greens are most appropriate. In smaller areas associated with buildings strong colours can be used more successfully to provide eye-catching accents.

Texture—This is the surface quality of a material and is less predictable than other qualities in plants. In the landscape texture is, at near view, the result of the detailed structure of the plant growth, including the size, spacing, disposition, grouping and attitude of leaves and twigs. At greater distances texture depends on whole plants and masses of plants. The textural pattern is made by the play of light and shade on the plant mass. Glossy leaves and small leaves tend to give a finer texture because light reflections are more broken up. Large leaves appear coarse in near view and this is accentuated when the leaves are widely spaced. Uniformity of texture will tie together any planting and emphasis of texture should be related to emphasis on the plan. Texture is very closely related to scale; wrong textures can easily disturb the apparent size of an area. Texture is especially important in choosing plants for backgrounds, for example, close matt textures make the best foil for sculpture or for specimen plants.

Time—Plants are unlike other basic materials of landscape design in that they continually change with the seasons and through the years, and it may be some time

145

before they reach a degree of development that matches the designer's vision of maturity. Only annuals and bedding plants reach their full potential in one season, other plants may require years in which to mature. Therefore it is important to consider the length of time that the site can be guaranteed to the plant. In most schemes, plants will be selected from quick-growing species for early maturity, together with slower-growing species that will not give much effect for several years. Many quick-growing plants are short lived, so only a temporary scheme should be based entirely on such species. Slower growing plants should always be included, either to take over from short-lived species after some years or to form the backbone of new planting. It is very expensive to buy slow-growing plants in large sizes but comparatively easy to move them on a site that is being redeveloped.

Planting near buildings—Growing conditions near buildings vary greatly according to the aspect and plants must be chosen to suit the amount of light and moisture available. Shrubs and herbaceous perennials may be planted as close to buildings as desired. Climbers may be used where adequate support can be provided; self-clinging climbers should be used only where the fabric of the building does not need painting and is suitably strong. Access should be provided to the outside of the building for window-cleaning and other maintenance; either borders should be narrow enough to reach over or a small service path must be provided between the planting and the building.

The distance at which trees may be planted from buildings will depend on a number of factors, e.g. type of subsoil, climate of the area, foundations of the building. Poplars and other quick-growing trees should not be used. Slow-growing trees will not normally harm foundations when planted at such a distance from a building that they have room to grow to their natural size; problems may develop when trees are planted on shrinkable clays in the drier parts of England, unless the building has suitably constructed foundations.

9.3 Plant material

9.3.1 Sources of plants

Plants may be obtained from a trade nursery or sometimes from private nurseries such as those maintained by a new town or a parks department. The advantages of a private nursery are that the plants are probably grown with soil and climatic conditions similar to those on the site to be planted and thus should establish themselves quickly after transplantation. It also permits plants to be available when required, thus decreasing the time that they are out of the ground. Furthermore, given regular root pruning in the nursery, trees and shrubs may be grown on to sizes not normally available from trade sources. The disadvantages of private nursery plants are that unless requirements can be specified well in advance, the range of plants available from such a source may be very limited, often being restricted to plants which are easily propagated or of limited landscape value.

To buy plants from trade sources means that it is usually possible to obtain the exact species required but it has the disadvantage that these may be delivered to suit the nursery's lifting programme rather than the planner's planting scheme, and it may be difficult to obtain plants at short notice. Also, the plants may be grown under soil and climatic conditions very different from those of the area for which they are intended. Plants grown in a light soil or in a warm part of the country may suffer a setback when moved to a heavy soil or a cold area; this must be considered when choosing plants from a trade source. Similarly, imported plants will take time to adjust themselves to our climate and should be grown on for at least one year under skilled care in a nursery before being used for permanent planting.

On large-scale developments lasting several years a temporary nursery should be established on part of the site where, by planning ahead, the required plants can be purchased and grown-on until their permanent positions are ready. In this way larger plants can be provided, for moving quickly and with the minimum of disturbance, to suit the progress of the work. They will also have adapted themselves to the site conditions and should rapidly establish themselves with the minimum of care. Such a nursery must be fenced and rabbit-proofed and skilled maintenance must be assured.

9.3.2 Buying plants

Plants bought for permanent planting as part of a landscape scheme should comply with the following requirements.

General. The plants should be true to name and each plant or bundle should be legibly labelled. Some plants grown from seed do not come true and may show a wide range of seedling variation. This may be acceptable for certain purposes, but a nursery should state if plants normally propagated vegetatively, have been grown from seed; if grafted or budded, this should be stated and the name of the root stock supplied on request.

The root systems should be suitable for successful transplantation. Where necessary, the root-ball should be preserved by supporting it with hessian or other suitable material.

The plants should be substantially free from pest and disease, and should be physically undamaged. Their roots should not have been exposed to adverse conditions (e.g.

Plate 9.3. The purple and grey of *Stachys! anata* backed by a group of *Macleaya cordata* with coral flower plumes.

Plate 9.4. *Gunnera manicata*. Great green plates six feet in diameter contrasting with the strong vertical emphasis of the weeping willow.

drying winds, frost) before delivery. The root-ball should be free from pernicious weeds.

The plants should be carefully packed to avoid heating or drying during transit.

Quality. The quality and condition of a plant is more important than its actual size.

Trees—These should have a sturdy, reasonably straight stem and, according to the species and intended use, either have a well-balanced branching head or a well-defined straight and upright central leader with the branches growing from the stem in reasonable symmetry.

Open-ground shrubs—Such shrubs should have been transplanted and, according to species, cut back or trimmed to encourage bushiness. Shrubs offered for hedges may have been slacked or undercut, instead of transplanted.

Roses—These should be growing on suitable stocks, and should have had one season's growth after budding.

Conifers—Most species should be well-furnished evenly to the ground on all sides; there are exceptions, e.g. *Cedrus*. A single central leader is desirable for most conifers unless required for hedging or other special purposes.

Pot-grown plants—These should be well established in their pots and may have been cut back or trimmed to encourage bushiness. Generally they should not have been more than two years in their final pot; otherwise they may have become root-bound. Plants in containers (other than flower pots) may not have been established in

them; plants are often lifted during the dormant season and placed in individual containers so that they may be transplanted easily at any time of the year.

Herbaceous plants—These should have been grown for at least one season after transplantation with room to develop as individual plants.

9.3.3 Plant specification

The following information is needed by the nursery so that it may supply the correct material for a planting scheme (see also Chapter 2—Practice, in which section 2.4 deals with specifications, etc.).

Name of plant. This should include the generic and specific names and supplementary botanical category such as varietas (variety), or the name of the cultivar (variety) where this applies (following the *International*

Plate 9.5. *Hypericum* is an ideal ground cover plant in deep shade, here making a pattern through the coursing of stone paving slabs.

147

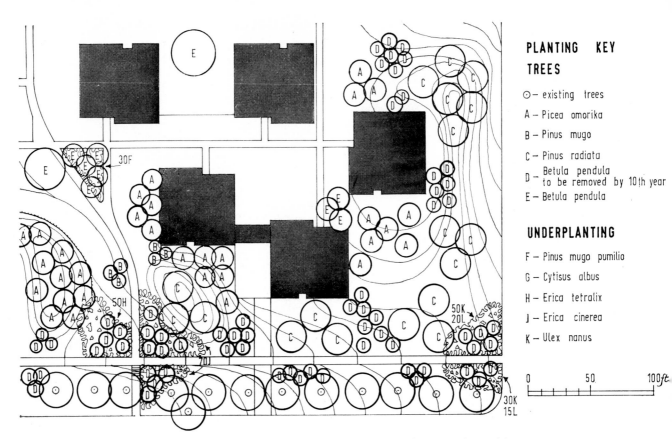

Fig. 9.1. A planting plan showing the use of a key to refer to planting positions.

Code of Nomenclature for Cultivated Plants), e.g. *Cotoneaster salicifolius floccosus, Berberis thunbergii* 'Atropurpurea'.

In practice plants are often referred to by their common names, but in many cases one common name covers several species and the Latin name must be quoted to the supplier to ensure that the correct plant is obtained and to avoid disputes. (This does not apply to forest transplants.)

Size.   *Trees*—Size and form should be quoted when ordering trees. Normal nursery stock will include the forms shown in Fig. 9.5:

RECOMMENDED SIZES

Form	Height from ground level to lowest branch	Diameter of stem measured between 2 and 3 ft from ground
Bush	1 ft 0 in–2 ft 6 in	—
Half standard	3 ft 6 in–4 ft 6 in	minimum ¾ in
Three-quarter standard	4 ft 9 in–5 ft 3 in	minimum ¾ in
Standard	5 ft 6 in–6 ft 0 in	minimum ¾ in
Tall standard	6 ft 3 in–7 ft 0 in	minimum 1 in
Weeping standard	minimum 5 ft 6in	minimum ¾ in

Shrubs, including conifers—For general planting the sizes requested should be those which fall within the range of normal nursery stock (a list of recommended sizes for many common shrubs, including roses, is included in the *British Standard Specification for Nursery Stock*, B.S. 3936). Plants of these sizes should transplant easily and grow away without special care. Very small sizes and rooted cuttings are not recommended for general planting because they give no immediate effect and are more likely to be damaged.

Low growing shrubs—Up to 24 in; specify the height in inches usually in 3 in series (6–9 in, 12–15 in, etc.).

Medium shrubs—Over 24 in (2 ft); specify height in feet in a 6 in series (2–2½ ft, 2½–3 ft, etc.).

Strong growing shrubs—Over 3 ft; specify height in feet in 1 ft series (3–4 ft, 4–5 ft, etc.).

Spreading shrubs—Give the average diameter in addition to or in place of the height.

Pot-grown plants—In addition to height or spread, state the diameter of the pot in which the plant is to be supplied (3, 4, 5, etc. inches).

148

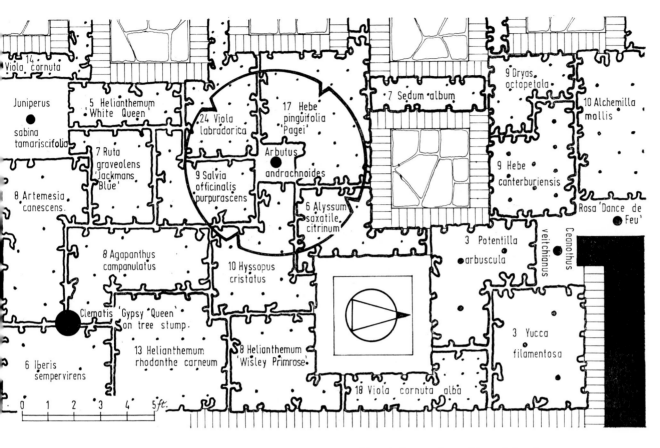

Fig. 9.2. A planting plan showing plant names and quantities of plants to be used in each location.

9.3.4 Planting plans

Planting plans are usually required to serve several different purposes and time will be saved when a single plan can be prepared with all these uses in mind. These plans should meet the following points:

(*a*) Be easily understood by the client who may wish to approve the choice of plants.

(*b*) Be accurate enough to prepare a detailed schedule of plants.

(*c*) Be suitable as working drawings for the planting foreman.

(*d*) Be suitable for inclusion in the maintenance schedule.

The planting plans should show the name of each plant or group of plants, the number of plants in each group and the distance between plants within a group. Each planting area should have a key letter or name, and the groups within that area should be numbered for easy reference. These references should be included on the plant schedule and may be put on the plant labels to assist in placing plants. It is much simpler to consult or work from a plan where the plant name appears in full at the position the plant is to occupy, but sometimes space on the plan does not permit this and symbols have to be used. In the latter case an explanatory key to the symbols must be given (see Figs. 9.1 and 9.2). Planting areas which can be viewed only from one direction, e.g. next to a building, should be so drawn and labelled that the plan can be read from that particular direction. Any alterations in position or in the substitution of plants at the time of planting, should be noted on the planting plan, to help in identifying plants later; this is particularly important in cases where plants die and have to be replaced. It is also necessary to have an accurate record of actual plantings to include in the maintenance schedule.

Scale of planting plans

For small areas and intricate planting: $\frac{1}{4}$ in to 1 ft.

Shrub borders and less detailed planting: $\frac{1}{8}$ in to 1 ft.

Tree groups and broad planting areas: 1/16, 1/500 etc. It is helpful, both in planning and in laying-out plants on the site, to have the planting areas on a plan covered with a grid in suitably sized squares e.g. 1 yard, 5 yards, 10 yards, 500 feet etc.

Planting Distances—Planting distances will depend on the vigour and size of the plant and the money available.

149

Plant	Distance apart (in)	Number of plants per square yard	Plant	Distance apart (in)	Number of plants per square yard
Shrubs—dwarf and slow-growing	18–24	2–4	Small herbaceous and ground cover	8–12	9–25
medium	36–48	1	Bulbs—		
vigorous	60–72	2–3 sq yd per plant	large, e.g. Narcissus	8–12	9–25
Bush roses	18–24	3–4	small, e.g. Crocus	6–8	25–36
			Hedging—		
Herbaceous perennials			Privet, Quickthorn	9–18	—
vigorous	24–48	1–3	Beech, Hornbeam	12–24	—
average	12–18	4–9	Yew, Holly	18–30	—

9.4 Ground preparation

9.4.1 General

The initial preparation of planting areas should aim to produce soil in its best physical condition and at the same time to improve its chemical condition by incorporating manures and fertilisers. Cultivations should provide a good root-run for plants without destroying the texture of the soil, and while maintaining sufficient consolidation for good anchorage. Water should be able to move freely and to be retained in sufficient quantity.

9.4.2 Cultivation

The physical preparation of the ground may be done by hand or mechanically, whichever is the more economical for the scale of operations. Hand cultivation consists in digging or forking and raking. Mechanical cultivation may include ploughing, disking, or the use of various modern cultivating machines. Areas which have been untouched by building operations can be prepared for planting by cultivation to a depth of 9 in to break up the topsoil; grass and annual weeds are turned under and large stones and rubbish removed. When the subsoil forms a hard or impermeable layer, this should be broken up to a further depth of 9 in, but without mixing the two layers.

Areas that have been stripped of topsoil and compacted (by heavy machinery or building materials) must be thoroughly broken up and any builders' rubbish removed, after the new formation level has been attained. The required depth of topsoil can then be spread, care being taken not to over-consolidate it during spreading.

9.4.3 Weed clearance

It is much easier to destroy weeds while the ground is still bare of plants, and the amount of future maintenance is greatly decreased when the soil is substantially free from perennial weeds and weed seeds before planting is done. Annual weeds can be dealt with by periodic cultivation (hoes, mechanical cultivators) preferably throughout the summer before planting begins. This will ensure that seedlings are killed and prevented from reseeding.

Perennial weeds are a bigger problem since cultivation will spread the roots and thus propagate rather than destroy them. On small areas the roots can be dug out by hand and burned. On larger areas it is easier to apply a suitable weedkiller to kill perennial weeds before any cultivation is done. The actual weedkiller used will depend on the weeds present. For deep-rooted perennials (e.g. docks) a translocated herbicide applied to the leaves will probably be most suitable and will not persist in the soil. Progress in chemical weed control is now very rapid and it would be wise to obtain advice on specific weed problems as they arise. In all cases it is essential that the directions of the manufacturer of a weedkiller should be followed in detail and that all precautions are observed.

9.4.4 Drainage

Planting areas will not normally require special drainage since plants will be chosen which suit the existing circumstances. It may, however, be necessary to provide special drainage in certain cases, particularly on heavy soils or where the natural drainage has been impeded by building operations or landshaping. Drains will be required for individual tree pits in clay subsoil; planting areas excavated into an area of clay 'cut' in which water will be trapped; and areas where the ground water table lies within 2 feet of the surface. Drains should be laid after ground shaping has been completed but before topsoil is spread or planting done (see also Chapter 4—Earthworks, especially section 4.9 on drainage).

9.4.5 Topsoil

The topsoil is the surface layer; it is usually darker and greyer than the subsoil and contains organic matter intimately mixed with the mineral particles. A minimum depth of 9 in of topsoil is needed for general planting so that plants can be planted with all their roots in this layer. Large plants will require a greater depth of topsoil or must be planted in individual holes deep and wide enough to contain enough topsoil for successful establishment.

This means a hole 24 in × 24 in × 18 in deep for an average shrub. A greater depth of topsoil should be allowed where the subsoil is unfavourable. To make planting areas more effective it is often desirable that the final level should stand 6–9 in above the adjoining areas. This may be accomplished either by introducing subsoil fill underneath the topsoil, or by adding more soil to the existing topsoil. On sites where regrading is necessary or on areas used for constructional purposes, stock-piling building materials or parking machinery, topsoil should have been stripped off and stock-piled to conserve it. Where soil has been stored for more than three years its mechanical condition may have deteriorated. For small areas this can be corrected by thoroughly rotovating the topsoil after spreading. For larger quantities, passing the topsoil through a high capacity shredder before respreading may be considered.

Importation of topsoil

Where there is insufficient topsoil on a site it may have to be imported, usually from grassland or cultivated areas that are being cleared for road building or industry. Imported topsoil should be free from large stones and rubbish, and it is particularly necessary that it be free from pernicious weeds (e.g. couch grass, ground elder). When the soil is needed for growing a particular class of plants it may be necessary to specify texture requirements, e.g. light, medium or heavy, and lime content. Topsoil which contains chalk should not be imported where plants which require an acid soil are to be grown, e.g. rhododendrons.

When specifying topsoil for a particular purpose the *British Standard Specification for Top Soil* (B.S. 3882) may be useful.

9.4.6 Fertilisers and manures (see also Chapter 10—Grass especially sections 10.5.2 and 10.5.3)

Under natural conditions various biological cycles of chemical elements ensure that the soil is not impoverished, but where plants are cultivated in restricted spaces with a limited root run and under unnatural conditions nutrients must be added at regular intervals. Manures must also be added to remedy any deficiencies in the soil before new planting is undertaken. Plants require sixteen or more chemical elements, most of which have to be obtained from the soil. In practice most elements are present in sufficient amounts, apart from nitrogen, potash and phosphorus (as phosphates) which are needed in large quantities. These nutrients can be supplied as organic manures (of animal or plant origin) or as inorganic fertilisers.

Bulky organic manures—These mostly supply several nutrients in comparatively low concentrations, but they are valuable also for their beneficial effects on the physical properties of the soil. They improve soil structure, aera-

Plate 9.6. The leaf of the *Acanthus* has been admired since the Greeks used it in the motif of the capital to the Corinthian column.

tion and water-holding capacity and promote microbial activity.

Concentrated organic manures—Because they supply nutrients gradually over a long period they are very useful.

Inorganic fertilisers—These supply certain plant foods in concentrated form and are most useful for application to soils where the humus content is already reasonably high.

Lime—This may be used to modify the pH value of a soil to make it less acid, or to improve the physical condition of clay soils. While it is easy to apply lime to a soil, it is virtually impossible to remove it and its presence may severely limit the choice of plants (see section 9.2.2 soils).

Peat—This supplies nitrogen in low concentration but is valued as organic matter to help retain moisture on light soils or to improve the texture of heavy soils.

151

79.4. Fertilisers and manures for planting areas (use chemical analysis to determine exact rate of application)

Material	Notes	Rate of Application	Time and method of application
BULKY ORGANIC MANURES	All bulky organics vary in composition according to source. Obtain analysis before ordering		Mix with top soil during preliminary cultivation or apply as top dressing and lightly fork in during early spring
Farmyard manure	Should be well rotted	1 cu yd to 25 sq yd	
Poultry manure	Store before use	4 oz per sq yd	
Sewage sludge, dried		1 cu yd to 50 sq yd	
Sewage sludge, activated		4 oz per sq yd	
Spent mushroom beds	Contains lime and is not suitable for plants needing acid soil	1 cu yd to 50 sq yd	
CONCENTRATED ORGANIC MANURES			
Bone meal Hoof and horn meal	The coarser the texture the more slowly the nutrients become available	2–4 oz per sq yd	Spread on surface after cultivation and rake in
Dried blood	Expensive, but quick acting and safe. Good for evergreens	2–4 oz per sq yd	Spread on surface after cultivation and rake in
LIME	Do not apply lime within 3 weeks of manuring as it reacts with many fertilizers and manures		
Carbonate of lime	Safe and slow in action	4–8 oz per sq yd	Thoroughly work into top 3–4 in soil during initial cultivation
Hydrated lime	Pure and fine: comparatively expensive	4–8 oz per sq yd	
PEAT			
Coarse sedge peat	High water holding capacity	4–6 lb per sq yd	Soak very dry soil before adding peat. Mix with topsoil at time of planting or use as a mulch after

9.5 Planting and establishment of plants

Type of Plant	Main Planting Season
Deciduous trees and shrubs; roses	End of October–end of March
Evergreen shrubs and conifers	End of September–early May
Herbaceous perennials	End of September–end of April
Alpines and rock plants	End of August–end of October or early March–end of April
Pot-grown plants and plants in containers	Throughout the year preferably September–early May
Water lilies and marginal aquatics	Mid-March–early June
Narcissus and crocus	Early September–October

9.5.1 Time to plant

Planting should normally be done within the recommended months of the year. When this is so, the specification may call upon a contractor to replace, free of charge, any plants which did not survive the first growing season after planting. Planting should not be done when the ground is wet or waterlogged or during periods of drought or frost. As a general rule planting is better done during the autumn on light soils and in drier areas, while spring planting is better on heavy soils and in colder and wetter areas. Whenever possible planting should be arranged so that all the plants in one layout or in one section of a layout, are put in at the same time.

9.5.2 Protection of plants while out of the ground

It is essential that roots should not be left exposed to

frost or to drying winds at any stage of transplantation. When it is necessary for plants to be left out of the ground the roots should be covered with damp sacking or other protective material. Trees and shrubs may be sprayed before lifting, using a proprietary wax or latex preparation to reduce transpiration. This treatment is particularly useful when moving evergreens and will assist towards their successful establishment. Plants that arrive and cannot be planted immediately can be stored for a short period in their packages, in a frost-free place. For prolonged storage during hard frost the packaging and ties should be loosened to admit air. When the ground is not hard frozen it is best to heel-in plants until they can be put into permanent positions. An open trench deep enough to hold the roots should be made and the plants placed in it so that the tops lay at an angle of about 45°; the trench is then filled-in and the soil trodden firmly over the roots.

Large bundles of plants should be opened before heeling-in so that all the roots are in contact with soil. It is important to make sure that all plants can be identified and that labels are not buried. Heeled-in plants should be watered when the soil is dry. It may be convenient to heel-in stock in several places near final planting positions. When needed for planting, the plants should be carefully lifted after removing the covering soil.

9.5.3 Planting, general

The ground should be prepared for planting and individual pits dug for trees and large shrubs before the plants arrive on the site, so that they will be out of the ground for as short a time as possible. Positions for groups of plants should be marked-out and labelled. Where a large area is to be planted, the deliveries should be phased to avoid the need to heel-in plants which cannot be dealt with immediately. Trees and large shrubs should be planted before ground cover, and bulbs last of all to avoid disturbance. All plants in one group or section should be set out before planting is begun to ensure correct placing and distribution, but more material than can be planted within a short time should not be set out. After an area of planting has been completed the surface soil should be lightly pricked over with a fork to prevent a hard crust forming and to leave the ground level and tidy.

Depth of planting. Most plants must be planted at such a depth that the final soil level will be where it was when the plant was previously growing in the nursery. This is particularly important on heavy soils where deep planting can kill susceptible plants. While it is safe to comply with this general rule there are certain exceptions; some plants will grow better when planted more deeply than in the nursery, e.g. heathers, lavenders, clematis, clumpy shrubs.

Plate 9.7. The mirrored plane of still water makes an ideal background for the strong architectural shapes of marginal and deep-water plants.

Planting bare-rooted plants. Most common nursery stock transplants readily, and can be lifted without soil attached to the roots for ease of packing and transport. A hole large enough to take all the roots without twisting or bending is dug with trowel or spade; broken or damaged roots are cut off and the plant is placed in the hole so that the roots are well spread and the plant is at the correct depth. Loose topsoil is carefully worked between the roots, each layer being firmed so that the roots are fixed and there are no air pockets. When the soil is dry, the hole should be filled with water after the plant has been set and the hole partially filled with soil. The water will settle the soil around the roots and back-filling can be completed after the water has drained away. Firm planting is essential, but care must be taken on heavy and wet soils that the ground is not over compacted and the soil structure destroyed (see Fig. 9.3).

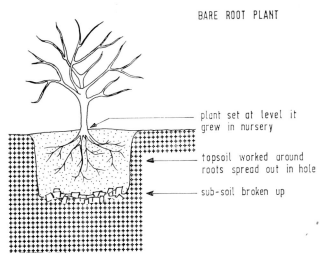

BARE ROOT PLANT

plant set at level it grew in nursery

topsoil worked around roots spread out in hole

sub-soil broken up

Fig. 9.3. Diagram showing points to watch in planting out a bare root plant.

Planting root-balled shrubs. Plants, such as conifers and rhododendrons, which make a dense mass of fibrous roots, giving a root-ball, are lifted with the soil attached and the root-ball is wrapped in sacking or other protective material, to hold it intact and to prevent damage and drying-out during transit. Such plants should always be handled by the root-ball and not by the top, to avoid damaging evergreen foliage and to prevent strain on the plant. The root-ball should be soaked in water on arrival without removing the sacking. The plant is then put in a prepared hole at the correct depth, ties holding the sacking cut and any sacking that is easily removable cut away. Any material left under the root-ball will quickly rot away; attempts to remove it are likely to damage the roots. When staking is necessary the stake should be driven into the ground at an angle (to avoid piercing the root-ball) with its head facing into the prevailing wind, otherwise guy wires may be used (see Fig. 9.4).

Planting pot-grown plants. Plants which do not transplant easily are grown in pots so that they can be moved with the root system intact. Small plants such as alpines are grown in pots for ease of handling. Other stock may be grown in pots or cans so that they can be moved at any time of the year or to make it easier to transplant material that is larger than the normal nursery stock. All pot-grown plants should be carried by the pot itself and not by holding the plant. The soil in the pot must be well moistened before planting. The plant should be knocked out of the pot, the young roots lightly loosened, without disturbing the main soil-ball, and placed in the prepared hole in the normal way. When a plant has become pot-bound and the roots protrude through the bottom hole it is best to break the pot away to avoid damaging the roots.

Plate 9.8. The correct choice of plants in a public area is difficult; doubly so when they are to be grown in pots. The well-filled concrete containers which stood on the terrace at the Festival Hall.

Planting climbers. Climbers and wall shrubs should be planted not less than 6 in from walls or fences. Stakes, wires, etc., for training the shrubs should be in a position before planting is done so that the shoots can be immediately tied in position to avoid damage.

Planting bulbs in grass. Narcissus and crocus are the most commonly used bulbs for naturalising in grass but many others may be grown successfully, particularly under trees where grass does not grow so strongly. Bulbs should be planted only where their foliage can be left to die down naturally and grass cutting can be postponed until the leaves are dead.

Narcissus—Bulbs with a smooth skin and which are firm when lightly pressed with the thumb should be chosen. 'Rounds' and 'small rounds' are suitable sizes for naturalising. Bulbs should be planted 4 in deep, either by using a trowel or a special tool to make individual holes, or by lifting the turf over the area to be planted, setting the bulbs and then replacing the turf. A bulb must be placed so that its base is in contact with soil and there is no air-pocket underneath. Bone flour at the rate of 2 oz per sq yd should be applied before planting and then yearly each February. Access to bulb-planted areas must be prohibited from early December when the shoots begin to emerge, and grass-mowing must be postponed until the bulb leaves are dead, some time in June.

Crocus—Bulbs with a circumference of 7 cm are suitable for naturalising. Planting is done by lifting the turf to a depth of 4 in, applying bone flour (2 oz per sq yd), setting the bulbs and replacing the turf.

9.5.4 Out-of-season planting
On landscape projects where several different contracts (building, road works, etc.) are involved, it is often im-

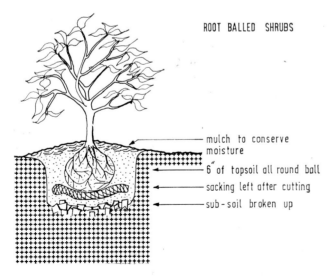

ROOT BALLED SHRUBS

— mulch to conserve moisture

— 6″ of topsoil all round ball

— sacking left after cutting

— sub-soil broken up

Fig. 9.4. Diagram showing the planting out of a root-balled shrub.

possible to plant during the normal season and it may be desirable to plant out of season in order to complete a contract by a fixed date. Out-of-season planting should not be considered unless there is an adequate water supply and maintenance staff is available to work as and when required. Given these essentials, suitable weather and soil conditions are more important than the time of year, and many plants can be moved at any time in the year provided that care be taken.

Plants in pots or cans and plants with fibrous root-balls can be moved fairly easily, but plants with coarse straggly roots should not be moved unless they can be lifted with soil attached.

The following procedures will minimise failures:

Trees and shrubs should be sprayed with a proprietary wax or latex preparation before lifting. This spray should be repeated after a few weeks if necessary.

Plants should be out of the ground for as short a time as possible. It is an advantage to have plants available in a private nursery, e.g. of a New Town; or on a large scheme it is often possible to plant part of the site as a nursery to be drawn from as other areas become ready for planting.

A period of dull cloudy weather should be chosen for planting.

The soil around open-ground plants should be thoroughly watered before they are lifted; other plants should be watered in their containers.

Plants should be watered into their holes to settle the soil; there is no need to soak the surrounding soil because roots will spread more quickly into dry soil. When a period of drought follows transplantation the areas at the roots should be thoroughly soaked at about weekly intervals. A mulch of well-rotted farm-yard manure, compost, damp peat or grass clippings applied on the surface around each plant after watering will help to conserve moisture.

Plants should be frequently sprayed with water with a fine overhead spray, to decrease water loss during dry weather. Water loss can also be decreased by protecting the plants from drying winds and direct sunlight by using temporary shelter such as wattle hurdles or hessian on supports.

9.5.5 Aftercare

Aftercare includes the operations which may be necessary during the first growing season after planting to ensure that the plants establish themselves quickly and begin to grow with minimum delay. (For care after the first year, see section 9.6 on maintenance.)

Firming—Hard frost may loosen roots and cause plants to rise out of the ground. These should be firmed-in by treading the soil round each plant when the ground is not sticky.

Watering—When planting is done at the best time it should not be necessary to water plants in order to establish them; but when planting is followed by a drought then water must be supplied if the plants are to survive. The soil around the plants should be thoroughly soaked once a week during dry weather.

Evergreens are particularly susceptible to drought and drying winds. The soil round their roots should be soaked in March and covered with a protective mulch; watering should be repeated in a prolonged drought. During dry and hot weather a fine water spray should be given in the evenings until July.

Pruning—Damaged growths should be cut away, after planting. Most shrubs will grow away better when their longest shoots are shortened by one third to balance any loss of roots and disturbance during transplanting. Care should be taken that the shape and symmetry of each plant is not spoilt by cutting, especially with evergreens.

Some shrubs, including bush and climbing roses, large-flowered clematis and *Buddleia davidii* grow best when cut back hard to encourage growth from the base.

Shrubs and Hedges	*Initial Pruning*
Quick thorn, Privet	Cut to within 4 in of ground level
Beech, Hornbeam, Box, Cotoneaster, Berberis, etc.	Cut down by ⅓ of their height and trim back side shoots
Conifers, Hollies, Yew	Shorten side shoots only
Bamboos	Cut back half-way and then to base as new canes appear

Grafted and budded plants—any suckers that appear should be removed at their point of issue, by pulling or cutting so that no stump is left.

Weeding—Weeds should be controlled by hoeing at intervals of about 14 days throughout the spring and summer after planting.

(See also Chapter 12—Administration and Maintenance.)

9.6 Maintenance

9.6.1 General

Plants are usually considered to be established when they survive the first growing season; but at the end of that period they may have made little new growth and their future care is very important if they are to grow to maturity and fulfil the designer's intentions. The maintenance of any planting should have been considered in the initial stages of design to ensure that it can be done with the manpower and machinery available. A maintenance schedule can then be prepared; this gives detailed guidance for the care of the planting after the initial establishment period. This schedule is essential if the maintenance staff are to produce the effect intended by the planner who may have no further contact with the scheme once it has been finished.

The maintenance schedule should include the following parts:

Plans showing details of the planting as actually completed, so that plants can be identified when labels become lost and any plants which may die can be replaced with the correct species. Where whole groups are unsatisfactory, it may be necessary to replace with a different species to give a similar effect. The plan should also show which plants are intended as fillers to be allowed to die out or to be removed as the permanent planting matures.

Sections or elevations to show the intended shape and height of hedges and of any other planting that requires pruning to the form intended, together with details of any special pruning and treatment needed.

Recommendations for weed control, feeding, pruning and general management of planted areas.

9.6.2 Cultivation and weed control
There is no need to cultivate between plants except as a method of weed control; indiscriminate forking or dig-

ging may damage the feeding roots near the surface and hamper growth. It is usually sufficient to prick over the soil once or twice yearly with a fork, to break up surface crust and to assist penetration of rain water. Manures or fertilisers can be incorporated during this cultivation when required.

Weed control is particularly important for the first few years after planting, until plants are established and the soil is covered by growing plants or leaf litter. If allowed to grow, weeds will use water and nutrients needed by the young plants and may eventually smother them. Shrubs planted in grass should have an area about 3 ft diameter kept clear of grass and weeds for several years after planting, if they are to establish themselves satisfactorily. Hoeing at regular intervals through the spring and summer will eradicate most weeds, but is time consuming. Chemical control may be appropriate in some cases, particularly round roses and a wide range of established deciduous and evergreen shrubs. The soil can be treated with a residual herbicide in February or March which will prevent the establishment of annual weeds for most of the year.

9.6.3 Feeding
Feeding will depend upon the type of plant and site conditions, particularly the character of the soil. It must be remembered that amenity planting is not intended to produce a crop and feeding should be limited to what is necessary to maintain health without producing excessive growth after the plants have filled the space intended. Plants that are clipped or hardpruned regularly (e.g.

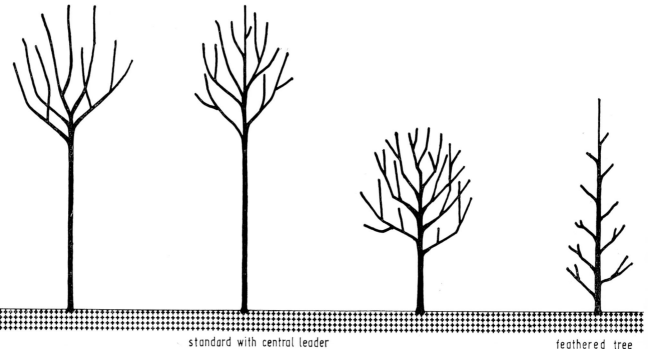

standard with central leader

standard with branching head

bush tree

feathered tree

Fig. 9.5. Forms of trees.

156

hedges, roses), will require more feeding than those which are left to grow naturally. Vigorous shrubs on a heavy clay or rich loam will probably not need manuring after the initial application at the time of planting; but plants growing on light sandy soils may need yearly feeding until they are well established and the soil has been enriched by natural leaf litter. When feeding is necessary farmyard manure or compost is the most suitable and should be lightly forked into the surface soil during early spring. Hoof and horn, and bone meal can be used where bulky manure is not available.

9.6.4 Pruning

Pruning is a general term that covers several cutting operations, including shortening growths, cutting-out old and weak shoots, thinning. Most advice about pruning is intended for the gardener who wishes to grow a wide range of shrubs within a confined space and to produce quantities of good quality blossom. In landscape work the problem is usually to encourage plants to fill an area and the quality of the flowers is less important than the overall effect of form and colour. Therefore any pruning needs careful consideration to ensure that it will produce the required results. Because of the different aims of pruning, many plants which are pruned regularly in a garden need be given less intensive pruning when used as part of a landscape scheme. Hard cutting will produce bushy or vigorous growth and more flowers, but the natural habit of a plant may be lost and the year-round effect sacrificed for a short period of floral display.

The reasons for pruning include the following:

To remove dead, damaged or diseased growth.
To help bring out the character of a plant's natural form by selective cutting.
To prevent overcrowding and plants outgrowing their positions.
To maintain health by removing old and weak shoots and thinning others.
To increase quantity or quality of foliage or shoots.
To maintain the shape of hedges or topiary by clipping. (see hedges).

Pruning should always be done to just above a bud, with no snags left. Quick growing shrubs which tend to get leggy unless trimmed regularly will not usually stand pruning back into the old wood. These shrubs are better used as fillers, e.g. *Cytisus, Cistus, Buddleia* and can be removed once the permanent planting has become established. Shrubs that are out-growing their positions may be kept in check by removing complete branches rather than by over-all trimming. If one third of the growth is cut back each year the size will be restricted but the natural habit of the plant retained.

Time to prune. Heavy pruning of deciduous shrubs is usually done in the winter months when other main-

Plate 9.9. The controlled jungle. An exercise in differing plant forms, needing careful maintenance to ensure that no one species eradicates or smothers another. Designed by Clifford R. V. Tandy.

tenance jobs are not so pressing. When time permits it is easier to identify and cut out dead and diseased growths when shrubs are in leaf and wounds heal quicker after spring pruning. Spring and summer time are also best for light pruning to encourage bushiness and to check over-vigorous growth. It is best not to prune evergreens in winter; this should always be left until spring or summer. Many shrubs, particularly evergreens, require no regular pruning provided they have space to develop naturally.

When necessary, pruning should be as follows:

Plant	Pruning	Season
Evergreens including conifers	Shape to natural form	April and throughout summer
Leggy and over-grown evergreens, e.g. Yew, Holly, Box, etc.	Cut hard back into old wood	End of February or early March
Deciduous flowering shrubs, e.g. Philadelphus, Syringa, Rosa, Weigela	Thin every three years by cutting back old and weak shoots to base	Dormant season or after flower-ing
Ground cover, e.g. Vinca, Hedera, Calluna, Erica, Hypericum calycinum	Clip over to encourage bushy growth	April
Shrubs grown for foliage effect, e.g. Ailanthus, Sambucus, Rhus typhina	Cut hard back to within a bud or two of old wood	March
Shrubs for winter effect of coloured bark, e.g. Cornus, Salix	Cut hard back to within a bud or two of old wood	Late March, early April

9.6.5 Hedges

After initial pruning hedges have to be built up gradually by trimming the leaders lightly and the side shoots hard, several times a year until the required shape and height are reached. Then all-over clipping at regular intervals will keep the hedge in shape. Formal hedges should be trimmed so that the top is narrower or the same width as the base; this helps to keep them well furnished to ground level.

Fast growing shrubs such as quickthorn, privet and *Lonicera* should be clipped in June and at intervals of about 6 weeks thereafter.

Yew, beech and hornbeam and slow-growing plants can be kept fairly neat by clipping once a year in August, but a neater appearance will result from two clippings, one at the end of May, the other in September.

Hedges of flowering shrubs must be clipped *after* flowering. Formal hedges of small leaved plants may be clipped with shears or a mechanical trimmer. Large leaved shrubs (e.g., laurel, rhododendron) and informal hedges of flowering plants look better when trimmed with secateurs.

Bibliography

Britain's Green Mantle, A. G. Tansley, Allen and Unwin.
Garden design, Sylvia Crowe, Country Life.

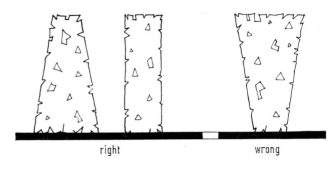

right   wrong

Fig. 9.6. The right and wrong ways to clip a hedge.

Grounds Maintenance Handbook, H. S. Conover, F. W. Dodge Corporation, New York.
Hardy Herbaceous Plants, Lanning Roper, Penguin Books.
Modern Florilegium, G. S. Thomas, Sunningdale Nurseries, Windlesham, Surrey.
Roses, F. Fairbrother, Penguin Books.
Trees and Shrubs Hardy in the British Isles, W. J. Bean, John Murray.
Water Gardens, Frances Perry, Penguin Books.
Weed Control Handbook, Blackwell Scientific Publications, Oxford.
World of the soil, Sir E. J. Russell, New Naturalist and Fontana.

10 Grass

IAN GREENFIELD

10.1 Soils

10.1.1 The soil and site preparation

The properties of the soil have their origins deep in geological history. While the differences between igneous, sedimentary and metamorphic rocks may appear largely academic, they do in fact greatly influence the nature and size of soil particles and therefore soil structure and drainage.

Quartz particles derived from igneous rocks form hard grains of sharp sand while silicates form the smaller silt and clay particles. The extreme forms of sedimentary rocks are the porous sandstones, the impervious clays and the alkaline limestones with a high calcium content, and in general the older they are, the harder they are. The metamorphic rocks are harder still.

When a pit is dug, the soil 'profile' usually reveals dissimilar layers, ranging from the topsoil down to the parent rock or in pedological shorthand, horizons A to D. While the upper part A is much modified by vegetation and other living organisms, C and D are little altered parent material; the intervening B horizon may be much influenced by minerals, notably iron, washed down from above; this iron may form a hard pan which hinders plant roots and drainage alike.

10.1.2 Soil texture and structure

An important feature of the soil, its ease of working, depends on its texture. This is a measure of the ultimate soil particles which are internationally defined in terms of size thus:

	Size (millimetres)
Stones and gravel	over 2·0
Coarse sand	2·0–0·2
Fine sand	0·2–0·02
Silt	0·02–0·002
Clay	below 0·002

In loams, sand, silt and clay are present in balanced amounts and thus allow easier working than heavy clays, but are heavier than sands (see also Chapter 3—Survey, section on soils, and Appendix 2·2, Soil).

Soil structure differs from soil textures and describes the ability of the ultimate particles to form stable aggregates under varying conditions, particularly varying water supply. The crumbs of loams tend to be stable while those of clays are amorphous and in wet conditions collapse and become sticky. It is this factor rather than individual particle size, that makes clay soils 'heavy' and sandy ones 'light'.

10.1.3 Humus

Among the soil particles, plant and animal debris degenerates into humus, the organic constituent of the soil. Although this is degraded by microbes, insects, worms and fungi, it plays a vital part in maintaining soil fertility by improving crumb structure, retaining water, and making soils darker and therefore warmer. An important group of soil bacteria ('nitrifying bacteria') convert the unavailable proteins of dead creatures into nitrates and ammonium ions soluble in water and readily taken up by grass roots.

10.1.4 Soil minerals

The mineral elements nitrogen, phosphorus, potassium, calcium and magnesium must be plentiful in order to produce good crops, but turf, especially fine bent/fescue turf, requires less nutrients than do farm crops. The importance of these nutrients, other than magnesium which is seldom either deficient or excessive in turf, are shown by Table 10.1. The most common cause of mineral deficiency is leaching; much nitrogen, phosphate and potash, lime and magnesium, are carried out of the reach of plant roots by drainage water. Nitrogen may, conversely, be inadequate in badly drained soils where waterlogging discourages the nitrifying bacteria and fosters other bacteria that actually reduce the available nitrogen. Much soil phosphate is unavailable to plants, especially in heavy soils where a large fraction of it is in an insoluble form.

Other elements required by the grass (sulphur, manganese, zinc, boron, copper, iron and molybdenum) are called 'trace' elements because the plant needs them only in minute traces. The commonest deficiencies are of iron, revealed by yellowing of leaves, and/or boron, shown by the collapse of growing points.

TABLE 10.1: PLANT NUTRIENTS AND THEIR EFFECTS ON GRASS SWARDS

Element	Normal Source	Effects of Deficiency	Effects of Excess
Nitrogen	Ammonium salts and nitrates, mostly in soil solution	Plants small, bright-tinted with pale older leaves.	Soft flabby growth, a risk of mechanical damage and disease
Phos-phorus	Organic and inorganic phosphates in soil, not all available to grass	Poor roots, weak bluish or purplish shoots, wearing badly	Encourages clover
Potassium	Potash salts in soil solution only scarce in peat, chalk or sands. Also in minerals, e.g. felspar	Growing points fail, shoots die back. Risk of disease	Seldom met with
Calcium	Limestone, chalk, soil solution. Plentiful except in very acid soil	Growing points fail. Leaf tips yellow or stunted	Causes iron shortage; favours weeds

10.1.5 Soil acidity

Under acid conditions the ions of potassium, calcium, magnesium and ammonium are replaced in the soil by those of hydrogen which affects soil fertility and the species of grass which will grow. Soil acidity can be measured both in terms of lime requirement (a high lime requirement indicating an acid soil and a low one, a basic one) or by the symbol pH. Some important figures are given in Table 10.2 and the reader will appreciate the importance of pH and its adjustment by the use of lime or, on acidic soils, by acid fertilisers like sulphate of ammonia.

TABLE 10.2

Acidity	pH	Colour of B.D.H. Universal Indicator	Soil Suitable for
Very acid	5	Red	Heaths
Acid	5·5–6	Orange	Fine turf
Slightly acid	6–6·5	Yellow	Sports turf
Neutral	7	Green	Sports turf, many weeds
Alkaline	8	Blue	Chalk grass-land, weeds

10.1.6 The suitability of soils for turf formation

The ideal soil for turf formation is deep enough for roots to grow and spread, and drains freely allowing them ample moisture and air. This implies an open and well-defined crumb structure, and a texture that of a loam, neither sticky nor too friable. Humus should be plentiful. The pH, fertility and nutrients should be appropriate; fertility is well indicated by the population of earthworms which increases with fertility and alkalinity. 'Trace' elements must be present though only in small amounts, and toxic chemicals absent—this last condition being difficult to control in air-polluted industrial towns and on reclaimed derelict land.

The five main deviations from this ideal are corrected as follows:

Soil	Problems	Treatment
Clay and clay loams	Heavy, compacted, waterlogged in winter, crack in summer, earthworms	Difficult. If possible, cover with several inches of good loam, otherwise dress with sharp sand
Sandy soils	Inadequate humus and minerals; summer drought	Readily improved by working in compost or peat. Adjust pH with lime
Infertile heath	Mineral shortage, poor drainage; acidity	Break up 'iron pan' in subsoil to improve drainage; add lime, compost and fertilisers. Irrigate in dry weather
Chalky soils	Shallowness, alkalinity, excessive drainage	Break up subsoil, add sulphate of ammonia (or other acid fertiliser) and compost
Derelict land (slag heaps, etc.)	Debris, unweathered rock, sometimes acidity	This takes time. Clear the worst debris, break up the soil and allow to weather. Preferably import topsoil

10.1.7 Seed bed preparation

After levelling and draining the topsoil is evenly returned, to a depth of 6 in for normal landscape work, or for preference 12 in for playing fields or fine turf. While it is sometimes desirable to seed areas associated with building or engineering projects immediately best results are only obtained if the site is first allowed to settle, is dug or ploughed to 6 in depth in the autumn, and allowed to overwinter.

In spring, further modifications may be necessary. Sandstones are improved with Keuper marl, gravels with manure, light soils with peat, green manure or sewage sludge, and heavy soils with sand. Cultivations such as harrowing and raking (alternately at right angles), mixes these materials with the soil, gives an even tilth, and kills weed seedlings. Analysis of soil nutrients and pH at this stage may reveal the need for fertilisers or lime. Weeds and insect pests may also require treatment. Successful fallowing should make weed killing with sodium chlorate

(4–12 oz per sq yd) unnecessary, but pre-emergence weed-killers may be used at this stage. Wireworms and other insect larvae encountered on ploughed up pasture and elsewhere, may be controlled by working D.D.T., B.H.C. or pest dusts into the soil surface, or by mixing $\frac{1}{2}\%$ lindane dust with the seed, 1 cwt per acre sown. Lead arsenate is less suitable as it may impair germination.

All these operations are designed to give a seedbed which is clean, free from weeds and their seeds, fine, moist, warm and above all, firm. In a well-tilled soil the particles approximate in size to wheat grains for the top few inches, grading downwards into a firm subsoil, well drained and aerated. 'Fluffy' seedbeds are bound to be disappointing.

10.2 Grasses

10.2.1 The grass

The plant family to which the grasses belong—the *Gramineae*—is one of the largest groups of plants, with over 10,000 species all told. It is, therefore, remarkable that all British turf needs are met from the 100 indigenous British species or plants clearly related to them.

The resistance of grass to close cropping by livestock due to its ability to provide a continuous foliage cover at ground level is its main virtue in the formation of good quality turf; in the perennial grasses it can be achieved in two ways. At one extreme, sheep's fescue forms compact tufts with many short erect shoots; at the other are the bent grasses with leafy shoots (stolons) creeping above ground, or couch grass with its whitish stems (rhizomes) ranging horizontally below ground level. Good quality turf contains a blend of tufted and stoloniferous species and the desirable fescues and bents can be found in grazed heathland as well as in well-managed lawns and greens.

In the more luxuriant meadows, the grass grows taller and it is here that cocksfoot, and meadowgrasses, rye-grass and timothy abound in nature. Though these are usually too coarse for use in fine turf, their vigour and productivity, especially when well fertilised, has suited them to agriculture and they may find a place in sports turf and extensive turf, especially in damper situations, or where a quick cheap attractive grass cover is the aim.

It is impossible to catalogue all the turf grasses, let alone all the wild British grasses, which, between them, can colonise almost any natural or manmade situation. Still less can all their English names be listed here, as some of them, like *Agrostis tenuis*, have as many as eight. Table 10.3 attempts to set out the most important of them, in order of their scientific names. The reader is advised to familiarise himself with the main scientific names, which will frequently be used in this text for reasons of clarity and brevity.

TABLE 10.3: COMMON GRASS SPECIES
(*In order of their scientific names*)

Scientific Name	English Name	Where Employed
Agropyron repens	Couch grass	A serious weed
Agrostis canina Subspecies canina-fascicularis	Velvet bent	Fine turf
Subspecies montana-arida	Brown bent	Fine turf
Agrostis gigantea	Black bent	Rough turf
Agrostis stolonifera—alba	Creeping or white bent	Fine turf, especially damp soil
A. stolonifera variety palustris	Fiorin	Rough turf or damp ground
A. stolonifera 'Emerald Velvet'		Rough turf; plant as stolons
Agrostis tenuis	Browntop common bent	Fine turf (important)
Aira, see *Deschampsia*		
Cynosurus cristatus	Crested dogstail	Cricket squares, playing fields (hard wearing–important)
Dactylis glomerata	Cocksfoot	Only very rough turf
Deschampsia flexuosa	Wavy hairgrass	On acid soils
Festuca longifolia	Hard fescue	Playing fields
Festuca ovina	Sheep's fescue	Tennis courts, lawns (important)
Festuca rubra S.59	Red fescue	Playing fields (important)
F.r. variety genuina glaucesens	Cumberland marsh fescue	Fine turf
Festuca rubra FR10	St. Ives fescue	Fine turf, developed at Sports Turf Research Institute Bingley

Scientific Name	English Name	Where Employed
Festuca rubra subspecies	Chewing's fescue	Fine turf and playing fields (important)
Festuca tenuifolia	Fine-leaved fescue	Cricket tables
Holcus lanatus	Yorkshire fog	Weed in fine turf
Lolium perenne S23 (There are other strains also)	Perennial ryegrass	Playing fields rough turf (important)
Nardus stricta	Moor mat grass	Weed in acid heathy places
Phleum pratense S50	Cat's tail, timothy	Playing fields on heavy damp soil
Phleum nodosum	Small timothy	Playing fields on heavy damp soil
Poa annua	Annual meadow-grass	Weed in fine turf, useful in urban turf
Poa nemoralis	Wood meadow-grass	Shady places
Poa pratensis	Smooth stalked meadow-grass, Kentucky bluegrass	Playing fields (important)
Poa trivialis	Rough stalked meadow-grass	Playing fields (important)
Puccinellia maritima and P. distans	Salt marsh grass	Poor constituents of sea washed turf
Sieglingia decumbens	Heath grass	Poor quality grass of heaths

10.2.2 Choice of seeds mixtures: general and fine turf

The main factors influencing the choice of seed mixtures are soil type and moisture content, climate, cost, the type and area of turf required, and the height of cut and foot traffic envisaged and the shade if any. The modern trend is to simplify the mixtures from 8–10 species down to 3 or 4, of which only one is stoloniferous, as grasses with this habit blend badly with each other. The best colour is obtained if species are used which mature at different seasons, the behaviour of grasses being as follows:

Bents	Best from July to October
Dogstail	Varies little with season
Fescues	Best from April to June; poor in winter
Meadowgrasses	Vary little with season
Ryegrass	Best in spring and autumn

Some fine turf mixtures (Table 10.4, column 1–3) usually contain 30% of *Agrostis tenuis*, but if it is scarce, as after the war, it can be replaced by fescue (columns 4–6).

Ryegrass is omitted except as an occasional 'nurse crop', to be eliminated later on by constant mowing and acidifying with sulphate of ammonia. Fertility must be kept low or fescues may be overrun by the bents.

TABLE 10.4: FINE TURF MIXTURES

Species	% Present					
	(1)	(2)	(3)	(4)	(5)	(6)
Agrostis tenuis	30	30	25	10	10	10
Chewing's fescue	70	30	50	70	90	60
S.59 fescue	–	40				30
Cumberland fescue			25			
Fine-leaved fescue				20		

10.2.3 Hard-wearing mixtures

Where short turf is subject to wear, dogstail comes into its own as seen in Tables 10.5 and 10.6. A lesser amount is required in tennis courts and hockey pitches, than in cricket squares.

TABLE 10.5: MIXTURES BASED ON DOGSTAIL

Species	% Present					
	Lawns		Cricket squares		Tennis	Hockey
	(1)	(2)	(3)	(4)	(5)	(6)
Crested Dogstail	40	35	20	15	25	10
Agrostis tenuis	10	5	10	10	30	15
Chewing's fescue	40	50	50	75	45	60
Red S.59 fescue			20			15
Poa species (see 10.2.5)	10	10				

TABLE 10.6: TENNIS COURTS AND HOCKEY PITCHES

Species	% Present						
	Tennis Courts				Hockey Pitches		
					Wet	Medium	Sandy
	(1)	(2)	(3)	(4)	(5)	(6)	(7)
Chewing's fescue	60	45	40	40	60	60	40
S.59 fescue	25		30		10	15	20
Fine-leaved fescue			10				
Agrostis tenuis	5	30	10	10	10	15	20
Dogstail	10	25		20	10	10	20
Timothy					10		
Poa species			10	10			
Ryegrass		useful on base lines		20			

10.2.4 Ryegrass mixtures

For reasons of suitability or cost, ryegrass is a major constituent of football pitches and other places where hard winter wear occurs on long turf (Table 10.7) and in extensive parks and outfields where cheapness is an asset (Table 10.8).

TABLE 10.7: RYEGRASS MIXTURES FOR FOOTBALL, RUGBY, HOCKEY, AND OTHER PITCHES: VERGES AND LAWNS

(the last 5 are most suitable for rugby and football)

Species	% Present							
	(1)	(2)	(3)	(4)	(5)	(6)	(7)	(8)
Chewing's fescue	10	10						
S.59 fescue	30	15	10–30	10				5–15
Hard fescue		5						
Agrostis tenuis	10	5	10					
Ryegrass S.23	50	50			80–70	60–65	80	75
Ryegrass short-seeded			80–60	60				
Dogstail		15		10	20–30	10	20–30	10
Poa species				20		20–15	0–20	10
Timothy						10		

10.2.5 Seeds mixtures for special situations

Grass seed mixtures should be carefully modified for different situations and many of these are catered for above. Ryegrass and *Poa trivialis* cope best with shade, while the presence of toxic and acid chemicals in urban atmospheres kills or disfigures most perennial grasses so that *Poa annua* which establishes itself naturally, should here be encouraged; it may need summer watering. The most important modifications to suit situations are:

Situation	More should be sown	At the expense of
Dry or light soil	Dogstail, *Poa pratensis*	Timothy, *P. trivialis*
Wet or heavy soil	Timothy, *P. trivialis*	Dogstail, *P. pratensis*
Shade	Ryegrass, *P. trivialis*	Most others

Situation	More should be Sown	At the Expense of
Chalky soil	Dogstail	Bents, fescues, or timothy
Acid or peaty soil	Fine-leaved fescue, wavy hairgrass or velvet bent	Most others
Dry, sandy heaths	*Poa pratensis*, fescues	Bents, fescues or timothy
Conifers	Wavy hairgrass	Most others
Urban situations	*Poa annua*	Perennials
Tennis base lines	Perennial ryegrass	Others in mixture

The following mixtures are suitable for shady places:

Heavy soil   50% ryegrass, 30% *P. trivialis*, 20% *Agrostis Stolonifera*.

Medium soil   50% *P. pratensis*, 25% each of ryegrass and either dogstail or sheep's fescue.

Towns   40% ryegrass, 30% each of *Poa trivialis* and *P. annua*.

Light soil   40% sheep's fescue, 20% fineleaved fescue, 10% S.59 fescue. 30% *Agrostis tenuis*.

Peaty heaths 40% wavy hairgrass, 30% each of S.59 fescue and hard fescue.

TABLE 10.8: RYEGRASS MIXTURES FOR PARKS, GOLF FAIRWAYS, AND CRICKET OUTFIELDS

Species	% in Mixtures								
	Cricket Outfields						Parks		Fair-ways
	Dry soils		Wet soils		S.59 mixtures				
	(1)	(2)	(3)	(4)	(5)	(6)	(7)	(8)	(9)
Chewings fescue	20	10					10	15	45
S.59 Fescue					40	40			
Agrostis tenuis	10	10	10	10			10	10	10
Ryegrass S.23	50	50	60	50	50	60	60	50	25
Dogstail	20	10	10	10	10		10	15	10
Poa trivialis			10	20			10	10	
Poa pratensis		20							
Timothy (see 10.2.5)			10	10	10				

10.3 Establishment of grassed areas

10.3.1 Sowing

Improved seed strains and site preparation methods have led to a steady fall in the prescribed seed rate over the last few years. Lawns, tennis courts, cricket squares and similar swards require $\frac{3}{4}$–1 oz per sq yd (200–300 lb/acre) but on well-prepared extensive areas, 50–75 lb/acre suffice.

A quick-acting fertiliser, evenly mixed and spread at

3 oz per sq yd, and raked into the soil surface, 1–2 weeks beforehand, enables grass seeds to develop rapidly and is particularly useful where the small non-ryegrass mixtures are at risk from damping off. A good formula (parts by weight) is as follows:

	Analysis
Sulphate of ammonia	2
Superphosphate	4 Nitrogen 5·4%
Bone meal	4 Phosphate 14·1%
Sulphate of potash	1 Potash 4·4%

Late summer, after adequate fallowing and cleaning, is the best time to sow, unless followed by an unusually cold, early or wet autumn. Mid-August is best in north Britain, late August or early September in the milder south, west and coastal districts. Less satisfactory are spring sowings, especially when the spring is late or May dry.

10.3.2 First-year management of turf from seed
When fine grass attains 1–2 in and rough turf 2–3 in the area is cleared of wormcasts and lightly rolled to firm the surface. 1–2 days later the top $\frac{1}{2}$–$\frac{3}{4}$ in of grass, not more, is removed by means of a side-wheel mower; this encourages tillering. Regular and frequent mowing should then continue, the height of cut being reduced each time until the final height is reached, usually $\frac{1}{4}$–1 in.

Coarse grasses have to be eradicated by hand, likewise the larger perennial weeds such as dandelions, docks and plantains. Annual weeds—chickweed, groundsel, fat hen, deadnettles, redshank and speedwells—unless very numerous as a result of poor site preparation, succumb readily under repeated close mowing. Only after six months can selective weedkillers and lawnsands be safely applied to fine turf.

Three months after a successful sowing, 3–4 lb finely-sieved compost per sq yd lightly worked in so as not to smother the grass, is beneficial. Nitrogen deficiency, revealed by weak yellow turf, is remedied by applying $\frac{1}{2}$ oz of sulphate of ammonia to each sq yd; spring sowings may need irrigation. Then bare patches should be re-seeded and the edges clearly marked out.

10.3.3 Turfing
A common and quicker alternative to seeding is turfing, but it is more costly and by perfectionist standards not usually as good. A balanced sward is necessary; see section 10.2.2.

Turf beds need less preparation than seedbeds but should be well settled. Autumn or early winter is a better time to lay than Spring as in the latter case dry weather can hinder rooting. $2\frac{1}{2}$ oz per sq yd of a fertiliser (bone meal 4 parts, superphosphate 4, sulphate of potash 1) raked in, should precede this.

Whatever type is desired, sown or turfed, it will be helpful to refer to *Specification* (1966) published by the Architectural Press.

10.4 Maintenance

10.4.1 Turf maintenance: machinery
Good turf maintenance results from good management—the ability to assess the labour, machinery and materials necessary to achieve good economic results. Labour and operations therefore must be undertaken with a proper understanding of the finances available and with a forward looking budget. Chemical fertilisers and sprays must be intelligently used and new techniques tried and where successful, adopted and worked into routine operations.

The capital outlay, and routine current expenditure, must be carefully judged beforehand, and before buying machinery one must consider:

Funds available for initial purchase.
Expected maintenance costs.
The labour available to handle it.
The turf itself—site, soil, size and quality.

10.4.2 Normal machinery requirements
This naturally depends on circumstances, but some idea of machinery needs may be gauged from *Turf Culture*, p. 201, by the author. In the next few years, one may expect this list to be modified a good deal, particularly as the agricultural tractor improves in versatility. The following fourteen machines can be operated with a standard tractor, though on smaller areas a 2-wheel universal tractor may suffice.

Gang mowing with up to 7 units.
Heavy or light duty piercers.
12 ft scarifier.
12 ft tilther rakes.
12 ft brushes.
6 ft liftable roller or gang roller.
Rotovator.
Rotary or reciprocating screens.
Chain harrow.
Disc harrow.
Cartage of 2–3 cu yd loads.
Spraying (units with 12–20 ft boom).
Fertiliser distributors.
Ploughing.

10.4.3 Mowing
Mowing, the most important of all turf maintenance

Plate 10.1. A hollow tining machine at work on a golf green.

Plate 10.2. A 'Sisis' HA6 aerator towed behind a tractor.

Plate 10.3. Levelling top dressing and filling holes and undulations.

operations, can dictate the whole appearance, durability and well being of the sward. It should be done regularly and not too keenly—'little and often'—so that only a modest amount of grass is removed at each cut. Once to twice per week is sufficient, and entails the removal of $\frac{1}{2}$–$\frac{3}{4}$ in at most, on each occasion, though the exact frequency can be modified by climate, season, grass species and fertiliser regime. Winter mowing, essential to prevent the sward becoming open and lank, must be carefully timed for dry, non-frosty conditions.

Mowing gradually eradicates many broad-leaved weeds, but also grasses such as ryegrass, given time. Turf is also much influenced by whether the clippings are boxed or returned; the latter produces a spongy sward and many earthworms especially on heavy soils, and distributes unwanted seeds, but in dry weather affords a valuable mulch. In rough work, the low budget and simple standards required favour frequent cutting without a grass box.

10.4.4 Choice of mower
Mowing machines fall into 8 categories according to their source of power and method of cutting:

(a) Hand mowers, driven by human effort. These have either a rear roller or two side wheels, and are respectively termed 'roller' and 'side-wheel' types.
(b) Cylinder-driven mowers, hand-pushed but with an engine to drive the cylinder.
(c) Fully driven motor mowers, powered by internal combustion engines.
(d) Heavy duty mowers, as (c) but with engines of $3\frac{1}{2}$ hp or more, capable of haulage as well as mowing.
(e) Machines powered by electricity, whether from mains or battery.
(f) Rotary mowers, with the cutting cylinder replaced by horizontally rotating blades.
(g) Miscellaneous—including clipper-type scythes and general purpose engines.

165

Plate 10.4. Hydraulic grass seeding being carried out on difficult rock surfaces.

10.4.5 Aeration and renovation

Aeration is second only to mowing in the production of healthy turf, a fact which is becoming increasingly realised. Correctly carried out and timed, it can promote free drainage under almost all conditions with but little interference to the playing surface. Moisture, air and top dressings can penetrate the turf, roots and fibre are pruned, helpful bacteria develop and grass roots can penetrate deeper. As a result aeration can play a leading and relatively inexpensive part in turf renovation, especially if this has to be done rapidly.

Aeration is achieved at two levels, surface and subsurface.

Surface aeration. Some of the fine turf grasses produce excessive fibre which hinders green growth and root development. Once this exceeds a certain minimum, mowing fails to remove it and raking and scarification becomes necessary.

Spiked and smooth chain *harrows*, commonly 7 ft × 6 ft or 7 ft × 14 ft are useful on fairways, removing old matted grass, but their use on fine turf needs great care, and slitting gives better results. On a larger scale, a sportsground aerator with light metal wheels and tines, 6, 9 or 12 in apart and capable of cutting 4–5 in deep, can be used monthly in winter, given suitable weather conditions.

Besides the above, *canes* are useful for scattering dew and wormcasts on fine turf; *mats* can work in top dressings, but are less good for this purpose than drag brooms in wet weather; and *pricking* to a depth of ½ in rejuvenates neglected turf.

Subsurface aeration. It is seldom adequate to confine the attention to the matted turf surface; soil compaction has to be avoided at all times by forking, spiking or slitting, and is most conveniently tackled as part of the autumn or early spring treatments, before applying top dressings. On a domestic lawn, the use of the ordinary garden *fork* at frequent intervals may suffice to remedy this.

Multipurpose aerators. Most of the above operations and also rolling, are done using multipurpose equipment for which reference should be made to the trade literature. The frame which carries the tools may be driven by hand, mower or tractor.

Rolling and other mechanical operations. Much turf suffers from the over-use of the roller, especially when wet or in a vain attempt to level depressions. This compacts the soil surface, excludes water and air, inhibits grass root growth and admits weeds and moss. Aeration must therefore follow whenever rolling takes place throughout the season; this is especially true on heavy soils.

10.5 Turf dressings

10.5.1 Chemical treatment of turf fertilisers

The nutrients removed by cutting must be frequently replaced; of these (see section 10.1.4) nitrogen, phosphorus and potash (loosely termed N.P.K. after their respective chemical symbols) are the most vital. The analysis and rate of application of many turf fertilisers appear in section 10.5.2 and they may be classified as follows:

High-nitrogen fertilisers—Of these sulphate of ammonia is widely used, being cheap, readily taken up by the plant, and rich in nitrogen. Its acidity brings the turf to the optimum pH for fine grasses, eliminates many weeds and scorches moss—hence its use in lawnsands. Pre-sowing, 3–7 lb per 100 sq yd should be applied. More recently urea of good quality (excluding biuret), near-neutral and non-scorching, has become a useful substitute, especially in the form of methylene–urea (38% N).

Alkaline nitrogenous fertilisers These have a high nitrogen content but their alkalinity harms fine turf, except on very acid soils, and favours weeds and earthworms. Except for nitrochalk they take up atmospheric moisture and 'cake' in store; cyanamide is phytotoxic while nitrate of soda leads to sodium clay and *Ophiobolus* disease.

Low-nitrogen fertilisers—Organics but with little nitrogen slowly available to grass, these are mostly soil improvers

Plate 10.5. Lawn outfit comprising turf piercing implement, whale-bone brush, fine rake scarifier, spiker slitter.

and top dressings rather than fertilisers, they are used on seedbeds more than on established turf. The richest and best is dried blood which gives readily available nitrogen without scorch, stores well and blends with most other fertilisers.

Phosphatic fertilisers—As the raw material, rock phosphate, is mostly unavailable to grasses, it is usually modified before sale by treatment with sulphuric acid, giving superphosphate, or with phosphoric acid, giving triple superphosphate. Both these revert to the insoluble form, slowly in storage and more rapidly in acid soils rich in iron or aluminium. If applied alone they temporarily scorch the turf. Basic slag or bone derivatives are a useful source of phosphate for turf on acid or light soils, but unfortunately encourage clover. Quite different chemically is ammonium phosphate which is water soluble, rapidly available to the turf and may also scorch it.

Potassic fertilisers—Potassium sulphate and chloride ('Muriate') are both effective sources of potash, the sulphate being the safest for use on grass and the most pure chemically. Kainit contains sodium and magnesium salts as well as potash.

Plate 10.6. Selekta feed fertiliser distributor.

Other inorganic nutrients—These are not listed in the table. They can be supplied as follows:

Calcium	In lime, chalk, gypsum and some nitrogenous fertilisers.
Sulphur	In superphosphate, ammonium sulphate and sulphate of potash.
Magnesium	In Epsom salts, agricultural magnesium sulphate, kieserite, kainit and dolomite.
Iron	In chelated iron compounds.
Boron	In borax.

10.5.2 The main turf fertilisers

Fertiliser	Analysis % Nitrogen	Rate of Application (lb/100 sq yd)	Remarks
HIGH NITROGEN			
Sulphate of ammonia	20·6	2–5	Strongly acidic 2
ALKALINE-NITROGEN			
Nitrate of soda	15·5	2–5	Alkaline 2
Nitro-chalk	15·5	¾–7	Mildly alkaline 2
Nitrate of lime	13	5	Alkaline 2
Calcium cyanamide	20·6	5	Strongly alkaline 2
LOW NITROGEN			
Dried blood	13	7–10	Use on light soil
Hoof and horn	7–15	14	Has 10% phosphate
Shoddy	up to 16	180	Use on heavy soil
Leather waste	6	48–72	For seedbeds
Rape meal	5·5	7	For sandy soils
Soot	4	7–14	Mildly acid 2
Sewage sludge	1–6	2–8 cwt	Sometimes alkaline
Malt culms	3·5	7–12	
Spent hops	3·5	1–2	
Farmyard manure	0·7	4–12 cwt	
	% (P_2O_5)		
PHOSPHATES			
Superphosphate	14–18	7	2
Triple superphosphate	47	1–3	
Basic slag	18	24–48	Alkaline
Bone meal, bone flour	21–25	14–24	Has some nitrogen
Ammonium phosphate	61	3–7	2
	% Potash		
POTASH			
Sulphate of potash	48	3–7	
Muriate of potash	50–6	3–7	
Kainit	14	5–12	

1. To convert the above rates of application to oz per sq yd divide by 6, to cwt per acre divide by $2\frac{1}{2}$.

2. Where figure 2 appears in the remarks column, the fertilisers should be bulked with compost, sand or sterilised soil, 6 parts per part of fertiliser (10 parts in the case of soot).

3. See also Chapter 9—General Planting sections 9.4.6 and 9.4.7 for fertilisers and manures.

10.5.3 Choice of fertilisers

When buying fertilisers, consider the following points:
Cost per unit weight of nutrient—This can be deduced from the stated N : P : K analysis given by all reputable manufacturers.

Suitability for the purpose in hand—e.g. alkaline fertilisers will probably be inappropriate, and the nitrogen content must suit the time of year.

Compatibility—Although cheaper than buying a proprietary mixture of all three major nutrients, making up a compound fertiliser from its primary constituents needs care. Dried blood and potash salts blend quite well with other materials but others, e.g. sulphate of ammonia and superphosphate, inter-react with harmful results. A fertiliser compatibility table like that on page 331 of *Turf Culture* must be studied first, and then the ingredients thoroughly mixed under dry conditions (see also Appendix 2.3.1, Mixing of manures and fertilisers).

Although space does not permit a full discussion of the fertiliser requirements of turf, the following table accounts for most seasons and situations. It will be seen that the nitrogen content is reduced in the autumn to avoid flabby growth and disease, and potash and phosphate correspondingly increased.

10.5.4 Fertiliser analyses for season and situation

Purpose	*% Nitrogen*		*% Phosphate*		*% Potash*
	Inorganic	*Organic*	*Soluble*	*Insoluble*	
SPRING					
Fine turf	4	3	6	1	4
Rough turf	4–6	3	6	1	6–7
AUTUMN					
Fine turf	1	1–2	6	6	6
Rough turf	1	1–2	9	3	12
Preseeding	4	1	10	3	5

Except for the last (3 oz) they are applied at 2 oz per sq yd.

10.5.5 Other turf dressings

The following may also be useful:
Lawn sand (sand with 30–40% sulphate of ammonia, 15% sulphate of iron) at 3–4 oz per sq yd, acts as nitrogen fertiliser and weedkiller.

Liquid fertilisers (e.g. 16:10:28) can be diluted and applied to greens.

Slowly released inorganic fertilisers, with nutrients borne on a carrier.

Lime, on very acid turf. 2 cwt of quicklime, $2\frac{1}{2}$ cwt of slaked lime, or $3\frac{1}{2}$ cwt of chalk or limestone are usually enough to raise the pH by one unit. Finely divided chalk is the kindest to the turf.

Top dressings, based on compost, improve the soil texture, the level, and the grass tillers. They are applied in the autumn, usually at 2 lb per sq yd occasionally at 4 lb, and must be thoroughly worked into the turf to avoid smothering it.

Charcoal or coke breeze, at 1–2 lb per sq yd, help to lighten heavy soils.

Peat improves lawns on heavy and clay soils. It is then applied at $\frac{1}{2}$–1 lb per sq yd, but much more may be used in the preparation of seedbeds.

10.5.6 Fertiliser distribution

Even distribution of fertiliser is essential and while it can be achieved by hand, specially designed equipment is almost indispensable on larger sports grounds. The largest quantities, up to 2 tons per acre, are spread by a tractor drawn spinning-disc distributor with a 5 cwt hopper, at 4 m.p.h. In most other models, the flow of material is regulated by a grooved roller or a canvas conveyor. These can sow fertiliser, seed (bulked), mowrah meal, etc., of differing texture. It is therefore advisable to check the actual flow rate of the given material by collecting it on brown paper, or a path, before applying it to large areas of turf.

10.5.7 Irrigation

The need for artificial watering of sports turf has been increasingly realised and several factors affect this need. Fine grasses are better adapted to withstand drought than are bents or annual meadowgrass; thin sandy soils need frequent irrigation in dry periods; and growing grass needs large amounts of water. Growth will always suffer if the groundsman waits for symptoms of drought before irrigating, and soil moisture should never be allowed to fall below half the field capacity. Irrigation equipment is likely to improve steadily in the next few years; for example the American practice of using remotely controlled golf-green watering units, may gain currency here. Irrigation water is, of course a useful vehicle for the delivery of chemicals to turf, and various fertiliser diluters can introduce accurately measured amounts of nutrients into it. Provided suck-back into the water mains can be avoided, the same methods can be likewise used for fungicides, insecticides, weed killers, and wormkillers.

10.6 Turf management

10.6.1 Different turf types and their management

The foregoing remarks apply to all kinds of turf, but according to its quality and purpose the various operations assume different degrees of importance. Sections 10.6.2 and 10.6.8 show how fine turf, rough-wearing turf, extensive turf and turf substitutes are treated in practice.

10.6.2 Fine turf establishment

Fine bent/fescue turf needs careful establishment to give a level surface, pleasing and uniform in appearance, with true running qualities. As found in golf, putting and bowling greens, and croquet and other lawns, it is usually flat, but may have gentle angles and undulations in golf greens and an 8–10 in central crown in crown bowling greens. Basic maintenance is the same for all.

Since Cumberland turf is increasingly difficult to obtain (see section 10.3.3), parkland and moorland turf may be substituted; the ousting of fescues by *Poa annua* and pearlwort may not always spoil the playing surface, but greens with excessive creeping bent may be slow running in wet conditions.

Turfing permits earlier play—autumn-laid turfs are usable by next June—but excellent results are obtained at low costs from New Zealand browntop/chewing's fescue sowings. Seeding requires careful management and takes a year to mature.

However turf is formed its site needs careful preparation. Golf greens require 8 in of good topsoil, and a lengthy procedure must be followed when making a bowling green. A full 42 yd square (45 yd in crown greens), allowing for ditches and banks, is excavated and levelled and a 4 in peg placed at its centre, its height depending on the thickness of material to be laid. Drains in rectangular or herringbone pattern, with 4 in tiles for mains and 3 in for laterals should fall from near ground level at one end to $2\frac{1}{2}$ ft down at the other; overdrainage must be avoided.

Then a 4 in clinker layer (broken stone if well consolidated is also permissible) should extend to the ditches; after levelling, 2 in of fine ash is spread on top. The build-up is completed by adding either 3–4 in of sandy soil or turfs boxed to 2 in, or 6 in of light loam plus seed. Turfs, if used, are laid starting diagonally from one corner, or on crown greens from the centre, rolled, dressed with sharp sand, and levelled from a long flat block of timber.

10.6.3 Fine turf maintenance

The usual principles apply to all fine turf. Mowing is most important; hand-pushed roller mowers are best but special precision motor mowers are also suitable. Fine turf usually requires mowing at least once a week and a height of $\frac{3}{16}$ in is the aim. On heavier soils a shorter cut, 2–3 times per week in the growing season, is necessary,

but is less kind to the turf. During winter, a light topping is the rule, depending on conditions and grass growth; it should not take place in frosty spells or cold winds.

An American study of golf greens revealed compaction in only the top 2 in; the resulting bad porosity is remedied there by using 3 cwt of krilium per acre and covering it with 4 in of a 7 : 1 sand/peat mixture, the sand being large grained.

Fertilisation, aeration and top dressing are similarly important. Spring treatment comprises raking, mowing at decreasing height, aeration and rolling with a roller 1 cwt or less. Cutting at $\frac{3}{16}$ in and the use of sharp sand, gives as fast a surface as closer cutting and frequent rolling. The spring fertiliser and that for small booster doses should be mainly sulphate of ammonia; the more complicated autumn ones are applied at 1–2 cwt per acre with sharp sand or top dressing at 6 tons. For formulae, see section 10.5.4 and also *Turf Culture* page 133.

Divots must be replaced and it is advisable to stagger the effects of wear, for example by moving the pins on golf greens frequently. Foot traffic in frosty weather harms greens and should be discouraged.

Fine turf needs protection against pests, diseases and weeds. *Poa annua* and pearlwort are common; plantains, daisies and other broad-leaved weeds may warrant grubbing by hand. Selective weedkiller application if decided upon, should not be delayed, and made a few days after fertilising and in settled non-drought conditions. Mat-forming mosses in otherwise well-maintained greens can be eradicated with mercury-based compounds, and earthworms can also seldom be tolerated. 'Switching' the dew reduces the risk of *Fusarium* disease but fungicidal treatment may also be necessary—before symptoms appear, if previous history shows that they are probable.

10.6.4 Turf subject to rough wear: winter pitches

Hardwearing turf falls into two categories with different management programmes, depending upon the time of year when it is used. This section deals with winter pitches for football and hockey; sections 10.6.5 and 10.6.6 deal with summer games such as cricket and tennis.

In a good winter pitch, with a firm even surface of close growing turf, the grass affords a cushioning effect against the compaction of the soil and injury to players following falls. Seeds mixtures as in section 10.2.3 should give an easily-managed hard-wearing sward, not necessarily fast growing which implies more mowing. From the outset, *football* pitches must be designed to endure 8–9 months play, often under bad conditions, for each of several subsequent years. Association football is more severe on turf than rugby. The soil must be a light medium, not heavy loam, levelled and well-drained. A First Division club may find it worthwhile to substitute large amounts of light soil for a heavy one, as did Tottenham Hotspur in 1952; smaller clubs can apply gypsum to advantage. Autumn play may follow a spring turfing, but after autumn turfing or seeding, a full year must elapse.

During the season, compaction due to play and rolling must be relieved by surface aeration and spiking, and applying sand. Rolling should be light and as infrequent as possible. Plantains, knotgrass and other weeds of bare patches may have to be removed. When play ends in April, the surface of muddy and compacted goal areas, etc., should be broken up with a disc harrow, or rotary cultivator set shallow, raked and forked. After dressing with gypsum and a fertiliser, it should be seeded with quick-growing ryegrass, or turfed from a turf nursery of similar soil type, and then kept well watered.

The whole pitch must be deep-pierced to 9 in using a slow moving tractor, and later pierced again to 4 in. It benefits from a general fertiliser, and should be lightly rolled and topped with the mower—not allowed to run to hay—in the summer. The ideal height is $1\frac{1}{2}$ in but $\frac{3}{4}$ in where it also serves as a cricket outfield. As the summer closes, the height of cut should tend to 1–$1\frac{1}{2}$ in. for association football, but $2\frac{1}{2}$–3 for rugby pitches. A fine surface is achieved by the use of a heavy roller before the association football season starts.

Hockey pitches need a firm level surface without minor undulations, to permit free-running of the ball. The soil must be well-drained and the grass kept short. A well-established bent/fescue turf is alone able to give the required clean resilient surface.

Divots removed during play must be quickly replaced. If it is necessary to roll in wet conditions to maintain an even surface, tining, slitting and dressings of sharp sand become vital. Frost presents a serious hazard and the use of electric warming wires should be considered if funds permit. Salt should never be applied to frozen ground as it destroys both soil structure and turf vigour. Renovation should begin early in April, obtaining a fine tilth and applying fertiliser. 1–2 cwt of grass seed should be sown per acre, covered with $\frac{1}{4}$–$\frac{1}{2}$ in of fine topsoil, raked and rolled and the seedlings mown when they reach 2 in high.

In summer the grass needs regular mowing at 1–$1\frac{1}{2}$ in with occasional top dressing and light rolling. Balanced fertilisers are preferable to sulphate of ammonia which produces quick flushes of growth. The height of cut should be reduced to $\frac{3}{4}$ in as the playing season approaches, and earthworms eliminated.

On *polo* grounds there is a short playing season in spring and early summer. Hard true level turf should be established on loam soil from a non-ryegrass mixture; light soil is subject to undue wear and clay soil to 'poaching'. The grass should be kept to 1–$1\frac{1}{2}$ in rolled and spiked; weeds and ryegrass must be controlled as they cause slippery patches and erratic movements of the ball. As the season ends, levelling, renovation and fertilising are needed.

10.6.5 Summer sports turf: cricket

Cricket grounds consist of two sections, the wicket and the outfield. The latter needs a well-mown, 'fast' and accurate surface, with a gradient of no more than 1 : 60. Its mowing should start early in the year, with the blades set high at first and later lowered. Compaction, commonly due to heavy gang mowers, must be relieved by spiking and aeration. Otherwise outfields are managed as are other extensive areas. Wicket management however demands great skill. Recent losses in Test Match takings, estimated at £25,000, have been blamed on the wickets at Lord's and Headingley and the popular demand for 'fast' wickets continues. The pace and bounce throughout the match should encourage the batsmen to play shots. Fast bowlers need to be able to move the ball off the seam early on, and wrist spinners to turn the ball from the first day onwards; then sufficient wear should assist finger spinners from the second afternoon onwards.

The wicket is prepared on a 30 yd square 'table' or 'cricket square', on excellently drained soil underlaid with ash or sharp stones. The top 3 in of existing soil may have to be replaced by the ideal heavy, water-retentive soil such as a heavy Surrey loam, or failing that by a 1 : 4 marl/lighter soil mixture, and the soil must be graded before seeding or turfing. A more simple way of making the soil heavier is by regular top dressing with heavy loam.

After seeding (see section 10.3.1) and management (section 10.3.2) the grass should be lightly 'topped' when 2–3 in, lightly rolled, and gradually brought to the required shortness. If turf is used, springy or matted ones must be discarded. Maintenance begins in September on those parts of the square no longer required for play, with a general fertiliser, scarifying and raking, several close mowings, and a thorough 9 in spiking to allow dressings to penetrate. The equipment used must not cause undulations in the ground, and should make holes at 3 in intervals.

The worst areas may need returfing from a good turf nursery, but most of the square should be reseeded with 5 lb of seed (see section 10.2.2) per 100 sq. yd. and covered with sacking or polythene. Top dressings of good loam, lime and sand are then worked in and levelled with a wooden lute and can be followed with a low-nitrogen fertiliser but bearing in mind that excessive organic matter makes the wicket matted or soft.

If the soil is still considered too light, the traditional autumn application of marl (1–2 lb per sq yd with up to 10 lb of loam) improves the surface. Control of earthworms and leatherjackets may also be necessary. In winter the square may need light mowing in dry weather. Fungal disease must be prevented by 'switching' the dew and by fungicidal treatment (see section 10.7). In February the turf should be well aerated and rolled—in different directions, to avoid ridges—using first a light roller, then a heavier one. From early March onwards, light mowing and aeration, if possible weekly, and at the end of the month a balanced fertiliser, develop a good wicket. Wormkiller may also have to be applied. As the first match approaches, particularly in the final fortnight, the pitch should be consolidated to a depth of 4 in, with a roller of up to 2 tons weight, the last rolling being along the line of the pitch. Frequent raking and mowing, with the blades steadily lowered, encourages vertical growth, especially valuable on wickets for early play. Debris should be swept off. This is the ideal time to apply selective weedkillers; any watering must be completed in time to allow the top 3–4 in to dry out before play begins.

After play, spiking and light dressings of loam and a sprinkling of fertiliser should be given, bowler's foot-marks returfed, and thin patches reseeded. Watering—copious in dry weather—must finish in good time and the sequence is then light rolling, heavier rolling (up to 30 cwt), hand raking and final very close mowing, before the next match.

10.6.6 Tennis courts

These must have a true even surface giving an accurate bounce—9 in of medium loam overlying 4–6 in of ashes give best results, and sandy soils need additional organic material. As the court must dry quickly and yet have negligible gradient, drainage needs careful attention. Courts are best oriented N.N.W–S.S.E or failing that, North–South; their surroundings should allow the ball to be easily seen against the background, and in this respect trees and shrubs are preferable to open sky. At least 20 yd of run back have to be allowed behind the base lines and similarly 4 yd on either side. The seed mixtures in section 10.2.3 are suitable.

Base lines may be renovated in September using turfs of hardwearing species, of $\frac{1}{2}$ oz per sq yd of 50% chewing's, 40% dogstail, and 10% browntop. Rye grass with its power of rapid establishment may also be useful here. The whole court must be forked or aerated and treated with a phosphate- and potash-rich autumn fertiliser. The usual principles of winter and spring mowing should be followed; in April a general fertiliser rich in nitrogen but poor in organic matter which would give a spongy surface, is necessary. During the season, light raking, whaleboning, fertilising, slitting, rolling, frequent close mowing, and the usual measures against pests, diseases, earthworms, weeds, moss and drought may all be required.

10.6.7 Road and motorway verges

Since the war a large area of hard-wearing turf has been laid down on the *verges* of residential roads and motorways. The former of these sites present special problems such as the cutting of strips of turf intersected by paths,

Plate 10.7. Grass is a major ingredient in landscape work in housing areas. Lawn standards are seldom appropriate and design must be for hard wear and minimum maintenance. Housing development by Wates Ltd. at Sydenham. Landscape consultants: Derek Lovejoy & Associates.

branch roads, drives and trees, and mowers have been considerably modified to meet them. Conventional motor mowers and gang mowers with easily raised cutting cylinders have been in use for some time, and more recently verge cutters have been developed with vertically rotating blades which cut the grass and direct the clippings downwards. Motorway verges receive similar attention although slope is here a more serious problem than obstacles. Grass growth retarding chemicals such as maleic hydrazide may be useful in these situations where grass quality is not a primary aim. New landscape problems on a grand scale have been presented by the development of our motorway programme. This has led to the development of hydraulic seeding, where seed is applied in liquid suspension from a special machine thus enabling the rapid treatment of large areas and the establishment of turf on all types of surface from fly ash to hoggin. In these situations grass may be replaced with grass/clover/ black medick and other mixtures (Plate 10.4).

On *dog tracks* and *athletic tracks* the necessary short, even, weed-free turf has to be well kept and frequently renovated. Frost may be a serious hazard and dog tracks benefit from protection with straw or by electrical warming wires. The height of cut is $\frac{3}{8}$–$\frac{1}{2}$ in for dog tracks and $\frac{1}{2}$–1 in for athletic tracks.

Racecourses, often sited on heaths where bents and fescues are indigenous, are ideally on light loam rather than sand or clay and form a fine matted springy turf. Their shock-absorbing quality is increased by keeping the turf fairly long—2 in between meetings allowing longer growth just before the races, especially for steeplechasing —without letting it run to hay. After racing, and replacing divots, the course requires spiking, rolling, regular mowing and occasional fertilising.

Moles and rabbits may warrant removal.

Orchards and *cemeteries* pose few special problems if advantage is taken of rotary mowers tailor-made to these conditions; large gang mowers are likewise the obvious choice on *airfields*. Lastly there is the more difficult matter of establishing and maintaining turf on derelict areas despite debris, toxic chemicals, and infertile subsoil or shale. Given time, a fair humus may be built up by growing nurse crops of grey alder, willow, Corsican pine or birch; later on grass seed may be broadcast (not drilled) with fertiliser, on the cleared site. The low pH which must be adjusted to 6, makes alkaline–nitrogen fertilizers and lime much more valuable than on most turf, and legumes may also probably be included in the seeds mixture. Even then, turf cannot be expected to establish itself rapidly as on better sites.

10.6.8 Grass substitutes
While the superiority of turf is undoubted, there are a few situations where it may be preferable to replace it with artificial 'all weather pitches' or with fine greens

composed of pearlwort, clover or yarrow, of aromatic plants like thyme, chamomile or pennyroyal. For details of these the reader is referred to pages 211–16 of *Turf Culture*.

10.6.9 The use of clover mixtures
In certain circumstances, clover may be better ecologically suited to a particular situation than grass, and can often be used to good effect. For example, for turf around factory premises, power stations, institutions, university parkland or campus, where maintenance and cutting may be carried out using a gang mower, and the length of grass is usually kept between one and two inches, the use of a mixture containing clover can be of particular value. In addition, clover confers a pleasant appearance, and supplies nitrogen, and also drought resistance.

Note: Ministry of Transport specification for roads:

	For Verges, Central Reserves and Side Slopes
Perennial rye grass S.23	60
Red fescue S.59	20
Smooth-stalked meadow grass	10
Crested dogstail	12
White clover S.100	10
Total	112 lb

The nitrogen-fixing properties of clover can be valuable where one is faced with the problem of difficult soil and subsoil conditions, such as occur on high pH soils which are subject to boron toxicity as in the case of P.F. ash which is used as an embankment fill. The desirable properties of clover in obtaining nitrogen from the air together with the effect of its extensive root system, all help to produce a better soil structure under these conditions where grass species alone would not give the most beneficial results.

Examples of mixtures which can be used in such situations are given below:

	Grass on P.F. Ash Embankment (on 4–8 in topsoil)
Perennial rye grass S.23	40
Red fescue S.59	20
Smooth-stalked meadow grass	10
Crested dogstail	12
White clover S.100	15
Red clover S.123	15
Total	112 lb

Plate 10.8. Major open spaces in New Towns include large areas of grass which can be kept quite rough and informal at a parkland standard. Stevenage New Town.

	Grass on P.F. ash		Grass on P.F. Ash
GRASSES		CLOVERS	
Italian ryegrass	15	S.123 broad red clover	12
S.23 perennial rye grass	15	Late flowering red clover	15
S.24 perennial rye grass	30	S.100 white clover	10
Rough-stalked meadow grass	15		
		Total	112 lb

10.7 Calendar of turf management

JANUARY

Drainage: Check outlets and note where drainage is ineffective.

Top dressings: Under cover, screen, mix, and transport top dressing and compost.

Aeration: Use aerating machinery where ground conditions permit, and apply coarse sand to wet, muddy surfaces. Hand fork wet areas on sportsgrounds, especially goalmouths, and brush and harrow frequently.

Renovation: Although late, turfing is still possible in January, and sometimes necessary to rectify holes in football pitches.

FEBRUARY

Seeding: Cultivate and work spring seedbeds, add appropriate top dressings and fertiliser, and leave fallow.

Aeration: Continue aerating and brushing under suitable conditions, harrow and rake when the soil is drying off after a wet period. Improve aeration of golf greens on heavy soils with solid tine fork and sharp sand; on light porous soils replace the sand with loam.

Pests: If worm casts tend to smother grass scatter with a cane in dry weather, and apply arsenical or non-poisonous wormkilling preparations in dull mild weather.

173

Weeds:	In dry weather towards the end of the month, apply lawn sand and other preparations to control pearlwort, daisy and clover.
Moss:	If moss invasion is serious, examine possible predisposing causes. Control by combination of cultural and chemical treatments.

MARCH

Seeding:	Make early spring sowings on well-prepared seedbeds; scarify and oversow thinly covered areas of established turf. Cover the seed with a fine layer of soil or sharp sand..
Fertilising:	Apply general fertiliser at the end of March, or early in April.
Mowing:	Mow with blades high, especially in cold and windy weather.
Rolling:	Counteract effects of frost by rolling but only when the surface is dry. Roll cricket pitches lightly at first and more heavily towards the end of the month.
Aeration:	Thoroughly rake all matted turf. Brush bowling greens, tennis courts and cricket pitches to distribute worm casts and top dressing.
Diseases:	Apply fungicides to turf prone to *Fusarium* patch disease.
Pests:	Tests for worms and leather jackets, and if necessary apply control measures.
Weeds:	Use lawn sand, selective weedkillers, and other preparations to control daisies, pearlwort, clover and other weeds.
Moss:	Continue treatment—scarify and apply moss control compounds.

APRIL

Seeding:	Sow seed, rake in, apply thin layer of soil and roll if the weather is dry.
Fertilising:	Apply the complete fertiliser if not done in March.
Mowing:	Mow little and often, especially after warm showery weather, lower cutter blades at each successive mowing, except in cold weather.
Rolling:	Roll periodically.
Renovation:	Treat winter pitches by mowing, aerating, fertilising, scarifying, sowing 1–2 cwt grass seed per acre, harrowing, covering with clean light loamy soil, rolling if dry, lay turf in goal areas.
Diseases:	Apply fungicides for control of *Fusarium* and *Helminthosporium* diseases.
Weeds:	7–10 days after fertiliser treatment, and at least 3 days after mowing, apply selective weedkillers. Remove persistent weeds and coarse grasses by hand.
Moss:	If not done in March, apply moss control compounds.

MAY

Fertilising:	Apply supplementary fertilisers and water in during dry weather.
Mowing:	Cut frequently with knives low. Prepare wickets by repeated raking, mowing and rolling until the surface is firm and true with the barest covering of grass. Cut newly-sown turf when 3 in high, using hand shears or a side wheel mower with sharp blades set high; avoid 'pulling' and early close mowing.

Diseases:	Apply fungicides for control of Dollar Spot.
Weeds:	Continue April treatment as necessary.

JUNE

Fertilising:	Apply sulphate of ammonia and water in, if weather is dry. Examine and turn the compost heap.
Mowing:	From June onwards until October, regulate the height of cut according to the weather—during drought raise the blades and cut without grass box.
Diseases:	Apply fungicides for the control of *Corticium* and Dollar Spot.
Weeds:	Continue selective weedkiller treatment except in drought.

JULY

Fertilising:	Turn over the compost heap to destroy weed seeds.
Irrigation:	Water before the effects of drought become obvious.
Diseases:	If the weather is hot and humid, prepare to treat Dollar Spot, *Fusarium* and *Corticium*.
Weeds:	Selective weedkillers may be necessary to deal with the second crop of weeds.

AUGUST

Seeding:	Finally rake and roll the autumn seedbed; sow in favourable weather after the middle of the month.
Renovation:	Prepare to renovate worn areas.
Diseases:	In close, damp conditions apply fungicides to control *Fusarium*, *Corticium*, Dollar Spot, and *Ophiobolus* Patch.
Weeds:	Prevent weed establishment on worn areas.

SEPTEMBER

Seeding:	Take advantage of adequate moisture and warm soil to sow grass seed.
Fertilising:	Apply autumn fertiliser with a large organic fraction and little or no nitrogen.
Renovation:	Scarify, reseed, rake, cover with soil or sand, and roll to finish worn spots on cricket tables, bowling greens, and tennis courts.
Aeration:	Use hand forks or turf aerators, and spike and hollow-tine tennis courts, bowling greens, and lawns followed by a dressing of sharp sand or compost, well brushed in.
Diseases:	Continue to spray areas prone to disease with turf fungicides.
Weeds and Moss:	Apply control measures.

OCTOBER

Drainage:	Remedy defective drainage.
Turfing:	October is the best month for laying turf.
Fertilising:	After aerating, apply composts or other organic top dressings, or autumn fertilizers; apply also Nottingham marl to cricket pitches.
Renovation:	Renovate and reseed bare patches on bowling greens, tennis courts, cricket pitches, and other turf which was still in use in September.
Aeration:	Aerate with solid spikes or hollow tines.
Diseases:	Continue preventive and curative fungicide treatment.
Pests:	Apply worm control measures.

Weeds and Moss:	Continue control measures in settled, dry weather.

NOVEMBER

Turfing:	Complete the laying of turf.
Drainage:	Carry out drainage operations while the weather remains suitable.
Fertilising:	Apply winter turf dressing, as necessary, and on wet days, mix and screen compost indoors.
Aeration:	Aerate by hand fork or machine.
Rolling:	Lightly roll turf formed from autumn sowings, avoiding over-consolidation of clay soils.
Mowing:	Machines can be brought in for overhaul as the need for mowing decreases.
Pests:	Test for presence of leatherjackets and if necessary apply control measures. Continue treatment against earthworms.

DECEMBER

Turf nursery:	Prepare the turf nursery for fresh sowing by digging over; add fresh soil, and well-rotted manure or sewage sludge.
Pests:	Continue treatment against leatherjackets.
General:	December is a good time for overhaul and obtaining details of new materials which have become available.

Bibliography

Turf Culture, Ian Greenfield, Leonard Hill Books, London.

Lawns, R. B. Dawson, Royal Horticultural Society, Penguin Books.

Lawns and Sportsgrounds, M. Sutton, Sutton and Sons Ltd, Reading.

Planning, Construction and Maintenance of Playing Fields, P. W. Smith, Oxford University Press.

11 Tree Planting

BRENDA COLVIN

11.1 Groups and specimens for functional or design purposes

11.1.1 Introduction

Trees play an all-important role in British landscape. For the landscape architect they are a material of design, used not only for their beauty but also for their functional value as shelter, screens, backcloth; also for their power of absorbing smoke, dust and noise. They define and separate the open spaces, thus serving as do the walls and pillars of a building. Most of these functions call for collective use of trees, in belts, spinneys, or woodland groups, rather than for single perfect specimens. Landscape architects often need to combine forestry and horticultural methods and require therefore a clear understanding of both systems. Only in rare cases is either system, undiluted, suited to the needs of landscape architecture. In addition to these two traditional methods, modern machinery enables us to transplant mature or semi-mature trees, and the rate of industrial development throughout the country provides a supply of trees which would otherwise not have been available. Many trees doomed to make room for new buildings can now be transplanted to new positions.

11.1.2 Types of planting

The choice for the landscape architect therefore lies between three types of tree planting:

Traditional forestry—Small seedlings, 9–15 in high, closely planted with minimum ground preparation and subsequent drastic thinning as plantations grow.

Traditional horticulture—Nursery-grown specimens of various heights up to 10 or 15 ft. Careful ground preparation and moderate subsequent thinning and trimming.

Mature or semi-mature trees transplanted as available and spaced as ultimately required with no allowance for subsequent thinning.

11.1.3 Choice of type

The choice will be influenced not only by the effect desired, but also by the speed with which it can be achieved, and by the availability and cost of suitable types. The cost of transplanting rises steeply with the size of the tree; the spacing, or number of trees per acre, is of secondary importance. Indeed, forest-type planting of small trees six feet apart costs less per acre than any other

landscape treatment (see section 11.4.3). It compares favourably in initial cost with land sown with agricultural grasses. Subsequent maintenance costs per acre are also low in relation to other land use. Their assessment, in normal forestry practice, is related to ultimate timber yields, and while this aspect is not to be overlooked in large scale landscape projects, timber values in landscape projects are usually secondary to visual considerations. Siting of woodland will have been determined by design factors. Tree species must conform to existing soil and climatic conditions as well as to visual needs. Many visual and cultural errors can be avoided by following the indications of ecology and using the trees native to the locality.

11.1.4 Siting

Siting trees near buildings can be a difficult problem as shade is unwelcome in the case of old houses with small windows. In the case of modern buildings with large windows, shade may be an advantage. The difference is particularly marked in the case of schools where outdoor classes may be held on hot days only if shade is available near classrooms. Unwelcome shade may often be reduced by removing whole limbs or large overhanging branches of trees without spoiling the balance and appearance of the tree. Top lopping increases the foliage density below the cut and ruins the shape of the tree (see section 11.8.4 on care of mature trees).

11.1.5 Effect

Quick effects are usually called for in landscape planting. Clients and architectural colleagues tend to press for immediate results even where these preclude slower but surer methods. The landscape architect may, therefore, seek some compromise to combine immediate effect with long-term value, perhaps by using a few specimen trees in a matrix of forest type planting, or by using each type of planting in separate areas. Professional probity requires that long-term results are assured, and it is part of the landscape architect's duty to demonstrate to clients and colleagues all the issues involved. The rapid but sparse effect which we get by the use of mature trees is well justified in certain types of work, especially in urban

Plate 11.1. Young trees of more than normal nursery size planted for a reasonably quick effect in an industrial setting. Bowater Paper Corporation, Northfleet offices. Landscape architect: Brenda Colvin.

housing and street planting, but such specimen trees can never take the place of dense woodland, either for visual or functional purposes. Their value, indeed, is mainly ornamental—they tend to be inadequate as shelter or screens, and they fail to give the 'mass' needed as foil or counterpart to the voids or open spaces in a design. The transplanting of big trees should, in such cases, be done in conjunction with, and not as a substitute for, traditional planting.

11.1.6 Cost
When it comes to the cost of tree planting, landscape systems will of necessity be more costly than orthodox forestry. It should be remembered that many of the standard forestry practices are based on economic considerations related to timber yields. These considerations, essential to the scale and circumstances of forestry, give way to other factors which are of primary importance in landscape design. The cost of tree planting, when considered in relation to the cost of the industrial or town planning undertakings which call for such planting, is infinitesimal. Charges of extravagance based on comparison with forest planting can be met by presenting a balanced view taking amenity into consideration. The amenity and psychological values of the results will far outweigh the relatively small additional costs required. It is therefore important for the landscape architect to distinguish between those forestry practices which are governed by timber values and those which depend on

ecologic factors such as type of soil, climate and habits of growth where the experience of forestry is equally relevant to landscape planting.

11.1.7 Choice of species
Choice of species, whether for woodland, shelter belt or amenity planting, depends on local conditions; also on whether the ultimate crop aimed at is 'shade tolerant' in the early stages. The Forestry Commission *Bulletin No.* 14, *Forestry Practice*, gives useful tables and advice on the choice of species for different situations and soils. In general the conditions of trees growing naturally in an area are the best guide as to the ultimate crop, but in the early stages additional shelter and protection provided by 'nurse trees' of some quicker growing species may be needed. These can be removed as thinnings when the main crop becomes established, and need not therefore be of importance in the landscape for more than a few years. A typical example occurs in the case of beech plantations. Although beech is the natural 'climax' growth in many chalk and limestone areas, it would, in the primitive forest, have developed under ash or some other shade tree which it ultimately overshadows. Beech is not easily established in the open without some shade and, therefore, shelter is normally given by interplanting with quick growing species such as pine. The market for thinnings is an important factor leading in most cases to the use of pine, larch or other conifers which are in demand as pit props and poles. Many lamentations

177

from the public about conifer plantations are due to misconceptions on this subject. Rarely does the Forestry Commission, or any other landowner, plant conifers as a final crop on land which is well suited to hardwood timber.

Species for park and garden should also be adapted to ecological and climatic site conditions, though in urban situations and gardens the smaller scale of plantations and the greater degree of after-care may justify the use of special soils, irrigation and other artificial devices calculated to overcome the natural conditions, enabling the designer to choose from a much wider range than he can in the case of woodland and countryside.

11.1.8 Natural regeneration

Foresters are growing more appreciative of natural increase and, with the advance of their own methods, are quick to observe and recognise tree seedlings at the earliest stages. Protection from rabbits and other damage may suffice to develop woodland of good quality and fast growth in areas where conditions favour natural regeneration, and such woods may be better adapted to the locality than man-made plantations (see Fig. 11.1).

The landscape architect can make use of many self-sown trees. By selection and trimming, small saplings, if left undisturbed, will make fine specimens sooner than transplanted trees. Such trees are less easily transplanted than nursery stock, and should therefore be preserved *in situ* where possible. The process of scrub clearance is often too drastic, and saplings are frequently destroyed even in areas destined for new planting, through lack of observation and care. The standard specification to 'clear all scrub and trees of less than 4 in in stem diameter' is short-sighted since the unnoticed saplings with stems of 1 or 2 in stem diameter may hold greater promise than old neglected trees. The correct action is to select and trim up the best saplings and to remove inferior competitors, trees, weeds or redundant seedlings, as the case may be.

In most cases, however, new planting is necessary in addition.

11.1.9 Preservation of existing trees on new sites during construction and development

Temporary fencing around existing trees or groups is essential to prevent damage. In most cases it is best to enclose the contractor's working area to give protection to all surrounding vegetation to be preserved. Effective penalty clauses should be included in the contract, and the responsibility for maintenance of temporary fencing and replacement of damaged trees placed on the contractor.

New services should be sited to avoid damage to existing trees so far as possible.

The existing soil level must be maintained around trees to be preserved. Most tree species are liable to die if soil or rubbish is piled around their stems or over their roots. Equally they suffer from drought and starvation if their roots are cut or unduly limited. Changes in the drainage conditions leading to excess or shortage of water damages mature trees more than young ones as the latter are more adaptable while still making vigorous growth.

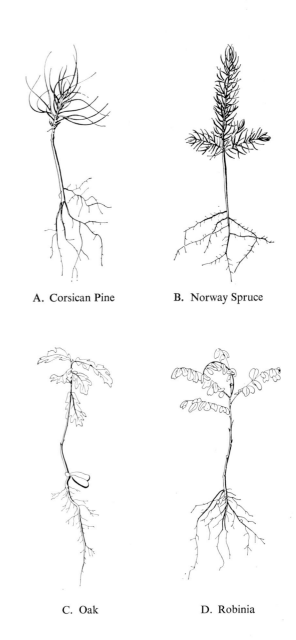

A. Corsican Pine   B. Norway Spruce

C. Oak   D. Robinia

Fig. 11.1. FOREST SEEDLINGS. Protection from rabbits and other damage may suffice to develop woodland of good quality and fast growth where conditions favour natural regeneration.

Plate 11.2. Esthwaite: a Forestry Commission mixed plantation blends naturally with the countryside and indigenous trees.

11.2 Drainage

11.2.1 General notes

The following brief notes do not cover this field. See Chapter 4, section 4.9 on Drainage. Reference to a standard work on the subject, such as *Principles of Field Drainage* by H. H. Nicholson, is also recommended.

Many trees flourish in moist ground, but few can endure stagnant water at the roots, and a well-aerated soil is necessary for healthy growth. Plantations on porous formations such as chalk, limestone or sand usually need no drainage, but the facts should be ascertained at the outset. Hardpans underlying sands can be troublesome and should be broken, for the sake of healthy growth, by deep ploughing or by subsoiling. Clay and other retentive soils (unless overlying porous rocks near the surface) should be drained.

A high water table may defy improvement by drainage and such areas are suitable only for alders, willows and poplars.

Open ditches (and/or ridge ploughing) are more suitable for woodland and hedgerow than covered agricultural drains, but for parkland planting of more open type normal pipe drains should be laid. Their depth depends on the soil profile. Normally they should be laid at the bottom of the topsoil. They may be useless if laid below clay.

Special drainage arrangements may be necessary in the case of stations prepared in retentive soils for trees whose roots require greater depth than the surrounding topsoil, as excavations in non-porous strata hold water and become bogs. Drains must in that case be as deep as the bottom of the pits, and the pipes covered with clinker or hardcore to the base of the topsoil (see Fig. 11.2).

Planting positions and drainage layout should be related in all cases, and records of drainage kept for reference. Other underground cables, ducts and services

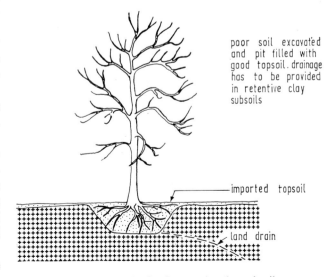

poor soil excavated and pit filled with good topsoil. drainage has to be provided in retentive clay subsoils

imported topsoil

land drain

Fig. 11.2. Tree planting in retentive clay subsoils.

179

of all kinds should also be related to, and recorded on planting plans.

11.2.2 Compaction of soil

On development sites, builders' vehicles and earth-moving machinery tend to compact the soil and to form hardpans, particularly in heavy retentive loams and on clay subsoils.

It is essential to ensure that the subsoil is friable and porous before planting on such ground. Deep cultivation by ploughing, mole drainage or subsoiling should be done

Plate 11.3. Natural regeneration of beech trees in a Chiltern wood.

to break up the subsoil and to ensure proper drainage conditions.

Water will often lie on the surface of such sites giving an erroneous impression of a high water table and water-logged subsoil, but, unless the pan is broken, drought will follow in dry seasons, as water is unable to pass either up or down through over-compacted subsoil.

Plate 11.4. A forest nursery in the Quantocks. Norway spruce being laid in a 'spacing board' to ensure correct distance between each transplant.

11.2.3 Damage to foundations and drains

Such damage by tree roots is liable to occur in soils of clay origin and in clay subsoils, where during periods of drought the roots seek moisture under these structures. Clay shrinks when dry and expands when moistened; it is this movement rather than any pressure of the root itself which causes damage. Where constant subsoil water is available, or where the soil is light and sandy, the risk does not exist. Roots do not penetrate sound waterproof drains, but may choke open land drains in heavy soils. Fast growing trees such as poplar and willow are not suitable for clay soils liable to shrink in drought. Research has shown roots twice as long as the height of the tree in such positions but in the moist situations to which such trees are adapted, such excesses do not occur.

In clay soils liable to shrinkage, it is better to keep all large trees well away from buildings and drains, unless water can be assured during periods of drought.

11.3 Young seedling trees

11.3.1 Selection and availability of nursery stock

Forest nurseries supply small seedling trees (from 6 in to 2 or 3 ft high) at very low rates for large quantities. Such trees seem very small to the uninitiated, but the younger the transplant the greater its adaptability and its power of fending for itself in new and perhaps adverse circumstances. All plants should have been transplanted, however, at least once by the grower before sale so they are usually not less than two years old, and are normally

sold for forest planting when not more than three or four years old (Plate 11.4).

'Sturdy transplants having a high ratio of root collar diameter to shoot length' are recommended by the Forestry Commission which, incidentally, is sometimes willing to supply seedling trees for landscape work.

Shortages of certain young stock occur occasionally and in these cases imports from the Continent may meet the need.

180

Transplanting helps to encourage a bushy root system and this can also be achieved by drawing a knife underneath the seed bed. This is known as undercutting. A plant grown in a seed bed one year, and then undercut and allowed to grow for a further year would be described in the trade as a 'two year u/c'. A plant grown in a seed bed for two years and then transplanted is called a '2 + 1'. A '1 + 1 + 1' refers to a three-year-old tree transplanted twice.

11.3.2 Park and garden trees of normal nursery size

Trees in a great range of variety for park and garden are supplied by growers of trees and shrubs at sizes ranging from 2–3 ft upwards to about 10 ft high, but stocks are usually limited in quantity to one hundred or less of a kind. No single grower ever seems able to supply the whole list required for any landscape project and great insistence is required to obtain all the species and varieties correctly as specified. Substitutes are often offered, or wrong varieties supplied in the hope that 'mistakes' will pass unrecognised. The specification should guard against this so far as possible, but actual experience of nursery and planting work is invaluable to the designer and this knowledge is not easily acquired from books.

Nursery-grown trees should have a well-developed compact root system as a result of frequent transplanting. Neglected trees and self-sown seedlings may have grown greater height for their age, but their straggling root system involves more risk in transplanting.

Sizes of trees for transplanting should be specified but as species vary greatly in regard to their tolerance to transplanting, it is necessary for the designer to be familiar with the sizes normally suitable and easily transplanted in each case, so that he can judge whether or not it may be safe in particular circumstances to specify larger than normal transplants. Many nursery firms are now growing trees and shrubs to sell at larger than average nursery sizes, especially for landscape work where maintenance and other site conditions are sufficiently good to justify the extra cost, and the growers in such cases can advise on this aspect of planting. In America it has long been the practice to provide an almost mature effect from the start, and to allow for little or no thinning at later stages.

In England stocks of large sizes are in short supply. Checking to ensure availability is essential before specifying quantities.

11.3.3 Size of trees for transplanting

In normal forestry where large areas are being close planted, very small seedlings are usually found to become established more readily than older plants. This is particularly true where weed competition is not great. On bare stony windswept hillsides in Derbyshire for instance, sycamores of 5 in in height survive better than those of 1 ft, and losses among 2 ft high transplants amount to nearly 100%. On the other hand, in areas of coarse weed growth it may be better to plant trees less likely to be suffocated by grasses. In such regions the best results have sometimes been attained by saplings started at 2 ft to 2 ft 6 in high, whose tips reach above the surrounding vegetation. The degree of aftercare and weeding has a close bearing on this subject and these aspects must be considered in relation to one another. One of the forester's reasons for using very small plants—though not his only reason—is their low relative cost, a matter of minor importance in most landscape projects.

We may indeed prefer, under certain circumstances, to use saplings of 4 or 5 ft in height, spaced 9 or 10 ft apart instead of the 6 ft by 6 ft forest, or even to interplant standard trees up to 12 ft high in critical positions amongst the rest, or in groups where quick height is needed.

11.3.4 Care of trees in transit and on arrival

Good packing and quick transport should be the responsibility of the supplier. Bundles of young trees should be opened, examined and 'heeled in' on arrival, and any complaints of dry or overheated roots should be registered without delay. The commonest cause of failures probably lies in wrong treatment between lifting and final planting. Plants tied up in bundles are liable to suffer irreparable damage from faulty aeration and moisture conditions. Once opened and laid in trenches with roots well covered by moist soil, the plants can await their turn without damage, but the shorter the period between lifting and planting, the better for the health of the trees.

11.4 Planting

11.4.1 Time of planting

Time of planting, depending on circumstances, may be from October to March inclusive. In wet seasons or high rainfall districts planting may continue into April. Periods of hard frost or high wind should be avoided. The choice between autumn and spring planting is a matter of judgment and foresight. In areas of high rainfall, or in moist soils, the risk of severe frost can be avoided by delaying planting until spring, but in dry areas and light sandy soils, the greater risk of spring droughts may be reduced by early planting. In parks and gardens where ample irrigation is available through periods of drought, spring planting is to be preferred.

In certain cases where site availability, weather conditions or other circumstances control planting periods, calculated risks have to be taken, with proper skill and precautions, to provide for planting earlier or later than normal practice would indicate. Adequate watering, and in some cases spraying the foliage with a retardative anti-transpiration spray (e.g. S.600) to prevent excessive evaporation are amongst the precautions to be taken. In this case a compensating fertiliser, consisting of equal parts of dried blood, hoof and horn and bonemeal, should be applied. The whole operation requires experienced supervision.

11.4.2 New plantations

New trees may be required:

(a) In areas of existing woodland to replace dead or diseased trees and to allow for future felling of mature timber without loss of amenity.

(b) In areas where former woods have been clear felled.

(c) On fresh ground formerly treeless.

(d) On difficult sites in industrial wastelands.

Woodland soils of (a) and (b) favour better tree growth than open land (even if cultivated) where no depth of leaf mould and forest humus has accumulated. Some trees fail completely in soils lacking the associated fungi. Trees such as *Prunus avium* and *Acer campestre* rarely attain full height in open sites but respond to the shelter and shade of light woodland by making quicker growth in the early stages. Some species are valuable in reclaiming derelict land in industrial areas.

11.4.3 Preparation of ground

In existing woodland. Some felling of poorly grown or senile trees, and clearance of undergrowth should be done to provide space and light conditions for new groups. The removal of old tree stumps and roots is not customary, but can now be done by machines such as the Vermeer stump-cutter or the Myers–Sherman 'stump-gobbler'—both American machines. This makes it

Plate 11.5. Deep ploughing on moorland.

possible to level over the ground, so easing future maintenance.

Adequate drainage should be restored where damaged or choked. Little further preparation is needed for small seedling trees; for standards and specimens, pits should be prepared as described in section on standard and park land trees p. 184.

Fertilisers are rarely needed in existing woodland soils at the time of planting, but light surface applications of general fertilisers in subsequent seasons will stimulate faster growth.

Trees planted in loose woodland soils must be well firmed in. Copious watering may be necessary in dry spring periods.

The above remarks apply equally to the replanting of areas recently clear felled.

Ploughed land. Well-drained ground which has been recently ploughed needs little or no further preparation unless weed growth is excessive. Freshly ploughed ground should be allowed to settle, or disc harrowed, so that no air pockets remain below the surface. Clean ground may be kept weed-free after planting by spraying with proprietary brands of weed killer containing 'Simazine'. This is a potent and long-lasting compound and must only be used with expert supervision.

Grassland. Established grassland provides many problems as some form of treatment is usually necessary before planting. The usual methods are ploughing, screefing or spraying. Ploughing is very satisfactory on deep soils, but on shallow soils over chalk it may do harm by bringing up the chalk and mixing it with the shallow suface loam.

Screefing, that is scraping away the vegetation and top layer of roots so as to leave a bare patch of soil about 18 in or 2 ft square where the tree is to be planted, is often used when ploughing is impracticable, and on shallow soils. It does not suppress the growth of vegetation so well as ploughing, but the soil below is not loosened and plants can be put in more firmly. There is less risk of them suffering from drought.

Spraying with Dalapon can be very effective when carried out at the right time, but grasses vary considerably in their resistance to this chemical.

Moor and heathland. Ploughing of moorland or heath in preparation for tree planting adds to the cost but is becoming more general as many foresters believe it to be justified by better results, particularly in wet peaty highland where it is difficult to establish trees. Where necessary the application of a fertiliser such as triple superphosphate is becoming standard practice. Ploughing is done with a special deep plough and the ground is usually left with high ridges and furrows, in some cases adjoining, as in normal farming), in others spaced at intervals of 5 or 6 ft according to the tree rows (Plate 11.5). The small trees are then planted on the ridge in the case of damp heathland on highland moors, in the furrow in dry eastern areas, or half way up the furrow when in doubt. On peat moors the system of placing the root between the two soil surfaces (the normal ground on one side and the upturned turf on the other) enables trees to be established where planting on the flat unploughed land would fail. Small trees planted low on the ridge gain some protection from wind.

The ridge and furrow should be aligned to accord with drainage requirements, leading surface water to open ditches along the contours. In porous soils and dry areas they may be planned to reduce run-off and delay loss of surface water. The ridge and furrow system is well suited for forestry plantations on large areas, using very small seedling trees (Plate 11.5).

On difficult sites. Difficult sites present special problems. Trees have been successfully established in pure chalk at the base of former quarries. Where the subsoil or underlying rock material is porous—as in the case of chalk or limestone—no drainage is needed; it is only necessary to ensure sufficient depth of good imported soil—say 6 yd diameter by 1 yd deep for trees whose spread will be approximately 20 ft when grown. But in retentive clay or other non-porous material such tree stations must be individually drained. In these cases it is better to build up mounds of topsoil to give adequate depth and drainage above the impermeable strata, and to group trees on these mounds (Fig. 11.3). Shallow drainage of the substrata may still be necessary but will be easier and less costly than individual drainage for each station. Mounding of additional topsoil above normal ground level may solve other problems also. For example, a low-lying site near the sea wall of an estuary, where the

Plate 11.6. Planting on shale tip at Brayton, Cumberland. Forestry Commission.

subsoil water is slightly saline, needs special treatment. Extensive mounds of topsoil, rising to 2 or 3 ft above normal ground level make it possible to establish trees which would otherwise fail; better root systems enable the trees to withstand high winds.

Too little is known as yet about the possibilities of tree planting without soil on difficult sites such as industrial waste materials, or in areas where soil or atmosphere, or both, may be polluted by industrial fumes. Much research is needed to enable such areas to be restored to health and balance. Many fairly good stands of trees have become established in unpromising situations such as colliery waste heaps, and where this can be achieved, eventual restoration of the soil will follow (Plate 11.6). On such difficult sites, any vegetation cover is valuable; care should be taken to preserve even pernicious weeds if they are colonising unfavourable ground. In such cases, screefing and ploughing are to be avoided; instead, seeds, cuttings or young seedlings should be tried in mounds of topsoil, peat or whatever suitable medium may be available, added to the surface.

Young trees—especially when self-sown—are more tolerant of indifferent soil conditions than is usually supposed; when good topsoil is in short supply, almost any material of suitable pH value and texture may be added to eke out the supply. The texture should be well mixed and the material must of course be free of toxins. Ash, city refuse, sand, brickbats and brickdust, lime rubble and other waste materials can all contribute to a growing medium. Analysis will indicate special deficiencies and imbalance which can be chemically rectified. In such

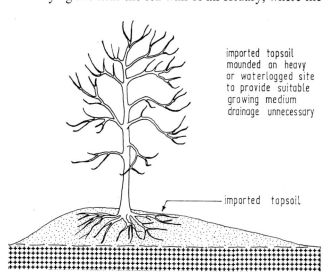

imported topsoil
mounded on heavy
or waterlogged site
to provide suitable
growing medium
drainage unnecessary

imported topsoil

Fig. 11.3. Tree planting on a mound formed on a heavy or waterlogged site.

183

unfortunate conditions humus and soil bacteria may be deficient. All colonising plants helping to make good these deficiencies, however slowly, are useful, as are also peat, sawdust, wood shavings, straw, bracken and other organic materials if they are available.

Small forest trees.　　　These are usually planted by spade. Special spades have been developed and these are useful where the ground is stony, hard or full of roots. The simplest method is a single 'notch'. Notching consists of making a slit with a spade, slipping in the young tree root before withdrawing the spade, and then treading the slit firmly together. A skilled forester may, under favourable conditions, plant up to one thousand a day by this method. Variations are the T notch and the L notch. In these, two cuts are made at right angles to each other, and a flap of soil is levered up with the spade and the plant roots spread out underneath. The flap is then lowered and the plant well firmed in. These methods enable the roots to be spread out better, and also avoid the dangers of compacted soil, or the roots being left in an air pocket.

A mechanical tree planter can be used under suitable conditions and is capable of planting many thousands of trees a day (eight thousand has been claimed). Two men are needed to operate tractor and planting trailer, but the machine is less subject to fatigue and uneven work than the human plantsman. The notches are regulated according to soil depth and tree root type, and any human tendency to shallow planting at the end of the day is obviated. It cannot operate in stony soil or in places where roots and rubbish are encountered, but will work well in many agricultural soils whether or not screefing and/or ploughing have been done previously. The distributors in Britain are Messrs. Jack Olding of Hatfield, Herts.

Standard and parkland trees.　　　Pit planting is the gardener's system suitable for larger transplants and standard trees. A hole is dug amply large enough to receive the roots without bending or confining them. Where grass is the existing ground cover, a thick turf is first cut, and after a hole of the required size has been excavated, is laid in upside down at the bottom of the hole to decompose and provide humus. Good quality loam with peat and a sprinkling of bone meal may be substituted for, or mixed with, the existing soil where this is of poor quality.

Cuttings or 'slips'.　　　In moist situations, stem cuttings of willows and certain poplars may be used instead of rooted plants. Shoots should be about 2 ft 6 in long and about $\frac{1}{2}$ in diameter. The thinner leading portion of the shoot is usually discarded; it is less likely to make good growth. Three-quarters of the shoot should be below the soil, and kept moist until roots have begun to form. Willow cuttings are supplied by certain nursery firms at low rates, or wands may be cut from local plants.

In order to make a dense bushy growth, and to obtain the brightest bark colouring, willows may be cut back in spring at regular intervals, to any desired height, thus making pollards or coppice forms. New shoots growing from buds below the cut, will make 6–8 ft annual growth from established root stocks.

Costs of planting.　　　These are so variable that figures are apt to be misleading.

Forest planting—Costs of recent date have varied between £100 and £170 (excluding the cost of fencing) per acre.

Park planting—Standard trees cost from £2 to £5 per tree, including supply, preparation and planting, stake and tie. Costs per acre depend on the density of the planting and may vary between £36 for very thin distribution and £150 for good parkland planting (excluding the cost of fencing). To this should be added the cost of preparation and sowing and mowing of grass (which is unnecessary in the case of forest planting). For grass of normal agricultural quality, allow £100 to £150 per acre. A local farmer may be able to sow pasture at a much lower cost.

The above figures assume in every case a sufficient depth of good topsoil *in situ*, and do not include the cost of fencing or tree guards.

11.4.4 Fertilisers

Additional fertilisers are sometimes applied, but experience indicates that subsequent surface mulching with organic material is better than the use of rich compost at the time of planting. The young tree should begin to grow and make contact with normal soil moisture before stimulants are given; moisture in the early stages is more urgently needed than plant food.

A good all-round fertiliser for general use is:

> 2 oz superphosphate of lime
> $\frac{1}{2}$ oz nitro chalk
> 2 oz bonemeal

This should be applied at the rate of 2 oz to the sq yd, and can be mixed with any organic mulch to make application easier.

11.5 Transplanting large trees

11.5.1 Introduction

The current extensive programme of factory, office and housing development has led to a considerable demand for the planting of large trees which will give some immediate effect. For the purposes of these notes on the general methods employed, large trees are regarded as being over 20 ft in height and over 4 in stem diameter. There is no upper size limit for trees that may be moved, but clearly with larger sizes the problem is correspondingly greater and the effects obtained may not warrant the greatly increased costs and risks involved.

11.5.2 Selection and preparation of trees
In general, trees selected for transplanting should be healthy young specimens, normally with well-balanced crowns. Where they are to be placed in groups some irregularity of form can be accepted, often with advantage to the scheme.

It is generally considered advantageous to prepare the tree a year or two in advance by root pruning. The object is to encourage the development of a compact fibrous root-ball that will be able to sustain the tree after moving and yet be of manageable proportions. Difficult species or very large trees benefit from a longer period of preparation. The suitable dimensions of the root-ball must be determined for each case, but, for trees of 4–11 in diameter stem at 1 ft from the ground, root-balls may vary from about 4–8 ft diameter and 18–36 in depth. Shallow soils which check deep rooting are of particular interest in that preparation costs may be reduced.

The root-balls of trees lifted from heavy soils hold together much better, and are easier to move without damage, than those from light soils. Good access to the lifting site is important to permit winter working.

11.5.3 Time for planting
Normal seasonal planting is the most satisfactory, but in many cases other considerations compel planting when trees are in leaf. In these cases an anti-transpiration spray such as S.600 should be used, and the remarks in section 11.4.1 are as applicable to mature trees as they are to young ones.

11.5.4 Availability of suitable trees
There is a general shortage of prepared nursery-grown trees, but as some nurseries are now specialising in large trees this situation should improve in future.

11.5.5 Costs
Prices vary substantially, depending on species, shape, size and amount of preparation already carried out by the nurseryman.

Prospective purchasers would be well advised to investigate as many sources of supply as practicable. A tree of 25–35 ft can cost from £25 to £80 to buy, transport and replant, so thorough investigation before planting is planned is essential if schemes are to be carried out satisfactorily. Awkward access to sites and long hauls with the heavy equipment required for the operation naturally cause significant increases where they occur.

Sometimes suitable trees can be found on the client's own land. In these cases, however, the saving is often disappointing as so much of the outlay is due to moving machinery from the contractor's base to the site and the subsequent transportation of the trees. A few of the firms who specialise in moving trees will guarantee their work, but this is naturally an additional cost.

11.5.6 Transplanting
There are three principal methods employed in this country at the present time.

Crane. After digging around and partly under the tree, the root-ball is securely wrapped. The stem is suitably protected and the crane lifts the tree by the stem, root-ball, or a combination of both. The trees are transplanted from site to site on lorries or low loaders and replanted again using a crane.

Cranes have been used successfully for many years, and the method has the advantage that several trees at a time may be transported long distances. Furthermore, cranes are capable of dealing with the larger sized trees.

Newman trailer. One tree at a time can be lifted, transported and replanted using only this simple two-wheeled trailer and a suitable four-wheel-drive towing vehicle. The root-ball is suitably wrapped and firmly secured by chains to a special clamp fixed around the stem. The trailer is tipped against the tree and fastened to the clamp. The trailer is then pulled down by the towing vehicle thereby prising the tree from the ground into a horizontal position. The underside of the root-ball is wrapped, the crown tied in as far as possible, and the tree is ready to travel. For planting the operations are reversed (Plate 11.7).

This method has the advantage that trees can be moved by comparatively light tackle and a small gang of two or three men. The size of the tree that can be moved using this trailer is limited by the maximum stem diameter that will fit the clamp (about 12 in) and the total weight of the tree (about 4 tons).

S.L.D. transplanter. This machine has been recently introduced from the U.S.A. It consists of a high-powered, four-wheel-drive tractor with a hydraulically operated trowel-shaped blade mounted on the front. Three to four cuts are made around the tree, and on the last the tree is prised from the ground, carried to its new site and lowered into a previously prepared hole. Guying is often unnecessary due to the wide and deep root-ball that is formed by the machine.

At the present time trees are being transplanted without previous preparation, and experience suggests that a relatively high degree of success may be achieved. The method has the advantage that large numbers of

Plate 11.7. A substantial tree about to be removed to another site by a Newman transplanting machine.

unprepared trees may be moved rapidly. The limiting factor is the distance the machine can economically carry the trees. Special self-loading trailers are being developed to extend the scope of the method.

11.5.7 Replanting

Certain fundamental considerations are applicable to all methods.

The planting hole should be dug at least 2 ft wider than the tree's root-ball, and sufficiently deep to allow drainage and 6 in of topsoil at the base if required. The tree should be placed at its former level and the trench firmly back filled with good topsoil. Watering, if considered necessary, should be copious and should be carried out before the last of the topsoil is placed. A mulch of 1–2 in of porous topsoil or peat is desirable.

Transplanted trees will normally benefit from an application of fertiliser, which may be incorporated in the backfill or applied as a surface dressing.

Most trees require guying for 3 to 4 years until they are re-established, and windfirm. The normal procedure is to place three guys about half way up the tree and secure them by stakes or sunken 'dead men'. The stem of the tree should be protected from rubbing and some means of periodically tightening the guys is desirable. Alternatively, underground guying may be carried out whereby

guys are fixed across the root-ball with suitable protection. The latter method has the advantage that there are no unsightly guys to cause an obstruction.

11.5.8 Aftercare

Attention to any maintenance required is essential. Watering may be necessary at regular intervals until the trees have recovered. The quantity of water required varies, but average requirements are about 40 gal per tree at 3–4 weekly intervals from April to September. Mulching over the entire root-ball to a depth of 2–3 in can greatly reduce watering requirements and stabilise soil temperature.

Care must be taken over drainage. Losses can be expected if surface and subsoil drainage are disturbed and the planting holes became waterlogged.

Thin barked species, particularly when planted in paved areas, can benefit considerably from hessian wrapping on the main stem. This also reduces the danger of sun scorch.

Further applications of fertiliser may be desirable to assist trees and complete a full return to health and vigour.

The tightening or replacing of guys may be required from time to time. All trees should be checked periodically and prompt attention given as required. Failure to do so may well result in the waste of all the previous time and effort.

11.6 Fencing and tree guards

11.6.1 Plantation fencing

Young trees need protection until thoroughly established against:

(*a*) Grazing animals, both domestic cattle, sheep, horses, etc. and wild rabbits, hares and deer.
(*b*) Human vandalism and carelessness.

The type of fencing must be adjusted accordingly. Deliberate, aggressive vandalism is difficult to overcome but casual vandalism and trespass can be discouraged by high fences of close strands of strong barbed wire without horizontal timber bars. Post and rails make good cattle fences and look well in the landscape, but they invite trespass. In cases where some seasonal trespass by hunt servants, keepers and sportsmen is to be tolerated, stiles or bars should be provided. Gates or moveable panels in the fencing, necessary for maintenance, should be sited inconspicuously to discourage trespass.

Damage by contractors' vehicles and tackle in the course of development work should be avoided by the provision of fences in the case of established as well as young trees, though a temporary definition may suffice for that purpose (see section 11.1.9).

With the exception of this type of temporary fencing, it is false economy to erect fencing insufficiently durable or insufficiently high to give full protection. Above all avoid easily climbable fencing where trespass is likely to occur.

Ornamental fencing, if required for special situations, must be designed to fulfil its functions also.

For general all-round use and to meet most types of hazard, the following specification is suggested:

Top of fencing to be 4 ft above ground. Posts 4 in × 5 in at top fully pressure creosoted, to be dug into the ground to a depth of 2 ft at 50 yd intervals. Stakes 3 in × 4 in at top fully pressure-creosoted, to be driven into ground to a depth of 14 in, fourteen per 50 yd. Corner posts to be securely strutted, fully pressure creosoted, dug in to a depth of 3 ft.

All posts and stakes, other than corner posts, to be sawn off on the slant 3 in above top strand of wire after erection.

Wire netting to be erected 36 in high, bottom edge turned out 6 in and buried in shallow trench. Wire netting: 17 gauge, 1¼ in mesh, 42 in wide. High tensile wire on which to hang netting, attached to the posts, to be 8 gauge. Above this fix three strands of barbed wire at 4 in intervals, making top strand 4 ft from ground.

11.6.2 Cost of fencing

This is usually reckoned per yard run. Recent costs have varied between 8*s*. 0*d*. and 12*s*. 0*d*. per yard for the specification above.

A more economical type of fence with post and wire to exclude stock but not rabbits may cost 5*s*. 0*d*. to 10*s*. 0*d*. per yard.

Posts and rails of good quality timber cost approximately 25*s*. 0*d*. per yard.

11.6.3 Tree guards for specimen standard trees or groups of trees and shrubs

In parks or agricultural areas where fencing is of the type specified above, tree groups may be protected by similar means. Individual standards, or hedgerow and roadside trees may be enclosed by close set barbed wire supported on three posts making triangular guards.

With the increasing use of mechanical hedgecutters steel guards for hedgerow saplings may be necessary on industrial sites or where maintenance is liable to be carried out by men with no forestry training.

In urban areas tree guards may be of painted or galvanised metal. Many standard types are commercially available. All guards should be removed before the increase of stem girth approaches their diameter. Neglect of this obvious precaution has caused the death of many urban trees.

11.6.4 Stakes and ties for standard trees

Stakes for standards over 4 or 5 ft high should be specified to suit the size of the tree. They should be stout enough to provide support until new roots are formed; say 1½–2 in diameter. They should be spiked at one end and driven 2 ft into the ground before planting the tree. In very windy sites two stakes per tree may be necessary. The length of the stake should equal that of the tree stem below the branching.

Two adjustable ties per tree should be specified. Ties should be inspected and adjusted frequently to allow for expansion of stem diameter. Easily adapted ties are commercially available.

11.7 Hedgerows and shelter belts

11.7.1 Hedgerow trees

With the use of bigger ploughs and harvesters, the sizes of fields in arable areas is increasing and many hedgerows are being destroyed. The Ministry of Agriculture and the Forestry Commission are concerned and have advised farmers and landowners to maintain trees where possible, as windbreaks, or as groups in the corners of large fields, to check the risk of wind erosion and to maintain biological balance, since much bird and insect life is lost along with the hedges. Ground temperature is raised perceptibly by means of hedges—a point of importance in some areas.

In grazing districts, so long as animals are pastured in the open, the need for enclosed fields and shade trees remains and biological balance better assured than under modern factory farming systems.

The landscape architect may appreciate the visual variety between the two types of landscape; he is also concerned to maintain biological balance and that traditional distribution of timber trees so characteristic of the British landscape. When we have few hedges and very large fields, the tree groups become outstanding features, and their siting and distribution an even more important element of the landscape. In such cases grouping is usually a key to success (Plate 11.8).

Most hedges contain numerous seedling trees, and traditionally the hedge cutter selected a few to replace those felled for timber or dying of old age. The machine hedge cutter is less sensitive and tends to cut everything regardless of future needs.

It has been estimated that one third of British standing timber consists of hedgerow trees and it should be realised that hedgerow timber, especially along country roads, has commercial as well as scenic value; the care needed to ensure continuity is well spent. To plant young trees in hedgerows is difficult and nearly always unnecessary. Selection and marking of natural saplings growing in the hedge is the best means of obtaining new trees where required, and this can be done by a woodman in anticipation of the hedge cutting holocaust. A few yards of hand clipping, and removal of redundant growths on either side of the selected trees, before the hedge cutter arrives, will

bring them to his notice and make it easier for him to follow previous instructions on the subject. The system has been found effective even without previous instruction.

Where no saplings are found and new trees are required, standards can be planted just alongside the hedge. Strong triangular tree guards and stakes (needing some attention for several years) should be supplied. Local types of trees should be chosen, and they should be planted far enough back to avoid slaughter by the hedging machine.

Groups planted in field corners should be fenced securely against trespass and grazing animals.

11.7.2 Shelter belts and screen planting

In upland or coastal districts the wind shelter provided by tree belts can contribute materially to the temperature and 'amenity' of the leeward area (Plate 11.9). The width of shelter given depends on wind strength and ground form, but in broad general terms, on flat ground there is a fifty per cent reduction of wind velocity at a distance of ten times the height of the trees at ground level (Fig. 11.

The siting of shelter belts should be a preliminary aspect of design, considered at the master plan stage.

Belts of fairly open texture, breaking the force but not deflecting the wind completely, are found to be more effective than complete dense growth, because the latter causes turbulence on the leeward side—as does a high wall. There are, however, means of overcoming this turbulence, such as a gradual lift, starting on rising ground with low shrubs, and increasing the height of the trees in the leeward rows, so that the wind is carried over

Plate 11.8. Good standing timber in hedges in a field and wood pattern typical of many parts of the country.

Plate 11.9. Clydesdale. A view showing useful shelter plantations in exposed country.

and not infuriated by abrupt frustration. One might draw the analogy of a horse approaching a hurdle set too high; a sudden stop and the jockey is flung in turbulence over the fence.

Forestry Commission grants are available for shelter belts if their width is not less than 2 chains, or 132 ft; this allows for felling of one half the width at maturity without loss of the screen. Even in the case of narrower belts where the timber factor is inapplicable, it is still necessary to ensure continuity by some means of rotational or selective felling and renewal to avoid the risk of the whole belt becoming senile at the same time.

Narrow widths may more often be available, but are less satisfactory for screening or shelter than wide belts. A single row of trees offers little opportunity for renewal, or for the mixture of evergreen and deciduous species which is a valuable feature of screens. A row of lombardy poplars suggests sewage works and draws attention to sites which might otherwise pass unnoticed. The principle of 'defence in depth' is applicable not only to military strategy; plantations to screen people from noise, fumes, smoke, smells and cold winds are effective only if wide enough to permit of a good mixture of height and texture. Visually, they should be well related to the ground plan and to other features in the area.

An effective screen can be planted for quick results on a 50 ft width. Fig. 11.5 shows a section of a plantation which served its purpose three years after planting, but does not allow for renewal, as it is not regarded as a permanent feature. This is a visual screen, not intended for wind shelter.

Close planting encourages rapid growth in the early stages but may need thinning (particularly if required for wind shelter) at successive stages of development (Fig. 11.5).

Where the ground is moist enough for willows and poplars, dense and rapid growth can be obtained by cutting back alternate rows in spring to form pollards or coppice growth at the height required. Good visual screens can be made on very narrow widths by this method.

11.7.3 Hedges with tree screens

In nearly all cases a hedge planted on the windward side of tree belts increases the rate of growth of the screen in the early stages and ensures low cover in the long term. Screens which are allowed to become 'leggy' may defeat their purpose, as draughts develop near the ground. Thorn hedges are usually the most suitable; they should be 'laid' when five or six years old to ensure good bottom growth, but may be left to develop freely thereafter if space permits.

189

11.8 Maintenance and care of trees

11.8.1 Maintenance of new plantations of forest type
The main maintenance necessary is:

Regular inspections after planting.
Replacement of losses.
Weeding round young trees.
Thinning at successive stages.

The work for the first few years after planting may be included in the planting contract and should be clearly specified.

The landscape architect himself also has a responsibility to make careful inspections after planting, and these may often be necessary for several subsequent years. This is a point which needs to be settled with the client as the extent of these visits largely depends on the calibre of the personnel in charge of a particular site.

Attention to fences includes, in addition to repairs, the clearance of rabbits and hares where they may have gained access.

Weeding to prevent overshadowing and suffocation of small trees is necessary until these outgrow surrounding vegetation. Two or three weeding operations in a summer depending on the soil and season, are usually enough to give the trees that initial advantage over the competition.

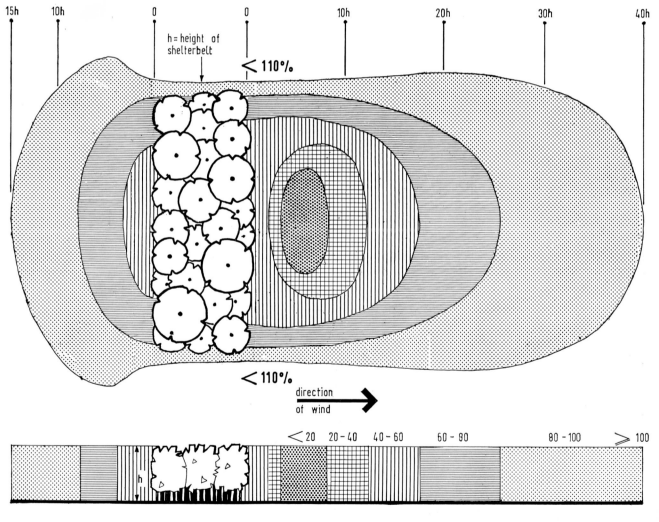

Fig. 11.4. Diagrams showing reduction of wind speed obtained from shelter belt protection
(based on Forestry Commission Forest Record No. 22—*Shelterbelts for Western Hill Farms*).

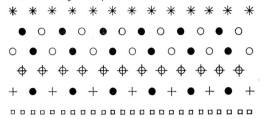

PLANTING PATTERN which achieves a very quick screen later thinning anticipated

KEY

* — cotoneaster salicifolia · 3′-4′
● — populus canescans · standards
○ — ligustrum lucidum · 2′-2·6″
⊕ — cotoneaster frigida · 4′-5′
+ — prunus lusitanica · 2′-2·6″
□ — ligustrum ovalifolium · 2′-2·6″

Fig. 11.5. Close planting for quick shelter and screening. To be thinned out at successive stages of development.

After a few years, their shade gradually suppresses most weed growth.

Replacement of losses, or 'beating up' to ensure up to ninety per cent 'take' of initial planting is usually included in the contract to be carried out within a year of planting.

Thinning begins at the stage when mutual competition among the trees must be checked. Numbers are successively reduced to fifty per cent, twenty-five per cent or less of original numbers according to the species and rate of growth. Details of such thinnings, depending on many circumstances, should be determined in the light of developments.

Brashing, or trimming off the lower branches up to a height of 6 or 7 ft, is commonly carried out before thinning, when the trees are about 20 ft high. Sometimes only every other row is brashed, but complete brashing is well worth while where landscape appearance is of importance. It lets in light and air, ensuring better development of the trees and of the ground flora.

High pruning is sometimes carried out on selected stems, and usually only those trees likely to form the final crop are pruned. This practice much improves the appearance of groups and plantations.

11.8.2 Weeding of young plantations

Weeding is usually done with a hook but may sometimes be done mechanically or chemically. Mechanical weeding may be carried out by hand-controlled reciprocating knives or rotary cutters, or by tractor-mounted rotary cutters. With all mechanical methods, it is difficult to weed close to the trees. Chemical methods are still rather limited. Dalapon may be used to control grass in planted areas but can only be safely applied when the trees are dormant and even then care must be taken not to get too much spray on the trees.

Some conifers are unaffected by some of the growth regulating herbicides such as 2,4.D and 2,4,5.T and these have been successfully used to control weed growth, but they tend to encourage grass to develop. Other contact herbicides have been tried in conjunction with shields, and experiments are being carried out to develop granular herbicides effective against grasses only.

11.8.3 Care of young specimen trees in park and garden

A high standard of care promotes quick sturdy growth and good formation of specimen trees. The operations include:

Attention to stakes and ties.
Weeding, mulching and watering.
Fertilising.
Trimming.

Stakes should be renewed if necessary until the tree is wind-firm, after which they should be removed. Failing to adjust ties to allow for stem growth (referred to in section 11.6.4) can ruin the shape of young standards.

Weeding, mulching and watering are considered together; correct mulching should obviate the need for weeding and reduce the need for watering. The soil over the roots of newly-planted standards should be kept free from grass and coarse weeds competing for moisture. Drought, before the roots are fully established, is accountable for many losses especially under urban conditions. Mulching consists of a 2 or 3 in litter of organic material laid over the roots, but *not touching the stem itself*. Straw, grass mowings, peat, garden compost or farmyard manure laid on the surface and thoroughly soaked by rain or copious watering will maintain soil moisture for many weeks and smother weed growth. Further watering may be necessary in the event of drought during the first spring and summer. If growth appears to be unsatisfactory, a fertiliser may be added to the mulch but is not necessary on good deep soils (see section 11.4.4). Dry root conditions are the commonest cause of failure among transplanted trees.

Trimming consists of shaping the tree gradually to form

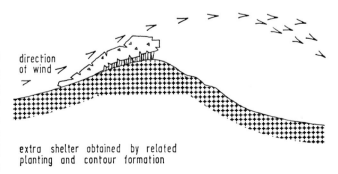

direction of wind

extra shelter obtained by related planting and contour formation

Fig. 11.6. Shelter planting. Additional shelter obtained by related planting and contour formation.

a balanced head with straight clean stem up to the required height (to be determined by the design). A few small branches, especially the lower ones, may be removed each winter, by clean cuts leaving no stubs. It is not good for a young tree to be cut much at a time, so skill and judgment must be exercised.

In the case of grafted trees such as copper beech or variegated maples all shoots arising below the graft should be removed, but double or triple stems on trees such as willows, birch, sycamore and maple growing on their own roots can be very attractive. They can be induced, by cutting a sapling almost to the ground once the root system is established, or by planting several in the same spot.

11.8.4 Care of mature trees
All dead wood should be removed, and mis-shapen or dangerous branches overhanging roads, buildings, etc. should also be cut away. The appearance of squalor and neglect given by dead wood and broken branches can be corrected and transformation brought about by skilled tree surgery. Some thinning out of redundant growth in the centre of the crown, and the removal of unbalanced branches may also improve the appearance and growth of the tree.

Damaged or decayed areas on branch and stem should be cut away leaving clean cuts in healthy wood. Cavities should be cleaned out and drained (either by drilling from below or by making V cuts at the base). The filling of cavities should only be undertaken by experts, and until there is greater agreement among these as to correct methods and indeed as to the value of the operation, it is perhaps better to be content with cleaning and draining alone.

All cuts and treated wounds should be left smooth and clean, and should be painted with Arbrex to discourage the entry of disease spores and to encourage the growth of 'callus' that fresh cambium layer which protects the wood and develops new bark to cover the wound. Cambium can grow fast over well-smoothed surfaces but is impeded by roughness and sharp angles so that the complete removal of stumps and irregularities hastens the growth of new bark even though the surface of the wounds is thereby enlarged. Irregularities and untrimmed stubs lead to the formation of cavities and so shorten the life of trees.

11.8.5 Maintenance calendar

JANUARY–MARCH
Replace losses in moist or high rainfall areas.
Remove dead branches and broken stubs.
Trim to shape required.

APRIL
Cut back willows and other pollard trees.

MARCH–AUGUST
Adjust tree ties on young standards.
Inspect stakes and renew where necessary.
Mulch young standards.
Water young standards during drought.
Remove weed growth around small trees and clean ground at foot of standards.

AUGUST–NOVEMBER
Inspect plantations, reckon losses to be replaced or thinnings to be removed.

NOVEMBER–DECEMBER
Plant replacements in dry areas or light soils.
Thin young plantations where necessary.

11.8.6 When to fell trees
To the forester, trees are a crop to be felled when the timber is at its best. The appearance of the tree at that stage, however, is just approaching its period of greatest beauty and will go on improving while its timber declines for perhaps another hundred years. Clients should be warned against the advice of timber merchants in this connection and reminded that landscape considerations may differ from those of economic forestry.

The safety factor often leads to the loss of fine trees. No expert can declare that any tree is 'safe' since storm or lightning may cause accidents. Nor, in this sense, is any wheeled vehicle 'safe'. Insurance against accident is the obvious remedy in both cases. Decaying and diseased trees should obviously be removed, but the landscape value of a sound tree continues long after the peak of its timber value and this gives time to plant and grow on young understudies to take the place of older trees threatened by senility.

Felling becomes necessary when the new annual growth fails to keep pace with dead or dying wood and the appearance of the tree declines. It may also be necessary to make room for new plantations or natural regeneration, particularly in woodland, where spaces can be cleared and replanted without loss of amenity. The decision whether or not to fell is more difficult in those cases of specimen trees, avenues and small groups where lack of space prevents new planting while the old trees remain. The ease with which large trees can now be transplanted provides a happy solution, far better than alternate felling and replanting with small standards which seldom flourish in competition with their elders.

The landowner who forbids the felling of any single tree does a disservice to posterity, since so many plantations are of one age and therefore liable to complete decay at the same stage. The need to ensure continuity is more important than short-sighted preservation of every individual tree; it is one of the landscape architect's special responsibilities, since many humans seem to think that trees are immortal.

11.9 Government grants

Grants for tree planting are available under the following schemes:

(*a*) Dedication of woodlands (Forestry Commission).
(*b*) Approved woodlands (Forestry Commission).
(*c*) Small woodlands planting (Forestry Commission).
(*d*) Shelter belts (Ministry of Agriculture).

The Forestry Commission pamphlet *Grants for Woodland Owners*, free on application to any office of the Forestry Commission, gives full particulars of these grants. Briefly summarised, the dedication scheme, which offers substantial grants, is applicable to woods permanently dedicated to timber production under a management scheme approved (or in some cases controlled) by the Forestry Commission.

'Approved woodland' grants are available for owners not wishing to enter into long-term legal commitments, for woods planned and managed under a system approved by the Forestry Commission.

Small woodland planting grants are for plantations of any size, which can be considered for this grant subject to certain conditions.

Scrub clearance grants are available under certain conditions in addition to the planting and management grants for (*a*), (*b*) and (*c*) above.

Shelter belts on upland stock-rearing farms are not administered by the Forestry Commission, but by the Ministry of Agriculture and Fisheries from whom information should be sought. The Forestry Commission will provide grants for belts with a width of 2 chains, or more. Poplar plantations no longer qualify for special grants as formerly, but may be included with other forestry schemes under (*a*), (*b*) and (*c*) above.

Loans for management of grant-aided woods are available from the Forestry Commission. Their leaflet No. 12, *Income Tax and Estate Duty on Woodlands* (H.M.S.O.) describes arrangements operating to the advantage of woodland owners.

The local Conservator of Forests, whose address is given in *Grants for Woodland Owners*, should be consulted in connection with all schemes likely to qualify for grants. He is able to provide forms of application and to give technical advice but does not prepare plans of operations. Woodland associations or forestry consultants will assist in these details of planting projects. They can be contacted through the Royal Forestry Society of England and Wales, 49 Russell Square, London, W.C.1 or the Royal Scottish Forestry Society, 7 Albyn Place, Edinburgh 2. The Secretary of the Institute of Landscape Architects can supply a list of forestry consultants.

The Forestry Commission Bulletin No. 14 *Forestry Practice* (H.M.S.O.) gives valuable information on approved conventional forestry methods. The warning given in the foreword, however, that such a textbook cannot cover the whole science of forestry and is no substitute for the advice of an expert after inspection of the site, should be heeded by the landscape architect no less than by the landowner to whom it is addressed.

Bibliography

British Isles and Their Vegetation, A. G. Tansley, Cambridge University Press.

Care and repair of ornamental trees, A. D. C. LeSueur, Country Life.

Field Drainage, H. H. Nicholson, Cambridge University Press.

Forestry Practice, Bulletin No. 14, Forestry Commission, H.M.S.O.

Grants for Woodland Owners, Forestry Commission, H.M.S.O.

Hedges, shelter belts and screens, A. D. C. LeSueur, Country Life.

How a Tree Grows, W. Somerville, Oxford University Press.

Income Tax and Estate Duty on Woodlands, Leaflet No. 12, Forestry Commission, H.M.S.O.

Practical British Forestry, C. P. Ackers, Oxford University Press.

Shelter-belts and Windbreaks, J. M. Coborn, Faber and Faber.

Shelter Belts for Western Hill Farms, Forest Record No. 22, Forestry Commission, H.M.S.O.

'Transplanting of large trees', A. D. B. Wood, *I.L.A. Journal*, Nos. 51 and 52.

'Transplanting semi-mature trees in redeveloped town areas', *Municipal Journal*, 11 January 1963.

Transplanting Trees and Other Woody Shrubs, U.S. National Parks Service, U.S. Government Printing Office, Washington D.C.

Tree Maintenance, P. P. Pirone, Oxford University Press.

Trees for Town and Country, Brenda Colvin and S. R. Badmin, Lund Humphries.

Trees in Towns, R. J. Morling, Estates Gazette Press.

12 Administration and Maintenance
J. T. CONNELL

12.1 Introduction

The objective of maintenance as applied to landscape work is to ensure that the completed scheme as envisaged by the landscape architect reaches maturity in the most economical manner possible. Unlike the work of the architect and engineer, the work of the landscape architect is seldom complete when handed over to the client at the end of the construction and planting period. As the work is largely in living materials it has at that point merely started on its long growing period to maturity. It is essential for the designer to understand the problems of maintenance and to appreciate the standards of upkeep which can be achieved. If the scheme is to develop in the way envisaged by the landscape architect the maintenance organisation should be fully informed of the designer's intentions, and be sympathetic to them. Different standards require different management and technique, and consultation with the appropriate maintenance organisation can be rewarding for all concerned. It is essential also that the organisation entrusted with maintenance be supplied with the lay-out of planting and drainage details to ensure the efficient working of the scheme.

Failure to appreciate the importance of the treatment afforded to the scheme after completion, can lead to serious disappointment at a later date and the scheme may not achieve the purposes intended. Accordingly, it is in the interest of the landscape architect to have some understanding of the organisation required for maintenance, and to be assured that the staff employed are competent to carry out the work to the required standards. It is equally vital that the team make use of the most efficient equipment, skill and modern methods in carrying out the work. This chapter outlines the principles involved in organising maintenance services.

12.2 Organisation and management

The size and complexity of any maintenance organisation will be directly related to the size and nature of open spaces to be maintained.

Where the establishments can be grouped together as in a city parks department, the maintenance organisation may be large and complex, dealing with intensively-developed parks, rest gardens, sports grounds, cemeteries, crematoria, etc., maintained efficiently and economically from geographical centres, with specialised mobile work gangs for the maintenance of the smaller areas, street trees, verges, etc. The organisation of the department will include for all ancillary services, stores, workshops, nurseries, propagation centres and similar. Whilst the allocation of duties to individual members of the staff will depend on the size of the organisation and the number of employees, the larger the organisation the more specialised become the duties and yet the whole must be closely related and bound together with the means of getting orders quickly from the top to all sectional heads, and to each employee, as may be required.

By extreme comparison is the landscape maintenance service provided by the single gardener in an isolated centre. If the carefully planned scheme is to be nurtured to maturity this will depend not only upon gardening skill but also the clear directions given and the sympathy and understanding with which they are carried out.

The nature of much present-day landscape work does not however relate to conventional open spaces in towns or to enclosed gardens, both with their well-established techniques of administration and maintenance. Landscape planning for New Towns, screening and site planning problems associated with large scale constructional development for power production, roads, reservoirs, etc., may involve acres of countryside hitherto managed under a farming economy which when displaced may need maintenance on an estate management scale. Recreation landscape work in mountain, coastal and other amenity areas may be directed so that the development of new facilities ensures that the landscape can absorb more people, with their transport, resort accommodation and associated services, without destroying the rural qualities sought in that particular area. This process of planned development coupled with preservation and enhancement is a landscape conservation problem for which adequate administrative and maintenance techniques have yet to be established.

194

Plate 12.1. Common land in Surrey, previously overgrown and impenetrable, now maintained to a high standard by a local authority estates management team.

12.3 Staffing

12.3.1 Grades

The staff required for competent maintenance will consist of managerial, technical and supervisory, administrative and clerical and manual grades, according to the size and complexity of the organisation, the acreage and nature of areas maintained and intensity of usage.

In the managerial, technical and supervisory categories of staff a sound knowledge of arboriculture, horticulture, sylviculture, entomology, soil and similar sciences, is a basic requirement. Experience of the applied use of these sciences in the maintenance of grounds, propagating centres, glasshouses, grass areas and the culture of plants generally, with a thorough understanding of the use, servicing and capabilities of relative mechanical equipment, is equally essential.

The small organisation may well include personnel acting in several categories, as in the case of the group hospital head gardener, who in addition to the management of his men, must have the technical ability to scheme and carry out minor improvements and renovations, and be able to undertake corresponding clerical duties.

12.3.2 Managerial

The manager must be a practical man with the ability to control staff, thorough competence in the basic skills of his men, and the professional ability to administrate. He must be far-searching in his endeavours to improve on past standards and in the application of new ideas. In the local government service with responsibility for developed public open spaces, sports grounds, woodlands, allotments and ornamental areas generally, such a man may be termed director, or superintendent, and the appropriate qualification would be the Diploma of the Institute of Park Administration (F.Inst.P.A. (Dip.)), coupled with considerable experience in the various capacities.

12.3.3 Technical and supervisory

This category of staff calls for specialist knowledge in constructional and maintenance work, the supervision of staff, and a thorough understanding of the maintenance and management of the various garden features.

The man with professional status and qualifications such as F.Inst. P.A. (Dip.) or N.D.H., or intermediate grades of these examinations, with adequate experience, including Botanic Garden or Horticultural Institute training, would be competent to deal with these matters.

The organisation would demand technical and specialist knowledge from these personnel and the ability to put the works into practice.

195

12.3.4 Administrative and clerical

The function of staff in this category is to ensure the efficient working of the organisation from the purely administrative aspect. The compilation of wage sheets, routine correspondence, the preparation of estimates and statistics, the ordering of materials, etc. are some of the works to be executed.

The personnel would range from chief clerk or administrative assistant to staff officer, responsible for engaging manual staff, finance officer, wage clerk, cost clerk, order clerk, etc., according to the size and scope of the organisation. Qualifications would be principally administrative or clerical in nature, coupled with adequate experience, and would range from the Diploma in Municipal Administration (D.M.A.), or Membership of the Chartered Institute of Secretaries (A.C.I.S.) for the higher assistants, to the clerical examinations of the N.J.C. for the more junior officers in local government service.

12.3.5 Manual

The manual grades of staff will generally be under the control of an area superintendent, where this is possible, or a head gardener for the smaller establishments. These men will have progressed through the various manual grades and will be practical men with outstanding experi-ence in all aspects of the work, preferably gained in a number of good establishments. Their function is to organise and deploy the men and machines and transport, according to the needs of maintenance.

The qualities required of such men will include sound judgment, initiative and keenness, and the ability to manage men. It is necessary also that the area super-intendent or head gardener has proven technical know-ledge, is capable of keeping the necessary management records, able to adopt his organisation to new ideas and, in appropriate cases, has the ability to deal with the general public.

The main body of manual staff will be in the foreman, propagator gardener, gardeners, garden labourer and apprenticeship classes. In addition there will be staff designated as tractor, dumper and motor drivers and in the larger establishments, there will also be attendants, watchmen, etc.

Generally, promotion to the higher grades (excepting the purely administrative and clerical grades) will be by progression from the gardener status. The main require-ment for a trained gardener is a sound practical training, usually an apprenticeship, and experience of the work involved. This should be coupled with an appropriate qualification gained as the result of passing a theoretical and practical test set by an approved body.

Plate 12.2. HEATON PARK, MANCHESTER. Informal parkland designed for minimum maintenance.

Plate 12.3. PRINCES PARKWAY, MANCHESTER. Broad highway verges, largely open parkland with permanent planting requiring minimum maintenance.

12.4 Administration

Efficient management of completed landscape schemes involving specialised maintenance, demands a set policy for the maintenance organisation relative to the standard, extent and limit of the work required. It is important that the scope, intention, usage, and future development of any particular scheme should be properly understood and assessed in terms of staff, equipment and materials required for maintenance, so that adequate finance can be made available in advance of the completion date. The function of the committee, management board, or authority in this respect is to receive professional advice and opinion with a view to setting and defining policy concerned with the proposed organisation, the facilities required, staffing, mechanical equipment, etc. to ensure satisfactory maintenance of the completed scheme. Administration is necessary to implement policy and to supply the needs of maintenance work when and where required and to ensure smooth and efficient working of the maintenance organisation.

Mention is made of the basic operations only which will have to be carried out. Quite obviously different local circumstances will require additional procedures, but in general the main outlines will apply to all maintenance establishments.

12.4.1 Preparation of wages sheets
These will be compiled by the staff from the certified time sheets submitted weekly by supervisory staff, such as head gardeners or superintendents. Various mechanised methods of compilation are now being adopted for the larger organisations; for example, the electronic accounting machine, as an extension to the punched card installation can be used. After calculation and documentation the required amounts will be drawn and payment of wages made at agreed times on the site to the staff concerned.

12.4.2 Personnel records
These are essential records of staff employed and may take the form of a card index system or individual reference files. Recorded information will include where employed, length of service, qualifications, grade of employee, previous experience and other relevant details. This will prove of value when internal promotions are under discussion.

12.4.3 Stores
Effective maintenance of the landscape and horticultural features cannot be achieved without the supply of essential materials and stocks. Such items as replacement tools, drains, grids and gullies, grass seed and fertilisers, tree stakes and ties, insecticides and fungicides, etc. will be required. This may be at short notice if brought about by vandalism, climatic fluctuations and similar occurrences.

197

The function of the stores in the organisation is to supply these items as and when required. The establishment will be controlled by a storekeeper whose duty will be to receive and issue goods and materials against authorised requests, and to keep the necessary records. The receipt and issue of a commodity will normally be recorded on an index bin card and when the stock in hand reaches an agreed low figure this will be the occasion for a request to head office for additional quantities of the material. In this way stocks of essential materials and goods are always available for supply.

12.4.4 Certification of accounts for payment

It is essential that the accounting procedure adopted for dealing with the certification of accounts for goods and services is efficient and flawless. Several methods of procedure are currently in practice, but all require that the full details of the actual material received are certified as being received on site by an authorised member of the staff. This is treated as evidence of delivery against a specific order and invoice. After deduction of discount, if due, the amount is passed forward for payment and the date recorded. In some cases it may prove worthwhile to keep purchase books for this purpose, whilst in others, copy orders only are kept and duly marked with the relative delivery details for checking against the supplier's invoice. Time and money can be saved if materials can be supplied in bulk.

12.4.5 Costing

This work consists of the assessment and allocation of labour, materials and transport used by the organisation on the various works. This can be extremely useful as a means of providing actual costs of the respective jobs, and as a means of proving inefficiencies where comparisons of costs are made against similar schemes. Work here is the basis for the provision of useful statistical records.

12.4.6 Use of forms

These can be of great value for given purposes, but their creation must be carefully controlled and efforts made to simplify procedures and not to add to them.

12.4.7 Servicing equipment

It is necessary that systems should be devised to ensure that the mechanical equipment in use is properly looked after. Regular inspections and servicing of vehicles and machinery, apart from ensuring a longer useful life, will

Plate 12.4. Maintenance with new development. Trees on this site, which is shown about to be developed, are covered by a Tree Preservation Order. It is also proposed that a residents' association will be formed to take over maintenance of the estate.

Plate 12.5. An example where some trees are under local authority control and others in private ownership are protected by Tree Preservation Orders.

also increase general efficiency. In the larger organisation it will prove economical to establish a workshop and employ tradesmen such as motor mechanics, black-smiths, painters, fitters, sawmillers and joiners, etc. Where this is possible it will mean that in addition to servicing mechanical equipment, staff can be called on to carry out repairs to games and playground equipment, fencing, repairs to seats, and maintenance repairs to small tools such as hedging shears, saws, etc. Where the establishments maintained are numerous and scattered, it may prove to be more efficient to create a mobile workshop. In such a case, it is possible to carry out essential repairs to equipment at any location at very short notice with the minimum interference with the maintenance programme. Alternatively a replacement machine can be delivered, where lengthy repairs are found to be necessary.

If records of the cost of repairs and the working hours of individual items of equipment are kept, this can serve as a useful guide when considering the purchase of new items. Such records can also indicate when it is no longer economic to repair a machine and this in turn will deter-mine the rate of depreciation, which will be reflected in the hourly hire rate charged to the individual maintenance works. To facilitate servicing and records, all machines should be numbered, prefixed with the year of origin. Thus the efficiency of any machine can be readily ascer-tained. It is necessary also that machine operators are made aware of the correct usage of the machines and the correct oils, greases and procedures to be adopted for routine maintenance.

12.5 Maintenance

12.5.1 Seasonal nature of maintenance

The day to day work varies considerably according to the season and climatic variations, and although it is possible to plan for normal maintenance work it is necessary to be prepared to make changes of operation at very short notice. This may be occasioned by an early or late season, gale damage, insect or fungoid attack, etc. any of which may bring about a change in normal routine.

Two main periods evolve for the maintenance man. Firstly, the growing season extending from March to early October, when the routine work of grass cutting and management operations generally, will predominate, and secondly, the dormant season, extending from the end of October to the end of March, according to seasonal variation, when the specialised tasks of planting, pruning, constructional and specialised turf and other maintenance will be executed.

12.5.2 Redesign for easy maintenance

Many maintenance problems can be eased if winter work on established sites includes a programme of redesign which is weighted towards simplification rather than the

199

more usual ambitious 'improvements'. Easing slopes and rounding off crowns and sharp arrises, resiting geometric beds and providing flush mowing edges, will allow the use of larger machines and eliminate time consuming edge trimming. Resiting flower beds away from lawn centres to border positions now more sheltered as hedging has matured, may permit different, more permanent, and less labour-demanding plant material to give improved effects. In mixed tree and shrub areas ecological needs may be met by clearing relatively short lived shrubs no longer thriving under naturally increasing shade of maturing trees.

12.5.3 Grass

The maintenance of grass (see Chapter 10—Grass) makes the greatest call on the labour force during the growing season. Areas of grass land may be dealt with in different ways, according to what is intended and the usage. Where bulbs are naturalised for instance, it will not be possible to carry out any cutting until the life cycle of the bulb has been completed, and this again will vary according to the species of bulb used. Grass cutting may have to be carried out daily in periods of heat with ample moisture, as in the case of lawns and areas of the highest standard, such as bowling greens, grass tennis courts and the immediate surrounds to buildings. If such areas can be grouped together maintenance costs will be less. Other areas of lesser importance such as grass on sports areas can be effectively dealt with at less frequent intervals and cutting may average once every ten days. In all cases, the quality and mixture of grass seed will dictate the future treatment. For example, the use of a ryegrass mixture would not be suitable for the close mowing treatment required for visible effect with a good lawn. In other cases, if the choice of seed species is not suited to the existing soil conditions and to the proposed pedestrian usage, the natural grasses may be favoured and patchy results can follow. Areas suitably located where usage is at a minimum and turf is not required may be kept as rough grass and the maintenance treatment consists of cutting two or three times a year with a mechanical reaper or similar. With steep banks where ground cover shrub planting cannot be used it may be a practical proposition to treat the area annually with a proprietary grass inhibitor containing maleic hydrazide.

Above all other considerations, the economic cutting of grass demands the use of the right machine for the right work. It is advisable, however, to bear in mind policy concerning the servicing of grass cutting equipment, and some attempt at standardisation of equipment is desirable for the larger maintenance organisation.

Grass areas require specialised treatment if a given standard is to be maintained. This means annual renovations, i.e. turfing or reseeding work areas as necessary, a balanced programme of fertiliser dressings, weedkilling,

worm eradication, aeration, rolling, and the application of insecticides and fungicides or other specialised treatment as may be necessary. In addition, the finer grass area will require the application of prepared top dressings.

It is necessary also on all grass areas to make periodic checks on the inspection chambers serving the land drainage system, to ensure the satisfactory working of the system. This should be a routine operation, aimed at preventing difficulties arising. Where sumps have been used in the drainage system, these also should be regularly inspected and emptied. Where blockages do occur in the system, these should be quickly located by the use of supple drainage rods and the blockage cleared. It is worthy of note also, that where a drainage system passes through a tree planted area, the use of salt glazed pipes suitably caulked can save difficulties arising at a later date.

12.5.4 Trees and shrubs

Permanent trees and shrub groups will require maintenance and pruning treatment at a time determined by the species and the particular requirements. For example, shrubs which flower on current wood in the late summer will require to be pruned hard back in the spring. Spring flowering species, flowering on old wood will require less drastic treatment immediately flowering has finished. Shrubs grown for the stem colour, such as *Salix* species, will again be pruned in the spring, in order to provide a sufficiency of branches for colour in the winter months. A record of species and relative locations, should be kept as a check against the ordering of suitable replacements when necessary. The maintenance of these features is a very worthwhile and economic proposition, provided that skilled staff are employed to preserve the habit of the species. It should be appreciated that the care of trees and shrubs can have a far reaching effect on their value in design.

Specimen trees ideally require a card index system of annual inspection. Note should be taken of the condition and the amount of annual growth and suitable action if any is decided upon.

12.5.5 Herbaceous borders

Well-planned borders are useful features providing colour and interest throughout the summer months. The labour consuming work lies in the staking and tying, cleaning, top dressing and the periodic division of the plants.

12.5.6 Rockeries

Care should be taken to limit the amount of maintenance work where these are created. This can be achieved by the effective arrangement of rocks and paths, the right choice of plants, omitting the more tender species which will require possible replacement, and weed control.

12.5.7 Bedding plants

This is a most costly item in maintenance, involving two

Plate 12.6. High flats in a parkland setting. At high residential densities special maintenance care is needed to retain parkland character.

and possibly three or more changes of plants during the year, using plants raised annually in the propagating centre. In present day landscape design this type of planting has very limited uses, confined to the areas of intense pedestrian usage.

12.5.8 Hard surfaces and fencing

Surfaces here may consist of asphalt, tarmacadam, paved areas, and semi-porous surfaces. In the case of paving and semi-porous surfaces, annual maintenance will consist of weedkilling, making good damage and defects and top dressing, watering, rolling, dragging and brushing the porous surfaces. Cobbles and setts will require little maintenance treatment but neglect of a few displaced stones may rapidly lead to wear, weathering and ill-use stripping large areas. Otherwise repairs to paths and sealed surfaces generally will be an annual operation, preferably carried out in the summer months, before leaf fall. Kerbs and edgings will need to be made good, grids and sumps checked and any surface potholes cleared out and filled with the required surfacing.

Fencing may be wooden, iron or wire in various sizes and designs, and maintenance work will consist of essential repairs where damage has occurred, and painting every two or three years. On average, depending on the gauge, and whether plastic coated or galvanised wire has been used, chain link cladding will require to be replaced every 5–8 years in industrial areas. Wooden fences, not painted, such as interwoven panels, will require to be dressed annually with creosote or a proprietary wood preservative.

Annual inspections of surfaces and fencing, when followed by effective action, can extend the period of usefulness enormously, and care should be taken to see that financial provision is made for this to be done. The larger establishments will employ specialised staff to carry out this work.

12.5.9 The propagation centre

This is essential where the maintenance of a number of establishments is to be effectively and economically carried out. However, the economics of raising plants locally as compared with commercial purchase must be very carefully considered. In the routine maintenance work of estates, private gardens, factory surroundings, land used by commercial, industrial transport and other undertakings, it will seldom be possible to produce the plants needed for replacements and improvements at costs competitive with those of commercial growers. There are dangers too that growing capacity will be taken up and even expanded beyond real site needs, leading to unnecessary elaboration of planting. Special exceptions are of two kinds. First where the propagation centre is needed to back up a development programme of the site as a whole over a known period of years or is very specialised as in the production of seedlings for woodland management and economic forestry on large estates. These are not of course strictly 'maintenance' needs. Secondly a propagation centre will be justified where a large direct labour force exists to use the regular output of the nursery and where there is a demand for flowering plants for public display, or for cut flowers; for example public parks and hospitals. Once such a centre is justified it should be made to serve the widest possible demand. Hence a local authority with responsibility for street planting, recreation grounds and public open spaces will probably supply its own plant material from nurseries established to supply display plants in parks and flowers for municipal events. The existence of such a centre would mean for example that successive changes of plants can be grown for bedding displays where provision has been made for these in the layout scheme. It would mean also that tubs and bowls of shrubs, etc. could be brought back and recuperated, whilst other seasonal displays take their place. The main function of the centre, however, will be the propagation and growing of trees and shrubs, and plants generally, for subsequent use as replacements or for improvement work. In the larger establishments, the centre will include frames for general nursery use and heated glasshouses equipped with modern devices such as the mist propagation technique unit, and automatic watering and glasshouse ventilation in order to extend the range of plants grown with the minimum labour force. In addition, nursery beds and plunge beds for rock plants will be available to further this end.

The staffing of such a centre will call for employees with considerable skill and experience in the raising and growing of plants and may consist of nursery manager, supervising several propagator gardeners, gardeners and labourers.

Where the centre is growing for several establishments it may function as a self-contained unit and it will be necessary for the yearly requirements of each establishment served to be assessed and compiled well in advance of the date wanted, in order that the basic materials may be acquired and the procedures for producing the plants put into early operation. The request for seeds and requirements generally, will be by requisition to the head office, where the request will be checked against an approved item of expenditure and duly supplied. The actual issue of plants, trees and shrubs, etc. from the propagating centre will be by nursery issue note, originated by head office against an approved item of expenditure, with delivery effected by propagating centre transport to the required location.

12.6 Landscape work by contract

12.6.1 Practical considerations affecting maintenance

Constant supervision of the work being carried out is essential, both from the point of view of ensuring high quality of materials and workmanship, and in order to authorise accurate progress reports and payments. Without this supervision, a contractor may, perhaps due to outside pressure, or because of the time factor, carry out work which is basically unsound. Examples of this can be seen in mixing topsoil with subsoil, in working the ground when conditions are unfit, to the detriment of the soil and often causing excessive compaction. These works can cause considerable future maintenance problems—for example if clay should be brought to the surface, then the rain water will not percolate through to the drains and that particular area will become waterlogged. Levelling and cultural operations specified should be closely supervised and if necessary modified as required by site conditions prevailing at the time of execution. The drainage work also should be checked for adequate falls and standard of workmanship. The boundaries of the site should be defined in advance of the work and secured without delay, bearing in mind the proposed finished levels. This will ensure the protection of the works and may bring to light problems affecting adjoining properties in the early stages of development.

Materials brought on to the site should be subject to the closest scrutiny. In the case of planting material, it should be ascertained that the source of supply is reputable, that the material itself is as specified, and that the trees and shrubs, etc. are planted at the right time in the correct place and in suitable conditions. Imported soil should be approved at the source or be conditional to the first load being approved on site. Grass seed and fertilisers should be the subject of test and analysis, and the purity and germination standards of the grass seed determined. The statutory statement applicable to the fertilisers to be used should also be produced by the contractor. Competent supervision will ensure that the right amounts are actually used in the manner specified, and at a time dictated by soil conditions. With schemes carried out for local authorities it may be useful for a qualified member of the maintenance staff to carry out the supervision of the site works as outlined in the contract and plans, as it is a common failing in practice for maintenance staff to blame contractors' work for difficulties which may later occur on the site. Where there has been a degree of co-

Plate 12.7. Informal gardens in local authority cottage type development. Wythenshawe Estate, Manchester.

operation and agreement with the maintenance organisation, before and during the layout work, then the reason for any subsequent failure in the work will have to be found elsewhere than in the specification and subsequent contract work.

12.6.2 Takeover

When the layout work has been executed, it is most necessary to ensure a smooth takeover by the maintenance staff. Nothing can be more disheartening than to find that there has been a lapse of time since completion and that the grass is now overgrown, and the planted areas infested with weeds. Such occurrences can mean, in the case of grass, that in failing to keep the grass short, the encouragement to 'tiller' has not been achieved and, consequently, the delay in maintenance will be reflected in the time it now takes to establish a satisfactory sward suitable for hard wear or the playing of games. In the case of weeds, particularly if allowed to seed, much trouble and extra expense can occur in eradication. The conditions of contract may call for the contractor to roll the grass seeded area and carry out the first cut. The defects liability clause will also include for areas to be reseeded where germination is unsatisfactory. The completion of these works may extend over a considerable period and care should be taken to ensure that both the contractor and the maintenance organisation are each aware of their respective responsibilities in this matter.

The most satisfactory approach to the problem is for the landscape architect to arrange a site meeting when the work is nearing completion, for the purpose of discussion between the parties concerned. In this way, the maintenance staff can profit by the experience of the contractor where difficulties have been encountered in carrying out the layout work, possibly due to local soil profiles, drains which have been picked up, etc. These and other matters may influence future maintenance treatment. It is opportune at this time also to acquaint the staff with the intentions of the scheme, where this might influence future pruning treatment, etc. and any proposals for extending or curtailing the plantings. It will also be necessary to supply a linen copy of the layout drainage and planting plans showing all relevant details. This is most important in the case of planting plans, as the continuity of the scheme can be lost if wrong species and varieties are put in as replacements.

12.6.3 Establishment period

The landscape contractor is responsible for the maintenance of plant material as soon as it is planted until the agreed maintenance period expires. Responsibiilty will be for protection, replanting in cases of failures, forking through, or any other item which a specification may require. This maintenance period following completion of the contract is usually a relatively brief defects liability period provided to ensure that all contract liabilities have been met and defects made good.

But after handing over, establishment of the plants must still be carried on. In the case of small shrubs establishment may be completed in three or four years; larger shrubs may take from five to ten. During this time, the spaces between young plants must be kept weed-free and forked through until the plants have effectively covered the allotted area. Ground cover such as vinca may be planted under shrubs with large spread. This will tend to suppress weed growth. It will also give a more satisfactory effect than bare earth during early years. Maintenance within public areas of housing estates may vary according to the design of the planting. Various berberis species and varieties have proved successful in

203

deterring trespass and reducing damage and it has also been found economical to obtain nursery specimens which have been allowed to grow on for an extra year or two and are therefore much bigger and less likely to be trampled underfoot. Planting closer than normally will also speed the mass effect. Some plants can be lifted for re-use if they appear to be overcrowded on reaching full size. Planting for protection should be unnecessary in an enclosed private garden, but close planting may still be used for early effect and here it is important that later maintenance should allow for planned thinning out to avoid overcrowding.

12.6.4 The maintenance schedule

Architects, painters and sculptors are in direct control of the culmination of the project that they envisaged at the design stage. The landscape architect is using materials that live and grow and his proposals may take many years to reach maturity. Those whose responsibility it is to carry on after the landscape contractor's maintenance period has expired should be given comprehensive guidance as to how the trees shrubs or other planting, etc. should be maintained until maturity is reached. The maintenance schedule together with a copy of the detailed planting plan can give most of the information needed. The schedule can take many forms, being set out as written instructions, tables, drawings, or various combinations of these.

The original planting detail for the project may be used marking on one or two prints all the same species of plant with a key number. It is assumed that the same species will require the same type of maintenance each year. Some plants may need thinning or cutting back for example while others may need training. Some shrubs may require dressing, liming (or not liming), mulching, forking through, spraying; some may suffer during times of drought, while others may be drought resistant. In many cases the work may not have to be done every year, but only every second or third year (Table 12.1) for one example of a maintenance schedule.

TABLE 12.1 MAINTENANCE SCHEDULE
(*Name of job and client*)

Name and address of landscape architect:
Telephone number:

Name and address of landscape contractor (if necessary):
Telephone number:

N.B. This schedule should be read in conjunction with drawing No. 000 revised date

Species Number (*see drawing*)	1967	1968	1969	1970	1971	1972	Key to letters
1, 5 and 9	a × 2† h × 3	a × 2 h × 2 d	a h × 2 d	a h × 2 d	h d		*a.* Fork through lightly area of species
3.	a × 2 h × 3	a 8 h × 2	a h × 2	h			*b.* Thin out last year's growth after flowering
7 and 10	a × 2	a	h				*c.* Prune as instructed‡
2 and 6	a × 2 h × 3	a h × 2	h × 2	h × 2 c	h × 2	h × 2 c	*d.* Surface dress as instructed‡
4. e.g. *Hypericum calycinum*	a	e	e				*e.* Cut off dead flower heads
8.	a × 2 h × 3	a h × 2 b	a h × 2 b	a h × 2 b	h b	h b	*f.* Close mowing.
11. (Lawns)	d × 2 f × 12–14	d × 2 f × 12–14	d × 2 f × 12–14	d × 2 f × 12–14	d × 2 f × 12–14	d × 2 f × 12–14	*g.* Mowing roto scythe
12. (Rough grass) etc.	g × 2	g × 2	g × 2	g × 2	g × 2	g × 2	*h.* Hoe through, etc.

† × 2 etc. means twice per annum, etc.

‡ Written instructions should be given as to methods of pruning or choice of fertilisers, height of cut, etc., etc.

Plate 12.8. Common greens in medium density private housing, Dulwich.

Schedules will of course vary with the complexity of the job and the number of years the schedule covers may be extended or reduced at the discretion of the landscape architect, taking full account of the nature of the site, project and probable use. Frequency of grass cutting should be estimated and guidance given on the management of those areas containing naturalised bulbs or for some other reason needing to be managed on a natural ecological basis. It is possible that for some reason certain items may not mature very well or that substantial modification may become necessary. The maintenance schedule cannot cover all eventualities, but should have a general note that substantial changes are to be referred to the landscape architect for his advice and approval.

The Ministry of Transport technical memorandum on grass maintenance on highways is a simple example of a written maintenance schedule setting out general requirements (*Technical Memorandum No. T2/65*). To guide maintenance routine important distinctions are made. The first is that for two years after sowing, management is concerned with *establishment* of a suitable turf; the height of the grass for first cut, and intervals of subsequent cutting during the growing season are indicated as an approximate guide for different kinds of grassed surface. After the *establishment* of a close weed-free sward it is recommended that *maintenance* should be kept to the minimum necessary to provide a satisfactory appearance in keeping with the surrounding topography. The important distinction here is that different categories of surroundings—dense urban, open country, moorland and woodlands—call for different kinds of maintenance treatment. An appropriate standard is suggested for each, ranging from 3 to 4 weeks between cuts for verges to urban roads, to leaving side slopes and embankments to moorland *uncut*.

For a particular length of road maintenance items could be scheduled to cover all categories of grassed surface, side slopes, verges, central reservations, etc., and extended to include treatment for shrubs and hedges, staked trees and forest planting.

12.6.5 Cost of maintenance

It may be necessary to attempt to estimate maintenance costs (see also Appendix 4.1). It is unwise to rely on overall cost averages from other examples for this purpose, but by assessing the various labours involved in working to the maintenance schedule an approximate estimate should be possible. The costs are best built up from unit of area rates. If built up from labour rates oncosts must be allowed, for loss of time due to inclement weather, sickness, holidays with pay, etc. A further allowance on gross labour costs would have to be added for plant depreciation, administration and general overheads. If estimates are based on previous experience and known rates for a similar area, careful adjustments should be made to take account of any significant difference.

In preparing estimates the variables to be taken into account will include the following:

Plate 12.9. Three storey, private housing with gardens requiring a high standard of maintenance.

Total area involved and the total interrupted area of each item—Large simple shrub areas, and particularly large unbroken areas of grass capable of being cut by large machines will lead to substantial economies.

Growing conditions—good conditions help up to a point, but a warm moist climate in which grass starts growing early and continues into November will add to cutting costs.

Conditions of use and mis-use—Intensive use because of popularity or lack of alternative space will cause unduly heavy wear beyond the naturally regenerative capacity of some open spaces, so leading to heavy maintenance costs. Management costs may be important here too in the effort to prevent misuse. In addition vandalism may give rise to high replacement costs.

Standards required—City gardens, floral displays, gardens to exhibitions, elaborately laid out 'prestige' entrances to factories or offices may properly require high standards and are likely to be costly to maintain. The maintenance schedule should attempt to ensure that at least, but no more, than appropriate standards are kept up. Meticulous clearance of leaves for example can add substantially to costs of otherwise low-cost informal greens which are well wooded. The proper enjoyment of the area by week-end crowds and children may require no more than simple tidiness and if this is the case an ecological balance of wear and regeneration encouraged by rough cutting and trimming may be more satisfactory than horticultural elaboration.

Order of magnitude costs vary widely. Maintenance of open spaces in a large city can cost an average of £300 per acre per annum. These are high acreage costs attributable to high standards including floral displays, botanical collections and representation at horticultural shows, all achieved in difficult circumstances including heavy use and misuse of open spaces which in total acreage are below those of recognised planning provision. Maintenance costs in the New Towns appear modest, with their generous but more simple and informal open spaces falling in the £100 per acre range. At the bottom of the scale, costs for wooded commons and heathland are very low at £6–£9 per acre. Between these figures, a survey taken some years ago indicated average local authority costs at £145 and a 1964 survey of a larger sample at £173 per acre per annum. For playing fields an average figure of £100 per acre may be taken as representative.

In some housing areas little landscape provision and maintenance service is found, with a 1964 local authority sample as low as £5 *per acre of housing*. But where it is on a reasonable scale, as in many New Towns, maintenance in cottage-type housing at low densities of ten to fourteen dwellings per acre may run at £2 to £3 *per house* per annum, and with terraces and flats at medium densities of say 20 per acre at £2 10s. to £4 10s. *per dwelling*.

Most experience and collected evidence is of wide variation in costs. This suggests that extreme care must be used to assess real costs rather than rely on crude averages which are unreliable as a basis of estimating.

206

Plates 12.10, 12.11, 12.12. TOWN CENTRE, STEVENAGE. A high standard of maintenance is required, but design includes a large proportion of durable pavings. Permanent planting restricted to trees, decorative planting in containers. Landscape Architect: Gordon Patterson.

12.7 Maintenance with new development

Two kinds of development must be considered here. The first is associated with new projects particularly those large in scale and extending over a number of years in their execution. The second is the development which a planning authority must control, at the same time attempting to conserve, enhance, and devise methods of maintaining the landscape environment.

12.7.1. Maintenance associated with new projects

During the construction period the landscape organisation will be concerned with new planting and other work but it must also devise economical methods of conserving what exists and can be kept. New projects for power stations, universities, New Towns, etc. occupy large land holdings. Those aspects of the existing landscape which for their economic and visual well-being depend upon a system of management or farm husbandry will rapidly deteriorate if neglected. Even on completion of constructional development large areas of land may remain which are not strictly required for urban or operational purposes and it is essential to put them in a form of land use which will ensure their careful management. Use for grazing or afforestation for example will help ensure that fencing, drainage, and the like will receive proper care and attention. The estate manager or farm bailiff form of supervision may be necessary to deal with these matters and to arrange proper tenancies. Landscape maintenance here can only be secured by first devising a proper management system.

Administrative problems can be complex and if great care is not taken there are many points at which continuity from design and construction, through to maintenance, can be broken. In a New Town for example for all landscape work there will be a master plan which should help co-ordinate separate landscape contracts associated with housing, roads, schools, playing fields and industry. But on completion only the town estate of woodlands, farming and green belt may remain under development corporation control. Housing and public playing fields are normally a district council responsibility; the county education authority will manage school playing fields, and the county highway authority at least the classified roads; industries may deal with their own open spaces and playing fields. This possible fragmentation can restrict visual and functional effectiveness of open spaces. Standards of maintenance of the different authorities will be far from uniform. But there are now indications of official encouragement for multiple use of land, with suggested joint use of school and other playing fields. It would seem logical to have further extensions of this principle to cover all open spaces and to have a single comprehensive maintenance organisation, giving services on an agency basis if necessary.

On large sites, such as a power station, a university campus, or the grounds of a major industrial establishment, hospital, etc. single ownership and management should remove administrative barriers. But adequate financial provision must be budgeted for and a proper landscape maintenance organisation planned from the very outset of design and development.

12.7.2 Planning authorities and maintenance

In its exercise of statutory planning powers (mainly derived from the Town Planning Acts as substantially consolidated in 1962, but also from the National Parks Act) the planning authority can preserve and enhance landscape. With care and administrative skill it can increase the long-term effectiveness of these powers by ensuring that proper arrangements are made for maintenance. Tree Preservation Orders for example (see also Chapter 2—Practice) may be dealt with in a way that encourages care of trees and provides for additional young planting as replacement for some felling. Development permissions which include planting conditions should include maintenance as part of these conditions. They will only be enforceable if due regard has been paid to the practical problems of maintenance.

The special problem which faces the planning authority is that of securing a management agency to take over maintenance responsibilities. Where the developer is also the occupier, as in the case of large institutions, the maintenance of new planting is a clear responsibility of the kind accepted in maintaining the fabric of buildings, Where development is followed by multiple occupation. as in the case of housing, the problem is much more difficult. Major greens and planted areas are best taken over by local authorities which are well equipped to do this work at low cost, although not always to high standards. Reluctance to take over these open spaces has had a cramping effect on the evolution of pleasant and convenient layout of housing. Present interest in the built environment, including segregation of pedestrians and motor vehicles for reasons of safety and noise, indicates that the conventional street pattern must be replaced or at least supplemented by common pedestrian routes and areas. If this amounts to open space away from the highway the developer selling freehold property may have to provide a capital sum, the interest on which would cover maintenance services. With tenanted properties, the rent can be adjusted to include landscape maintenance costs by direct or contract labour. Where properties are leasehold a residents' association may be the agency to arrange for maintenance. There are many forms which such an association may take, but usually a management committee is made up from the residents, and its responsibilities include maintenance of private open spaces included within the total leasehold area. The money needed for this work is raised from annual subscriptions as required by the residents' leasehold agreements, provision being made for contributions to be varied in accordance with the current cost of maintenance.

12.8 Conservation and maintenance

12.8.1 Amenity open spaces, National Park areas, commons, coastal amenity areas, National Trust lands

The natural beauty of these areas is a primary reason for their popularity. Maintenance will usually be directed towards conserving natural qualities of the landscape. According to the type of area this may rely upon continued farming, management of rough grazing, maintenance of natural drainage; or protection of existing flora in its wild and undisturbed state. But it must be appreciated that changed conditions of public access call for appropriate management and maintenance. This is likely to be needed in proportion to the intensity of use. The basic principle should be to make maintenance as unobtrusive as possible, over-zealous improvements being as erosive of natural landscape qualities as public pressure.

Simple attention is needed to traditional fencing, reinforced in places to deflect rather than channelise in areas of frequent access—near car parks for example. Continued farming is usual in our National Parks, but skilful sign-posting, fencing and siting of car parks can help protect economic use and restrict interference with grazing and cropping. On commons some clearance of scrub and gorse burning, may occasionally be necessary, but under very intensive public use some effort may be required to protect areas where natural regeneration would be severely checked with unrestricted access. New tree planting needed—to give added tree cover or as long-term compensation for lack of natural regeneration, should be selected from species growing locally or be well matched ecologically. Supplementary planting should be of plants from the natural shrub layer and during establishment should be forked through only sufficient to ensure survival and not to produce a cleanly cultivated border. Paths should be left as natural tracks in the turf unless use is so heavy that they get really muddy. Even then, simple gravel should be used, and not kerbed or tidied up into straight lines or uniform widths. It will seldom be necessary to cut the grass. But regular clearance of litter should be arranged, as an untidy appearance rapidly leads to further neglect.

A warden patrol is a deterrent to open vandalism and provides an inspection service to report on broken fencing, litter, etc. and any other maintenance needs.

Bibliography

Grounds Maintenance Handbook, H. S. Conover, F. W. Dodge Corporation.

A.1.1 Linear measure

CONVERSION TABLES

	Centimetres	Metres	Kilometres
1 inch	2·54	0·025	0·00002
1 foot	30·48	0·304	0·00030
1 yard	91·44	0·914	0·00091
1 mile	—	1609·344	1·60934

	Inch	Foot	Yard
1 centimetre	0·393	0·032	0·010
1 metre	39·370	3·280	1·093
1 kilometre	—	3280·8	1093·6

CONVERSION FACTORS

To convert	Multiply by
Metres to inches	39·37
Metres to feet	3·280
Metres to yards	1·093
Kilometres to miles	0·6214
Inches to metres	0·025
Feet to metres	0·304
Yards to metres	0·914
Miles to kilometres	1·609

A.1.2 Area

CONVERSION TABLES

	Square metres	Hectares
1 square foot	0·093	—
1 square yard	0·836	—
1 acre	4046·860	0·405
1 square mile	—	258·999

	Square feet	Square yards	Acres
1 square metre	10·76	1·196	—
1 hectare	—	11959·9	2·471

CONVERSION FACTORS

To convert	Multiply by
Square feet to square metres	0·093
Square yards to square metres	0·836
Acres to hectares	0·405
Square miles to hectares	258·9
Square metres to square feet	10·76
Square metres to square yards	1·196
Hectares to acres	2·471
Hectares to square miles	0·0039

NOTE
1. An acre is equivalent to a square of 208 ft 8 in side. A hectare is equivalent to a square of 100 m side.
2. Irish, Scottish and Welsh acres may occasionally be encountered. They vary in different parts of the British Isles from 3,240 sq yd to 9,780 sq yd.

A.1.2.2 Thickness per square yard to cubic yards per acre

CONVERSION TABLE

Inch thickness per square yard	Cubic yards per acre	Inch thickness per square yard	Cubic yards per acre
$\frac{1}{2}$	67*	$3\frac{3}{4}$*	500
$\frac{3}{4}$*	100	4	538*
1	$134\frac{1}{2}$*	6	$806\frac{2}{3}$
$1\frac{1}{2}$*	200	$7\frac{1}{2}$*	1000
2	269*	12	$1613\frac{1}{3}$
$2\frac{1}{4}$*	300	24	$3226\frac{2}{3}$
3	$403\frac{1}{3}$	36	4840

* approximate

A.1.2.1 Acres to square yards

Acres	Square yards	Acres	Square yards
0·005	24·2	0·20	968
0·01	48·4	0·207	1000
0·02	96·8	0·30	1452
0·021	100	0·40	1936
0·03	145·2	0·413	2000
0·04	193·6	0·50	2420
0·041	200	0·60	2904
0·05	242	0·619	3000
0·062	300	0·70	3388
0·083	400	0·80	3872
0·10	484	0·826	4000
0·103	500	1·0	4840

A.1.3 Volume

CONVERSION TABLES

	Cubic metres	Litres	U.S. liquid pints	U.S. gallons
1 cubic foot	0·028	28·316	59·844	7·480
1 cubic yard	0·764	764·5	—	—
1 U.K. pint	—	0·568	1·201	0·150
1 U.K. gallon	0·0045	4·546	9·607	1·201
	Cubic feet	Cubic yards	U.K. pints	U.K. gallons
1 cubic metre	35·315	1·308	—	—
1 litre	0·035	—	1·760	0·220
1 U.S. liquid pint	0·017	—	0·833	0·104
1 U.S. gallon	0·134	—	6·661	0·833

CONVERSION FACTORS

To convert	Multiply by
Cubic inches to cubic centimetres	16·39
Cubic feet to cubic metres	0·028
Cubic yards to cubic metres	0·764
Cubic Metres to cubic feet	35·315
Cubic metres to cubic yards	1·308
U.K. pints to U.S. liquid pints	1·201
U.K. gallons to U.S. gallons	1·201
U.K. pints to litres	0·568
U.K. gallons to litres	4·546
U.S. liquid pints to U.K. pints	0·833
U.S. gallons to U.K. gallons	0·833
U.S. liquid pints to litres	0·473
U.S. gallons to litres	3·785

NOTE
An Imperial Bushel is a dry measure equivalent to 8 U.K. gallons or 4 pecks, and contains 1·28 cubic feet (e.g. 10 in × 10 in × 22 in)

A.1.3.1 Volume per unit area

CONVERSION TABLE

Pints per square yard	Gallons per acre	Inches of rainfall
$\frac{1}{6}$	100	
$\frac{1}{3}$	200	
$\frac{1}{2}$	302·5	
$\frac{2}{3}$	400	
1	605	
$1\frac{1}{3}$	800	
$1\frac{2}{3}$	1,000	
2	1,210	
4	2,420	
8	4·840	
$2\frac{1}{3}$	11,300	$\frac{1}{2}$
$4\frac{2}{3}$	22,600	1
$9\frac{1}{3}$	45,200	2

A.1.3.2 Rainfall

CONVERSION TABLES

Inches of rainfall	Gallons per acre	Cubic feet per acre	Tons per acre
1	22,635	3,630	101·1
2	45,270	7,260	202·2
3	67,905	10,890	303·3
4	90,539	14,520	404·4
5	113,174	18,150	505·5
10	226,348	36,300	1011·0

A.1.4 Weight

CONVERSION TABLES

	Kilo-gramme	Tonne	U.S. short cwt	U.S. short ton
1 lb	0·45	0·00045	0·01	0·0005
1 cwt	50·8	0·0508	1·12	0·056
1 ton	1,016	1·016	22·4	1·12

	Pound	Hundred-weight	Ton
1 tonne	2,204·62	19·684	0·984
1 kilogramme	2·205	0·020	—
1 U.S. short hundred-weight	100	0·893	0·045
1 U.S. short ton	2,000	17·857	0·893

CONVERSION FACTORS

To convert	Multiply by
Hundredweights to kilogrammes	50·8
Hundredweights to tonnes	0·051
Hundredweights to U.S. short hundredweights	1·12
Hundredweights to U.S. short tons	0·056
Tons to kilogrammes	1,016
Tons to tonnes	1·016
Tons to U.S. short hundredweights	22·4
Tons to U.S. short tons	1·12
Tonnes to hundredweights	19·684
Tonnes to tons	0·984
Tonnes to U.S. short hundredweights	22·046
Tonnes to U.S. short tons	1·102
U.S. short hundredweights to hundredweights	0·893
U.S. short hundredweights to tons	0·045
U.S. short hundredweights to kilogrammes	45·359
U.S. short hundredweights to tonnes	0·045
U.S. short tons to hundredweights	17·857
U.S. short tons to tons	0·893
U.S. short tons to kilogrammes	907·185
U.S. short tons to tonnes	0·907

A.1.4.1 Weight per unit area

CONVERSION TABLES

	Grammes per square metre	Kilogrammes per hectare
1 oz per sq yd	33·906	339·057
1 lb per acre	0·112	1·121

	Ounces per square yard	Pounds per acre
1 g per sq m	0·029	8·922
1 kg per hectare	0·0029	0·892

CONVERSION FACTORS

To convert	Multiply by
oz per sq yd to g per sq m	33·906
oz per sq yd to kg per hectare	339·057
lb per acre to g per sq m	0·112
lb per acre to kg per hectare	1·121
g per sq m to oz per sq yd	0·029
g per sq m to lb per acre	8·922
kg per hectare to oz per sq yd	0·003
kg per hectare to lb per acre	0·892

A.1.4.2 Weight per unit area

CONVERSION TABLE

Ounces per square yard	Pounds per acre	Hundredweights per acre	Tons per acre
$\frac{3}{8}$*	112	1	
$\frac{1}{2}$	151$\frac{1}{4}$	1$\frac{1}{3}$*	
$\frac{3}{4}$*	224	2	
1	302$\frac{1}{2}$	2$\frac{2}{3}$*	
1$\frac{1}{2}$*	448	4	
1$\frac{3}{4}$*	560	5	$\frac{1}{4}$
2	605	5$\frac{1}{2}$*	
2$\frac{1}{4}$*	672	6	

Ounces per square yard	Pounds per acre	Hundredweights per acre	Tons per acre
3*	896	8	
3$\frac{3}{4}$*	1,120	10	$\frac{1}{2}$
4	1,210	10$\frac{3}{4}$*	
7$\frac{1}{2}$*	2,240	20	1
15*	4,480	40	2
29*	8,960	80	4
60*	17,920	160	8
74*	22,400	200	10

* approximate

212

A.1.5 Gradients

CONVERSION TABLE

Gradient	Angle	%
1 in 1	**45°**	**100**
1 in 1·732	**30°**	5
1 in 2	26° 34′	**50**
1 in 2·747	**20°**	
1 in 3	18° 26′	33⅓
1 in 4	14° 02′	**25**
1 in 5	11° 19′	**20**
1 in 5·671	**10°**	
1 in 10	5° 43′	**10**
1 in 11·430	**5**	
1 in 14·301	**4°**	
1 in 15	3° 49′	6⅔
1 in 19·081	**3°**	
1 in 20	2° 52′	**5**
1 in 28·65	**2°**	
1 in 40	1° 25′	2½
1 in 57·290	**1°**	
1 in 60	0° 57′	1⅔
1 in 80	0° 43′	1¼
1 in 100	0° 34′	**1**
1 in 114·59	**0° 30′**	
1 in 150	0° 23′	

NOTE
All gradients in this table are calculated 1/horizontal distance

A.1.5.1 Foot rise per 100 yards

CONVERSION TABLES

Gradient*	Foot rise per 100 yards	Gradient*	Foot rise per 100 yards
1 in 1	300	1 in 20	15
1 in 2	150	1 in 40	7½
1 in 3	100	1 in 60	5
1 in 4	75	1 in 80	3¾
1 in 5	60	1 in 100	3
1 in 10	30	1 in 150	2
1 in 15	20	1 in 300	1

* (1/horizontal distance)

A.1.6 Temperature

CONVERSION TABLE

Fahrenheit	Centigrade	Fahrenheit	Centigrade
212*	100*	98·6†	37†
200	93·3	90	32·2
180	82·2	80	26·6
160	71·1	70	21·1
140	60	60	15·5
120	48·8	50	10
100	37·7	40	4·4
		32‡	0‡

* Boiling point   † Blood heat   ‡ Freezing point

CONVERSION FACTORS

To convert degrees Centigrade to degrees Fahrenheit multiply by $\frac{9}{5}$ and add 32.

To convert degrees Fahrenheit to degrees Centigrade subtract 32 and multiply by $\frac{5}{9}$.

A.1.7 Cost

CONVERSION TABLE

Cost per square yard s. d.	Cost per acre £ s. d.	Cost per square yard £ s. d.	Cost per acre £ s. d.
0¼	5 0 10	1 6	363 0 0
0½	10 1 8	1 8*	**400 0 0**
1	20 3 4	2 0	484 0 0
1¼*	**25 0 0**	2 0¾*	**500 0 0**
2	40 6 8	2 6	605 0 0
2½*	**50 0 0**	4 1½*	**1,000 0 0**
3	60 10 0	5 0	1,210 0 0
5*	**100 0 0**	6 2½*	**1,500 0 0**
6	121 0 0	8 3*	**2,000 0 0**
9	181 10 0	10 0	2,420 0 0
10*	**200 0 0**	1 0 0	4,840 0 0
1 0	242 0 0	1 0 8*	**5,000 0 0**
1 3*	**300 0 0**	2 1 4*	**10,000 0 0**

* approximate

A.2.1 Weights of Materials

Material	Weight per cubic foot (lb)	Weight per cubic yard (cwt)	Cu feet per ton
Granite	166		
Marble	170		
Portland stone	135–145		
Slate	160–180		
York stone	130–150		
Brickwork (average)	115		
Concrete: lightweight	90		
Concrete: precast	130		
Concrete: reinforced	150		
Lime	53		
Plaster	50		
Timber: hardwood (av.)	45		
Timber: softwood (av.)	35		
Cast iron	450		
Steel	490		
Bronze	513		
Pebbles	110		
Humus: dry	35		
Humus: wet	82		
Subsoil, *in situ*: dry	110		
Subsoil, *in situ*: wet	125		
Mud	100		
Clay soil: compacted, dry	75–100		16–18
Clay soil: Compacted, wet	125		
Clay soil: loose dug		26	18–22
Loam: *in situ*: dry	80		23–25
Loam: *in situ*: wet	120		
Loam loose dug	75	23	25–27
Sandy loam: *in situ*			21–23
Sandy loam: loose dug		23	15–17
Dry sand	95–110	22	23–25
Wet sand	110–130	30	17–19
Gravel	110	28	16–20
Chalk	125	34	13–15
Limestone	135	40	13–14
Marl		25	19–21
Sandstone	125	37	14–16
Shale	150	38	12–14
Peat: dry		7	60–70
Peat: wet		14	33–36
Shingle	110	36	
Flints		48	

A.2.1.1 Area covered by pavings

Material*	Area covered approx. (sq yd)
1 ton of York stone, in slabs 2 in thick	11
1 ton of York stone, in slabs 2½ in thick	9
1 ton of concrete paving slabs 1½ in thick	15
1 ton of concrete paving slabs 2 in thick	12
1 ton of concrete paving slabs 2½ in thick	10
1 ton of slate, in slabs 1 in thick	17
1 ton of gravel, well rolled 2 in thick	15
1 ton of gravel, well rolled 3 in thick	10
1 ton of setts, 6 in × 4 in × 4 in	4½
1,000 bricks, in simple rows, on edge	20
1,000 bricks, in simple rows, flat	30
1,000 bricks, in pattern, with cutting, on edge	18
1,000 bricks, in pattern, with cutting, flat	27

* The above table allows for normal jointing, but not for cutting to boundaries, breakage, or waste.

A.2.1.2 Water

1 Imperial gal = 10 lb = 0·16 cu ft = 4·54 l.
1 U.S. gal   = 8.33 lb = 0·13 cu ft = 3·79 l.
1 ton of water   = 36 cu ft
                       = 224 gal
1 ft head of water   = 0·434 lb per sq in (p.s.i.)
1 lb per sq in (p.s.i.) = 2·3 ft head of water
1 atmosphere   = 34 ft head of water
                       = 14·7 lb per sq in (p.s.i.)
                       = 30 in of mercury (inHg)

$$\text{Water horsepower} = \frac{\text{gal per min} \times \text{total head in ft}}{3,300}$$

$$\text{Horsepower required to drive pumps} = \frac{\text{water hp} \times 100}{\text{efficiency percentage of motor or engine}}$$

A.2.2   Textural composition of soils

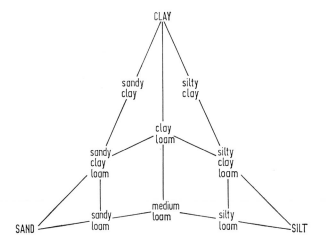

A.2.2.1 Soil: Hand test for texture

Work a handful of *moist* soil in the fingers:

If it is gritty and fails to soil the fingers	**Sand**
If it is gritty but soils the fingers and can be pressed roughly into a ball	**Sandy-loam**
If it is 'sticky', easily moulded in the fingers and quickly 'polished' by sliding between the finger and thumb	**Clay-loam**
If it is sticky, stiff and plastic enough to be rolled into long flexible 'worms'	**Clay**
If it is not sticky, nor can be polished, but feels 'silky' or 'soapy', and can be moulded but is not cohesive	**Silty-loam**
If it is neither gritty, sticky nor silky	**Medium-loam**

DEFINITIONS

Loam: a mixture of clay, sand and silt in fairly balanced proportions

Marl: a mixture of clay and chalk

A.2.2.2 Soil: Water holding capacity (expressed as a percentage of weight)

Coarse sandy soil	15–30
Light loam	22–34
Stiff clay	36–50
Sandy peat	53–60

A.2.2.3 Number of agricultural drain pipes to the acre number of pipes 12 in long: or ft run of pipes)

6 ft apart	7,260	24 ft apart	1,815
9 ft apart	4,840	27 ft apart	1,613
12 ft apart	3,630	30 ft apart	1,452
18 ft apart	2,420	42 ft apart	1,037
21 ft apart	2,074	60 ft apart	726

A.2.2.4 Angle of repose of various soils

Firm earth (*in situ*)	50°
Loose earth or vegetable soil	28°
Firm clay	45°
Wet clay	16°
Dry sand	38°
Wet sand	22°

A.2.2.5 Constituents of soils (main constituents given as a percentage: according to Dr Voelcker)

	Organic matter	Clay	Sand	Lime	Potash	Phosphoric acid	Alkalies (incl. magnesia)
Fertile loam	4·38	18·09	76·16	1·37	0·49	0·12	—
Orchard soil (under turf)	11·70	48·39	35·95	1·54	0·91	0·08	—
Calcareous clayey soil	11·08	52·06	24·53	11·53	0·32	0·12	—
Heavy clay	4·87	72·29	9·26	1·15	0·06	1·37	—
Sterile sandy soil	5·36	4·57	89·82	0·25	—	(trace)	0·49

A.2.3 Principal constituents of manures (figures given are average gross percentages)

	Water	Organic matter	Nitrogen (or ammonia)	Phosphoric acid or phosphates	Potash	Lime	Magnesium
Farmyard manure	72·6	27·4	0·77	0·39	0·6		
Poultry manure (dried)	7		4	2·3	1·2		
Hoof and horn			12·5	1·0			
Dried blood			12·5				
Bone meal			3·7	22			
'Improved' blood, meat and bone meal			3	9	5		
Fish meal	14	50	4·5	9	5	12	
Wood ash				2·8	9	4·3	3·8
Sewage sludge (dried)	5–10		2·0	2·0			
Sewage sludge (activated)	5–10		6·0	3·0	0·5		
Spent mushroom beds			1·0	0·7	1·5		
Basic slag				15		45	
Guano (very variable)	5–20	7–40	2–14	40 av.	0·5–3·0	10–40	
Human faeces	77	20	1	1·1	0·3	0·6	0·5
Garden compost (av.)	10–15	10–20	0·8	0·45	1·45	1·25	0·3

A.2.3.1 Mixing of manures and fertilisers (Geehen's Chart)

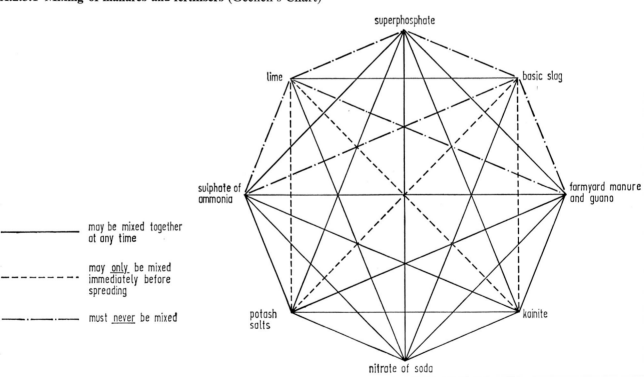

A.2.4 Comparative rates of growth of trees

Heights given in the tables are approximate and show the likely growth in 20 years and 50 years of trees growing in *average* conditions in Britain. Slower rates of growth should be expected in difficult exposure or town conditions.

Expected height in 20 years	Expected height in 50 years	Expected height in 20 years	Expected height in 50 years
LESS THAN 20 FEET	**LESS THAN 40 FEET**	**20 FEET TO 40 FEET**	**40 FEET TO 60 FEET**
Arbutus	Arbutus	Oak	Oak
Almond	Almond	Scarlet Oak	Scarlet Oak
Japanese Cherry	Japanese Cherry	Holm Oak	Holm Oak
Cedar		Turkey Oak	
Crab Apple	Crab Apple	Corsican Pine	
Catalpa		Scots Pine	Scots Pine
	Eucalyptus		Plane
Gleditschia	Gleditschia	Serbian Spruce	
Hawthorn	Hawthorn	Sycamore	
	Holly	Walnut	Walnut
Laburnum	Laburnum	Willows	Willows
Hornbeam			
Magnolia	Magnolia	**OVER 40 FEET**	**OVER 60 FEET**
Field Maple	Field Maple	Acacia	Acacia
Oak (or more)			Ailanthus
	Willow-leaf Pear		Birch
Plane			Lawsons Cypress
Rowan	Rowan		Wych Elm
Whitebeam	Whitebeam	Noble Fir	Noble Fir
Yew	Yew		Gingko
			Larch
20 FEET TO 40 FEET	**40 FEET TO 60 FEET**		Turkey Oak
Ailanthus			Corsican Pine
Alder	Alder	Grey Poplar	
Ash	Ash		Spruce
Beech	Beech		Serbian Spruce
Birch			Norway Spruce
	Catalpa		Sycamore
	Cedar	Thuya plicata	Thuya plicata
Eucalyptus		Tulip Tree	
Horse Chestnut	Horse Chestnut	Tsuga	
Red Chestnut	Red Chestnut		Willows
Sweet Chestnut	Sweet Chestnut	White Willow	
Lawsons Cypress		Wellingtonia	
Swamp Cypress	Swamp Cypress		
English Elm	English Elm	**OVER 60 FEET**	**OVER 80 FEET**
Cornish Elm	Cornish Elm	Douglas Fir	Douglas Fir
Wych Elm		Giant Fir	Giant Fir
Gean		Black Poplar	Black Poplar
Gingko			Grey Poplar
Holly		Lombardy Poplar	Lombardy Poplar
	Hornbeam	Sitka Spruce	Sitka Spruce
Larch			Tulip Tree
Lime	Lime		Tsuga
Silver Maple	Silver Maple		Wellingtonia
			White Willow

A.2.4.1 Plants which assist in indicating soil conditions

Sphagnum mosses	Wet, acid, peaty soil
Heather and ling *Erica and Calluna spp.*	Dry acid soil
Rushes and reeds *Juncus and Carex spp.*	Wet, poor (boggy) soil
Common (perennial creeping) stinging nettle—*Urtica dioica*	Potentially fertile soil
Chickweed *Stellaria media*	Potentially fertile soil
Canterbury bells *Campanula glomerata*	Chalky or limey soil
Thistle *Carduus spp.*	Waste ground
Sheep's sorrel *Rumex acetosella*	Poor, light, dry acid (sour) soil
Foxglove *Digitalis purpurea*	Dry, sandy or gravelly soil
Hoary plantain *Plantago media*	Dry, hard, stony, alkaline soil
Barren (wild) strawberry *Potentilla fragaria*	Dry, stony, barren soil
Common furze *Ulex europaeus*	Poor, infertile soil
Heath bedstraw *Galium saxatile*	Dry, light, acid soil
Silverweed *Potentilla anserina*	Damp places (profuse on clay)

A.2.4.2 Number of plants to the yard (lineal)

Distance apart	Number per lineal yard	Number per 100 yards	Number per mile
3 in	12	1,200	—
4 in	9	900	—
6 in	6	600	—
8 in	$4\frac{1}{2}$	450	—
9 in	4	400	7,038
12 in	3	300	5,280
15 in	$2\frac{2}{5}$	240	4,224
18 in	2	200	3,520
24 in	$1\frac{1}{2}$	150	2,640
30 in	$1\frac{1}{5}$	120	2,112
36 in	1	100	1,760
5 ft	—	60	1,056
10 ft	—	30	528
15 ft	—	20	352
20 ft	—	15	264
30 ft	—	10	176

A.2.4.3 Number of plants to the square yard (area)

Distance apart*	Number per square yard	Number per acre
6 in	36	174,240
9 in	16	77,440
12 in	9	43,560
15 in	$5\frac{4}{5}$	27,878
18 in	4	19,360
2 ft	$2\frac{1}{4}$	10,890
3 ft	1	4,840
4 ft	—	2,722
5 ft	—	1,742
6 ft	—	1,210
7 ft	—	889
8 ft	—	680
9 ft	—	537
10 ft	—	435
12 ft	—	302
14 ft	—	222
15 ft	—	193
20 ft	—	108
25 ft	—	70
30 ft	—	48
40 ft	—	27
50 ft	—	18

* In rows at the same distance apart.

A.3.1 Sources of Information: a short list of references

A. H.M.S.O. publications

Ministry of Agriculture, Fisheries and Food: 'Fixed Equipment on the Farm' series
  Leaflet No. 5 *Permanent Farm Fences*
  Leaflet No. 15: *Shelter Belts for Farmland*
  Leaflet No. 19: *Soil Cement Roads*
Ministry of Housing and Local Government
  Trees in Town and City
  Landscaping for Flats
  Caravan Parks
  The Green Belts
  New Life for Dead Lands
  Circular 92: *Standard system of notation for Planning maps* (1951)
  Memorandum on the Preservation of Trees and Woodlands (and subsequent amendments)
Ministry of Transport
  Specification for Road and Bridge Works (1963)
  Technical Memorandum No. T. 2/65. Instructions on the establishment and maintenance of grass side slopes, verges and central reservations
  Traffic Signs. Report of the Committee on Traffic Signs for All-purpose roads

Department of Agriculture and Fisheries for Scotland:
Administrative Leaflet No. 5 (new series). *Shelter Woods or Belts*—revised by Sir John Holm, 1959

Forestry Commission
Grants for Woodland Owners
Leaflet No. 12: *Income Tax and Estate Duty on Woodlands*—revised 1959
Bulletin No. 14: *Forestry Practice* (8th Edn 1964)
Bulletin No. 29: *Shelter Belts and Microclimate*
Forest Record No. 22: *Shelter Belts for Western Hill Farms*

Road Research Laboratory
Road Note No. 15: *Specification for the Construction of Housing Estate Roads using Soil-cement*
Road Note No. 25: *Sources of White and Coloured Aggregates in Great Britain*

Building Research Station
B.R.S. Digests contain much useful information on building materials and construction

Ordnance Survey Office
Maps generally. Those most likely to be used for landscape work are to scales of 1 in, 2½ in, 6 in, 25 in and 50 in to 1 mile
Small scale maps of special interest, including geology, soil types, land use, types of farming, vegetation, etc, etc.
Geological handbooks on particular regions

Legislation
All Acts of Parliament are published by H.M.S.O.

B. Trade publications

Cement and Concrete Association
'Paving Patterns and their uses' *Concrete Quarterly*, vol. 43, 1959
Terraces in Concrete
Wexham Springs—pavings described
Concrete in Garden Making

Electrical Development Association
Electricity in Your Garden
Electricity for the Grower

Federation of Coated Macadam Industries
The Types and Scope of Coated Macadam
Model Specification for School Playgrounds
Model Specification for Roads and Footpaths on Housing and Factory Estates and Parks
Recommendations for the Construction and Surfacing of Vehicle Parking Areas
Recommendations for the Construction and Surfacing of Paved Areas for Recreation and Sport

Mono Concrete Ltd
Paved Areas

National Federation of Brick Industries
Brick Information Sheets, Nos. 7, 8, and 12

Redland Group
Information Sheets on Landscape Work

Sutton's Grass Advisory Service
The Identification of Grasses by the Leaf Method
The Identification of Grass Seeds
Turf Weeds: Identification and Control

Timber Research and Development Association
Timber Fencing and Gates for Housing and Other Buildings
Timber Fencing and Gates for Agricultural and Open Space Purposes

Trade and Nurserymen's Catalogues (many of which are now comprehensive and informative handbooks)

C. Periodicals on landscape design

Anthos (Zurich)
Garten und Landschaft (Munich)
Journal of the Institute of Landscape Architects (London)
Havekonst (Copenhagen)
Landscape Architecture (Washington D.C.)

D. Miscellaneous

Architectural Press
Element Design Guides (published in *The Architects' Journal*)
SfB (11) Ground: general
(12) Drainage: general
(13) Retaining Structures
(14) Roads and Pavings: general
(15) Garden: general
(15) Garden: Fences, Gates, Walls
Ba4 (78) Building Investigation and Planning: External Circulation
(78) External Fixtures and Equipment: general

British Standards Institution
British Standard Specifications (see A.3.4)
Codes of Practice (see A.3.41)

Central Electricity Generating Board
Design Memorandum on the Use of Fences

Civic Trust
Derelict Land

Institute of Landscape Architects
List of Publications (see A.3.2)

National Association of Groundsmen
An Outline of Field Drainage with particular reference to the drainage of Sports Fields: A. L. Turner

National Playing Fields Association
Playgrounds for Blocks of Flats: Notes on Use and Surfacing
Selection and Layout of Land for Playing Fields and Playgrounds

Royal Horticultural Society
Lawns, Essentials of Establishment and Maintenance: R. B. Dawson

Pruning Hardy Shrubs: A. Osborn
The Choice and Care of Trees for the Small Garden:
F. P. Knight
Sunset Books, Lane Book Co., California
How to Build Fences and Gates
Walls, Walks, Patio Floors
Garden Work Centres
Patio Roofs
Swimming Pools
Verlag Georg D. W. Callwey, Munich
Dachgarten und Dachterrassen: Gerda Gollwitzer and
Werner Wirsing

A.3.2 Publications of the Institute of Landscape Architects

The following publications are available from the Secretary, Institute of Landscape Architects, 12 Carlton House Terrace, London, S.W.1.

The Landscape of Housing Estates
Forestry
The Landscape Treatment of Roads (C.P.R.E.)
Private Enterprise Housing and Landscape Design
The Organisation of Space in Housing Neighbourhoods
Landscape Maintenance
Memorandum No. 1 on the phasing of the Landscape Architect's work on development projects
The Landscape Architect—Landscape Architecture as a Career
Industry and Landscape
Landscape Design in the Countryside
Scale of Professional Charges
Form of Agreement and Conditions of Contract

A.3.3 List of professional and similar bodies connected with landscape work

Agricultural Engineers Association,
6 Buckingham Gate, London, S.W.1.
Arboricultural Association,
The Secretary, 38 Blythwood Gardens, Stanstead, Essex
British Waterways Board,
Melbury House, Melbury Terrace, London N.W.1.
Building Research Station,
Bucknalls Lane, Garston, Watford, Herts.
Civic Trust,
Walter House, Bedford Street, Strand, London W.C.2
Chartered Land Agents' Society,
21 Lincolns Inn Fields, London W.C.2.
Commons, Open Spaces & Footpaths Preservation Society,
166 Shaftesbury Avenue, London, W.C.2

County Naturalists Trusts (Headquarters in each county)
Country Landowners' Association,
7 Swallow Street, London, W1R 8EN.
Countryside Commission,
1 Cambridge Gate, Regents Park, London, N.W.1.
Council for the Preservation of Rural England,
4 Hobart Place, London S.W.1.
Council for the Preservation of Rural Wales,
Y Plas, Machynlleth, Montgomeryshire.
Crown Estate Commissioners,
Crown Estate Office, Whitehall, London S.W.1.
Fauna Preservation Society,
c/o Zoological Society of London, Regents Park, London N.W.1.
Field Studies Council,
9 Devereux Court, Strand, London W.C.1.
Forestry Commission,
25 Savile Row, London, W1X 2AY.
Horticultural Education Association,
65 Tilehurst Road, Reading, Berks.
Institute of Landscape Architects,
12 Carlton House Terrace, London S.W.1.
Institute of Park and Recreation Administration,
The Grotto, Lower Basildon, nr. Reading, Berks.
Institution of Civil Engineers,
Great George Street, London, S.W.1.
National Vegetable Research Station Association,
Wellesbourne, Warwick
Nature Conservancy,
19 Belgrave Square, London S.W.1.
(also Regional Offices and Research Stations)
National Trust,
42 Queen Anne's Gate, London S.W.1.
National Trust Committee for Northern Ireland,
82 Dublin Road, Belfast 2.
National Trust for Scotland,
5 Charlotte Square, Edinburgh 2.
National Playing Fields Association,
57B Catherine Place, London S.W.1.
Ramblers Association,
124 Finchley Road, London N.W.3.
Royal Horticultural Society,
Vincent Square, London S.W.1.
Royal Institute of British Architects,
66 Portland Place, London, W1N 4AD.
Royal Institution of Chartered Surveyors,
12 Great George Street, London, S.W.1.
Royal Forestry Society of England & Wales,
49 Russell Square, London W.C.1.
Royal Scottish Forestry Society,
7 Albyn Place, Edinburgh 2.
Town and Country Planning Association,
28 King Street, Covent Garden, London W.C.2.
Town Planning Institute,
26 Portland Place, London, W1N 4BE.

Wildfowlers Association of Great Britain and Ireland,
43 The Albany, Old Hall Street, Liverpool 3

Horticultural Colleges
  Kent Horticultural Institute
  Pershore Institute
  Nottingham University
  Reading University
  Waterpenny College
  Wye College, London University

Botanic Gardens and Arboreta
  Royal Botanic Gardens, Kew
  Royal Botanic Gardens, Edinburgh
  Royal Horticultural Society, Wisley
  Cambridge Botanic Garden
  Oxford Botanic Garden
  Liverpool Botanic Garden
  Botanic Gardens, University of Liverpool
  Bath Botanic Garden
  Harlow Car, Harrogate
  Bedgebury Arboretum
  Westonbirt Arboretum
  Winkworth Arboretum
  Alice Holt, Forestry Commission

Research Stations
  East Malling Research Station
  Long Ashton Research Station
  Rothamsted Experimental Station
  John Innes Institute
  McCaulay Institute of Soil Research
  Scottish Horticultural Research Institute
  Rosewarne Experimental Horticultural Station
  Sports Turf Research Institute

List of trade associations connected with landscape work

Association of British Tree Surgeons and Arborists
  Pembroke Cottage, 11 Wings Road, Upper Hale,
  Farnham, Surrey
Association of Swimming Pool Contractors
  12 Durrants Drive, Croxley Green, Rickmansworth,
  Herts.
Association of Tree Transplanters
  Secretary, 100 Colney Hatch Lane, London N.10.
British Association of Sportsground & Landscape
  Contractors Ltd
  12 Durrants Drive, Croxley Green, Rickmansworth,
  Herts.
Horticultural Traders Association
  6th Floor, Cereal House, Mark Lane, London E.C.3.
  a specialist groups
    Forest Trees
    Herbaceous Plants and Alpines
    British Orchid Growers' Association

Retail Seed Association
Rose Tree Group
  b affiliated, but autonomous
    British Chrysanthemum Trade Association
    British Dahlia Growers' Association
    Bulb Distributors Association
    Scottish Seed Trade Association
Land Settlement Association
  43 Cromwell Road, London S.W.7.
National Association of Agricultural Contractors
(Garden Section)
  140 Bensham Lane, Thornton Heath, Surrey
National Association of Groundsmen
  108 Chessington Road, Ewell, Surrey.
National Farmers' Union
  Agricultural House, Knightsbridge, London S.W.1.
National Farmers' Union for Scotland
  17 Grosvenor Crescent, Edinburgh 12.
Seed Trade Association of the United Kingdom
  Cereal House, Mark Lane, London E.C.3.
Timber Growers' Association
  35 Belgrave Square, London S.W.1.

A.3.4 British Standards applicable to land-scape work

B.S.12: 1958		*Portland cement (ordinary and rapid hardening)*
B.S.65: 1963		*Glazed vitrified clay drain and sewer pipes*
B.S.76: 1943		*Tars for road purposes*
B.S.340: 1963		*Pre-cast concrete kerbs, channels, edgings and quadrants*
B.S.368: 1956		*Precast concrete flags*
B.S.435: 1931		*Granite and whinstone kerbs, channels, quadrants, and setts*
B.S.497: 1952		*Cast manhole covers, road gully gratings and frames for drainage purposes*
B.S.539—		*Dimensions of drain fittings*
	Part 1: 1951	*Salt-glazed ware and glass (vitreous) enamelled salt-glazed fireclay*
	Part 2: 1951	*Scottish type. Salt-glazed ware and glass (vitreous) enamelled saltglazed fireclay*
B.S.540: 1964		*Glass (vitreous) enamelled salt-glazed fireclay pipes*
B.S.556: 1955		*Concrete cylindrical pipes and fittings including manholes, inspection chambers and street gullies*
B.S.594: 1961		*Rolled asphalt*
B.S.657: 1950		*Dimensions of common clay building bricks*
B.S.659: 1963		*Light gauge copper tubes for water, gas and sanitation*
B.S.706: 1936		*Sandstone kerbs, channels, quadrants and setts*

B.S.743:1951	*Materials for damp-proof courses*	Part 9: 1963	*Mild steel or wrought iron unclimbable fences with round or square verticals and flat standards and horizontals*
B.S.802:1958	*Tarmacadam with crushed rock or slag aggregate*		
B.S.864: 1953	*Capillary and compression fittings of copper and copper alloy for use with copper tube complying with B.S.659 and B.S.1386*	Part 10: 1963	*Anti-intruder chain link fences*

B.S.743:1951   *Materials for damp-proof courses*

B.S.802:1958   *Tarmacadam with crushed rock or slag aggregate*

B.S.864: 1953   *Capillary and compression fittings of copper and copper alloy for use with copper tube complying with B.S.659 and B.S.1386*

B.S.882, 1201: 1965   *Concrete aggregates from natural sources for concrete (including granolithic)*

B.S.892: 1954   *Glossary of highway engineering terms*

B.S.913: 1954   *Pressure creosoting of timber*

B.S.1010:1959   *Draw-off taps and stopvalves for water services (screwdown pattern)*

B.S.1014:1961   *Pigments for cement, magnesium oxychloride and concrete*

B.S.1185: 1963   *Guards for underground stopvalves*

B.S.1194: 1955   *Concrete porous pipes for underdrainage*

B.S.1196: 1944   *Clayware field drain pipes*

B.S.1198–1200: 1955   *Building sands from natural sources*

B.S.1217: 1945   *Cast stone*

B.S.1221: 1964   *Steel fabric for reinforcement of concrete*

B.S.1222: 1945   *Battery operated electric fences*

B.S.1241: 1959   *Tarmacadam and tar carpets (gravel aggregate)*

B.S.1242: 1960   *Tarmacadam tarpaving for footpaths, playgrounds and similar works*

B.S.1282: 1959   *Classification of wood preservatives and their methods of application*

B.S.1286: 1945   *Clay tiles for flooring (dimensions and workmanship only)*

B.S.1324: 1962   *Asphalt tiles for paving and flooring (natural rock asphalt)*

B.S.1377: 1961   *Methods of testing soils for civil engineering purposes*

B.S.1386: 1957   *Copper tubes to be buried underground*

B.S.1447: 1962   *Mastic asphalt (limestone aggregate) for roads and footways*

B.S.1485: 1948   *Galvanized wire netting*

B.S.1621: 1961   *Bitumen macadam with crushed rock or slag aggregate*

B.S.1690: 1962   *Cold asphalt*

B.S.1722—   *Fences*

   Part 1: 1963   *Chain link fences*

   Part 2: 1963   *Woven wire fences*

   Part 3: 1963   *Strained wire fences*

   Part 4: 1963   *Cleft chestnut pale fences*

   Part 5: 1963   *Close-boarded fences including oak pale fences*

   Part 6: 1963   *Wooden palisade fences*

   Part 7: 1963   *Wooden post and rail fences*

   Part 8: 1951   *Mild steel or wrought iron continuous bar fences*

Part 9: 1963   *Mild steel or wrought iron unclimbable fences with round or square verticals and flat standards and horizontals*

Part 10: 1963   *Anti-intruder chain link fences*

Part 11: 1965   *Woven wood fences*

B.S.1831: 1965   *Recommended common names for pesticides*

B.S.1926: 1962   *Ready-mixed concrete*

B.S.1972: 1961   *Polythene pipe (Type 425) for cold water services*

B.S.2040: 1953   *Bitumen macadam with gravel aggregate*

B.S.2468: 1963   *Glossary of terms relating to agricultural machinery and implements*

B.S.2660: 1955   *Colours for building and decorative paints*

B.S.2760: 1956   *Pitch-impregnated fibre drain and sewer pipes*

B.S.2787: 1956   *Glossary of terms for concrete and reinforced concrete*

B.S.2847: 1957   *Glossary of terms for stone used in building*

B.S.3178—   *Playground equipment for parks*

   Part 1: 1959   *General requirements*

   Part 2A: 1959   *Special requirements for static equipment (except slides)*

   Part 2B: 1960   *Special requirements for slides*

   Part 3A: 1960   *Special requirements for swinging apparatus. Section A. Pendulum see-saws*

   Part 3B: 1962   *Plane swings*

   Part 3C: 1964   *Plank swings*

   Part 3D: 1964   *Swings*

   Part 3E: 1964   *Rocking boats*

   Part 3F: 1964   *Rocking horses*

B.S. 3284: 1964   *Polythene pipe (type 710) for cold water services*

B.S.3445: 1961   *Field water troughs*

B.S.3470: 1962   *Field gates and posts*

B.S.3505: 1962   *Unplasticized PVC pipe (type 1140) for cold water supply*

B.S.3589: 1963   *Glossary of general building terms*

B.S.3656: 1963   *Asbestos cement pipes and fittings for sewerage and drainage*

B.S.3690: 1963   *Bitumen for road purposes*

B.S.3798: 1964   *Coping units (of clayware, unreinforced cast concrete, unreinforced cast stone, natural stone and slate)*

B.S.3826—   *Silicone based water repellents for masonry*

   Part 1: 1964   *For clay brickwork*

B.S.3854: 1965   *Farm stock fences*

B.S.2028: 1953   *Precast concrete blocks*

B.S.3882: 1965   *Topsoil*

B.S.3810: 1964   *Colours for specific purposes*

B.S.3892: 1965   *Pulverised-fuel ash for use in concrete*

B.S.3921: 1965   *Bricks and blocks of fired brickearth, clay or shale*

B.S.3936: 1965   *Nursery stock*
  Part 1: 1965   *Trees and shrubs*
  Part 2: 1966   *Roses*
  Part 3: 1965   *Fruit*
  Part 4: 1966   *Forest trees*

B.S.3969: 1965   *Recommendations for turf*

B.S.3975: —   *Glossary for landscape work*
  Part 4:   *Plant description*

B.S.3998: 1966   *Tree work*

B.S.4043: 1966   *Transplanting semi-mature trees*

NOTE: British Standards are also being drafted for the following subjects:

Domestic metal gates
Domestic wooden gates
Steel palisade fences
Fencing wire
Operations involving semi-mature trees
Other landscape operations
Grounds maintenance
Peat products for landscape purposes
Tree wound dressings
Personal safety equipment for use when working in trees
Precast concrete flags for landscape purposes
Silicone based water repellents for use on stone-work and hydraulic cement based products
Litter bins
P.V.C. hoses

NOTE: British Standards can be obtained from the British Standards Institution, 2 Park Street, London, W1Y 4AA. (01-629 9000).

British Standard Codes of Practice applicable to landscape work

Building

CP 121.101: 1951 *Brickwork*
CP 121.201: 1951 *Masonry. Walls ashlared with natural or cast stone*
CP 121.202: 1951 *Masonry. Rubble walls*
CP 122: 1952   *Walls and partitions of blocks and slabs*
CP 123.101: 1951 *Dense concrete walls*
CP 202: 1959   *Tile flooring and slab flooring*
CP 221: 1960   *External rendered finishes*
CP 231: 1952   *Painting*

CP 301: 1950   *Building drainage*
CP 303: 1952   *Surface water and subsoil drainage*
CP 310: 1965   *Water supply*
CP 325: 1953   *Farm and horticultural electrical installations*
CP 402: 101: 1952   *Hydrant systems*

Electrical engineering

CP 1004—   *Street lighting*
  Parts 1 and 2: 1963 *General principles. Lighting for traffic routes*
  Part 2A: 1956 *Roads other than traffic routes*

Civil Engineering

CP 2001: 1957   *Site investigations*
CP 2003: 1959   *Earthworks*

These Codes of Practice can be obtained from British Standards Institution, 2 Park Street, London, W1Y 4AA. (01-629 9000)

A.4.1 Maintenance rates

Summary of average labour requirements and average annual costs for local authority work (1962)

	Number of acres per man		Cost per acre	
	Minimum	Maximum	Minimum	Maximum
Wooded commons and heathland	75	100	£6	£9
Large scale grass, cutting only		22	£15	
Housing estates street verges, etc.*				
(a) low bracket	4	14	£50	£100
(b) high bracket	2½	5	£75	£100
Sports playing pitches and recreation grounds		8†	£80	£100
Parks, gardens and open spaces	2½	7	£150	£350
Nurseries and intensive formal bedding		¾	£800	£1,200

* Figures vary widely due to different standards of upkeep and different methods of assessing acreage.
† Labour rates for playing pitches vary widely and can be as high as one man to four acres.

Index

Numbers in *italics* refer to plates or figures.

Readers are also referred to the chapter contents pages which set out the contents of each chapter in considerable detail.